M000305596

Managing Information Security Risks

Managing Information Security Risks

The OCTAVE^{SM} Approach

Christopher Alberts

Audrey Dorofee

✦Addison-Wesley

Boston • San Francisco • New York • Toronto
Montreal • London • Munich • Paris • Madrid
Capetown • Sydney • Tokyo • Singapore • Mexico City

The SEI Series in Software Engineering

Many of the designations used by manufacturers and sellers to distinguish their products are claimed as trademarks. Where those designations appear in this book, and Addison-Wesley, Inc. was aware of a trademark claim, the designations have been printed in initial capital letters or in all capitals.

CMM, Capability Maturity Model, Capability Maturity Modeling, Carnegie Mellon, CERT, and CERT Coordination Center are registered in the U.S. Patent and Trademark Office.

ATAM; Architecture Tradeoff Analysis Method; CMMI; CMM Integration; CURE; IDEAL; Interim Profile; OCTAVE; Operationally Critical Threat, Asset, and Vulnerability Evaluation; Personal Software Process; PSP; SCAMPI; SCAMPI Lead Assessor; SCE; Team Software Process; and TSP are service marks of Carnegie Mellon University.

ANY MATERIAL FURNISHED BY CARNEGIE MELLON UNIVERSITY AND THE SOFTWARE ENGINEERING INSTITUTE IS FURNISHED ON AN "AS IS" BASIS. CARNEGIE MELLON UNIVERSITY MAKES NO WARRANTIES OF ANY KIND, EITHER EXPRESSED OR IMPLIED, AS TO ANY MATTER INCLUDING, BUT NOT LIMITED TO, WARRANTY OF FITNESS FOR PURPOSE OR MERCHANTABILITY, EXCLUSIVITY OR RESULTS OBTAINED FROM USE OF THE MATERIAL. CARNEGIE MELLON UNIVERSITY DOES NOT MAKE ANY WARRANTY OF ANY KIND WITH RESPECT TO FREEDOM FROM PATENT, TRADEMARK, OR COPYRIGHT INFRINGEMENT.

Special permission to use materials from the *OCTAVE Method Implementation Guide,* copyright © 2002 by Carnegie Mellon University, has been granted by the Software Engineering Institute.

The authors and publisher have taken care in preparation of this book but make no expressed or implied warranty of any kind and assume no responsibility for errors or omissions. No liability is assumed for incidental or consequential damages in connection with or arising out of the use of the information or programs contained herein.

The publisher offers discounts on this book when ordered in quantity for special sales. For more information, please contact:

Pearson Education Corporate Sales Division
One Lake Street
Upper Saddle River, NJ 07458
(800) 382-3419
corpsales@persontechgroup.com

Visit A-W on the Web: *www.awprofessional.com/*

Library of Congress Cataloging-in-Publication Data

Alberts, Christopher J.
  Managing information security risks : the OCTAVE approach / Christopher J. Alberts, Audrey J. Dorofee.
    p. cm.
  ISBN 0-321-11886-3
  1. Computer security—Management.   I. Dorofee, Audrey J.   II. Title.
  QA76.9.A25 A43 2002
  658.4'78—dc21   2002024939

Copyright © 2003 Pearson Education, Inc.

All rights reserved. No part of this publication may be reproduced, stored in a retrieval system, or transmitted, in any form or by any means, electronic, mechanical, photocopying, recording, or otherwise, without the prior consent of the publisher. Printed in the United States of America. Published simultaneously in Canada.

For information on obtaining permission for use of material from this work, please submit a written request to:

Pearson Education, Inc.
Rights and Contracts Department
75 Arlington Street, Suite 300
Boston, MA 02116
Fax: (617) 848-7047

ISBN 0-321-11886-3
Text printed on recycled paper
2 3 4 5 6 7 8 9 10—HT—060504
Second printing, April 2004

To Carol,
for her love and encouragement

—Christopher Alberts

For Ronald Higuera,
for putting me on the path
to risk management
so long ago

—Audrey Dorofee

Contents

List of Figures

List of Tables

Preface

Many people seem to be looking for a silver bullet when it comes to information security. They often hope that buying the latest tool or piece of technology will solve their problems. Few organizations stop to evaluate what they are actually trying to protect (and why) from an organizational perspective before selecting solutions. In our work in the field of information security, we have found that security issues tend to be complex and are rarely solved simply by applying a piece of technology. Most security issues are firmly rooted in one or more organizational and business issues. Before implementing security solutions, you should consider characterizing the true nature of the underlying problems by evaluating your security needs and risks in the context of your business.

Considering the varieties and limitations of current security evaluation methods, it is easy to become confused when trying to select an appropriate method for evaluating your information security risks. Most of the current methods are "bottom-up": they start with the computing infrastructure and focus on the technological vulnerabilities without considering the risks to the organization's mission and business objectives. A better alternative is to look at the organization itself and identify what needs to be protected, determine why it is at risk, and develop solutions requiring both technology- and practice-based solutions.

A comprehensive information security risk evaluation approach

- Incorporates assets, threats, and vulnerabilities
- Enables decision makers to develop relative priorities based on what is important to the organization
- Incorporates organizational issues related to how people use the computing infrastructure to meet the business objectives of the organization

- Incorporates technological issues related to the configuration of the computing infrastructure
- Should be a flexible method that can be uniquely tailored to each organization

One way to create a context-sensitive evaluation approach is to define a basic set of requirements for the evaluation and then develop a series, or family, of methods that meet those requirements. Each method within the approach could be targeted to a unique operational environment or situation. We conceived the Operationally Critical Threat, Asset, and Vulnerability Evaluation^{SM} (OCTAVE^{SM}) project to define a systematic, organizationwide approach to evaluating information security risks comprising multiple methods consistent with the approach. We also designed the approach to be self-directed, enabling people to learn about security issues and improve their organization's security posture without unnecessary reliance on outside experts and vendors.

An evaluation by itself only provides a direction for an organization's information security activities. Meaningful improvement will not occur unless the organization follows through by implementing the results of the evaluation and managing its information security risks. OCTAVE is an important first step in approaching information security risk management.

History of OCTAVE

Before we developed OCTAVE, we performed expert-led Information Security Evaluations (ISEs) for organizations. A team of security experts would visit a site, interview selected information technology personnel and users of key systems, and examine selected pieces of the computing infrastructure for technological weaknesses. The assessors used their expertise to create a list of organizational and technological weaknesses (vulnerabilities). When the managers at a site received the list of vulnerabilities and corresponding recommendations, they often did not know how to begin to overcome the weaknesses. Which issues

---

^{SM}Operationally Critical Threat, Asset, and Vulnerability Evaluation and OCTAVE are service marks of Carnegie Mellon University. OCTAVE was developed at the CERT Coordination Center (CERT/CC). Established in 1988, it is the oldest computer security response group in existence. The center both advises Internet sites that have had their security compromised and offers tools and techniques that enable typical users and administrators to protect systems effectively from damage caused by intruders. The CERT/CC's home is the Software Engineering Institute (SEI), a federally funded research and development center operated by Carnegie Mellon University, with a broad charter to improve the practice of software engineering.

should they address first, the organizational or the technological? With limits on the funds and staff available, what are the top five priorities? These are good questions. Unfortunately, when you examine only vulnerabilities, it is hard to establish appropriate guidelines. *You need to look at the vulnerabilities in the context of what the organization is trying to achieve before you can start establishing priorities.*

In addition to our experience with vulnerability evaluations, we had also developed and applied a variety of software development risk evaluation and management techniques [Williams 00 and Dorofee 96]. These techniques focused on the critical risks that could affect *project* objectives.

With these experiences, we decided to focus on a risk-based approach rather than a vulnerability-based approach. A risk-based approach could help people understand how information security affects their organization's missions and business objectives, establishing which assets are important to the organization and how they are at risk. Vulnerability evaluations could then be performed in the context of this risk information. Because information security risks are tied to an organization's missions and business objectives, it became necessary to include business staff in addition to information technology personnel in the evaluation.

A second important observation from our vulnerability evaluation days concerned a given site's level of involvement and subsequent ownership of the results. Because the vulnerability evaluations were highly dependent on the expertise of the assessors, site personnel involved in the process participated very little. When we were able to go back to a site, we saw the same vulnerabilities from one visit to the next. There had been little or no organizational learning. People in those organizations did not feel "ownership" of the various evaluations' results and had therefore not implemented the findings. We decided that sites needed to be more involved in security evaluations in order to learn about their security processes and participate in developing improvement recommendations. We started to develop a self-directed evaluation approach that

- Focused on risks to information assets
- Focused on practice-based mitigation using recognized, good security practices[1]

---

1. Practices in the catalog of practices (Appendix C) were derived from several sources of security practices including CERT/CC, the British Standards Institute, the National Institute for Standards and Technology, and government regulations.

- Included business personnel as well as staff from the information technology department
- Involved a site's personnel in all aspects of the evaluation

In June 1999 we published a report describing the OCTAVE framework [Alberts 99], a specification for an information security risk evaluation. This was refined into the OCTAVE Method [Alberts 01a], which was developed for large-scale organizations. In addition, we are developing a second method targeted at small organizations. During these efforts, we determined that the OCTAVE framework did not sufficiently capture the general approach to, or requirements for, the self-directed information security risk evaluations that we wanted. We refined the framework into the OCTAVE criteria [Alberts 01b], namely, a set of principles, attributes, and outputs that define the OCTAVE approach.

Contents of This Book

This book focuses on four key aspects of information security risk evaluation.

- It defines an approach for self-directed information security risk evaluations (OCTAVE criteria).
- It illustrates how the evaluation approach can be implemented in an organization using the OCTAVE Method.
- It shows how the OCTAVE Method can be tailored to different types of organizations.
- It describes how this approach provides a foundation for managing information security risks.

To address these key issues, we have divided the contents of the book into three parts.

- Part I, the Introduction, summarizes the OCTAVE approach and presents the principles, attributes, and outputs of self-directed information security risk evaluations.
- Part II, The OCTAVE Method, illustrates one way in which the OCTAVE approach can be implemented in an organization. This part begins with an "executive summary" of the OCTAVE Method and then presents the method in detail.
- Part III, Variations on the OCTAVE Approach, describes ideas for tailoring the OCTAVE Method for different types of organizations. This part also

presents basic concepts related to managing information security risks after the evaluation.

Three appendices supplement the material provided in the main text.

- Appendix A presents a sample final report from an OCTAVE example scenario.
- Appendix B shows OCTAVE Method worksheets and instructions.
- Appendix C lists a catalog of practices (a structured collection of commonly used good security practices).

Who Should Read This Book?

This book is written for a varied audience. Some familiarity with security issues is helpful, but not essential; we define all concepts and terms as they appear. The book should satisfy people who are new to security as well as experts in security and risk management.

Information security risk evaluations are appropriate for anyone who uses networked computers to conduct business and thus may have critical information assets at risk. This book is for people who need to perform information security risk evaluations and who are interested in using a self-directed method that addresses both organizational and information technology issues. Managers, staff members, and information technology personnel concerned about and responsible for protecting critical information assets should all find this book useful.

In addition, consultants who provide information security services to other organizations may be interested in seeing how the OCTAVE approach or the OCTAVE Method might be incorporated into their existing products and services. Consumers of information security risk evaluation products and services can use the principles, attributes, and outputs of the OCTAVE approach to understand what constitutes a comprehensive approach for evaluating information security risks. Consumers can also use the principles, attributes, and outputs as a benchmark for selecting products and services that are provided by vendors and consultants.

The OCTAVE Method requires an interdisciplinary analysis team to perform the evaluation and act as a focal point for security improvement efforts. The primary audience for this book, then, is anyone who might be on the analysis team or work with them. The book includes "how to" information for conducting an evaluation as well as concepts related to managing risks after the evaluation. For an analysis team, the entire book is applicable.

Those who want to understand the OCTAVE approach should read Part I. Those who just want an overview of the OCTAVE Method and a general idea of how it might be used should read Chapters 1 and 3. People who already perform information security risk evaluations and are looking for additional ideas for improvement should first read Chapters 1 and 3 and then decide which areas to explore further. Those ready to start learning how to conduct self-directed information security evaluations in their organizations should read Part II. Finally, people who are interested in customizing the OCTAVE Method or learning about what to do after an evaluation should read Part III.

How to Get OCTAVE

OCTAVE and OCTAVE-related materials can be downloaded at no cost from the following website: <http://www.cert.org/octave>

- *OCTAVE Method Implementation Guide*—a complete set of guidelines, worksheets, instructions, and examples that can be used by an analysis team to conduct the OCTAVE Method for larger organizations
- *OCTAVE-S Implementation Guide*—a complete set of guidelines, worksheets, instructions, and examples that can be used by an analysis team to conduct the OCTAVE-S method for smaller organizations
- *OCTAVE Criteria*—the basic requirements for an OCTAVE-consistent information security risk evaluation
- miscellaneous presentations, white papers, and other information pertinent to OCTAVE

Acknowledgments

Writing a book requires an intense effort. We would like to acknowledge the support of everyone who helped us in writing this book, without which we would never have been able to complete it.

The following people spent countless hours reviewing the material in this book and providing invaluable feedback: Julia Allen, Rich Caralli, Jeff Collmann, Carol A. Sledge, Andrew Moore, William Wilson, and Carol Woody.

We would especially like to thank Rich Pethia, program manager of the Networked Systems Survivability Program, and William Wilson, technical manager of the Survivable Enterprise Management Team, for their encouragement and support of our work. Such an ambitious project requires unwavering support from management, and we are grateful for their help.

Many people made contributions to the technical content of this book. Specifically, Julia Allen helped us develop the catalog of practices, Rich Caralli contributed lessons learned from his experiences with OCTAVE, Jeff Collmann offered insightful and detailed comments on our early prototypes, and Bradford Willke made important contributions to the technological pieces of OCTAVE.

We would also like to acknowledge those who have provided us with production assistance. Linda Pesante helped design the book and served as our technical editor, and David Biber created many of the graphics used throughout the book.

The technical content of this book evolved from many previous efforts within the Software Engineering Institute. We leveraged technical material from several projects, including Continuous Risk Management, Software Risk Evaluation, Information Security Evaluation, and the early work on the OCTAVE framework. Many people contributed to these projects, and we would like to thank all of them for providing such a rich foundation upon which to build.

We would also like to acknowledge all the organizations that provided funding and pilot opportunities as we developed the OCTAVE Method.

Finally, Chris would like to thank his wife, Carol Feola, for her support and encouragement. To put up with the frustrations, deadlines, and last-minute reviews required incredible generosity and patience.

PART I

Introduction

Part I provides an executive overview of self-directed information security risk evaluations and how they fit into the overall management of information security risks. Specifically, it introduces the Operationally Critical Threat, Asset, and Vulnerability Evaluation[SM] (OCTAVE[SM]) approach to assessments and the OCTAVE Method. Chapter 1 gives background on information security risk evaluations and the OCTAVE approach to assessing information security risks. Chapter 2 discusses the principles, attributes, and outputs that define a comprehensive, self-directed evaluation.

[SM]Operationally Critical Threat, Asset, and Vulnerability Evaluation and OCTAVE are service marks of Carnegie Mellon University.

1

Managing Information Security Risks

It is easy to overlook the fact that information security affects an entire organization. But ultimately, it is a business problem whose solution involves more than deploying information technology such as firewalls and virus patches. Some surveys on security incidents and breaches have indicated that the majority of security breaches occur from the inside, not from the notorious teenage attackers trying to get in from the outside. More recent surveys indicate that the majority of attacks do come from outside. There are yet other indicators that the most *costly* attacks come from the inside, even though the highest *frequency* of attacks come from the outside. With little consistency in the information available, it is difficult to pin down exactly where your threats lie. What is consistently reported, however, is an increase in the numbers of security incidents and vulnerabilities.[1]

No matter which way the current statistics swing, you need to consider both internal and external threats. Your organization is only as secure as its weakest link, and that link, more often than not, is one of you. How many people can state

---

1. From CERT Coordination Center: The number of vulnerabilities reported in 2001 is 2,437 (up from 1,090 in 2000), and the number of security incidents is 52,658 (up from 21,756 in 2000). See *http://www.cert.org/stats/cert_stats.html* for additional information.

with certainty that they have not deliberately or inadvertently revealed their pass-words in the past year? How many have a file on their personal data assistant (PDA) that lists passwords or contains confidential information? How many have "yellow stickies" under the keyboard? How many employees load games on their workstations or open up unknown email attachments? How many companies spend the time and money to keep up with the latest patches and technological security tools? Without good organizational practices in place and enforced, in addition to technological safeguards, the organization and its assets are at risk.

1.1 Information Security

Consider the following scenario. A former network administrator at a manufac-turing plant thought he had destroyed not only his former employer's manufac-turing capabilities but also the evidence that would link him to the crime. The trusted, 11-year employee built and maintained the network at the company. When he fell from corporate grace and knew he was to be fired for performance and behavioral problems, he built a software time bomb to destroy the system.

Three weeks after the network administrator was fired, a plant worker started the day by logging on to the central file server. Instead of booting up, a message came on the screen saying an area of the operating system was being fixed. Then the server crashed, and in an instant, all of the plant's 1,000 tooling and manufac-turing programs were gone. The server wouldn't come back up. The plant man-ager ordered that the manufacturing machines be kept running with the previous set of programs. It didn't matter if the orders already had been filled. He had to keep the machines running.

Then the plant manager went to get his salvation—the backup tape, kept in a filing cabinet in the human resources department. But the tapes were gone. He then turned to the workstations connected to the file server. The programs, at least a good chunk of them, should have been stored locally on the individual workstations. But the programs weren't there.

The fired network administrator, the only employee responsible for maintaining, securing, and backing up the file server, hadn't yet been replaced. In the days that followed the crash, the company called in three different people to attempt data recovery. Five days after the crash, the plant manager started shifting workers around the department and shutting down machines that were running out of raw materials or creating excess inventory. He took steps to hire a fleet of programmers to start rebuilding some of the 1,000 lost programs.

The company's chief financial officer testified that the software bomb destroyed all the programs and code generators that allowed the company to manufacture 25,000 different products and customize those basic products into as many as 500,000 different designs. The company lost its twin advantages of being able to modify products easily and produce them inexpensively. It lost more than $10 million, forfeited its position in the industry, and eventually had to lay off 80 employees.

What Is Information Security?

Information security is more than setting up a firewall, applying patches to fix newly discovered vulnerabilities in your system software, or locking the cabinet with your backup tapes. Information security is determining what needs to be protected and why, what it needs to be protected from, and how to protect it for as long as it exists.

The burning question, of course, is how to assure your organization an adequate level of security over time. There are many answers to this challenging question, just as there are many approaches to managing an organization's security. Unfortunately, there is no silver bullet, no single solution that will solve all of your problems. There are four common approaches:

- Vulnerability assessment
- Information systems audit
- Information security risk evaluation
- Managed service providers

Following is a brief description of each of the above approaches.

Vulnerability Assessment

A vulnerability assessment is a systematic, point-in-time examination of an organization's technology base, policies, and procedures. It includes a complete analysis of the security of an internal computing environment and its vulnerability to internal and external attack. These technology-driven assessments generally

- Use standards for specific IT security activities (such as hardening specific types of platforms)
- Assess the entire computing infrastructure
- Use (sometimes proprietary) software tools to analyze the infrastructure and all of its components
- Provide a detailed analysis showing the detected technological vulnerabilities and possibly recommending specific steps to address those vulnerabilities

Information Systems Audit

Information systems audits are independent appraisals of a company's internal controls to assure management, regulatory authorities, and company shareholders that information is accurate and valid. Audits will typically leverage industry-specific process models, benchmarks, standards of due care, or established best practices. They look at both financial and operational performance. An audit may also be based on proprietary business process risk control and analysis methods and tools. Audits are generally performed by licensed or certified auditors and have legal implications and liabilities. During an audit, the business records of a company are reviewed for accuracy and integrity.

Information Security Risk Evaluation

Security risk evaluations expand upon the vulnerability assessment to look at the security-related risks within a company, including internal and external sources of risk as well as electronic-based and people-based risks. These multifaceted evaluations attempt to align the risk evaluation with business drivers or goals and usually focus on the following four aspects of security:

1. They examine the corporate practices relating to security to identify strengths and weaknesses that could create or mitigate security risks. This

procedure may include a comparative analysis that ranks this information against industry standards and best practices.

2. They include a technological examination of systems, reviews of policy, and an inspection of physical security.

3. They examine the IT infrastructure to determine technological vulnerabilities. Such vulnerabilities include susceptibility to any of the following situations:

    a. The introduction of malicious code

    b. Corruption or destruction of data

    c. Exfiltration of information

    d. Denial of service

    e. Unauthorized change of access rights and privileges

4. They help decision makers examine trade-offs to select cost-effective countermeasures.

Managed Service Providers

Managed security services providers rely on human expertise to manage a company's systems and networks. They use their own or another vendor's security software and devices to protect your infrastructure. Usually, a managed security service will proactively monitor and protect an organization's computing infrastructures from attacks and misuse. The solutions tend to be customized for each client's unique business requirements and to use proprietary technology. They can either actively respond to intrusions or notify you after they occur. Some employ automated, computer-based learning and analysis, promising decreased response time and increased accuracy.

Vulnerability assessments, information system audits, and information security risk evaluations help you characterize your security issues, but not manage them. Managed service providers manage your security for you. Although each of these approaches can be useful to an organization trying to protect itself, all of them have some limitations, based on their context of use. A small company may have no choice but to use a managed service provider. A company with limited IT resources may not be able to do much more than manage vulnerabilities, and, depending on what it has to protect, may not need to do much more. The next section looks at a more comprehensive approach that builds upon the previous approaches, allowing an organization to assume responsibility for characterizing and managing its security issues.

Implementing a Risk Management Approach

Risk is the possibility of suffering harm or loss. It refers to a situation in which a person could do something undesirable or a natural occurrence could cause an undesirable outcome, resulting in a negative impact or consequence. The first step in managing risk is to understand what your risks are in relation to your organization's missions and its key assets. This understanding is reached by carrying out a comprehensive risk evaluation to identify your organization's risks. Once these risks are identified, the organization's personnel must decide what to do to address them. *Risk management* is the ongoing process of identifying risks and implementing plans to address them.

In this book, we propose a risk management approach to establish and improve an organization's information security posture. A comprehensive information security risk management approach incorporates asset, threat, and vulnerability information and enables decision makers to develop relative priorities based on what is important to the organization. It is a flexible approach that is uniquely tailored to each organization.

A risk management approach involves the entire organization, including personnel from both the information technology department and the business lines of the organization [GAO 98]. Solution strategies derived by using this approach are practice-based, that is, they are driven by best or accepted industry practices. By implementing these practice-based solutions across the information technology department and the business lines, an organization can start institutionalizing good security practices and making them part of the way the organization routinely conducts business. This approach enables an organization to improve its security posture over time. The next section takes a closer look at an information security risk evaluation and management.

1.2 Information Security Risk Evaluation and Management

Think about how much you rely upon access to information and systems to do your job. Today, information systems are essential to most organizations, because virtually all information is captured, stored, and accessed in digital form.

We rely on digital data that are accessible, dependable, and protected from misuse. Systems are interconnected in ways that could not have been imagined ten years ago. Networked systems have enabled unprecedented access to information. Unfortunately, they have also exposed our information to a variety of new threats. Organizations today have implemented a wide variety of complex computing infrastructures. They need flexible approaches that enable them to understand their information-specific security risks and then to create strategies to address those risks. An organization that wishes to improve its security posture must be prepared to take the following steps:

1. Change from a reactive, problem-based approach to proactive prevention of problems.
2. Consider security from multiple perspectives.
3. Establish a flexible infrastructure at all levels of the organization capable of responding rapidly to changing technology and security needs.
4. Initiate an ongoing, continual effort to maintain and improve its security posture.

An information security *risk evaluation* is a process that can help you meet these objectives. It generates an organizationwide view of information security risks. It provides a baseline that can be used to focus mitigation and improvement activities. Periodically, an organization needs to "reset" its baseline by conducting another evaluation. The time between evaluations can be predetermined (e.g., yearly) or triggered by major events (e.g., corporate reorganization, redesign of an organization's computing infrastructure). However, an information security risk evaluation is only one part of an organization's continuous information security risk management activities.

Evaluation Activities

Consider what happens during an evaluation. When an organization conducts an information security risk evaluation, it performs activities to

- **Identify** information security risks
- **Analyze** the risks to determine priorities
- **Plan** for improvement by developing a protection strategy for organizational improvement and risk mitigation plans to reduce the risk to critical organizational assets

The evaluation only provides a direction for an organization's information security activities; it does not necessarily lead to meaningful improvement. No evaluation, no matter how detailed or how expert, will improve an organization's security posture unless the organization follows through by implementing the results. After the evaluation, the organization should take the following steps:

1. **Plan** how to implement the protection strategy and risk mitigation plans from the evaluation by developing detailed action plans. This activity can include a detailed cost-benefit analysis among strategies and actions.

2. **Implement** the selected detailed action plans.

3. **Monitor** the plans for progress and effectiveness. This activity includes monitoring risks for any changes.

4. **Control** variations in plan execution by taking appropriate corrective actions.

Note that these activities are simply a *plan-do-check-act* cycle.

Risk Evaluation and Management

Risk evaluation is only the first step of risk management. Figure 1-1 illustrates an information security risk management framework and the "slice" that an evaluation provides. The framework highlights the operations that organizations can use to identify and address their information security risks. Chapter 14 examines the framework in some detail and presents the basic concepts behind information security risk management. One important point to note is that most information security risk management approaches rely upon the evaluation to focus subsequent mitigation and improvement activities.

The evaluation thus plays a central role in managing information security risks. It can help an organization assess both its organizational practices and installed technology base and can enable personnel in an organization to make information protection decisions based on potential impact on the organization. Information security risk evaluations can enable the selection of cost-effective and useful countermeasures by balancing the costs of addressing a risk against the benefits derived from avoiding the negative impact. They can also allow an organization to focus its security activities on what is important. If the organization's policies, practices, and tools are improperly "aimed," management in that organization is not effectively using its staff's time.

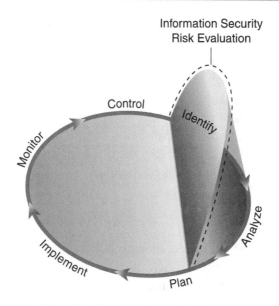

Information Security
Risk Evaluation

Control

Identify

Monitor

Analyze

Implement

Plan

FIGURE 1-1 Information Security Risk Evaluation Activities in Relation to an Information Security Risk Management Framework

There are many types of information security risk evaluations available to potential users. The quality and scope of products and services vary across an extremely wide range. Many of the evaluations do not lend themselves to an organizationwide security improvement approach. The next section outlines a flexible approach to evaluating information security risks in an organization.

1.3 An Approach to Information Security Risk Evaluations

An information security risk evaluation must identify both organizational and technological issues to be effective. It must address both the computing infrastructure and the way in which people use it as they perform their jobs. Thus, an evaluation needs to incorporate the context in which people use the infrastructure to meet the business objectives of the organization as well as technological security issues related to the infrastructure. It must consider what makes the organization succeed and what makes it fail.

We view using information security risk evaluations to improve an organization's security posture as a sound business practice. Since most organizations rely upon access to electronic data to conduct business, the data need to be adequately protected from misuse. The ability of an organization to achieve its mission and meet its business objectives is directly and strategically linked to the state of the computing infrastructure and to the manner in which personnel interact with it. For an organization to be in the best position to achieve its mission, its people need to understand which information-related assets are most important and what they should be doing to protect those assets. In other words, people in the organization need to be involved in the evaluation.

OCTAVE Approach

The Operationally Critical Threat, Asset, and Vulnerability Evaluation (OCTAVE) enables an organization to sort through the complex web of organizational and technological issues to understand and address its information security risks. OCTAVE defines an approach to information security risk evaluations that is comprehensive, systematic, context driven, and self-directed.

At the core of OCTAVE is the concept of self-direction, which means that people from an organization manage and direct the information security risk evaluation for that organization. Information security is the responsibility of everyone in the organization, not just the IT department. The organization's people need to direct the activities and make the decisions about its information security improvement efforts. OCTAVE achieves this by establishing a small, interdisciplinary team drawn from an organization's own personnel, called the analysis team, to lead the organization's evaluation process.

The analysis team includes people from both the business units and the information technology department, because information security includes both business- and technology-related issues. People from the business units of an organization understand what information is important to complete their tasks as well as how they access and use the information. The information technology staff understand issues related to how the computing infrastructure is configured as well as what is important to keep it running. Both of these perspectives are important in understanding the global, organizational view of information security risk.

Information Security Risk

An information security risk breaks down into four major components: asset, threat, vulnerability, and impact. An information security risk evaluation must account for all of these components. OCTAVE is an asset-driven evaluation approach, framing the organization's risks in the context of its assets. Using the organization's assets to focus the evaluation's activities is an efficient means of reducing the number of threats and risks that you must consider during the evaluation [Fites 89]. In addition, assets are used to form a bridge between the organization's business objectives and the security-related information gathered during an evaluation.

OCTAVE requires an analysis team to (1) identify the information-related assets (e.g., information, systems) that are important to the organization and (2) focus risk analysis activities on those assets judged to be most critical to the organization.

The analysis team has to consider the relationships among critical *assets,* the *threats* to those assets, and *vulnerabilities* (both organizational and technological) that can expose assets to threats. Only the analysis team can evaluate risks in an operational context. In other words, OCTAVE focuses on how operational systems are used to conduct an organization's business and how those systems are at risk due to security threats.

When a team completes an OCTAVE, it creates a protection strategy for organizational improvement and risk mitigation plans to reduce the risk to the organization's critical assets. Thus, the process incorporates both strategic (long-term or organizationwide) and tactical (mid-term or asset-specific protections) views of risk.

Three Phases

The organizational, technological, and analysis aspects of an information security risk evaluation lend themselves to a three-stage approach. OCTAVE is built around these three phases to enable organizational personnel to assemble a comprehensive picture of the organization's information security needs.

Phase 1: Build Asset-Based Threat Profiles. This is an evaluation of organizational aspects. Staff members from the organization contribute their perspectives on what is important to the organization (information-related assets) and what is currently being done to protect those assets. The analysis team consolidates the information, selects the assets that are most important to the organization (critical assets), and identifies the threats to these assets.

Phase 2: Identify Infrastructure Vulnerabilities. This is an evaluation of the computing infrastructure. The analysis team identifies key information technology systems and components related to each critical asset. The team then examines the key components for weaknesses (technology vulnerabilities) that can lead to unauthorized action against critical assets.

Phase 3: Develop Security Strategy and Plans. During this part of the evaluation, the analysis team identifies risks to the organization's critical assets and decides what to do about them. The team creates a protection strategy for the organization and mitigation plans to address the risks to the critical assets, based upon an analysis of the information gathered.

OCTAVE Variations

The specific ways in which business practices (e.g., planning, budgeting) are implemented in different organizations vary according to the characteristics of the organizations. Consider the differences between management practices at a small start-up company and those required in a large established organization. Both organizations require a set of similar management practices for planning and budgeting, but the practices are implemented differently. Similarly, the OCTAVE approach defines an information security risk as a management practice. We have found that the ways in which organizations implement information security risk evaluations differ based on a variety of organizational factors. OCTAVE implemented in a large multinational corporation is different from OCTAVE in a small start-up. However, some common principles, attributes, and outputs hold across organizational types.

Common Elements

The common elements of the OCTAVE approach are embodied in a set of criteria that define the principles, attributes, and outputs of the OCTAVE approach. Many methods can be consistent with these criteria, but there is only one set of

OCTAVE criteria. The Software Engineering Institute (SEI) has developed one method consistent with the criteria, the OCTAVE Method, which was designed with large organizations (more than 300 employees) in mind. The institute is presently developing a method for small organizations (fewer than 100 employees). In addition, others might define methods for specific contexts that are consistent with the OCTAVE criteria. Figure 1-2 illustrates these points.

The next chapter explains the principles, attributes, and outputs of OCTAVE, defining the criteria for information security risk evaluations. Part II presents the OCTAVE Method as an example of a method consistent with the criteria. Although the method was designed for large organizations, the concepts described are applicable to organizations of any size.

You can think of the OCTAVE Method as a baseline or starting point from which you can adapt to a particular operational environment or industry segment.

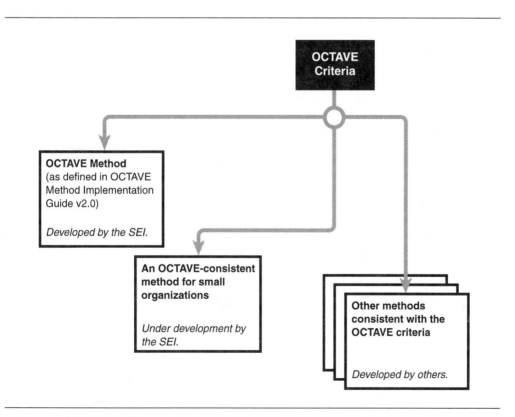

FIGURE 1-2 The OCTAVE Approach

The activities it requires can be tailored for a variety of organizational sizes. There are, however, limits to tailoring the OCTAVE Method. For example, the organizational dynamics of very small organizations are quite different from those of large organizations. An information security risk evaluation specifically designed for the needs of small organizations may have a distinctly different look and feel from the OCTAVE Method. Part III looks at tailoring options and how to adapt the OCTAVE approach to meet the needs of both small and complex organizations while still remaining true to its principles, attributes, and outputs. Part III also lays the groundwork for continuing the management and improvement of information security.

2

Principles and Attributes of Information Security Risk Evaluations

The journey of learning about information security risk evaluations begins with the fundamentals. This chapter presents the principles, attributes, and outputs of the OCTAVE approach, defines the basic characteristics of OCTAVE, and lays the foundation for the more detailed discussions about specific implementations of OCTAVE and information security risk management that come later in this book.

2.1 Introduction

The OCTAVE approach is defined in a set of criteria that includes principles, attributes, and outputs [Alberts 01b]. *Principles* are the fundamental concepts driving the nature of the evaluation. They define the philosophy that shapes the evaluation process. For example, self-direction is one of the principles of OCTAVE. The concept of self-direction means that people inside the organization are in the best position to lead the evaluation and make decisions.

The requirements of the evaluation are embodied in the attributes and outputs. *Attributes* are the distinctive qualities, or characteristics, of the evaluation. They are the requirements that define the basic elements of the OCTAVE approach and define what is necessary to make the evaluation a success from both the process and organizational perspectives. Attributes are derived from the OCTAVE principles. For example, one of the attributes of OCTAVE is that an interdisciplinary team (the analysis team) staffed by personnel from the organization leads the evaluation. The principle behind the creation of an analysis team is self-direction. Finally, *outputs* define the outcomes that an analysis team must achieve during the evaluation.

Table 2-1 lists the structure of the principles, attributes, and outputs that we will examine in this chapter. We begin our exploration of the OCTAVE approach in the next section by looking at principles.

2.2 Information Security Risk Management Principles

This section focuses on information security risk management principles. This is where we look at some of the philosophical underpinnings of an information security risk management approach. The principles shape the nature of risk management activities and provide the basis for the evaluation process. We group principles into the following three areas:

1. **Information Security Risk Evaluation Principles:** key aspects that form the foundation of an effective information security risk evaluation

TABLE 2-1 Information Security Principles, Attributes, and Outputs

Principles	Attributes	Phase 1	Outputs Phase 2	Phase 3
• Self-direction	• Analysis team	• Critical assets	• Key components	• Risks to critical assets
• Adaptable measures	• Augmenting analysis team skills	• Security requirements for critical assets	• Current technology vulnerabilities	• Risk measures
• Defined process	• Catalog of practices	• Threats to critical assets		• Protection strategy
• Foundation for a continuous process	• Generic threat profile	• Current security practices		• Risk mitigation plans
• Foward-looking view	• Catalog of vulnerabilities	• Current organizational vulnerabilities		
• Focus on the critical few	• Defined evaluation activities			
• Integrated Management	• Documented evaluation results			
• Open communication	• Evaluation scope			
• Global perspective	• Next steps			
• Teamwork	• Focus on risk			
	• Focused activities			
	• Organizational and technological issues			
	• Business and information technology participation			
	• Senior management participation			
	• Collaborative approach			

2. **Risk Management Principles:**[1] basic principles common to effective risk management practices

3. **Organizational and Cultural Principles:**[1] aspects of the organization and its culture essential to the successful management of information security risks

The ten information security risk management principles, shown graphically in Figure 2-1, are discussed in turn in the next section.

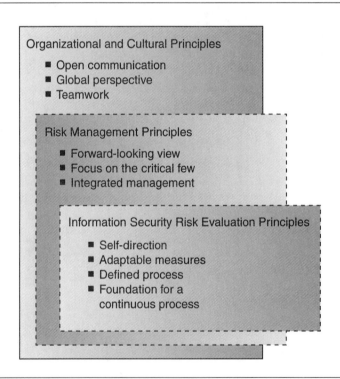

FIGURE 2-1 Information Security Risk Management Principles

---

1. These principles are similar in scope and intent to those documented in the *Continuous Risk Management Guidebook* [Dorofee 96].

2.2.1 Information Security Risk Evaluation Principles

We begin our examination of principles by focusing on the concepts that drive information security risk evaluations. This category includes the following four principles:

1. Self-direction
2. Adaptable measures
3. Defined process
4. Foundation for a continuous process

These principles provide the foundation for a successful evaluation. They focus on the roles of organizational personnel, key aspects of the process, and the link to ongoing security improvement activities. The first principle that we look at is self-direction.

Self-Direction

Self-direction describes a situation in which certain people in an organization manage and direct information security risk evaluations for that organization. These people are responsible for directing the risk management activities and for making decisions about the organization's security efforts. This approach allows the evaluation to consider the organization's unique circumstances and context. Self-direction requires

- Taking responsibility for information security by leading the information security risk evaluation and managing the evaluation process
- Making the final decisions about the organization's security efforts, including which improvements and actions to implement

Adaptable Measures

A flexible evaluation process can adapt to changing technology and advancements. It is not constrained by a rigid model of current sources of threats or by what practices are currently accepted as "best." Because the information security and information technology domains change very rapidly, an adaptable set of measures against which an organization and its unique context can be evaluated is essential. Adaptable measures require

- Current catalogs of information that define accepted security practices, known sources of threat, and known technological weaknesses (vulnerabilities)
- An evaluation process that can accommodate changes to the catalogs of information

Defined Process

A defined process describes the need for information security evaluation programs to rely upon defined and standardized evaluation procedures. Using a defined evaluation process can help to institutionalize the process, ensuring some level of consistency in the application of the evaluation. A defined process requires

- Assigning responsibilities for conducting the evaluation
- Defining all evaluation activities
- Specifying all tools, worksheets, and catalogs of information required by the evaluation
- Creating a common format for documenting the evaluation results

Foundation for a Continuous Process

An organization must implement practice-based security strategies and plans to improve its security posture over time. By implementing these practice-based solutions, an organization can start institutionalizing good security practices, making them part of the way the organization routinely conducts business. Security improvement is a continuous process, and the results of an information security risk evaluation provide the foundation for continuous improvement, which requires

- Identifying information security risks using a defined evaluation process
- Implementing the results of information security risk evaluations
- Setting up the ability to manage information security risks over time
- Implementing security strategies and plans that incorporate a practice-based approach to security improvement

2.2.2 Risk Management Principles

Now that we have presented the information security risk evaluation principles, we broaden our focus to risk management. The principles in this category are common to general risk management practices; they are not unique to information security. We first identified these principles when we were developing risk management techniques for software development projects [Dorofee 96]. This category includes the following three principles:

1. Forward-looking view
2. Focus on the critical few
3. Integrated management

Forward-Looking View

A forward-looking view requires an organization's personnel to look beyond the current problems by focusing on risks to the organization's most critical assets. The focus is on managing uncertainty by exploring the interrelationships among assets, threats, and vulnerabilities and examining the resulting impact on the organization's mission and business objectives. A forward-looking view requires thinking about tomorrow, focusing on managing the uncertainty presented by a range of risks. It also requires managing organizational resources and activities by incorporating the uncertainty presented by information security risks.

Focus on the Critical Few

This principle requires the organization to focus on the most critical information security issues. Every organization faces constraints on the number of staff members and funding that can be used for information security activities. Thus, the organization must ensure that it is applying its resources efficiently, both during an information security risk evaluation and afterwards. A focus on the critical few requires (1) using targeted data collection to collect information about security risks and (2) identifying the organization's most critical assets and selecting security practices to protect those assets.

Integrated Management

This principle requires that security policies and strategies be consistent with organizational policies and strategies. The organization's management proactively considers trade-offs among business and security issues when creating policy, striking a balance between business and security goals. Integrated management means (1) incorporating information security issues into the organization's business processes and (2) considering business strategies and goals when creating and revising information security strategies and policies.

2.2.3 Organizational and Cultural Principles

The final type of principle that we will examine is the broadest of all: organizational and cultural principles. Like the risk management principles, these are not unique to the information security domain. Organizational and cultural principles help to create an organizational culture conducive to effective risk management. From our experience, if these principles are not part of the way an organization conducts business, many issues will go unnoticed. People will not communicate key risks, nor will they work together to address them. Since information security is such a complex discipline, it spans the entire organization. Implementing these principles is essential to create an environment that supports an open exchange of ideas. Those organizations that are unsuccessful in implementing a risk management approach often fail because they violate these principles. This category includes the following three principles:

1. Open communication
2. Global perspective
3. Teamwork

Open Communication

One of the most important principles, open communication, is also the most difficult to implement. Yet information security risk management cannot succeed without open communication of security-related issues. Information security risks cannot be addressed if they aren't communicated to and understood by the organization's decision makers. A fundamental concept behind most successful risk management programs is a culture that supports open communication of risk information through a collaborative evaluation approach. Often, evaluation methods provide staff members with ways of expressing issues so that the information is not attributed to them, allowing for a free expression of ideas. Open communication involves three aspects:

- Developing evaluation activities that are built upon collaborative approaches (e.g., workshops)

- Encouraging exchanges of security and risk information among all levels of an organization
- Using consensus-based processes that value the individual voice

Global Perspective

This principle requires members of the organization to create a common view of what is most important to the organization. Individual perspectives pertaining to information security risk are solicited and then consolidated to form a global picture of the information security risks with which the organization must deal. Such a global perspective means (1) identifying the multiple perspectives of information security risk that exist in the organization and (2) viewing information security risk within the larger context of the organization's mission and business objectives.

Teamwork

No individual can understand all of the information security issues facing an organization. As noted, information security risk management requires an interdisciplinary approach, including both business and information technology perspectives. The teamwork involved requires

- Creating an interdisciplinary team to lead the evaluation
- Knowing when to include additional perspectives in the evaluation activities
- Working cooperatively to complete evaluation activities
- Leveraging people's talents, skills, and knowledge

The principles defined in this section are broad concepts that form the foundation for information security risk evaluation activities. The next section explores how these concepts can be implemented in an information security risk evaluation approach by focusing on information security risk evaluation attributes.

2.3 Information Security Risk Evaluation Attributes

We now turn our attention directly toward information security evaluation, moving from the more abstract nature of risk management principles to information security risk evaluation attributes. The remainder of this chapter focuses on the attributes and outputs of the OCTAVE approach.

First, we examine the tangible characteristics of information security risk evaluations and define what is necessary to make the evaluation a success from both the process and organizational perspectives. We begin by exploring the primary relationships between the principles and attributes, illustrated in Table 2-2.

TABLE 2-2 Mapping OCTAVE Principles to Attributes

Principle	Attribute
Self-direction	Analysis team
	Augmenting analysis team skills
Adaptable measures	Catalog of practices
	Generic threat profile
	Catalog of vulnerabilities
Defined process	Defined evaluation activities
	Documented evaluation results
	Evaluation scope
Foundation for a continuous process	Next steps
	Catalog of practices
	Senior management participation
Forward-looking view	Focus on risk
Focus on the critical few	Evaluation scope
	Focused activities
Integrated management	Organizational and technological issues
	Business and information technology participation
	Senior management participation
Open communication	Collaborative approach
Global perspective	Organizational and technological issues
	Business and information technology participation
Teamwork	Analysis team
	Augment analysis team skills
	Business and information technology participation
	Collaborative approach

Note that some of the attributes map to more that one principle, as is to be expected in such a complex activity as an information security risk evaluation. By looking at the attribute names, you will notice that they are focused on tangible characteristics of the evaluation process and are process oriented rather than activity oriented. We will start looking at activities in the next section when we present the outputs. Let's turn our attention now to the information security risk evaluation attributes, starting with the analysis team.

Analysis Team

An analysis team staffed by personnel from the organization must lead the evaluation activities. The analysis team must be interdisciplinary in nature, including people from both the business units and the information technology department. The analysis team must manage and direct the information security risk evaluation for its organization, and it must be responsible for making decisions based on the information gathered during the process.

This attribute is important because it ensures that ultimate responsibility for conducting the evaluation is assigned to a team of individuals from the organization. Using an analysis team to lead it helps to ensure the following results:

- People who understand the business processes and who understand information technology work together to improve the organization's security posture.
- The evaluation is run by personnel who understand how to apply all worksheets and tools used during the evaluation.
- The method is applied consistently across the organization.
- People in the organization feel "ownership" of the evaluation results, making them more likely to implement the recommended strategies and plans.

Augmenting Analysis Team Skills

The evaluation process must allow the analysis team to augment its skills and abilities by including additional people who have specific skills required by the process or who possess needed expertise. These additional people can be from other parts of the organization, or they can be from an external organization.

The analysis team is responsible for analyzing information and making decisions during the evaluation. However, the core members of the analysis team may not have all of the knowledge and skills needed during the evaluation. At each point in the process, the analysis team members must decide if they need to augment their knowledge and skills for a specific task. They can do so by including others in the organization or by using external experts. This attribute is important because it ensures that the analysis team has the required skills and knowledge to complete the evaluation. This attribute also allows an organization to conduct an information security risk evaluation even when it does not have all of the required knowledge and skills within the organization. It provides an avenue for working with external experts when appropriate.

Catalog of Practices

The evaluation process must assess an organization's security practices by considering a range of strategic and operational security practice areas. These are formally defined in a catalog of practices. The catalog of practices used by an organization should be consistent with all laws, regulations, and standards of due care with which the organization must comply. A more detailed description of the catalog of practices appears in Chapter 5 and in Appendix C.

Using a catalog of practices is important because it allows an organization to evaluate itself against a known and accepted measure. This helps the organization to understand what it is currently doing well with respect to security (its current security practices) and what it is not doing well (its organizational vulnerabilities). The catalog of practices is also important because it creates the structure for an organization's protection strategy. Finally, the catalog also provides a basis for selecting actions to include in risk mitigation plans.

Generic Threat Profile

The evaluation process must assess threats to the organization's critical assets by considering a broad range of potential threat sources that are formally defined in a generic threat profile. The profile contains potential threat sources ranging from insiders deliberately modifying critical information to power outages, broken water pipes, and other dangers beyond the organization's control.

Using a generic threat profile is important because it allows an organization to identify threats to its critical assets based on known potential sources of danger. The profile also uses a structured way of representing potential threats and yields a comprehensive summary of threats to critical assets, thus providing a complete and simple way to record and communicate threat information. A detailed look at the generic threat profile is presented in Chapter 6.

Catalog of Vulnerabilities

The evaluation process must assess the current technological weaknesses (technology vulnerabilities) in the key components of the computing infrastructure by considering a range of technology vulnerabilities based on platform and application. Vulnerability evaluation tools (software, checklists, scripts) examine infrastructure components for technology vulnerabilities contained in the catalog. Two examples of catalogs of vulnerabilities are CERT®[1] Knowledgebase[2] and Common Vulnerabilities and Exploits (CVE).[3]

Using a catalog of vulnerabilities is important because it allows an organization to evaluate its technology base against known technology vulnerabilities. Identifying which vulnerabilities are present in the organization's key components provides the organization with information about how vulnerable its computing infrastructure currently is. Chapters 7 and 8 discuss how to use the catalog of vulnerabilities.

Defined Evaluation Activities

The procedures for performing each evaluation activity and the artifacts (worksheets, catalogs, etc.) used during each activity must be defined and documented. These include

- Procedures for preparing for the evaluation
- Procedures for scoping the evaluation
- Procedures for completing each evaluation activity
- Specifications for all tools and worksheets required by each activity
- Specifications for catalogs of information that define accepted security practices, known sources of threat, and known technological weaknesses

---

1. CERT is registered in the U.S. Patent and Trademark Office.

2. The CERT® Knowledgebase contains a public database describing vulnerabilities and a restricted access catalog containing descriptive information regarding more than 1,300 vulnerabilities. It can be accessed at http://www.cert.org/kb/.

3. CVE is a community effort led by the MITRE Corporation. It can be accessed at http://www.cve.mitre.org.

Implementing defined evaluation activities helps to institutionalize the evaluation process in the organization, ensuring some level of consistency in the application of the process [GAO 99]. It also provides a basis upon which the activities can be tailored to fit the needs of a particular business line or group.

Documented Evaluation Results

The organization must document the results of the evaluation, either in paper or electronic form. Organizations typically document and archive risks to the organization's critical assets as well as security strategies and plans to improve the organization's security posture.

It is important to establish a permanent record of evaluation results. A database of information can serve as source material for subsequent evaluations and is also useful when tracking the status of plans and actions after the evaluation. For example, the information recorded can also be used as lessons learned. When risks to a critical asset are identified, staff members can look at the mitigation plans for risks to similar assets. Organizational personnel can then understand which mitigation actions have been effective in the past and which haven't, enabling them in turn to create more effective mitigation plans.

Evaluation Scope

The extent of each evaluation must be defined. The evaluation process must include guidelines to help the organization decide which operational areas (business units) to include in the evaluation. Determining the scope of an evaluation is important for ensuring that its results are useful to the organization. If the scope of an evaluation becomes too broad, it is often difficult to analyze all of the information that is gathered. If it is too small, it will not yield an accurate picture. Setting a manageable scope for the evaluation reduces the size of the evaluation, making it easier to schedule and perform the activities. In addition, the areas of an organization can be prioritized for the evaluation. Essentially, the highest-risk areas can be examined first or more frequently.

Next Steps

The evaluation must include an activity whereby organizational personnel identify the next steps required to implement security strategies and plans. This activity often requires active sponsorship and participation from the organization's senior managers. Next steps typically include the following information:

- What actions the organization will take to follow up on the results of the evaluation
- Who will be involved in implementing security strategies and plans
- Plans for future activities to evaluate information security risks

The task of identifying the next steps that people in the organization must take to implement the protection strategy and the mitigation plans is essential for security improvement. The people in the organization need to build upon the results of the evaluation. Getting senior management sponsorship is the first critical step toward making this happen.

Focus on Risk

The evaluation must focus on assessing an organization's information security risks by examining the interrelationships among assets, threats to the assets, and vulnerabilities (including both organizational and technological weaknesses). This attribute is important because it requires the organization's personnel to focus on security issues and their effect on the organization's business objectives and mission. Personnel must look beyond the current organizational and technological weaknesses and examine how those weaknesses relate to the organization's critical assets and the threats to those assets, thus establishing the risks to those assets.

Focused Activities

The evaluation process must include guidelines for focusing evaluation activities, for example:

- Workshops that efficiently elicit security-related information from an organization's staff members
- Analysis activities that use asset information to focus threat and risk identification activities
- Analysis activities that use asset and threat information to set the scope of the technology vulnerability evaluation
- Planning activities that establish risk priorities using risk measures (impact, probability)

Focusing each activity on the most critical information security issues is important to ensure that the organization applies its resources efficiently. If you gather too much information, it may be difficult to analyze. Focusing on the most important information reduces the size of the evaluation, making it easier to perform the activities while still collecting the most meaningful data and producing the most significant results.

Organizational and Technological Issues

The evaluation process must examine both organizational and technological issues. Information security risk evaluations typically include the following practice- and vulnerability-related information:

- Current effective security practices used by staff members
- Missing or ineffective security practices (also called organizational vulnerabilities)
- Technological weaknesses present in key information technology systems and components

Because security has both organizational and technological components, an evaluation must deal with both organizational and technological issues. When creating the organization's protection strategy and risk mitigation plans, the analysis team considers both types of issues in relation to the mission and business objectives of the organization. By doing so, the team is able to address security by creating a global picture of the information security risks the organization must confront.

Business and Information Technology Participation

The evaluation process must include participants from both the business units and the information technology department, allowing for the establishment of an interdisciplinary analysis team (see the analysis team attribute). Participants from key areas (business units) of the organization also need to contribute their perspectives on security-related issues during activities designed to elicit knowledge. Note that participants must include representatives from multiple organizational levels (senior management, middle management, and staff).

Incorporating multiple perspectives is essential to ensure that a broad range of risk factors is considered. Staff members who work in the business lines of an organization understand the relative importance of business operations and the systems and information that support them. In general, they are in the best position to understand the business impact of disruption or abuse to business systems and operations and the impact of potential mitigation actions. It is information technology personnel and information security experts who best understand the design of existing systems and the impact of technology-related vulnerabilities, just as it is they who are also in the best position to evaluate the trade-offs of mitigation actions when evaluating their effect on system performance.

Senior Management Participation

Senior managers in the organization must have defined roles during the evaluation process. Typically, an organization's senior managers demonstrate active sponsorship of the evaluation, participate in workshops to contribute their understanding of security-related issues and their effect on business processes, review and approve security strategies and plans, and define the steps required to implement security strategies and plans.

Senior management participation is the single most important success factor for information security risk evaluations, as it demonstrates strong sponsorship of the evaluation. This level of sponsorship helps to ensure that staff members are available and willing to participate in the evaluation, take the evaluation seriously, and are prepared to implement the findings after the evaluation.

The senior managers' active participation in an information security risk evaluation is also important to the success of the initiative. Senior managers can help to define the scope of the assessment and to identify participants. If senior managers support the evaluation, people in the organization tend to participate actively. If senior managers do not support the evaluation, staff support for the evaluation will dissipate quickly.

Collaborative Approach

Each activity of the evaluation process must include interaction and collaboration among the people who are participating in that activity. Collaboration can be achieved through the use of workshops or other interactive methods.

A collaborative approach is an essential attribute of information security risk evaluations. Because security is interdisciplinary in nature, completing the evaluation activities requires interdisciplinary knowledge and skills. It is therefore important for each evaluation activity to require all participating individuals to interact and collaborate, thus ensuring that the necessary skills and knowledge are applied to complete that activity satisfactorily.

As you can see, all of the attributes just described focus on the evaluation process and how that process is implemented in an organization. Next, we build on this view by exploring the results of information security risk evaluations.

2.4 Information Security Risk Evaluation Outputs

Outputs are the results, or outcomes, that an analysis team must achieve during the evaluation; they are the tangible products of the evaluation. An organizationwide information security risk evaluation produces three basic types of outputs: (1) organizational data, (2) technological data, and (3) risk analysis and mitigation data.

In designing the OCTAVE, we decided to organize the evaluation activities according to these data classifications, producing a three-stage information security risk evaluation approach. The three phases illustrate the interdisciplinary nature of information security by emphasizing its organizational and technological aspects. The OCTAVE phases and the required outputs are illustrated in Figure 2-2.

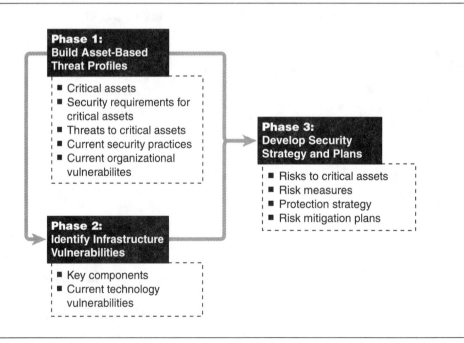

FIGURE 2-2 OCTAVE Phases

Sections 2.4.1–2.4.3 describe each phase of OCTAVE and highlight the outputs of each phase.

2.4.1 Phase 1: Build Asset-Based Threat Profiles

In today's business environment the computing infrastructure is distributed across organizations. Many business processes are also distributed, with staff members performing specialized job functions. Thus, all staff members play a role in information security. Each person has unique knowledge of what information is important to completing his or her job tasks, as well as a unique perspective on which security practices are effectively protecting the organization's information-related assets and which are missing or inadequate. In phase 1, the staff members from across an organization have the opportunity to contribute what they know about the organization's information security issues through a series of knowledge elicitation workshops.

Organizational View

Phase 1 is an organizational evaluation that includes knowledge elicitation, data consolidation, and analysis activities. In the knowledge elicitation activities, staff members from across the organization contribute their perspectives on what is important to the organization (information-related assets), what is currently being done to protect those assets (security practices), and missing or inadequate security practices (organizational vulnerabilities).

To consolidate the different viewpoints, the analysis team consolidates information from the knowledge elicitation workshops, selects the assets that are most important to the organization (critical assets), describes security requirements for the critical assets, and identifies threats to the critical assets.

The knowledge elicitation workshops are an important way of identifying what is really happening in the organization with respect to information security. Consolidating and analyzing the data are important tasks because they provide different perspectives on the organizational view of information security. These perspectives are used to focus subsequent evaluation activities and create the basis for the organization's protection strategy and risk mitigation plans created during phase 3.

Outputs

Table 2-3 highlights each required output of phase 1, provides a brief description of that output, and indicates where you can find more information about it in this book.

TABLE 2-3 Phase 1 Outputs

Output	Description
Critical assets	Critical assets are the information-related assets that are believed to be most important in meeting the missions of the organization. Section 5.2 presents asset identification, and Section 6.3 addresses critical asset selection.
Security requirements for critical assets	Security requirements for a critical asset indicate the important qualities of that asset with respect to its confidentiality, integrity, and availability. Section 5.4 defines security requirements, and Section 6.4 shows how to define these requirements for critical assets.
Threats to critical assets	A threat to a critical asset explicitly indicates how someone or some event can violate that asset's security requirements. Section 5.3 defines threats, and Section 6.5 discusses how to identify threats to critical assets.
Current security practices	Security practices are those actions presently used by the organization to initiate, implement, and maintain its internal security. Section 5.5 looks at security practices.
Current organizational vulnerabilities	Organizational vulnerabilities are indications of missing or inadequate security practices. Section 5.5 examines organizational vulnerabilities.

2.4.2 Phase 2: Identify Infrastructure Vulnerabilities

Phase 2 is an evaluation of the current information infrastructure. Phase 2 includes data gathering and analysis activities. This phase reflects what the majority of people think of when they hear the term "security evaluation," namely, an assessment of the computing infrastructure. The analysis team

- Scopes the examination of the computing infrastructure using the critical assets and threats to those assets
- Identifies key information technology systems and components that are related to each critical asset
- Evaluates key components for vulnerabilities
- Analyzes the resulting data to identify weaknesses (technology vulnerabilities) that can lead to unauthorized action against critical assets

Technological View

Phase 2 captures the technological view of information security, highlighting the technology vulnerabilities that are present in and apply to network services, architecture, operating systems, and applications. Phase 2 is important because the assets, security requirements, and threats of phase 1 are examined in relation to the computing infrastructure. In addition, the outputs of phase 2 document the present state of the computing infrastructure with respect to technological weaknesses that could be exploited by threat actors.

Outputs

Table 2-4 highlights each required output of phase 2, provides a brief description of that output, and indicates where you can find more information about it in this book.

TABLE 2-4 Phase 2 Outputs

Output	Description
Key components	Key components are devices that are important in processing, storing, or transmitting critical assets. Sections 7.2 and 7.3 address key components.
Current technology vulnerabilities	Technology vulnerabilities are weaknesses in systems that can directly lead to unauthorized action. Sections 8.2 and 8.3 define technology vulnerabilities.

2.4.3 Phase 3: Develop Security Strategy and Plans

Phase 3 includes risk analysis and risk mitigation activities. During risk analysis, the analysis team identifies and analyzes the risks to the organization's critical assets. Specifically, the team does three things:

1. It gathers data used to characterize and measure the risks to critical assets.
2. It defines the risk evaluation criteria for measuring the impact of threats to the organization.
3. It evaluates risks against the evaluation criteria.

During risk mitigation, the analysis team creates a protection strategy and mitigation plans based on an analysis of the information gathered. Specifically, the team does two things:

1. It develops a protection strategy for organizational improvement and risk mitigation plans to protect the organization's information-related assets.

2. It identifies next steps that will be taken to implement the protection strategy and the mitigation plans.

Risk Analysis

Phase 3 is important, because it is during this phase that the analysis team makes sense of its information security issues and develops a strategy and plans for improvement. The risk analysis activities of phase 3 are important for two reasons:

*   They put information security threats into the context of what the organization is trying to achieve, resulting in explicit statements of risk to the organization's critical assets.

*   They establish the criteria for measuring risks and a basis for setting priorities when developing risk mitigation plans.

The risk mitigation activities of phase 3 are important for several reasons:

*   They result in a protection strategy designed to improve the organization's security posture.

*   They create a risk mitigation plan for each critical asset designed to protect that asset.

*   They require the organization's senior managers to review the protection strategy and risk mitigation plans from the organizational perspective, developing senior management sponsorship of the evaluation results.

*   They define what the organization will do to implement the results of the evaluation, enabling ongoing security improvement.

Outputs

Table 2-5 highlights each required output of phase 3, provides a brief description of that output, and indicates where you can find more information about it in this book.

TABLE 2-5 Phase 3 Outputs

Output	Description
Risks to critical assets	A risk to a critical asset explicitly indicates how a threat to a critical asset can result in a negative impact or consequence to the organization. Section 9.2 discusses risk identification.
Risk measures	Risk measures are qualitative assessments of the ultimate effect on an organization's mission and business objectives (impact value) and the likelihood of occurrence (probability). Sections 9.3, 9.4, and 9.5 address how to establish risk measures.
Protection strategy	An organization's protection strategy defines its direction with respect to information security improvement efforts. Section 10.4 presents protection strategies.
Risk mitigation plan	Risk mitigation plans are an organization's plans for reducing the risks to its critical assets. Section 10.5 covers risk mitigation plans.

As indicated in Chapter 1, many methods are consistent with the OCTAVE approach. Part II focuses on one implementation of these criteria, the OCTAVE Method.

PART II

The OCTAVE Method

Chapter 2 presented the principles, attributes, and outputs of the OCTAVE approach, providing a foundation for information security risk evaluations. Part II builds upon that foundation by examining how the OCTAVE approach can be implemented in an organization. The OCTAVE Method is an example of an evaluation consistent with the principles, attributes, and outputs. This method is designed for larger organizations and is a starting point from which to adapt to a particular operational environment or industry segment.

Chapter 3 provides an overview of the OCTAVE Method, and Chapters 4 to 11 describe the activities required to conduct the method. Throughout Part II, each activity is illustrated using a sample scenario set in a hospital.

3

Introduction to
the OCTAVE Method

This chapter will introduce you to the basic structure of the OCTAVE Method, providing the foundation for a more detailed examination of the method in the following chapters. We also illustrate how the method is consistent with the general information security risk evaluation approach previously described.

3.1 Overview of the OCTAVE Method

The OCTAVE Method uses a three-phase approach to examining organizational and technology issues, thus assembling a comprehensive picture of the organization's information security needs. The method comprises a progressive series of workshops, each of which requires interaction among its participants. The OCTAVE Method is broken into eight processes: four in phase 1, two in phase 2, and two in phase 3. In addition, several preparation activities need to be completed before the actual evaluation. The three phases and preparation for the OCTAVE Method are depicted in Figure 3-1.

OCTAVE Workshops

The OCTAVE Method involves two types of workshops: (1) facilitated discussions with various members of the organization and (2) workshops in which the analysis team conducts a series of activities on its own. All workshops have a leader and a scribe. The leader is responsible for guiding all workshop activities

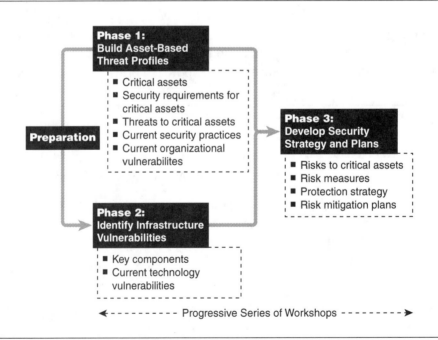

FIGURE 3-1 The OCTAVE Method

and ensuring that all of these (including preparatory and follow-up activities) are completed. The leader is also responsible for ensuring that all participants understand their roles and that any new or supplementary analysis team members are ready to participate actively in the workshop. All workshop leaders should also make sure that they select a decision-making approach (e.g., majority vote, consensus) to be used during the workshops. Scribes are responsible for recording information generated during the workshops, either electronically or on paper. Note that you might not have the same leader or scribe for all workshops. For example, a leader with more facilitation or interviewing skills may be suitable for the phase 1 workshops, whereas a leader with strong planning and analysis skills might be preferable for the phase 3 workshops.

The next four sections provide an overview of preparation activities and the processes of the OCTAVE Method.

3.1.1 Preparation

The initial focus of the OCTAVE Method is preparing for the evaluation. We have found the following to be key success factors:

Getting senior management sponsorship. This is the top success factor for information security risk evaluations. If senior managers do not support the process, staff support for the evaluation will dissipate quickly.

Selecting the analysis team. The analysis team is responsible for managing the process and analyzing information. The members of the team need to have sufficient skills and training to lead the evaluation and to know when to augment their knowledge and skills by including additional people for one or more activities.

Setting the appropriate scope of the OCTAVE Method. The evaluation should include important operational areas, but the scope cannot get too big. If it is too broad, it will be difficult for the analysis team to analyze all of the information. If the scope of the evaluation is too small, the results may not be as meaningful as they should be.

Selecting participants. During the knowledge elicitation workshops (processes 1 to 3), staff members from multiple organizational levels will contribute their knowledge about the organization. They should be assigned to workshops because of their knowledge and skills, not solely based on who is available.

The goal of preparation is to make sure that the evaluation is scoped properly, that the organization's senior managers support it, and that everyone participating in the process understands his or her role. The following preparation activities provide the right foundation for a successful evaluation:

- Obtain senior management sponsorship of OCTAVE.
- Select analysis team members.
- Select operational areas to participate in OCTAVE.
- Select participants.
- Coordinate logistics.

Once the preparation for the OCTAVE Method has been completed, the organization is ready to start the evaluation. Chapter 4 presents a detailed discussion of preparation activities, and the next section looks at phase 1 of the method.

3.1.2 Phase 1: Build Asset-Based Threat Profiles

In phase 1 you begin to build the organizational view of OCTAVE by focusing on the people in the organization. Figure 3-2 illustrates the four processes in phase 1.

Processes 1 to 3

The analysis team facilitates knowledge elicitation workshops during processes 1 to 3. Participants from across the organization contribute their unique perspectives about what is important to the organization (assets) and how well those assets are being protected. The following list highlights the audience for each of the processes:

Process 1: Identify Senior Management Knowledge. The participants in this process are the organization's senior managers.

Process 2: Identify Operational Area Management Knowledge. The participants in this process are the organization's operational area (middle) managers.

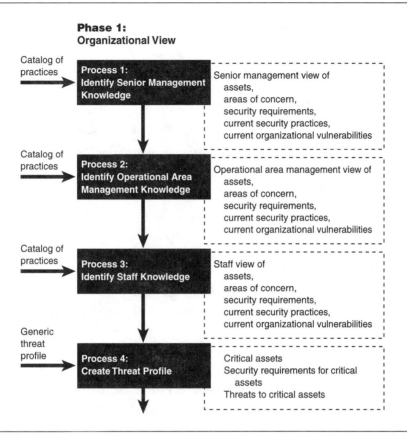

FIGURE 3-2 Phase 1: Build Asset-Based Threat Profiles

Process 3: Identify Staff Knowledge. The participants in this process are the organization's staff members. Information technology staff members normally participate in a separate workshop from the one attended by general staff members.

Four activities are undertaken to elicit knowledge from workshop participants during processes 1 to 3 (the basic activities are the same for each of the processes):

1. Identify assets and relative priorities.
2. Identify areas of concern.

3. Identify security requirements for the most important assets.

4. Capture knowledge of current security practices and organizational vulnerabilities.

Chapter 5 examines processes 1 to 3 in detail.

Process 4: Create Threat Profiles

The participants in this process are the analysis team members. During process 4, the team identifies the assets that are most critical to the organization and describes how those assets are threatened. Process 4 comprises the following activities:

- Consolidating information from processes 1 to 3
- Selecting critical assets
- Refining security requirements for critical assets
- Identifying threats to critical assets

See Chapter 6 for an in-depth discussion of process 4. The next section looks at the phase 2 processes.

3.1.3 Phase 2: Identify Infrastructure Vulnerabilities

Phase 2 is also called the "technological view" of the OCTAVE Method, because this is where you turn your attention to your organization's computing infrastructure. The second phase of the evaluation includes two processes, depicted in Figure 3-3.

Process 5: Identify Key Components

The participants in this process are the analysis team and selected members of the information technology (IT) staff. The ultimate objective of process 5 is to select infrastructure components to be examined for technological weaknesses during process 6. Process 5 consists of two activities:

1. Identifying key classes of components
2. Identifying infrastructure components to be examined

Chapter 7 looks at the activities of process 5 in more depth.

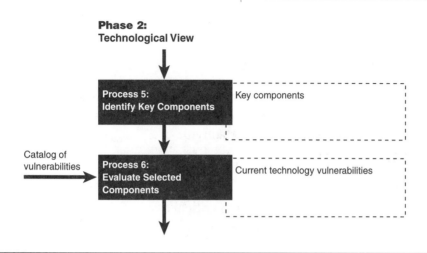

FIGURE 3-3 Phase 2: Identify Technological Vulnerabilities

Process 6: Evaluate Selected Components

The participants in this process are the analysis team and selected members of the IT staff. The goal of process 6 is to identify technological weaknesses in the infrastructure components that were identified during process 5. The technological weaknesses provide an indication of how vulnerable the organization's computing infrastructure is. Process 6 comprises two activities:

1. Running vulnerability evaluation tools on selected infrastructure components

2. Reviewing technology vulnerabilities and summarizing results

Chapter 8 provides more details about process 6. The next section completes our overview of the OCTAVE Method by looking at phase 3.

3.1.4 Phase 3: Develop Security Strategy and Plans

Phase 3 is designed to make sense of the information that you have gathered thus far in the evaluation. It is during this phase that you develop security strategies and plans designed to address your organization's unique risks and issues. The two processes of phase 3 are shown in Figure 3-4.

Process 7: Conduct Risk Analysis

The participants in process 7 are the analysis team members, and the goal of the process is to identify and analyze risks to the organization's critical assets. Process 7 includes the following three activities:

1. Identifying the impact of threats to critical assets
2. Creating risk evaluation criteria
3. Evaluating the impact of threats to critical assets

    Chapter 9 explores the details of process 7.

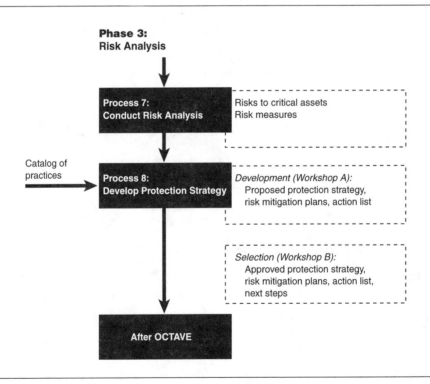

FIGURE 3-4 Phase 3: Develop Security Strategy and Plans

Process 8: Develop Protection Strategy

Process 8 includes two workshops. The participants in the first workshop for process 8 are the analysis team members and selected members of the organization (if the analysis team decides to supplement its skills and experience for protection strategy development). The goal of process 8 is to develop a protection strategy for the organization, mitigation plans for the risks to the critical assets, and an action list of near-term actions. The following are the activities of the first workshop of process 8:

1. Consolidate information from processes 1 to 3.
2. Review risk information.
3. Create protection strategy.
4. Create mitigation plans.
5. Create action list.

In the second workshop of process 8, the analysis team presents the proposed protection strategy, mitigation plans, and action list to senior managers in the organization. The senior managers review and revise the strategy and plans as necessary and then decide how the organization will build on the results of the evaluation. The following are the activities of the second workshop of process 8:

1. Prepare to meet with senior management.
2. Present risk information.
3. Review and refine protection strategy, mitigation plans, and action list.
4. Create next steps.

After the organization has developed a protection strategy and risk mitigation plans, it is ready to implement them. At this point, the organization has completed the OCTAVE Method. We examine the first workshop of process 8 in Chapter 10 and the second workshop in Chapter 11.

Nonlinear Nature of the OCTAVE Method

From the above description, the OCTAVE Method appears to be linear in nature. The method has three phases and eight processes, all numbered sequentially. It would be easy for you to assume that this is a lockstep process, that is, that when you complete one process, you are finished with it and can move to the next.

However, since information security addresses such complex organizational and technological issues, it does not lend itself to a linear process.

As you will find, the OCTAVE Method is nonlinear and iterative in nature. For example, you might identify issues in later processes that lead you to review (and possibly change) decisions that you made during earlier processes. There are actually many potential feedback loops in the method. As we present the detailed overview of the OCTAVE Method in Chapters 4 to 11, we do highlight some of the more common instances in which you should review your decisions and test your assumptions in light of new information that you have gathered. However, because of the overall complexity of security issues, there are too many potential feedback loops in the process to identify them all. Be aware of the need to revisit decisions and assumptions and do so when necessary. One guideline that we use often in this part of the book is "use your best judgment." In this case, you need to do just that—be aware of the nonlinear, iterative nature of the OCTAVE Method and go where the data lead you.

This concludes our brief introduction to the OCTAVE Method. The next section builds on this introduction by examining how the method is consistent with the attributes and outputs presented in Chapter 2.

3.2 Mapping Attributes and Outputs to the OCTAVE Method

The OCTAVE Method is consistent with the principles, attributes, and outputs of the OCTAVE approach described in Chapter 2. This section illustrates how the attributes and outputs map to the OCTAVE Method. Since Chapter 2 provided a mapping between principles and attributes, we do not explicitly map the principles to the OCTAVE Method here.

3.2.1 Attributes and the OCTAVE Method

Recall from Chapter 2 that attributes are the distinctive qualities, or characteristics, of the evaluation. They define the basic elements of an information security risk evaluation from both the process and organizational perspectives. Table 3-1 summarizes how each attribute is reflected in the OCTAVE Method.

The next section focuses on how the outputs map to the OCTAVE Method.

TABLE 3-1 Mapping of Attributes to the OCTAVE Method

Attribute	Implementation in the OCTAVE Method
Analysis team	An interdisciplinary analysis team consisting of personnel from the business units and the information technology department leads the OCTAVE Method.
Augmenting analysis team skills	The activities for the OCTAVE Method are documented in Chapters 4 to 11 of this book. We provide guidance about the types of skills required to conduct each process. If your analysis team believes that it does not possess sufficient knowledge and skills to conduct a process, it is instructed to include supplementary personnel who possess the required knowledge and skills for that process.
Catalog of practices	The OCTAVE Method requires the organization's security practices to be evaluated against a defined catalog of practices. Security practice–related information in worksheets is consistent with the practices in the catalog. (See Appendix B for the worksheets.)
Generic threat profile	The OCTAVE Method requires threats to the organization's critical assets to be evaluated against a generic threat profile. Threat-related information in the worksheets is consistent with the threats in the generic threat profile. (See Appendix B for the worksheets.)
Catalog of vulnerabilities	The OCTAVE Method requires the organization's computing infrastructure to be evaluated against a defined catalog of vulnerabilities. The method requires using vulnerability evaluation tools that check for known technology vulnerabilities.
Defined evaluation activities	The activities for the OCTAVE Method are documented in Chapters 4 to 11 of this book. They include • Guidance for setting the scope of the evaluation and for selecting participants • Guidance for conducting each process • Worksheets and templates for recording information gathered during each process (see Appendix B) • Catalogs of information required by the process (see Appendix C and Sections 5.1, 6.1, and 8.1)
Documented evaluation results	The OCTAVE Method requires the analysis team to document the results of the evaluation.
Evaluation scope	Guidance for setting the scope of the evaluation (e.g., selecting three to five operational areas) is provided in Chapter 4 of this book.
Next steps	The last activity in the OCTAVE Method requires senior managers to define actions to implement their organization's protection strategy and risk mitigation plans. The activity also requires the managers to assign responsibility for completing the actions.
Focus on risk	The OCTAVE Method is an information security risk evaluation. It addresses four components of risk: assets, threats, vulnerabilities and impact.

(continued)

TABLE 3-1 Mapping of Attributes to the OCTAVE Method (*continued*)

Attribute	Implementation in the OCTAVE Method
Focused activities	Each process of the OCTAVE Method focuses on identifying and analyzing the information security issues most important to the organization. • In processes 1 to 3 the facilitators focus the activities on the assets the participants believe to be most important. • In process 4 the analysis team focuses its analysis activities using the critical assets that it selects. • In processes 5 and 6 the analysis team sets the scope of the infrastructure vulnerability evaluation using the organization's critical assets and the threats to those assets. • In processes 7 and 8 the analysis team establishes risk priorities based on the organizational impact of risks.
Organizational and technological issues	The OCTAVE Method focuses on both organizational and technological issues. Phase 1 is an *organizational* evaluation whereby people from across the organization identify organizational information. Phase 2 is an evaluation of the information technology infrastructure, resulting in the identification of *technological* issues. The organizational and technological data are then analyzed during phase 3.
Business and information technology participation	An interdisciplinary analysis team that includes representatives from operational areas and the information technology department leads the evaluation. Personnel from both the business units and information technology department of the organization (including representation from multiple organizational levels) participate in processes 1 to 3.
Senior management participation	In the OCTAVE Method, senior managers are required to participate in process 1, in which the managers contribute their perspectives about what assets are important to them and how well those assets are being protected. The senior managers also participate in the second workshop of process 8, in which they review, refine, and approve the protection strategy and mitigation plans. In that workshop they also define the next steps for implementing the strategy and plans.
Collaborative approach	The OCTAVE Method comprises a progressive series of workshops, each of which requires interaction and cooperation among the participants.

3.2.2 Outputs and the OCTAVE Method

Outputs define the results that an analysis team must achieve during the evaluation. Table 3-2 shows where in the OCTAVE Method each required output is generated.

This section demonstrates how the attributes and outputs of the OCTAVE approach are implemented in the OCTAVE Method. We are now just about ready

TABLE 3-2 Mapping of Outputs to the OCTAVE Method

Output	Implementation in the OCTAVE Method
Critical assets	During processes 1 to 3 staff members from across the organization contribute their perspectives about which assets are important in completing their jobs. In process 4 the analysis team selects the assets that are most critical to the organization.
Security requirements for critical assets	Staff members from across the organization define security requirements for their important assets during processes 1 to 3. The analysis team uses this information during process 4 to establish the security requirements for the organization's critical assets.
Threats to critical assets	Staff members from across the organization identify scenarios that threaten their most important assets during processes 1 to 3. The analysis team uses these areas of concern as input when it creates a threat profile for each critical asset during process 4.
Current security practices	During processes 1 to 3 staff members from across the organization contribute their perspectives about which security practices are currently being used by the organization. The participants fill out surveys and talk about key issues during a follow-up discussion. During process 8 the analysis team consolidates security practices identified during the first three processes.
Current organizational vulnerabilities	During processes 1 to 3 staff members from across the organization contribute their perspectives about missing or inadequate practices in the organization (organizational vulnerabilities). These are identified in conjunction with security practices using surveys and follow-on discussions. During process 8 the analysis team consolidates organizational vulnerabilities identified during the first three processes.
Key components	The analysis team identifies key components of the computing infrastructure during process 5. The team uses the critical assets and the threats to the critical assets to focus their selection of components to evaluate for technology vulnerabilities.
Technology vulnerabilities	During process 6 the analysis team evaluates each key component from process 5 using vulnerability evaluation tools. The team interprets data generated by the tools, identifying the technological weaknesses (technology vulnerabilities) present in each component.
Risks to critical assets	During process 7 the analysis team identifies the potential impact on the organization of the threats to critical assets, resulting in explicit statements of risk.
Risk measures	The analysis team evaluates the impacts of risks based on a set of qualitative measures (high, medium, low) during process 7. Probability is viewed as optional in the OCTAVE Method.
Protection strategy	During process 8 the analysis team creates a protection strategy for organizational security improvement. The team bases the strategy on the organizational and technological information it identified throughout the OCTAVE Method.
Risk mitigation plans	The analysis team creates risk mitigation plans to reduce the risks to the organization's most critical assets during process 8. The team selects mitigation actions based on the organizational and technological information it identified throughout the evaluation process.

to dive into the details of the OCTAVE Method, but before we take a detailed look at it, we need to introduce you to the sample scenario used throughout this part of the book to illustrate the concepts behind the evaluation.

3.3 Introduction to the Sample Scenario

As we explore the details of the OCTAVE Method in Chapters 4 to 11, we illustrate major concepts using examples from a running scenario. The organization in the scenario is a fictitious, medium-sized, medical facility called MedSite. MedSite is a hospital with several clinics and labs, some of which are at remote locations. The hospital includes the following functional areas:

- A permanent administrative organization
- Permanent and temporary medical personnel, including physicians, surgeons, and medical staff
- Permanent and temporary maintenance personnel, including facility and maintenance staff
- A small information technology department (three people) responsible for on-site computer and network maintenance and upgrades and for help desk activities (e.g., handling simple user requests)

MedSite's Organizational Structure

The MedSite administrator is the chief administrator for the hospital and has a small staff responsible for overseeing MedSite operations. In addition, each major functional area of the organization (administrative, medical, labs, and remote clinics) reports directly to the chief administrator. MedSite's senior management team includes the MedSite administrator and the individuals who lead the functional areas of the organization. Each functional area of MedSite contains one or more operational areas. The head of each operational area is considered to be a middle manager in the organization. Figure 3-5 shows the organizational chart for MedSite.

MedSite's System

MedSite's main computer system is the Patient Information Data System (PIDS). PIDS includes the main PIDS server, the network, desktop PCs, and a variety of

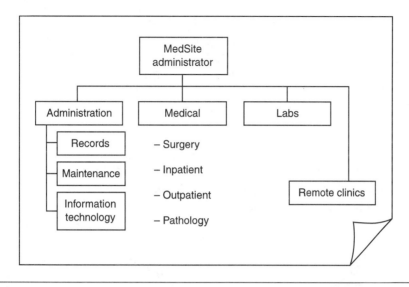

FIGURE 3-5 High-Level MedSite Organizational Chart

medical applications. The system also links and integrates a set of smaller, older databases related to patient care, lab results, and billing.

Patient data can be entered into PIDS or one of the other databases at any time from any workstation. Physicians, administrative clerks, lab technicians, and nurses have authorization to enter data into PIDS as well as other systems. Personal computers, or workstations, are located in all offices, treatment rooms (including emergency rooms), nursing stations, and labs. In addition, physicians can also access PIDS remotely using their home personal computers. In fact, there is talk around the hospital that medical personnel will soon be able to access PIDS using personal digital assistants (PDAs).

An independent contractor, ABC Systems, provides support for most of the systems at MedSite as well as for the network. MedSite's information technology personnel and another contractor each maintain some of the legacy systems still being used by MedSite's staff. The information technology staff members from MedSite provide on-site help desk support and basic system maintenance. ABC Systems provided MedSite's information technology personnel with limited systems and network training about a year ago.

MedSite's senior managers decided they wanted a comprehensive review of information security evaluation within their facility. Several new regulations are expected to be mandated by the government in the upcoming year, requiring MedSite to document the results of an information security risk evaluation. The regulations will also require MedSite to implement a practice-based standard of due care, meaning they would have to institutionalize recognized good security practices. After some discussion and consultation with other medical facility managers, they decided to use the OCTAVE Method. Funding for internally staffed activities was easier to find than more money for contractors, and senior managers hoped that their staff would learn better security practices while doing this evaluation.

During each activity in Part II, we will chart MedSite's progress as it conducts the OCTAVE Method. Chapter 4 starts exploring the OCTAVE Method in detail and examines how to prepare for the evaluation.

4

Preparing for OCTAVE

As we pointed out in Chapter 3, you need to prepare before you can success-fully conduct an organizationwide information security risk evaluation like the OCTAVE Method. The objective of preparing for the evaluation is to build a solid foundation for coordinating and executing all subsequent evaluation activities. This chapter examines the activities that need to be undertaken to prepare for the OCTAVE Method.

4.1 Overview of Preparation

Since the OCTAVE Method looks at a cross-section of an organization, it involves many people and requires a lot of coordination. The preparation activities are important, because they set the stage for the evaluation. During preparation you must overcome any organizational inertia and build momentum for conducting the evaluation.

Chapter 3 identified the following success factors for information security risk evaluations:

- Getting senior management sponsorship for the evaluation
- Selecting the analysis team to lead the evaluation
- Setting the scope of the evaluation
- Selecting participants for evaluation activities

It is during preparation that you directly address these key success factors and set the direction for your organization's evaluation.

Preparation for the OCTAVE Method

While there are many ways in which organizations can prepare to conduct the OCTAVE Method, this section focuses on a likely scenario for many organizations, making the following two assumptions:

1. There is a *champion,* someone within the organization who has an interest in conducting the OCTAVE Method.
2. The analysis team does *not* exist prior to gaining senior management approval.

The champion should help the senior managers understand the benefits of performing the OCTAVE Method and thereby gain their sponsorship for conducting the evaluation. After the organization's senior managers decide that the organization should conduct the OCTAVE Method, they work with the champion to select members of the analysis team. The analysis team then becomes the focal point for completing all evaluation activities.

Table 4-1 illustrates the preparation activities, while the rest of this chapter describes the basic activities that must be completed prior to conducting the evaluation in the context of the above scenario.

TABLE 4-1 OCTAVE Preparation Activities

Activity	Description
Obtain senior management sponsorship of OCTAVE	The champion works with the organization's senior managers to gain their sponsorship of the evaluation. The champion is responsible for making the managers aware of the evaluation process, the expected outcomes, and the time and personnel commitments that must be made.
Select analysis team members	The champion assembles the analysis team after obtaining senior management sponsorship of the evaluation. Alternatively, senior managers might designate someone in the organization to work with the champion or to lead the selection of the analysis team. Once analysis team members have been selected, they need to become familiar with the OCTAVE Method through formal training or through informal means.
Select operational areas to participate in OCTAVE	The analysis team guides the organization's senior managers in selecting which operational areas to examine during the OCTAVE Method.
Select participants	The analysis team selects people from multiple organizational levels (senior managers, operational area managers, staff) to participate in processes 1 to 3. The analysis team can, if necessary, augment its skills, experience, and expertise for specific activities in processes 4 to 8 by including additional participants if necessary.
Coordinate logistics	One member of the analysis team should be the focal point for coordinating logistics. The logistics coordinator must reserve rooms for all workshops, make sure that any required equipment (e.g., overhead projectors, flip charts) is available, and inform all participants when and where workshops will be held.

The next section looks at how an organization prepares for the evaluation by presenting a few ideas about developing senior management sponsorship of the OCTAVE Method.

4.2 Obtain Senior Management Sponsorship of OCTAVE

Senior management sponsorship is the top critical success factor for information security risk evaluations. Any successful evaluation requires the time of people in the organization, and senior managers need to participate in the OCTAVE Method. If they support the process, people in the organization tend to participate actively. If senior managers do not support the process, staff support for the evaluation will dissipate quickly. People will miss workshops, and the analysis team will not be able to persuade people to attend. If people know that senior management is committed to the evaluation process, the analysis team will have the authority and backing to persuade people to attend the workshops.

What Is Sponsorship?

First, let's address what we mean by sponsorship. We use the term to imply the following:

- Visible, continued support of OCTAVE activities
- Active encouragement of staff participation
- Delegation of responsibility and authority for accomplishing all OCTAVE activities
- Commitment to allocate the necessary resources
- Agreement to review the results and make decisions about next steps

The last item is particularly important, because an evaluation is worthless if little or nothing is done with its results and recommendations. An evaluation that goes nowhere is, in fact, worse than no evaluation at all, because participants and managers will be less inclined to do another one in the future.

Getting Sponsorship

Now that we've established what we mean by sponsorship, we need to think about how to get it. Although sponsorship from your organization's senior managers is a vital requirement for successful conduct of the OCTAVE Method, there is no simple formula for obtaining it. In some cases the senior managers in an organization have taken the initiative in getting the OCTAVE Method implemented in their organizations, thus guaranteeing sponsorship, but this is not typical.

Often, one person in the organization learns about the OCTAVE Method and decides to conduct an evaluation in his or her organization. We refer to that person as the champion. In order to develop senior management sponsorship of the OCTAVE Method, the champion needs to make appropriate senior managers aware of the evaluation process, the expected outcomes, and the expected time and personnel commitments. So an obvious question is, Who are the appropriate senior managers? In general, they are any individuals high enough up in the company to commit the organization and its resources to this effort. These senior managers are often chief executive officers, directors, or members of the organization's governing board.

It's Not Just an Information Technology Problem

We have seen cases in which despite strong sponsorship from the chief information officer in an organization, the organization nevertheless has trouble successfully conducting the OCTAVE Method. In such cases, broad support from the organization's business units was lacking because their personnel perceived the evaluation as only an information technology issue. For the OCTAVE Method to be effectively deployed in an organization, it also needs the support of a senior manager outside the information technology area.

The OCTAVE Method requires broad sponsorship because it requires the participation of people from both the business units and the information technology department. Staff members who work in the business lines of an organization understand the relative importance of business operations and the systems and information that support these operations. In general, they are in the best position to understand the business impact of disruption or abuse to business systems and operations and of potential mitigation actions. Information technology staff members, including information security experts, understand the design of existing systems and the impact of technology-related vulnerabilities. They are also in the best position to evaluate the trade-offs of mitigation actions when evaluating their effect on system performance. Senior managers need to be made aware that information security is not solely an information technology issue. In addition, the managers who sponsor an initiative such as the OCTAVE Method need to have the authority to commit the time of staff members from the organization's business units as well as from the information technology department.

Regulations and Standards of Due Care

Regulations are becoming more common in many industry segments these days. The Health Information Portability and Accountability Act (HIPAA) [HIPAA 98] establishes a standard of due care for information security for health care organizations, while Gramm-Leach-Bliley [Gramm 00] legislation does the same for financial organizations. Most information security standards of due care require an organization to conduct an information security risk evaluation and to manage its risks. If your organization must perform an information security risk evaluation because of regulations, bring this requirement to the attention of your organization's managers. We have seen the senior managers of organizations sponsor information security risk evaluations after learning about regulations and the requirements for compliance.

Anecdotal Information

Although there are no substantial "return on investment" data available at this time with respect to security improvement activities, you can present anecdotal information to inform senior managers about the benefits of using information security risk evaluations. You can emphasize how some organizations use these evaluations as the central component of a security improvement initiative. Those organizations often view a security improvement initiative as a competitive advantage.

Conducting a Limited Evaluation

The champion in one organization decided to conduct a limited evaluation to build sponsorship for a more extensive implementation of the OCTAVE Method. He was able to recruit an analysis team and get middle-management sponsorship from one operational area. The team conducted the OCTAVE Method on the operational area and then presented the results to senior managers. This approach enabled senior managers to see what the results of the evaluation looked like and was a good way to get them interested in expanding the effort.

In the end, of course, there is no single way to assure sponsorship for conducting an evaluation like the OCTAVE Method, but the ideas presented here should start you thinking about how to build sponsorship of the OCTAVE Method in your organization. The next section examines how to select analysis team members.

4.3 Select Analysis Team Members

The analysis team is the focal point for conducting the OCTAVE Method. This team is responsible for the ultimate success of the evaluation. Because the analysis team plays such a pivotal role in the evaluation, it is important to select a core team that has sufficient skills, experience, and expertise to lead the evaluation.

Who Is on the Analysis Team?

The champion often assembles the analysis team after obtaining senior management sponsorship of the evaluation. Senior managers might also designate someone in the organization to work with the champion or to lead the selection of the analysis team.

The core analysis team consists of three to five people from the organization's business units and information technology department; typically, the majority are from the business units of the organization. Some organizations also select people from the operational areas participating in the evaluation to be on the analysis team. In such cases this activity, Select Analysis Team Members, should be performed only after the next activity, Select Operational Areas to Participate in OCTAVE is completed.

The analysis team can add supplemental team members (e.g., an operational area manager or a vulnerability evaluation tool expert) to particular workshops as needed. These additional people augment the skills of the core team by providing expertise needed during designated workshops.

One member of the core analysis team normally handles logistics for the evaluation. However, an additional person can be assigned to the analysis team specifically to address logistics. (Section 4.6 discusses coordinating logistics for the OCTAVE Method.)

In summary, the analysis team includes between three to five people in the core group, represents both business/mission and IT perspectives, and is knowledgeable about business and IT processes.

Roles and Responsibilities

The analysis team helps to set the scope of the evaluation, leads the selection of evaluation participants, facilitates the initial set of knowledge elicitation workshops, and gathers and analyzes information. The roles and responsibilities of the analysis team include

- Working with managers to set the scope of the evaluation, select participants, and schedule OCTAVE activities

- Coordinating with senior managers, operational area managers, and information technology staff to conduct a vulnerability evaluation for the computing infrastructure
- Gathering, analyzing, and maintaining evaluation data during the OCTAVE Method
- Enabling the assessment activities, particularly ensuring that designated personnel attend their specific workshops
- Coordinating logistics for the evaluation

Skills Needed to Conduct OCTAVE

Although the OCTAVE Method is a complex process, analysis team members do not require extensive or unique skills. The OCTAVE Method is not a typical vulnerability evaluation that focuses solely on technological issues. Because it addresses both business and technological issues, the OCTAVE Method is similar to other business processes or management evaluations. Thus, it is helpful if someone on the analysis team is familiar with or has done assessments or evaluations. At least one member of the analysis team must have some familiarity with information technology and information security issues. Information technology representatives who participate in the evaluation should bring broad perspectives and have pragmatic viewpoints. They don't have to understand all aspects of security, but they need to be aware of their technical limits and identify others to include in the evaluation when necessary.

The specific skills needed for each OCTAVE process are detailed in the beginning of each of the remaining chapters in Part II (Chapters 5 to 11). By looking at the skills that we suggest for your team, you can determine whether it is necessary to supplement the skills of the core analysis team by including an additional person for a selected workshop. In general, the core members of the analysis team should have the following qualifications:

- Facilitation skills
- Good communication skills
- Good analytical skills
- Ability to present to and work with senior managers, operational area managers, and staff
- Knowledge of the organization's business environment

- Knowledge of the organization's information technology environment and how the business staff legitimately uses information technology in the organization

In addition, at different times the core team will need the following skills and knowledge or should be able to acquire them by adding supplemental team members:

- Knowledge of the organization's network topology
- Knowledge of common exploits of technology vulnerabilities
- Ability to interpret the results of vulnerability evaluation software tools
- Knowledge of the organization's planning practices
- Ability to develop plans

Training the Analysis Team

Once analysis team members have been selected, they need to become familiar with the OCTAVE Method. Team members can either participate in formal training or become familiar with the process by working on their own, for example, through reading and understanding the material in this book or the *OCTAVE Method Implementation Guide* [Alberts 01a].

If you, the analysis team, decide to get started without training, there are some things you can do to facilitate the learning process. First, all your team members should spend three to five days reading about the OCTAVE Method and discussing it among yourselves. You would then perform a very limited pilot by selecting one asset that you consider critical to the organization. Analyze that asset using the appropriate pieces of the method to perform the following activities for that asset:

- Define security requirements.
- Identify threats and risks.
- Develop risk mitigation plans.

You might also complete the surveys from process 3 and determine what kind of organizationwide protection strategy you would recommend based on the results. Running vulnerability tools is not likely to be something you can do without a recognized effort. If the organization does routinely run these tools, perhaps someone from the information technology department can help you incorporate the vulnerability information into the pilot.

Working through a limited pilot of the OCTAVE Method can go a long way toward understanding each evaluation process and how to work with information generated throughout the evaluation. As you complete your pilot, you should talk about what was easy and what was difficult. You should also review the guidance for the processes and begin to plan for an expanded evaluation. Use your results from the pilot to help persuade senior managers to sponsor the OCTAVE Method. Finally, if you choose to proceed without formal training, make sure your managers understand that you are learning as you go and that the evaluation may take longer than planned.

Once the analysis team has been selected and understands the evaluation process, it can set the scope of the evaluation. This activity is addressed in the next section.

4.4 Select Operational Areas to Participate in OCTAVE

One of the key OCTAVE principles is *focus on the critical few*. This principle implies that you can focus the evaluation on selected areas of the organization rather than performing an exhaustive search of the entire organization. Setting a manageable scope for the evaluation reduces its size, making it easier to schedule and perform the activities. It also allows you to prioritize the areas of an organization for the evaluation, ensuring that the highest-risk or most important areas can be examined first or more frequently.

Setting the Scope of the Evaluation

The analysis team works with the organization's senior managers to select which operational areas to examine during the OCTAVE Method. You can use the following guidelines when choosing operational areas for the evaluation:

- At least four operational areas are generally recommended, one of which *must* be the information technology or information management department.
- If the information technology or information management department is dispersed, or managed as separate support groups, select a cross-section of those groups.
- Select operational areas that reflect the primary operational or business functions as well as the important support functions of the organization.

- Consider areas that are in remote locations or are different in terms of the type of work or support that they need.

- Consider the time commitment that personnel will be required to contribute. Determine whether there will be significant conflicts with ongoing operations.

- Consider areas that require *electronic* information to accomplish their functions.

Remember that these are only guidelines. The senior managers and analysis team members need to use their best judgment as to which areas to select to participate in the evaluation.

Key Questions for Selecting Operational Areas

In addition to taking into account the guidelines suggested above, answer the following questions as you select operational areas:

- What areas of your organization are critical to achieving the mission of your organization?

- What additional areas are critical? Have you considered your entire organization, including support functions?

- Which areas would you (senior managers) like to participate in the risk assessment?

At this point your organization has selected the analysis team and operational areas that will participate in the evaluation. In the next activity you select participants from each operational area to participate in processes 1 to 3 of the OCTAVE Method.

4.5 Select Participants

Since the OCTAVE Method is an organizationwide evaluation, it requires people from throughout the organization to participate in it. The core analysis team members lead all activities during the evaluation; other members of the organization are required to participate in selected activities. The analysis team selects people from multiple organizational levels to participate in processes 1 to 3, and the team can augment its skills, experience, and expertise for specific activities in processes 4 to 8 by including additional participants if necessary.

Evaluation Participants

Table 4-2 provides a summary of the participants for each process required by the OCTAVE Method, as well as estimates for their time. In most cases the people participating in processes 1, 2, and 3 can provide supplementary support for the analysis team in other processes if necessary. For example, one of the information technology staff members from process 3 could also be a supplemental analysis team member for processes 5, 6, and 8. Note that all of the times in Table 4-2 are estimates. The actual time required to complete each workshop depends upon factors such as the abilities and experience of analysis team members, the extent to which the analysis team members are familiar with the evaluation process, and the scope of the evaluation.

Peer-Level Workshops for Processes 1 to 3

As shown in Table 4-2, participation in processes 1 to 3 is restricted according to organizational level. After developing a variety of risk evaluation techniques, we

TABLE 4-2 Participants in the OCTAVE Method

Process	Participants	Estimated Time
Process 1	At least 3 senior managers	½ day
Process 2	At least 4 operational area managers, including one manager from each operational area being evaluated	½ day
Process 3	3 to 4 staff members from each operational area being evaluated	½ day
Process 4	1 staff member with good analysis skills to supplement the analysis team (optional)	1 day
Process 5	1 to 3 information technology staff members to supplement the analysis team in selecting key infrastructure components (optional)	½ day
Process 6	1 to 2 information technology staff members to supplement the analysis by running vulnerability assessment tools (optional)	½–1 day
Process 7	1 operational area manager and/or 1 staff member with sufficient insight into the organization to supplement the analysis team (optional)	1 day
Process 8A	1 operational area manager with good planning skills and organizational insight, 1 staff member with good planning skills, and/or 1 to 2 information technology staff members with strong technology skills to supplement the analysis team (optional)	1 day
Process 8B	At least 3 senior managers	½ day

have learned that each knowledge elicitation workshop should contain a group of peers in the organization; there should be no real or perceived reporting relationships among the participants in any of the workshops for processes 1 to 3.

Remember that one of the most important risk management principles is *open communication*. In risk evaluations, people discuss sensitive information about what is not working well in an organization and how the organization's critical assets are at risk. To build an environment where people will share such sensitive information, it is essential that there be no reporting relationships among the people in a workshop. People tend to keep issues to themselves if they are in a workshop with someone to whom they report. We have even seen people refrain from active participation when they perceive that someone in the workshop has a higher position in the organizational hierarchy (e.g., a manager to whom a person does not directly report, a senior member of the general staff). When this happens, you will not get a free exchange of information so be careful when you select participants for the workshops of processes 1 to 3.

We have one final caution for you about processes 1 to 3. You should make sure that no information discussed in a workshop is attributed to a specific individual. People who know that information will not be attributed to them, tend to be more open in the knowledge elicitation workshops. You need to structure processes 1 to 3 to ensure that people openly discuss risk-related information, and you need to make sure that you let them know how the information will (and will not) be used after the workshop.

Selecting Senior Managers

As indicated in Table 4-2, you need senior management participation in processes 1 and 8B (the second workshop of process 8). Typically, the senior managers will decide which of them will participate; the analysis team can coordinate the selection process and provide guidance as necessary. In process 1, at least three senior managers are needed who

- Are familiar with the types of information-related assets used in your organization
- Are able to commit to the time required for this assessment
- Have the authority to select and authorize time for operational area managers
- Preferably have been in their position for at least a year

The managers who participate in process 1 generally also participate in the evaluation's final workshop, process 8B.

Selecting Operational Area Managers

Operational area managers need to participate in the process 2 knowledge elicitation workshop. Senior managers select managers from the operational areas that are being evaluated during the OCTAVE Method. The analysis team provides guidance during the selection of operational area managers. There is usually only one operational area management workshop (process 2), although additional workshops can be held if needed. At least four operational area managers, including the information technology manager, participate in the process 2 workshop. You should guide senior managers to select operational area managers who

- Have key responsibilities for the selected operational areas
- Are familiar with the types of information-related assets used in your organization
- Are familiar with the ways in which these information-related assets are used
- Are able to commit to the time required for this assessment
- Preferably have been in their position for at least a year
- Have the authority to select and authorize time for staff members

Operational area managers in your organization will contribute a half day of their time to attend the process 2 workshop. In addition, you might want to supplement your team's skills during processes 7 and 8A (the first workshop of process 8) by including an operational area manager.

Selecting Staff Members

General staff members and information technology staff members participate in the process 3 knowledge elicitation workshops. Operational area managers select three to four key staff members from their areas to participate in process 3. There should be at least three workshops involving staff: two for general staff and one for IT staff. Depending upon the number of operational areas selected, you may need more than two workshops for the general staff.

You should limit the size of the staff workshops to five people. If you include more than five people in a workshop, it will be difficult for all of them to participate actively, and some participants might be too overwhelmed to contribute. Higher numbers of participants can also be difficult to manage for a new analysis team. For the process 3 knowledge elicitation workshops, you should select at least three to four staff members from each selected operational area who

- Are familiar with the types of information-related assets used in their area
- Are familiar with the ways in which the information-related assets are used
- Are able to commit to the time required for this assessment
- Preferably have been in their position for at least a year

Additional members of the general staff may be needed to supplement the knowledge or skills of the analysis team during processes 4, 7, and 8. During process 4, someone with analysis skills might be included to help with threat identification. In processes 7 and 8A, additional help may be needed to analyze risks, define evaluation criteria, or develop mitigation plans. You will probably find that you will be better able to identify specific people to help with targeted pieces of the evaluation when you start preparing for those parts of the evaluation process. Refer to Table 4-2 for ideas about whom to include.

Briefing All Participants

After you have identified the participants, you will need to help them understand the purpose of the evaluation and define their roles for them before any of the workshops begin. We suggest that you hold a briefing for the selected participants. Make sure you mention that any information identified during the knowledge elicitation workshops will not be attributed to specific individuals; this is a good place to emphasize the need for open communication of sensitive issues. It is also a good idea for one or more senior managers to be present for the briefing. These managers can then use this opportunity to reinforce their sponsorship of the evaluation.

This concludes our overview of selecting participants and brings us to the last preparation activity remaining before you can begin the evaluation: coordinating logistics for the evaluation.

4.6 Coordinate Logistics

Logistics refers to the following items:

- Setting the evaluation's schedule
- Coordinating meeting rooms and equipment (viewgraph projectors, etc.)
- Handling unexpected events, such as scheduling additional workshops and/or substituting personnel in workshops

This activity is deceptively difficult in nature. The steps for coordinating logistics are straightforward and easy to understand, but they tend to present some of the bigger obstacles that you will face during the evaluation. Much of this activity involves arranging dates for workshops and coordinating the schedules of participants. Anyone who has ever tried to set up a meeting for five or six busy individuals knows how difficult this activity can be.

Scheduling and Logistics

We provide a general schedule of activities in Figures 4-1 and 4-2. Figure 4-1 highlights the preparation activities, while Figure 4-2 outlines the evaluation processes. The major assumption underlying this schedule is that the analysis team understands the evaluation process and has sufficient skills and expertise to conduct the evaluation. Teams who are attempting to conduct the evaluation for the first time might find this schedule aggressive. In addition, you will likely find that there is a time lag between preparation activities and the evaluation; you will probably not start the evaluation the moment after you have set the schedule. The time lag is not shown in Figures 4-1 and 4-2.

Also, note that the sample schedule makes several implicit assumptions, such as the following:

- The analysis team spends only three days learning about the evaluation process, either through some form of training or through a self-directed effort.

Preliminary Activities	Days													
	1	2	3	4	5	6	7	8	9	10	11	12	13	14
Preparation sessions	▨	▨												
Select analysis team				●										
Train analysis team							▨	▨	▨					
Select participants											●			
Participants' briefing														●

Legend:

▨ Partial to several days for a workshop or other activites

● Briefing, usually 1 to 2 hours

FIGURE 4-1 Sample Schedule for Preliminary OCTAVE Activities

Workshop/Action	Days																			
	1	2	3	4	5	6	7	8	9	10	11	12	13	14	15	16	17	18	19	20
Phase 1: Build Asset-Based Threat Profiles																				
P1: Identify senior management knowledge	▪																			
P2: Identify operational area knowledge		▪																		
P2: Identify operational area knowledge (optional)			▪																	
P3: Identify staff knowledge				▪																
P3: Identify staff knowledge					▪															
P3: Identify staff knowledge (IT)						▪														
P4: Create threat profiles							▪													
Phase 2: Identify Infrastructure Vulnerabilities																				
P5: Identify key components								▪												
P6: Prework (run tools)										▪	▪	▪	▪	▪						
P6: Evaluate selected components															▪					
Phase 3: Determine Security Strategy and Plans																				
P7: Conduct risk analysis																▪				
P8,wA: Develop protection strategy																	▪			
P8,wB: Develop protection strategy																			▪	
Results briefing																				●

FIGURE 4-2 Sample Schedule for OCTAVE Workshop Activities

- Only two general staff workshops are required in process 3.
- A week of elapsed time will be needed to run the vulnerability tools on the computing infrastructure (not a total of a week's effort, but rather a week with the tools run at different times and shifts to avoid interrupting key operations).

The OCTAVE Method is conducted using a series of short workshops; the schedule for conducting the workshops is quite flexible. The shortest possible time for completing an entire evaluation is slightly less than two weeks, assuming a full-time, dedicated analysis team. Practical constraints, such as problems scheduling participants for workshops, usually extend the calendar time required to conduct the OCTAVE Method. You need to consider any organizational constraints when scheduling evaluation activities. Also, remember that some workshops require data consolidation activities before they are conducted; allow time to complete all preparation activities.

One member of the analysis team should be the focal point for coordinating logistics for conducting the OCTAVE Method in your organization. Be sure to consider the following when you address evaluation logistics:

- Room reservations for all workshops
- Availability of required equipment (e.g., overhead projectors, flip charts)
- Time needed to complete all data consolidation and preparation activities
- Schedule for all workshops (be sure to inform all participants when and where workshops will be held)

Once you have set the schedule, you are ready to start the evaluation. The last section of this chapter presents what MedSite, the organization from our sample scenario, did to prepare for the evaluation.

4.7 Sample Scenario

The senior managers at MedSite held a meeting to select analysis team members. The team that they selected is shown in Table 4-3. With the exception of the logistics coordinator, all analysis team members were assigned to this effort on a

TABLE 4-3 Analysis Team Members

Name of Core Analysis Team Member	Job Function in MedSite
L. Pierce (analysis team leader)	Operational manager for Surgery A
J. Cutter (recorder)	Mid-level administrative clerk from Records
S. Nolan	Information technology staff member
K. Brown for logistics (part-time)	Facilities assistant manager
R. Green (alternate)	Information technology staff member

half-time basis. An information technology member was identified as an alternate, because the work schedules of all information technology staff members were subject to emergency interruptions.

Selecting Participants

The analysis team members (including the alternate) received OCTAVE Method training about a month before they were scheduled to begin the evaluation. They worked with the senior managers to determine who would participate in process 1. The team and the senior managers then selected the operational areas to be evaluated and identified the managers of those areas. Table 4-4 shows the senior managers who will participate in process 1, while Table 4-5 shows the operational areas and managers selected to participate in process 2.

Once the operational area managers were identified, the analysis team met with them to select the staff participants. The information technology staff was to participate in a separate workshop from the one attended by general staff members. The analysis team decided to mix the representatives from the other operational areas into two workshops. The layout of the workshops is shown in Table 4-6.

TABLE 4-4 Senior Managers

Senior Manager	Position
P. Rollins	Chief administrator
B. Houston	Director of admissions
M. Samuelson	Director of medical operations
R. Smith	Director of pathology
C. Davidson	Manager, Clinic D

TABLE 4-5 Operational Areas and Operational Area Managers

Operational Area	Operational Area Manager
Information technology	J. Donaldson
Outpatient records	M. Davis
Inpatient treatment	L. Roland
Lab 2	J. Livingston

TABLE 4-6 General and Information Technology Staff Members

Operational Area	Name of Staff Member	Workshop
Information technology	C. Jones	Information technology staff workshop
	L. Gunnar	Information technology staff workshop
	S. Leeds	Information technology staff workshop
Outpatient records	K. Ambrose	General staff workshop 1
	S. Woods	General staff workshop 2
	W. Goodman	General staff workshop 2
Inpatient treatment	J. Simmons	General staff workshop 1
	S. Caller	General staff workshop 2
	M. Davidson	General staff workshop 2
	L. Madison	General staff workshop 1
Lab 2	J. Fleet	General staff workshop 1
	K. Harriman	General staff workshop 1
	S. Thomas	General staff workshop 2

MedSite's Schedule

Once the staff members were selected, the analysis team met and developed the schedule for the evaluation. Figure 4-3 shows MedSite's schedule for conducting the OCTAVE Method. All participants were invited to an initial briefing before the evaluation was conducted. Two senior managers attended the briefing and talked about their commitment to making the evaluation a success.

You are now ready to start the evaluation. Chapter 5 looks at the first three processes of the OCTAVE Method.

Events	1/14	1/21	1/28	2/4	2/11	2/18	2/25
Participants' briefing	■						
P1: Senior management workshop	■						
P2: Operational area management workshop	■						
P3: Staff workshops (2)		■					
P3: IT staff workshop		■					
P4: Threat profile workshop		■					
P5: Key components workshop			■				
P6: Run vulnerability tools							
P6: Vulnerability evaluation workshop				■■■■			
P7: Risk analysis workshop					■		
P8: Protection strategy workshop A					■		
P8: Protection strategy workshop B (with senior management)						■	

FIGURE 4-3 MedSite's OCTAVE Schedule

5

Identifying Organizational Knowledge (Processes 1 to 3)

OCTAVE is an evaluation that examines operational information security risk. The evaluation starts by focusing on operational issues in the organization. In this method processes 1 to 3 mark the beginning of phase 1, Build Asset-Based Threat Profiles. In these processes you gather multiple perspectives about information security based on the knowledge of the people in the organization.

One of the objectives of phase 1 is to create an organizational, or global, perspective of operational security issues. To do this, you need to elicit individual views about security issues and then consolidate them into an organizational perspective, creating a foundation for all subsequent analysis activities in the evaluation.

5.1 Overview of Processes 1 to 3

All organizations face constraints with respect to the staff and funding that can be put toward information security efforts. The key is to determine where to direct organizational resources most effectively. The first step along this path is to determine what is important to the organization and what people are already doing to protect that which they believe to be important.

The best approach to understanding what is going on in an organization is to ask the people who work there. This is where phase 1 of OCTAVE starts, with a series of knowledge elicitation workshops. Here, you collect information from people in different levels of the organization as well as from those with business and information technology expertise. The workshops are important, because participants from throughout the organization contribute their unique knowledge of what is important to the organization and how well it is being protected. Each workshop focuses on an audience from a particular organizational level and features a series of brainstorming activities.

Workshops for Processes 1 to 3

Processes 1 to 3 comprise a series of knowledge elicitation workshops facilitated by the analysis team. Each workshop can be conducted in two to three hours if led by experienced facilitators. When recording information, the scribe needs to check with the participants to see if the wording is correct and carry out any suggested revisions. The key is to capture all information in the words of the participants. To enable all participants to see easily what is being recorded, the scribe should document all information on flip charts, viewgraphs, or some other easily viewable medium. The scribe's role is extremely important, because the documented information serves as the official record of the workshop. In general, your team should have the following skills to conduct knowledge elicitation workshops:

- Facilitation skills
- Ability and willingness to present to and work with senior managers, operational area managers, general staff members, and information technology staff members

Each knowledge elicitation workshop requires a peer-level group of participants from an organizational level. The format of all knowledge elicitation workshops is the same for each process, but the audience differs. The following list highlights the audience by process:

- Process 1: senior managers
- Process 2: operational area managers
- Process 3: general staff, information technology staff

Note that in process 3, general staff members and information technology staff members participate in separate workshops to allow information technology staff to focus on more technical issues. Thus, there are four types of knowledge elicitation workshops. Depending on the size of your organization and how you scope the evaluation, you could end up with multiple workshops for any organizational level. For more information about how to select participants for processes 1 to 3, see Chapter 4.

Activities

Table 5-1 summarizes the workshop activities for processes 1 to 3.

A key activity of processes 1 to 3 is the fourth one, in which participants evaluate the organization's security practices against a catalog of good practices. The results of this activity provide a snapshot of organizational practice and a basis for improvement.

TABLE 5-1 Processes 1 to 3 Activities

Activity	Description
Identify assets and relative priorities	The participants identify the assets used by the organization. They then select the assets most important to the organization and discuss their rationale for selecting those assets.
Identify areas of concern	The participants identify scenarios that threaten their most important assets based on typical sources and outcomes of threats. They also discuss the potential impact of their scenarios on the organization.
Identify security requirements for most important assets	The participants identify the security requirements for their most important assets. In addition, they examine trade-offs among the requirements and select the most important requirement.
Capture knowledge of current security practices and organizational vulnerabilities	Participants complete surveys in which they indicate which practices are currently followed by the organization's personnel and which are not. After completing the survey, they discuss specific issues from the survey in more detail.

Catalog of Practices

Security practices are actions that help initiate, implement, and maintain security within an enterprise [BSI 95]. A specific practice is normally focused on a specific audience. The audiences for practices include managers, users (general staff), and information technology staff. An example of a good security practice is that all staff members should be aware of and understand the organization's security-related policies.

We call a documented collection of known and accepted good security practices a catalog of practices. Chapter 2 introduced the idea of using a catalog of practices during an evaluation. The catalog of practices is used to evaluate the current security practices used by the organization. During the final activity of each knowledge elicitation workshop, participants fill out surveys and then discuss any issues arising from the survey that they feel are important. The surveys are specific to an organizational level. Each survey is developed by selecting practices from the catalog that should be used by staff members from that organizational level. For example, senior managers are more likely to know if corporate strategy and plans include or address security issues, whereas information technology personnel are more likely to be familiar with particular aspects of managing technological vulnerabilities and configuring firewalls.

The catalog of practices is divided into two types of practices: strategic and operational. Strategic practices focus on organizational issues at the policy level and provide good general management practices. Strategic practices address business-related issues as well as issues that require organizationwide plans and participation. Operational practices, on the other hand, focus on technology-related issues dealing with how people use, interact with, and protect technology. Since strategic practices are based on good management practice, they should be fairly stable over time. Operational practices are more subject to changes as technology advances and new or updated practices arise to deal with those changes.

The catalog of practices is a general catalog of security-related practices; it is not specific to any domain, organization, or set of regulations. It can be modified to suit a particular domain's standard of due care or set of regulations (e.g., the medical community and Health Insurance Portability and Accountability Act (HIPAA) [HIPAA 98] security regulations, the financial community and Gramm-Leach-Bliley regulations [Gramm 00]). It can also be extended to add organization-specific standards, or it can be modified to reflect the terminology of a specific domain. Figure 5-1 depicts the structure of a basic catalog of practices that was developed at the time this book was written; the details of the specific practices can be found in Appendix C.

The catalog was developed using several sources: [BSI 95], [Gramm 01], [HIPAA 98], and [Swanson 96]. In addition to these security-related references, we also used our experience developing, delivering, and analyzing the results of the Information Security Evaluation (ISE), a vulnerability assessment technique developed by the Software Engineering Institute and delivered to a variety of organizations over the past six years.

Section 5.5 shows how to use the catalog to evaluate your organization's current security practices and organizational vulnerabilities, while the next section looks at the knowledge elicitation workshop activities, starting with asset identification.

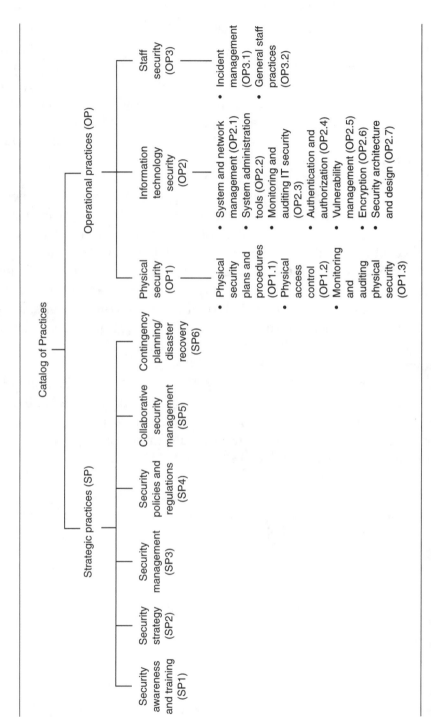

FIGURE 5-1   Structure of the OCTAVE Catalog of Practices

5.2 Identify Assets and Relative Priorities

Asset identification is the first activity in each knowledge elicitation workshop. During this activity, participants focus on the information-related assets they use in their jobs. From our experience of watching people learn how to perform the evaluation, we have singled out asset identification as a critical success factor for analysis teams. If you collect good information about assets in this activity, you lay the foundation for a successful and meaningful evaluation.

We call OCTAVE an asset-driven evaluation because assets are used to focus all subsequent activities. Assets guide the selection of devices and components to evaluate in phase 2, and the risk mitigation plans that you develop in phase 3 focus on protecting your organization's most critical assets. So it's important to get this activity right and gather as much meaningful information about assets as you can. If you allow participants to identify assets that are too broad or assets not relevant to information security, you will have trouble with later activities and will have to revisit this important activity.

What Is an Asset?

Before we explore how to conduct step 1, we need to define what we mean by the term "asset." An *asset* is something of value to the enterprise [Hutt 95]. In general, information technology assets combine logical and physical assets and can be grouped into the following categories:[1]

- Information—documented (paper or electronic) data or intellectual property used to meet the mission of an organization
- Systems—information systems that process and store *information* (systems being a combination of information, software, and hardware assets and any host, client, or server being considered a system)
- Software—software applications and services—such as operating systems, database applications, networking software, office applications, custom applications, etc.—that process, store, or transmit *information*

---

1. This list was created using information in the following references: [Fites 89], [BSI 95], [Hutt 95], and [Caelli 91].

- Hardware—*information technology* physical devices—such as workstations, servers, etc.—that normally focus solely on the replacement costs for physical devices
- People—the people in an organization who possess *unique skills, knowledge, and experience* that are difficult to replace

An *information* security risk evaluation must focus on an organization's information-related assets. Note that each asset category is linked to information in some way. To differentiate between these types of assets and others that might be important to an organization, we refer to assets in the above categories as "information-related assets." Table 5-2 describes additional considerations for each category.

TABLE 5-2 Considerations for Asset Categories

Asset Category	Considerations
Systems	Systems assets constitute the broadest of the asset categories, representing a grouping of information, software, and hardware assets. Most people think of a system as a whole; they don't break it down into its components. Because of this, systems assets are often identified during an information security risk evaluation.
Information	Information assets are intangible in nature and are closely linked to systems assets. Systems store, process, and transmit the critical information that drives organizations. Thus, when an organization creates strategies and plans to protect its systems assets, it is also protecting its critical information (as well as its software and hardware assets). Don't forget that some information assets are represented physically (on paper, fiche, etc.).
Software	When people identify software assets, you should try to determine whether they mean software applications or services or are actually referring to systems. For example, when someone identifies a software application, such as a database application, you should determine whether he or she believes that the software or the database system is the important asset. In many cases the person will be looking at the asset more broadly and will be referring to the database system (which includes the information). In another example, the participants might identify office automation software (word-processing applications, spreadsheet applications, etc.) as assets. Here, they are likely to be referring to the applications, not to systems.
Hardware	When people identify hardware assets, you should try to determine whether they mean physical hardware or are actually referring to systems. For example, if someone identified personal computers as an asset, you should determine whether he or she believes that the PC hardware or the PC host (system) is the important asset. Often the person will be referring to the PC as a systems asset.
People	People assets are a special case. When people are identified, it is because of some special skill that they have or because of a service that they provide. When people are identified as assets, determine whether there are related assets that may be more appropriate to identify. For example, identify a key system that they use or a type of information that they provide for others to use.

Note that the asset categories are contextual for any organization and must be defined in order for a meaningful evaluation to be conducted. You can tailor the list by adding or deleting categories to meet your organization's needs.

Step 1: Brainstorm a List of Assets

To conduct step 1, ask the participants to think about assets that they use in their jobs. Recall the five categories of assets that you are considering (information, systems, software, hardware, and people). You are trying to get the participants to identify assets that *they* use to help the organization meet its mission and business objectives. You start asset identification by specifically asking the participants the following question: What are your important assets?

As the participants are brainstorming assets that they use, you might find it necessary to focus the conversation. Consider using the following types of follow-up questions:

- Are there any other assets that you are required to protect (e.g., by law or regulation)?
- What related assets are important?
- What about _____ makes it an asset?
- Have you considered your entire organization? What other assets do you use?

Remember that the point of this activity is for the participants to identify assets that they use to help the organization meet its mission and business objectives. Some facilitators might be tempted to start by explicitly identifying the mission of the organization and using that as a common reference point for the participants. However, this could also lead to confusion among the participants.

For example, think about a knowledge elicitation workshop with the information technology staff at MedSite. From their perspective, the mission of MedSite is to deliver quality health care to patients. If you start by identifying the organization's mission, you might bias the IT staff members' views of assets. They would likely identify assets such as patient-identifiable information and medical records. However, this is not the information with which *they* work on a daily basis. They maintain the infrastructure that enables doctors and nurses to work with patient-identifiable information and medical records. Thus, you would want them to identify specific assets that are related to their work on the infrastructure.

The lead facilitator must play an active role in helping participants identify assets. For example, when a participant identifies a system as an asset, what is the asset that is really being identified? Is the information on the system the asset? Is an application or service on the system the asset?

Assets that are identified should be unique, specific, meaningful, and related to information technology in some way. A common pitfall is that participants will identify assets that have no relation to information or information technology, for example, a business process, a piece of physical equipment, or facility that has no link to the organization's computing infrastructure (e.g., the building that houses the organization).

A second pitfall is identifying assets that are too general in nature. For example, participants often start off by saying, "Our systems and our people are our two most important assets." To which systems and which people are they referring? How do those assets relate to information security? The facilitator must always keep the group focused on information-related assets.

Senior Management Assets

- Patient Information Data System (PIDS)*

- Paper medical records*

- Email

- Providers' credentials*

- Internet connectivity

- Medical Logistics System (MLS)

- Financial Record-Keeping System (FRKS)*

- Emergency Care Data System (ECDS)

- Personnel Management System

FIGURE 5-2 Senior Management Assets

Let's examine what the senior managers at MedSite identified as their important assets. At MedSite, the senior managers had a lively discussion about assets. Figure 5-2 shows the assets that were recorded by the scribe. The asterisk (*) by an asset indicates that the managers identified it as an important asset. (See step 2 of this activity for more details on important assets.)

Table 5-3 provides additional context about the senior managers' assets. The managers focused on assets that they use. Items such as provider credentials and the financial system, FRKS, were not identified by other groups, because they are uniquely important to senior managers. Appendix A summarizes all assets identified during processes 1 to 3. As you review that appendix, take a look at the assets identified by each organizational level for similarities and differences.

TABLE 5-3 Description of Senior Management Assets

Asset	Description
Patient information data system (PIDS)	PIDS is a database containing most of the important patient information at MedSite. Role-based access (e.g., appointment scheduler, pharmacist, lab technicians, providers) is required to access PIDS. ABC Systems, an IT contracting organization, maintains PIDS for MedSite.
Paper medical records	Complete patient records are recorded on paper. If a record is lost, there's no way to re-create it. Patients can hand-carry their paper medical records within the facility.
Email	MedSite's email system is a standard system. Email is used extensively by all staff members at MedSite. It most likely contains some sensitive information (e.g., patient information, financial information, personal information).
Providers' credentials	These are the credentials of MedSite's medical personnel.
Internet connectivity	MedSite's staff members access research and medical sites on the Internet as part of their day-to-day tasks. The link to MedSite's ISP is important for providing access to those sites.
Medical logistics system (MLS)	MLS tracks supplies, property, and equipment. In addition, all orders are entered in this system.
Financial record-keeping system (FRKS)	FRKS contains all of the insurance records, billing records, and payment schedules, as well as related financial information.
Emergency care data system (ECDS)	ECDS is essential to the efficient operation of emergency rooms. It is used to maintain and update patient records and billing related to emergencies, but it is not used to provide patient-related information during emergency care. It is also representative of systems that are linked to PIDS but maintained by the local staff.
Personnel management system	Personnel Management System contains demographics, work histories, assignments, skills, and disciplinary records.

At this point in processes 1 to 3 the participants will have identified a number of assets that they use on a regular basis.

Step 2: Select Important Assets

In this step the participants select the assets they consider most important. We recommend limiting the number of assets that participants can select to five. If too many assets are carried forward, later analysis activities can become more time-consuming and difficult. Requiring participants to select important assets also provides you with insight into the participants' perspectives that you might not otherwise have had.

Ask the participants to consider the following questions:

- From the assets that you have identified, which are the most important?
- What is your rationale for selecting these assets as important?

Document the important assets and the rationale for their selection.

PIDS

This system contains most of our important patient information.

We rely on PIDS to deliver health care on a day-to-day basis.

Paper medical records

These are the official medical records. If they are lost, we cannot re-create them.

FRKS

This system contains all of our financial information.

Providers' credentials

They are the credentials for all of our medical personnel.

FIGURE 5-3 Most Important Senior Management Assets and Rationale for Selection

The senior managers at MedSite selected their important assets. An asterisk (*) by an asset in Figure 5-2 denotes that it is important. Note that the senior managers selected only four important assets. Figure 5-3 shows the managers' rationale for selecting the important assets.

This step concludes the first activity of processes 1 to 3. In the next activity you will identify scenarios that describe how participants believe their important assets are being threatened.

5.3 Identify Areas of Concern

As people work with information-related assets when performing their jobs, they develop an understanding of the operational procedures related to accessing and using information. They learn about the way operations really work in their organization. They know where written procedures must be followed to the letter, and they know where they have to "make things work" by deviating from formally written protocols. The knowledge about what is really happening in the organization is vital when creating threat scenarios.

In this activity participants express concerns about how their most important assets are threatened. They create the scenarios using prompts based on known sources and outcomes of threat, resulting in highly contextual threat information from the people who use and depend upon the organization's assets. This information forms the basis for constructing threat profiles during process 4.

Step 1: Describe Areas of Concern

A *threat* is an indication of a potential undesirable event [NSTISSC 98]. It refers to a situation in which a person could do something undesirable (an attacker initiating a denial-of-service attack against an organization's email server) or a natural occurrence could cause an undesirable outcome (a fire damaging an organization's information technology hardware). An area of concern is a situation in which someone is concerned about a threat to his or her important assets. Typically, areas of concern have a source and an outcome, that is, a causal action that has an effect on the organization. Figure 5-4 shows typical sources and outcomes for areas of concern.

The threat sources and outcomes in Figure 5-4 are based on known sources of threat from the generic threat profile. For a more in-depth discussion of the generic threat profile, see Chapter 6. Table 5-4 provides a definition for each category of threat source, while Table 5-5 provides a definition for each outcome.

To conduct step 1, ask the participants the following question: What scenarios threaten your important assets? To help them think about threat scenarios, have the participants focus on how the sources and outcomes contained in Figure 5-4 related to their important assets.

Note that the participants might consider one asset at a time, or they might consider and discuss all important assets simultaneously when they identify areas of concern. Identifying areas of concern is a brainstorming activity, in which participants will likely focus on multiple assets and sources simultaneously.

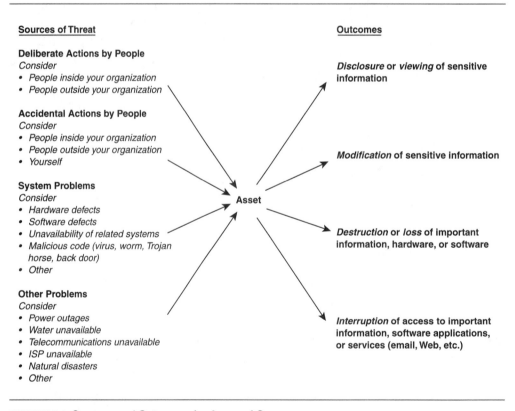

FIGURE 5-4 Sources and Outcomes for Areas of Concern

TABLE 5-4 Threat Sources

Category of Threat Source	Definition
Deliberate actions by people	This group includes people inside and outside your organization who might take deliberate action against your assets.
Accidental actions by people	This group includes people inside and outside your organization who might accidentally harm your assets.
System problems	These are problems with your information technology systems. Examples include hardware defects, software defects, unavailability of related organizational systems, viruses, malicious code, and other system-related problems.
Other problems	These problems are beyond your control. Threats in this category include natural disasters (e.g., floods and earthquakes) that can affect your organization's information technology systems, unavailability of systems maintained by other organizations, and interdependency issues. Interdependency issues refer to problems with infrastructure services, such as power outages, broken water pipes, and telecommunication outages.

TABLE 5-5 Threat Outcomes

Threat Outcome	Definition
Disclosure	The viewing of confidential or proprietary information by someone who should not see the information
Modification	An unauthorized changing of an asset
Loss/destruction	The limiting of an asset's availability, either temporarily or because it is unrecoverable
Interruption	The limiting of an asset's availability, mainly in terms of services

At MedSite, the senior managers identified areas of concern for their important assets. Figure 5-5 shows a few of the areas of concern for PIDS.

Note that the areas of concern in Figure 5-5 are written as complete sentences. One of the biggest mistakes, made by many inexperienced analysis teams, is to record partial phrases that do not completely capture the meaning of the concern. When the teams review areas of concern later in the process, they cannot always remember the exact concern if only a few words were recorded. Appendix A summarizes the areas of concern identified during processes 1 to 3.

Areas of Concern

- Personnel access information that they are not authorized to use: access is used inappropriately or legitimately accessed information is distributed inappropriately.

- Staff could intentionally enter erroneous data into PIDS.

- It's difficult to find and retain qualified personnel to help maintain PIDS.

- PIDS is not compatible with newer systems, leading to system crashes.

- The risk of an outside intrusion into PIDS is much higher than with newer systems, because of the need to bypass the firewall.

- Power outages, floods, and other external events can lead to a denial of access to PIDS. This essentially shuts the hospital down.

- Accidental loss of any important information is a concern.

FIGURE 5-5 Senior Management Areas of Concern for PIDS

Step 2: Describe the Impact on the Organization

The second step of this activity centers on collecting information about the potential impact on the organization. This information will be useful when you start to construct risks in process 7. It will help link the outcomes of threats to business goals and objectives. (See Chapter 9 for more information about process 7.)

For each scenario elicited, ask the following questions:

- What could happen if this scenario were to occur?
- What would be the impact on your organization?

Area of Concern	Impact
• Staff could intentionally enter erroneous data into PIDS.	• Incorrect modifications could affect the productivity of staff members. • The life and health of our patients could be affected.
• Power outages, floods, and other external events can lead to a denial of access to PIDS. This essentially shuts the hospital down.	• Our organization cannot deliver efficient health care without PIDS.

FIGURE 5-6 Impact on the Organization for Areas of Concern

Note that there can be more than one impact for each area of concern. Figure 5-6 illustrates the potential impact on the organization for two of the senior managers' areas of concern for PIDS.

This concludes the second activity of processes 1 to 3. In the next activity you will identify security requirements for the participants' most important assets.

5.4 Identify Security Requirements for Most Important Assets

In OCTAVE you are ultimately trying to create a protection strategy and risk mitigation plans geared toward protecting your organization's critical assets. To protect critical assets, you must first establish what is important about each of those assets. Then you can determine to what extent you will protect each asset.

At this point in the workshop, participants discuss what qualities are important about the assets that they have identified. In many cases you will find that an asset is identified as important to more than one organizational level. However, the quality of the asset that is most valued might differ among participants from different levels. It is important to understand such differences in perspective, so that you can consider them later in the evaluation when you are deciding how best to use organizational resources to protect critical assets.

Security Requirements

Security requirements outline the qualities of an asset that are important to protect. There are three typical security requirements that organizations need to consider:

- Confidentiality—the need to keep proprietary, sensitive, or personal information private and inaccessible to anyone who is not authorized to see it
- Integrity—the authenticity, accuracy, and completeness of an asset
- Availability—when or how often an asset must be present or ready for use

The categories of security requirements are contextual for any organization and must be defined in order to conduct a meaningful evaluation. They can be tailored to meet your organization's needs. For example, some organizations might want to add authenticity and nonrepudiation to their list of security requirements. First, you need to decide what categories of security requirements to incorporate into the evaluation, and then you need to use those requirements consistently throughout all activities. In this book we consider only confidentiality, integrity, and availability.

The concept of security requirements has also been difficult for people to understand when they are learning about OCTAVE. Most people have an intuitive sense about the extent to which information needs to be private, accurate, and available. However, it is hard for many participants to create concise and precise statements that reflect their knowledge, and in many cases, they will need additional assistance from you during this activity.

Step 1: Identify Security Requirements for Each Important Asset

In step 1, participants identify the security requirements for each important asset that has been identified. We have found that this activity can be difficult for participants; for example, some become confused and think that the security requirements are the protection strategies. Instead of stating that an asset needs to be kept confidential, they will state the actions needed to keep it confidential. Ask the participants the following questions for each of their important assets:

- Is this asset proprietary or sensitive? Does it contain personal information? Should it be inaccessible to anyone who is not authorized to see it? If the answer to any of these questions is yes, what is the specific confidentiality requirement?

- Are authenticity, accuracy, and completeness important for this asset? Do you need to be sure that only authorized people have modified the asset? Do you need to be certain that nothing was inadvertently deleted or changed? If the answer to any of these questions is yes, what is the specific integrity requirement?

- Is accessibility of the asset important? Who should be able to get to this asset? When or how often? What is the specific availability requirement?

- Are there any other security-related requirements that are important to this asset? What are they?

The security requirements for PIDS from the senior managers' perspective are shown in Figure 5-7. Note that a security requirement is a general statement. Each category of requirement (confidentiality, integrity, and availability) can have one or more statements that express the specific requirements for an asset. For example, the information on PIDS is medical information that is vital to treating patients. Because it is so important, one would assume that not just anyone should be allowed to change a patient's medical information. If we examine the requirement for integrity, we see that this is the case. The managers indicated that "only authorized users should be able to modify information." This requirement restricts legitimate access for the purpose of modifying medical information.

Step 2: Prioritize Security Requirements

In step 2 you examine the relative trade-offs among the requirements. Ask the participants the following types of questions for each of their important assets:

- What is the relative ranking of the security requirements for each information asset?

- Which security requirement is the most important?

Security Requirements for PIDS

Availability*

System availability is required 24/7.

Confidentiality

Information should be kept confidential.

Federal compliance with Privacy Act of 1974—anyone accessing can be prosecuted for passing data to others.

Integrity

Only authorized users should be able to modify information.

FIGURE 5-7 Security Requirements for PIDS from the Senior Managers' Perspective

Participants often have difficulty making this decision. People will often say that all of the requirements are equally important. However, in reality they rarely are. Is availability more important than confidentiality of the asset? If you could preserve only one of the requirements for an asset, which one would it be? These are important questions to consider, because they will help form the basis for making trade-offs in your risk mitigation plans later in the evaluation.

The senior managers at MedSite had a long discussion about the relative merits of the requirements. In the end they selected availability as the most important requirement as indicated by the asterisk (*) in Figure 5-7 They reasoned that information needed to be available to doctors and nurses when a patient needed care. They really focused on emergency situations. If the attending physicians could not get to information when it was needed during an emergency, lives could be lost.

Security Requirements for Different Types of Assets

In general, when you are trying to describe a security requirement for an asset, you need to understand what aspect of the asset is important. This is especially true for the more complex assets (systems). During this activity participants might have trouble describing the requirements. You can help them by suggesting a security requirement and letting them modify it. You will probably need to take a more active facilitation role for the first asset. Once the participants get the idea, they will need less help.

For *information assets,* the security requirements will focus on the confidentiality, integrity, and availability of the information. For example, the following is an example for information assets:

- The information must not be viewed by unauthorized personnel (confidentiality).
- The information can be modified only by authorized personnel (integrity).
- The information must be available whenever requested (availability).

Remember that *systems assets* generally represent groupings of information, software, and hardware assets. The specific aspect or quality of the system that is important will drive the security requirements. If the information stored, processed, and transmitted by the system is the most important aspect, the following example describes the security requirements:

- The information on system XYZ must not be viewed by unauthorized personnel (confidentiality).
- The information on system XYZ can be modified only by authorized personnel (integrity).
- The information on system XYZ must be available whenever requested. Downtime for system XYZ can be only 15 minutes every 24 hours (availability).

If the service provided by the system is the most important aspect, then the following example describes the security requirements:

- The service provided by system XYZ must be complete and consistent (integrity).
- The service provided by system XYZ must be available whenever requested. Downtime for system XYZ can be only 15 minutes every 24 hours (availability).

Notice that no confidentiality requirement was listed. Typically, confidentiality does not apply to services. However, confidentiality may apply, depending on the specific nature of the service.

For *software assets,* you should focus on the software application or service when you identify security requirements. Do not focus on the information that is processed, transmitted, or stored by the application. If you find that this is how you are thinking about the software asset, then you are really thinking about a systems or information asset. If the software is commercially or freely available, confidentiality probably does not apply. If the software is proprietary to your organization, there might be a confidentiality requirement. The following example relates to proprietary software assets. For commercially or freely available applications, ignore the confidentiality requirement.

- Application ABC must not be used by unauthorized personnel (confidentiality).
- Application ABC can be modified only by authorized personnel (integrity).
- Application ABC must be available during normal working hours (availability).

For *hardware assets,* you should focus on the physical hardware when you identify security requirements. Do not focus on the information that is processed, transmitted, or stored by the hardware. If you find that this is how you are thinking about the hardware asset, then you are really thinking about a systems or information asset. Confidentiality generally does not apply to physical hardware. Modification of a hardware asset focuses on adding or removing hardware (e.g., removing a disk drive or adding a modem). Availability focuses on whether the asset is physically available or accessible. The following is a guideline for hardware assets:

- The hardware can be modified only by authorized personnel (integrity).
- The hardware must be accessible to authorized personnel during normal working hours (availability).

For *people assets,* you should focus only on the availability requirement. Remember, people assets are a special case. When people are identified, it is because of some special skill that they have or because of a service that they provide. Thus, availability of the service or asset is the primary requirement. The following is a guideline for people assets:

- The IT staff must provide ongoing and consistent system and network management services (availability).

Remember, when people are identified as assets, determine whether there are related assets. For example, identify a key system that they use or a type of information that they know. When you examine the security requirements for people assets, you might start to find out that the systems the people use are also important. However, be careful with extending this activity too far. If the people are part of another organization, you can stop after you identify them as an asset. Your main concern is the service that they provide to you. Their systems are beyond the scope of your information security risk assessment. If the people are part of your organization, you can explore related assets.

5.5 Capture Knowledge of Current Security Practices and Organizational Vulnerabilities

If you want your organization to improve with respect to how it handles information security, you need first to establish where you currently are, that is, what you are currently doing well and where you need to improve. You do this by examining the security practices within your organization.

In this activity you evaluate your organization's current security practices against a catalog of known good security practices. You elicit detailed information about your organization's current security policies, procedures, and practices, thus providing a starting point for improvement. In OCTAVE we suggest using multiple means to collect information about current security practices used by the organization. This method uses surveys to collect the information and open discussion to reveal gaps, inconsistencies, and areas requiring clarification.

Step 1: Complete Security Practice Surveys

In this step you distribute a short survey on security practices to the participants and give them time to complete the survey. The surveys should be based on known security practices as documented in the catalog of practices. (See Section 5.1 for more information on the catalog of practices.) Figure 5-8 shows part of a survey for senior managers. You will find complete examples of surveys in Appendix B of this book.

Hand out surveys to the participants and ask them to take a few minutes to fill them out. Note that the example in Figure 5-8 requires participants to select the best response for each practice. Respondents must consider which practices are used in their organization. They have three options:

Name (optional): _P. Rollins_

Position: _chief administrator for MedSite_

Senior Management Survey	
Practice	**Is this practice used by your organization?**
Security Awareness and Training	
Staff members understand their security roles and responsibilities. This is documented and verified.	Yes No (Don't know)
There is adequate in-house expertise for all supported services, mechanisms, and technologies (e.g., logging, monitoring, or encryption), including their secure operation. This is documented and verified.	Yes No (Don't know)
Security awareness, training, and periodic reminders are provided for all personnel. Staff understanding is documented and conformance is periodically verified.	(Yes) No Don't know
Security Strategy	
The organization's business strategies routinely incorporate security considerations.	Yes (No) Don't know
Security strategies and policies take into consideration the organization's business strategies and goals.	Yes (No) Don't know
Security strategies, goals, and objectives are documented and are routinely reviewed, updated, and communicated to the organization.	Yes (No) Don't know
Security Management	
Management allocates sufficient funds and resources to information security activities.	(Yes) No Don't know

FIGURE 5-8 Excerpt of a Security Practice Survey

- Yes—the practice is used by the organization.
- No—the practice is not used by the organization.
- Don't know—the respondent does not know if the practice is used by the organization or not.

At MedSite, the senior managers completed the surveys. Each participant answered the question from his or her own perspective. Figure 5-8 shows part of the survey that was completed by MedSite's chief administrator. Note that surveys are just one means of collecting information about current practice.

Another way to collect very contextual information about current practice is to facilitate a discussion around the practices in the survey. You do this in step 2.

Step 2: Discuss Current Security Practices and Organizational Vulnerabilities

A facilitated discussion about current security practices in the organization will uncover detailed information that cannot be elicited by using surveys. In this step you use the surveys as a point of departure for a discussion about organizational security practices.

During this step the participants identify security practices that they currently use as well as organizational vulnerabilities that are present in the organization. *Organizational vulnerabilities* are weaknesses in organizational policy or practice that can result in unauthorized actions. These vulnerabilities include missing or inadequate security practices. Two examples of organizational vulnerabilities are staff members sharing their passwords with others and a lack of written security policies. In essence, you can think of organizational vulnerabilities as the reverse of good security practices.

To conduct step 2, ask the participants the following types of questions:

- Which issues from the survey would you like to discuss in more detail?
- What important issues did the survey not cover?
- Are there specific policies, procedures, and practices unique to specific assets? What are they?
- Do you think that your organization's protection strategy is effective? How do you know?

The first question addresses areas of the survey that the participants would like to discuss. Usually, they will focus on issues that are important to them and the organization. The second question addresses any important issues not covered by the survey. The third question focuses on specific actions that staff members take to protect certain assets. Sometimes an organization requires special policies, procedures, or practices for important information technology assets. The last question is broader and is intended to create a discussion of the general state of information security in the organization.

The resulting discussion should provide more details about issues covered in the survey and should elicit unique security practices and organizational vulnerabilities that were not covered in the survey. This discussion should also uncover issues that are important to or unique to the organization.

When discussing the first question, you should use the practice areas (e.g., security awareness and training, security strategy) as well as questions from the survey as prompts for focusing the participants' attention. For example, you might ask, "What is your impression of the organization's policies and procedures? Are they working?" Concentrate as much as possible on the direct experience of the participants with respect to the practices (e.g., ask probing questions, such as, "What security training have *you* had?"). The discussion should address what the organization is doing well (its current security practices) as well as poorly (its organizational vulnerabilities).

Remember that when the scribe records contextual information, the key is to capture all information in the words of the participants (and in complete sentences). Later in the evaluation, the analysis team reviews this information when creating your organization's protection strategy and risk mitigation plans. If you do not record the information as completely as possible, you will lose important contextual information.

Security Practices

+ We have training, guidance, regulations, and policies.

− Personnel understand systems, but not incident management and/or recognizing and reporting anomalies.

+ Policies and procedures exist.

− Consequences, or lack thereof, for violating policies and procedures are not well known; we're not enforcing our own policies.

− We don't have a business continuity plan.

FIGURE 5-9 Contextual Security Practice Information from the Senior Managers' Perspective

You also need to document whether a statement represents a security practice or whether it is an organizational vulnerability. Many times during this step, people focus only on what isn't working. Make sure that you also prompt them to think about what *is* working. Figure 5-9 shows the results of the discussion that senior managers at MedSite had about their organization's current security practices and organizational vulnerabilities. From the example, you can see that the senior managers believe that there are two security practices that *are* used within MedSite (marked with a "+") and three that are not (marked with a "–"), the latter being their organizational vulnerabilities.

The analysis team collected information like this from each workshop in processes 1 to 3. The team compiled the survey and discussion data prior to the first workshop of process 8. Team members used the data as background information when they developed MedSite's protection strategy and risk mitigation plans.

This concludes the knowledge elicitation workshop activities. After you have conducted all of these workshops, you will have gathered security-related information from throughout the organization. In the next step, process 4, you consolidate the information and start analyzing it.

6

Creating Threat Profiles (Process 4)

One of the principles of OCTAVE is to *focus on the critical few*. In an asset-based evaluation, the term "critical few" refers to your organization's most critical assets. In all subsequent data collection and analysis activities, you use critical assets as the basis for scoping each activity. This underscores the importance of carefully selecting critical assets.

Process 4 completes phase 1 of OCTAVE by consolidating and refining the individual perspectives elicited during the first three processes. You gain insight into how each asset is threatened by examining individual areas of concern in the context of a known range of threats.

6.1 Overview of Process 4

During process 4 you perform two vital functions. First, you consolidate the information that you documented during the first three processes, formatting the information for data analysis. Consolidating the information enables you to look for inconsistencies and gaps among individual perspectives. The analysis activities constitute the second vital function. You examine the individual perspectives and create a global picture of which assets are important to the organization and how those assets are being threatened.

Process 4 is important because this is where you set the scope for the rest of the evaluation. You use critical assets to focus the infrastructure evaluation in phase 2, and you use threat profiles as the basis for the risk analysis conducted in phase 3.

Process 4 Workshop

Process 4 is implemented using the core analysis team members and any supplemental personnel that they decide to include. An experienced team can complete this workshop in about three to four hours. Remember to review all activities for process 4 and decide whether your team collectively has the required knowledge and skills to complete all tasks successfully. We suggest that your team have the following mix of skills for this process:

- Understanding of your organization's business environment
- Understanding of your organization's information technology environment

- Good communication skills
- Good analytical skills

Process 4 requires data consolidation prior to the workshop. Obviously this consolidation could also have been done progressively at the end of each of the knowledge elicitation workshops. Table 6-1 summarizes the data consolidation activities. Table 6-2 summarizes the activities that the analysis team must perform during the workshop.

TABLE 6-1 Preparation Activities for Process 4

Activity	Description
Group assets by organizational level	The assets that were identified during processes 1 to 3 are grouped by organizational level to easily identify common assets and viewpoints.
Group security requirements by organizational level and asset	Security requirements that were identified during processes 1 to 3 are grouped by asset and organizational level to easily identify commonalities and conflicts.
Group areas of concern and impacts by organizational level and asset	Areas of concern that were identified during processes 1 to 3 are grouped by asset and organizational level to easily identify common concerns and gaps in perception at different levels.

TABLE 6-2 Process 4 Activities

Activity	Description
Select critical assets	The analysis team determines which assets will have a large adverse impact on the organization if their security requirements are violated. Those with the greatest impact to the organization are the critical assets. Normally, the analysis team selects five critical assets.
Refine security requirements for critical assets	The analysis team creates or refines the security requirements for the organization's critical assets. In addition, the team selects the most important security requirement for each critical asset.
Identify threats to critical assets	The analysis team identifies the threats to each critical asset by first mapping the areas of concern for each critical asset to a generic threat profile, creating the unique threat profile for that asset. Then the analysis team performs a gap analysis to determine additional threats to the critical asset.

Before we look in detail at the activities for process 4, let's take a look at the generic threat profiles, one of the key attributes of the OCTAVE approach and this method.

Generic Threat Profile

A threat profile is a structured way of presenting a range of threats to a critical asset. It is based on tree-based analysis techniques, such as fault tree analysis, and scenario-based planning. The threat profile uses a structured way of representing threats and provides a comprehensive summary of all of the threats to an asset.

In the OCTAVE Method, threats are represented visually in the profile using the following properties:

- Asset—something of value to the enterprise
- Actor—who or what may violate the security requirements (confidentiality, integrity, availability) of an asset
- Motive (or objective)—whether the actor's intentions are deliberate or accidental (applies only to human actors)
- Access—how the asset will be accessed by the actor, e.g., network access, physical access (applies only to human actors)
- Outcome—the immediate outcome (disclosure, modification, destruction, loss, interruption) of violating the security requirements of an asset

The resulting representation is called an asset-based threat tree. There is one asset-based threat tree for each of four categories of threat (see Table 6-3). Notice that two of the categories of threat in the table are different from the threat sources presented in Table 5-4. The reason for the difference in classifications lies with the manner in which they are used. We have found the threat sources in Table 5-4 useful when eliciting areas of concern from workshop participants, while the threat categories in Table 6-3 are useful for risk analysis and mitigation activities.

The *generic threat profile* is a catalog of threats that lists all potential threats under consideration. You use this as a starting point to create a unique *threat profile for each critical asset*. You essentially tailor the generic threat profile for each critical asset by deciding which threats in the range of possibilities actually apply to a critical asset.

TABLE 6-3 Threat Sources

Category of Threat Source	Definition
Human actors using network access	The threats in this category are network-based threats to an organization's critical assets. They require direct action by a person and can be deliberate or accidental in nature.
Human actors using physical access	The threats in this category are physical threats to an organization's critical assets. They require direct action by a person and can be deliberate or accidental in nature.
System problems	The threats in this category are problems with an organization's information technology systems. Examples include hardware defects, software defects, unavailability of related enterprise systems, malicious code (e.g., viruses, Trojan horses, etc.), and other system-related problems.
Other problems	The threats in this category are problems or situations beyond the control of an organization. This category of threats includes natural disasters (such as floods, earthquakes, and storms) that can affect an organization's information technology systems as well as interdependency risks. Interdependency risks include the unavailability of critical infrastructures (telecommunications, electricity, etc.). Other types of threats beyond an organization's control—power outages, broken water pipes, etc.—can also be included here.

Figures 6-1 through 6-4 present the asset-based threat trees that form the generic threat profile. Section 6.5 provides an example of how to create a threat profile for a critical asset. The generic threat profile in Figures 6-1 through 6-4 might not include all of the threats for your particular operational environment. There are a number of ways to tailor the generic threat profile:

- Adding threats in a category
- Including more detailed threat actor, access, and motive information in the profile
- Deleting threats in a category
- Adding a new threat category
- Deleting a threat category

Chapter 12 addresses tailoring issues for the generic threat profile.

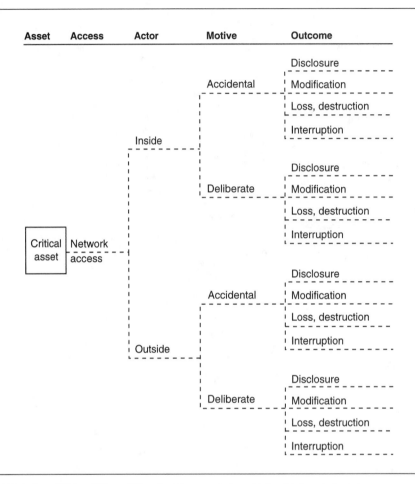

FIGURE 6-1 Asset-Based Threat Tree for Human Actors Using Network Access

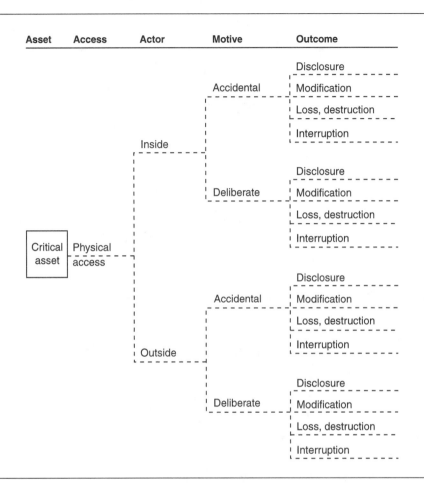

FIGURE 6-2 Asset-Based Threat Tree for Human Actors Using Physical Access

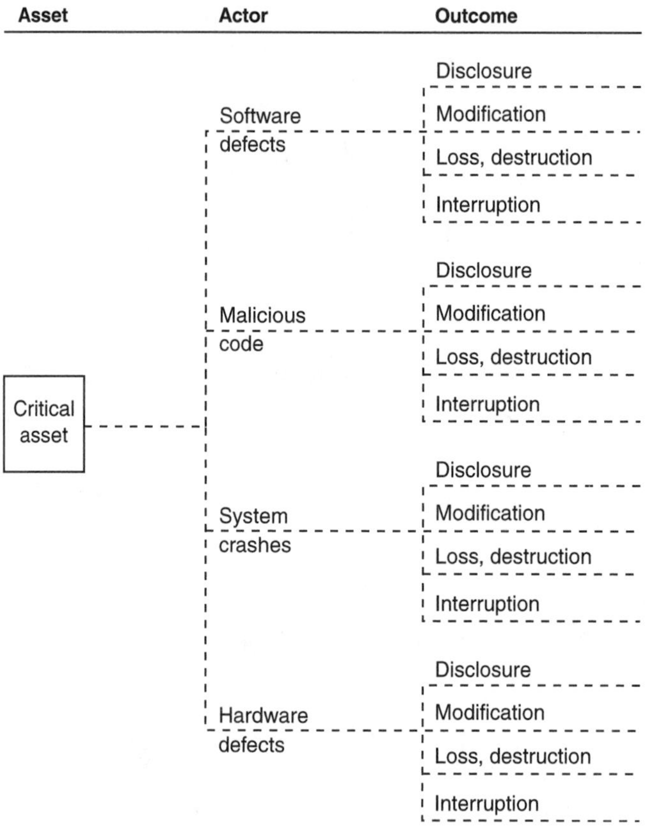

Asset	Actor	Outcome
		Disclosure
	Software	Modification
	defects	Loss, destruction
		Interruption
		Disclosure
	Malicious	Modification
	code	Loss, destruction
Critical		Interruption
asset		Disclosure
	System	Modification
	crashes	Loss, destruction
		Interruption
		Disclosure
	Hardware	Modification
	defects	Loss, destruction
		Interruption

FIGURE 6-3 Asset-Based Threat Tree for System Problems

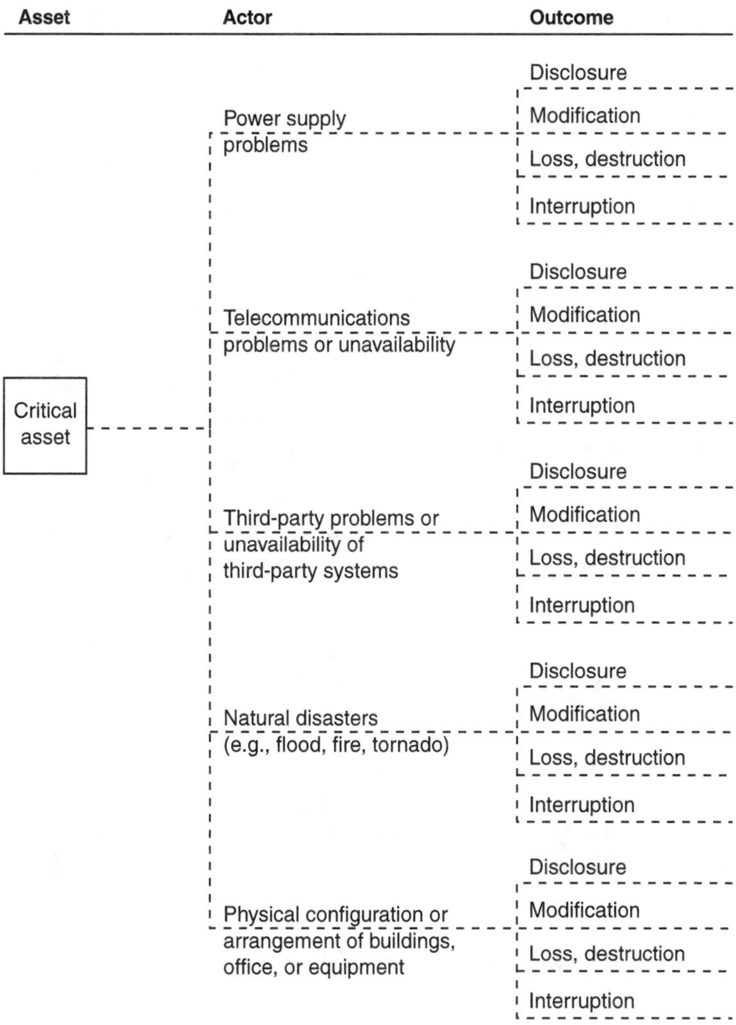

Asset	Actor	Outcome

Asset	Actor	Outcome
Critical asset	Power supply problems	Disclosure
		Modification
		Loss, destruction
		Interruption
	Telecommunications problems or unavailability	Disclosure
		Modification
		Loss, destruction
		Interruption
	Third-party problems or unavailability of third-party systems	Disclosure
		Modification
		Loss, destruction
		Interruption
	Natural disasters (e.g., flood, fire, tornado)	Disclosure
		Modification
		Loss, destruction
		Interruption
	Physical configuration or arrangement of buildings, office, or equipment	Disclosure
		Modification
		Loss, destruction
		Interruption

FIGURE 6-4 Asset-Based Threat Tree for Other Problems

6.2 Before the Workshop: Consolidate Information from Processes 1 to 3

Before you can analyze the information that you collected during processes 1 to 3, you need to organize it. Consolidating, or grouping, data provides information in a format you can easily read and understand. This section presents three activities in which the focus is grouping information from processes 1 to 3. These activities do not require decision making and can be carried out by one team member or performed incrementally at the end of processes 2 and 3. They can also be automated.

When you consolidate data from processes 1 to 3, you need to represent the data as originally recorded. You shouldn't paraphrase, edit, or interject opinions into the data as you consolidate them. This preserves the integrity of the data for all later analysis tasks.

This section presents the following data consolidation activities:

1. Group assets by organizational level
2. Group security requirements by organizational level and asset
3. Group areas of concern and impact by organizational level and asset

Group Assets by Organizational Level

In this activity you group the assets from processes 1 to 3 according to the organizational level that identified them. For each organizational level you document the following:

- Important assets identified by the participants
- The reason(s) behind workshop participants' identification of an asset as important
- Other assets that were identified by the participants

Let's look at consolidated asset information in the context of our example. Figure 6-5 shows part of the consolidated list of important assets identified by the operational area managers at MedSite.

Asset Group	
Operational area management	
Important asset	**Rationale for selection**
Patient Information Data System (PIDS)	PIDS has everything: pharmacy, appointment history, patient history, billing, admissions, and all the ancillary stuff. 400 modules in it, a massive system.
Paper medical records	Paper records contain all patient information, lab results, etc. These are paper for now, but some data are now also in PIDS.

FIGURE 6-5 Asset Group

Group Security Requirements by Organizational Level and Asset

The security requirements identified during processes 1 to 3 are grouped according to the organizational level that identified them and according to asset. Since more than one workshop group might have selected an asset as important, you can have more than one set of security requirements per asset. When you record security requirements information, make sure that you also indicate the security requirement(s) each workshop group considered most important.

Let's look at how the analysis team at MedSite consolidated security requirements information. Figure 6-6 shows the security requirements for PIDS. Notice that senior managers and staff considered availability to be the most important

Security Requirements Group	
Asset: Patient Information Data System (PIDS)	
Security requirements **(* indicates most important)**	**Security requirements** **(* indicates most important)**
Senior management	**Operational area management**
Availability* System availability is required 24/7. Confidentiality Information should be kept confidential. Compliance with Privacy Act of 1974 is required (anyone accessing can be prosecuted for passing data to others). Integrity Only authorized users should be able to modify information.	Availability* Access to records is required 24/7. Records must be available for patient encounter. Confidentiality* Records can be viewed only by those with "need to know." Integrity* This must be complete, and all information should be available for patient encounters. Patient information is subject to the Privacy Act.
Staff	**IT staff**
Availability* Access to information is required 24/7. Confidentiality "Need to know." Privacy statement is the first thing you see when you log in (Privacy Act). Integrity Information can be modified only by those with appropriate security keys.	Availability Confidentiality Integrity

FIGURE 6-6 Security Requirements Group

security requirement, while the operational area managers viewed all requirements as equally important. The words that were recorded during the knowledge elicitation workshops are included on the worksheet. Remember that you want to document all information in the words of the participants in order to help you resolve conflicts in viewpoints. There are no PIDS security requirements recorded for the information technology staff, because PIDS was not selected as an important asset during their workshop in process 3.

Group Areas of Concern and Impact by Organizational Level and Asset

In the final consolidation activity you group the areas of concern identified during processes 1 to 3 according to the organizational level that identified them and according to asset. Remember also to record any information about the resulting impact to the organization if it was identified. The consolidated information helps highlight any conflicts or similarities.

Figure 6-7 shows areas of concern for PIDS identified by the operational area managers at MedSite. Notice that the third area of concern does not have an

Areas of Concern Group	
Asset: PIDS	
Operational area management areas of concern	**Impact**
Connectivity is an issue, including problems with availability of and access to PIDS. The uptime requirement in the contract is for the servers, not for our connectivity.	If PIDS is down, then we can't function. We are rendered virtually helpless without PIDS capability.
Too many people are entering the wrong data, resulting in incorrect records, and/or there may be multiple files and records for an individual.	A patient's life and health could be affected due to improper changes to treatment plans or medical records.
Too many people have access to too much information. Role-based access builds over time, and replacements inherit all of those access privileges.	

FIGURE 6-7 Areas of Concern Group

associated impact. During the workshop, this impact was not discussed, nor did the analysis team actively pursue the information. As you consolidate information, you will often find that the information is incomplete in places. Part of your job during the process 4 workshop is to fill in these blanks as best as you can.

This completes the consolidation activities. Next, we move to the process 4 workshop, starting with the selection of your organization's most critical assets.

6.3 Select Critical Assets

This activity requires you to make decisions that shape the remainder of the evaluation—selecting your organization's critical assets. Depending upon the size of the organization, the number of information assets identified during processes 1 to 3 could easily exceed a hundred. To make the analysis manageable, you need to narrow the focus of the evaluation by selecting the few assets that are most critical to achieving the mission and meeting the business objectives of your organization. These are the only assets that you will analyze during later activities.

Step 1: Identify Critical Assets

Select your organization's five most critical assets. When you select critical assets, you are not bound to choose only five. Five assets are normally enough to enable you to develop a good set of mitigation plans during phase 3. However, you must use your judgment—you can select fewer than five or more than five if you desire. As you select critical assets, consider which assets will result in a large adverse impact on the organization in one of the following scenarios:

- Disclosure to unauthorized people
- Modification without authorization
- Loss or destruction
- Interrupted access

Remember that each of you brings a unique perspective to the discussion. Make sure you review the consolidated list of important assets from the processes 1 to 3 workshops. It is important that you review what was judged to be important from the participants' perspectives. Remember that you must consider the organizational view when you make your selections. When you reach a decision and select the critical assets, make sure that you record your selections.

Let's review which critical assets the analysis team at MedSite selected. Before reaching a decision, each analysis team member reviewed the assets identified as important by each organizational level, the rationale for selecting them, the security requirements for each important asset, and the areas of concern for each important asset. They then engaged in a lively discussion about the relative merits of selecting each asset. In the end, they selected the five assets shown in Figure 6-8.

You should not feel overly bound to the assets identified as important during the knowledge elicitation workshops. Often, an organization's critical assets will have been identified as important during earlier workshops. However, if you feel that one of the other assets from those workshops is critical to your organization, you can select it.

For example, in this case study, at MedSite, personal computers were not identified as an important asset by any of the groups during processes 1 to 3. However, when the analysis team was selecting MedSite's critical assets, it realized how important personal computers were for accessing all of the organization's systems. Thus, the analysis team decided to make personal computers one of the critical assets.

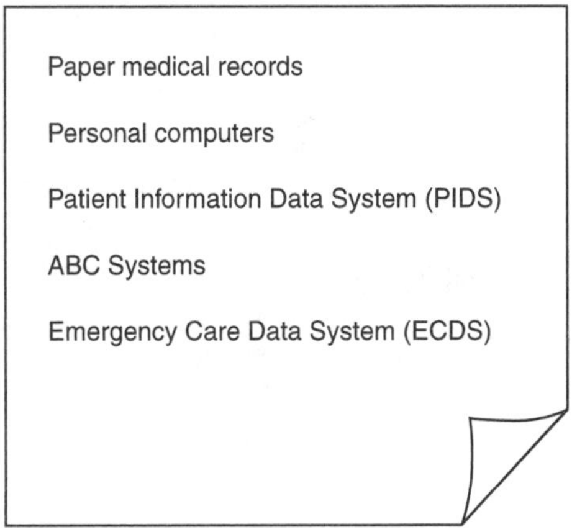

Paper medical records

Personal computers

Patient Information Data System (PIDS)

ABC Systems

Emergency Care Data System (ECDS)

FIGURE 6-8 Critical Assets

Step 2: Record the Rationale for Selecting Each Critical Asset

While selecting critical assets in step 1, you will discuss a lot of issues related to these assets. In this step you document your rationale for selecting each critical asset so that if you are asked subsequently why you designated an asset as critical after the evaluation, you will be able to provide an answer. In addition, by understanding why an asset is critical, you will be better able to define security requirements and threats in later process 4 activities. For each critical asset, consider and record your answer to this question: Why is the asset critical to meeting the mission of your organization?

At MedSite, the analysis team recorded information related to the organization's critical assets. Figure 6-9 shows information related to PIDS. The rationale for including PIDS as a critical asset is simple: MedSite depends upon it to deliver patient care. PIDS stores, processes, and transmits many types of patient information for various departments at MedSite. The other piece of information that the team recorded is a description of PIDS. Step 3 deals with how to create a description for each critical asset.

Critical Asset Information	
Asset	**PIDS**
Rationale for selection as a critical asset	98% dependency in order to deliver patient care
Brief description	The information technology department is responsible for maintaining the PIDS system and keeping it running. The clinical departments in MedSite own information on PIDS.
	Medical providers need PIDS information to deliver care. Administrators also need PIDS information for their job duties.
	PIDS is used to provide medical information to our providers as part of routine and emergency patient care.

FIGURE 6-9 Critical Asset Information

Step 3: Record a Description for Each Critical Asset

Discuss the operational aspects of each asset. Consider the following questions for each critical asset.

- Who controls it?
- Who is responsible for it?
- Who uses it?
- How is it used?

These questions focus on how assets are used and why they are important. If you can't answer all of these questions, you may need to ask people in your organization who can answer them. The information that you identify by answering these questions will be useful later in this process when you identify threats to the critical assets and in process 8 when you build mitigation plans. Make sure that you record this information.

At MedSite, the analysis team discussed the questions relative to PIDS. Two of the team members wrote a brief description based on their experiences using PIDS. Figure 6-9 shows the results.

Now that you have identified the critical assets for your organization, you next need to document what about each asset is important by describing or refining its security requirements. In the next activity we examine this topic.

6.4 Refine Security Requirements for Critical Assets

This activity can be difficult for many analysis teams, as it requires defining security requirements for each critical asset, focusing on the organizational perspective. As you review security requirements from earlier workshops, you will start to see conflicts and gaps among the data.

For example, senior managers may have selected confidentiality as the most important security requirement, while staff members valued availability most. Your task is to view the information from the perspective of the organization and resolve the differences in the data. You must consider trade-offs in selecting one security requirement over another. Which aspect of security would you sacrifice to protect another? Is easy availability of data more important than preserving confidentiality? These are the types of issues that you must resolve during this activity.

Step 1: Describe the Security Requirements for Each Critical Asset

Consider the following questions when refining or describing security requirements for each critical asset:

- Is this asset proprietary or sensitive? Does it contain personal information? Should it be inaccessible to anyone who is not authorized to see it? If the answer to any of these questions is yes, what is the specific confidentiality requirement?
- Are authenticity, accuracy, and completeness important for this asset? If yes, what is the specific integrity requirement?
- Is accessibility of the asset important? If yes, what is the specific availability requirement?
- What other security-related requirements, if any, are important to this asset?

As you think about the questions, review the security requirements and areas of concern that were recorded for that asset during processes 1 to 3. Remember that if the critical asset was not identified as important during the earlier processes, you will have neither areas of concern nor security requirements information for it. In that case you will have to create security requirements without the benefit of this additional information. Discuss the questions among yourselves. When you reach a decision about the security requirements for a critical asset, make sure that you record this information.

The analysis team at MedSite reviewed the security requirements and areas of concern for PIDS that were identified by earlier workshop participants (see Figures 6-6 and 6-7). The team then used its collective judgment and experience to create a refined list of security requirements. You can see the results in the right column of Figure 6-10.

Once you have refined (or in some cases, created) the security requirements for each critical asset, you need to determine which requirement is most important.

Step 2: Prioritize Security Requirements for Each Critical Asset

Consider any conflicts among the security requirements. As you do this, discuss the trade-offs among the requirements. Is confidentiality more important than availability? How important is integrity relative to the other requirements? This trade-off can be difficult. You need to avoid taking the easy way out and declaring that all requirements are equally important. When you get to mitigation in phase 3,

Security Requirement Type	Priority	Specific Requirement
Confidentiality		Information should be kept confidential (restricted to those with "need to know"). Information is subject to the Privacy Act.
Integrity		Records must be kept accurate and complete. All information should be available for the patient encounter. Only authorized users should be allowed to modify information.
Availability	X	Access to information is required 24/7; it must be available for patient encounters. It is essential to have an adequate number of terminals for data entry operators.
Other		

FIGURE 6-10 Security Requirements for Critical Assets

you may find that you need to make a choice between mitigation strategies or actions based on the relative priorities of security requirements. Will you need to sacrifice some confidentiality for availability? When you reach a decision about the most important security requirement for a critical asset, make sure that you record this information.

The analysis team from MedSite discussed the trade-offs among the requirements. They decided that availability was the most important requirement and then documented this decision by placing an *X* in the middle column of the table in Figure 6-10. You could also put all of the security requirements in priority order.

If you look at the security requirements for PIDS created by the operational area managers during process 2, you will see that they selected all requirements as being equally important (see Figure 6-6). Although the facilitator captured the wishes of the managers during that workshop, the analysis team members understood that they needed to evaluate the trade-offs and make a decision during this step. They selected availability as the top requirement for PIDS because the primary mission of MedSite is to treat its patients.

Now you understand what assets are most critical to your organization, and you have examined what aspects of those assets are important. It is time to examine what threatens your critical assets.

6.5 Identify Threats to Critical Assets

At this point in the evaluation you begin to examine the range of threats that can affect your critical assets. You perform a gap analysis of the areas of concern you elicited earlier in the evaluation, creating a complete threat profile for each critical asset.

Recall that a generic threat profile is a structured way of presenting a range of potential threats to a critical asset. In this activity you essentially tailor the generic threat profile for each critical asset by deciding which threats in the range of possibilities actually apply to a critical asset. This information helps to form the basis for examining the computing infrastructure for vulnerabilities as well as for identifying and analyzing risks to critical assets.

Step 1: Map Areas of Concern to Generic Threat Profile

For each critical asset, review the consolidated areas of concern that affect that asset. Consider the following question: How do the areas of concern map to the threat profile?

To map an area of concern to the threat profile, you must first determine which category of threat (e.g., human actors using network access) is represented by the area of concern. You then determine which threat properties (asset, access, actor, motive, outcome) are represented by the area of concern. Finally, you map the threat properties to the corresponding asset-based threat tree.

Let's examine how the analysis team at MedSite performed the mapping. Figure 6-11 shows three areas of concern for PIDS. Each is from the *human actors using network access* category. The team determined which threat properties were represented by each area of concern. In the first area of concern, the asset is the information on the PIDS system. The concern focuses on staff members using network access to enter data into PIDS. Thus, network access and people inside the organization are part of the concern, and the motive in this case is accidental. Finally, the outcome is modification—the data are entered incorrectly.

Notice how much interpretation is required when mapping areas of concern, which can be ambiguous. That is why it is important to be as precise as possible when capturing areas of concern during the knowledge elicitation workshops. For example, in the first item in the table, the threat actor is stated as "too many people." The analysis team interpreted this to mean insiders (staff members). Figure 6-12 shows the threat properties for the areas of concern from Figure 6-11.

Once you have identified the threat properties for each area of concern, you can easily map the threat properties to the generic threat profile. Figure 6-13 shows the asset-based threat tree for human actors using network access, including the mapping of the properties from Figure 6-12. The numbers in parentheses on Figure 6-13 refer to the areas of concern. Note that a solid line in Figure 6-13 indicates the existence of a threat, while a dashed line indicates no threat to the asset. Also note that an area of concern could be mapped to multiple branches.

PIDS Areas of Concern

1. Too many people are entering the wrong data, resulting in incorrect records, and/or there may be multiple files and records for an individual.

2. Personnel access information on PIDS that they are not authorized to use.

3. Inherent flaws and vulnerabilities in critical applications could be exploited.

FIGURE 6-11 Areas of Concern for PIDS

Area of Concern	Threat Properties
1. Too many people are entering the wrong data, resulting in incorrect records, and/or there may be multiple files and records for an individual.	Asset—PIDS Access—network (data entered into records on a system) Actor—insiders (i.e., staff with legitimate access) Motive—accidental Outcome—modification (data incorrect due to modification)
2. Personnel access information on PIDS that they are not authorized to use.	Asset—PIDS Access—network (information received by actor from PIDS) Actor—insiders (i.e., staff with legitimate access as well as outsiders) Motive—deliberate Outcome—disclosure (i.e., people viewing the information)
3. Inherent flaws and vulnerabilities in critical applications could be exploited.	Asset—PIDS Access—network (records received by actor from the system) Actor—inside and outside (both people inside and outside MedSite able to exploit vulnerabilities) Motive—deliberate Outcome—disclosure, modification

FIGURE 6-12 Threat Properties for Areas of Concern

This completes the mapping process. However, your task of identifying threats is not finished. You must now perform a gap analysis of the remaining (unmarked) threats on the profile to determine if any of them affect the critical asset.

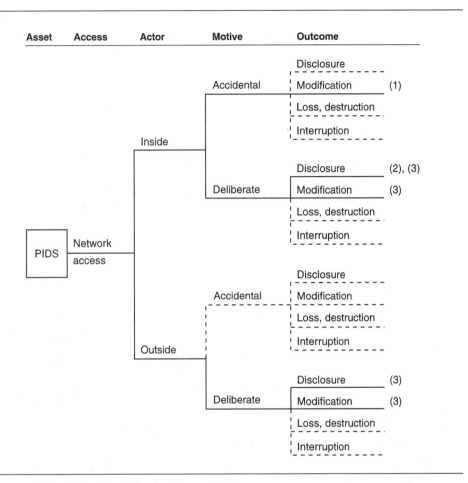

FIGURE 6-13 Threat Tree After Mapping Areas of Concern

Step 2: Perform a Gap Analysis

During this step you must remember that the areas of concern were elicited during the knowledge elicitation workshops. It is unlikely that all threats for an asset will be elicited during those workshops. Your job during this step is to determine what other threats could affect your organization's critical assets.

Consider the following questions:

- For which remaining potential threats is there a more than negligible possibility of a threat to the asset? Mark these branches in the threat profile.

- For which remaining potential threats is there a negligible possibility or no possibility at all of a threat to the asset? Do not mark these branches in the threat profile.

When discussing the questions, remember to consider all remaining branches for each threat tree. When you reach a decision, mark each additional more than negligible threat on the appropriate asset-based threat tree.

Always remember to record relevant contextual information on the threat profile. This information elaborates on the information represented by the trees. If a branch of the *human actors using network access* tree indicates an outside threat actor, you might want to add contextual notes to supplement the areas of concern. For example, if the threat refers specifically to threats from corporate spies, make sure that you add a note indicating this.

In some cases you might find that an area of concern contains a threat actor not in the generic threat profile. This is especially true in the *systems problems* and *other problems* threat categories. These categories might contain threats that are unique to a system or to your environment, or new threats that haven't been added to the generic threat profile. Since these unique threats might not easily map to the threat actors in the generic threat profile, you must add them to threat profiles for the affected critical assets. Depending on the nature of the threat actor identified from an area of concern, you might decide to add it to the generic threat profile.

The analysis team at MedSite performed a gap analysis on the PIDS threat profile. During the analysis the team members decided that if insiders could deliberately disclose and modify PIDS information, they could also destroy or deny access to the information. The team then identified other threats to the PIDS information. In fact, the analysis team felt that all threats except accidental actions by outsiders were applicable to the information on PIDS. They felt that PIDS was too difficult to access by accident. Only a determined outsider would be able to get in. Figure 6-14 shows the asset-based threat tree for human actors using network access after the gap analysis. The team used the same process for the other categories of threats, yielding a threat profile for the critical asset. (Appendix A presents the entire threat profile for PIDS.)

In addition, the team noticed that some of the areas of concerns contained threat actors not in the generic threat profile. Team members extended the threat profile for the affected critical assets to include those threat actors. Figure 6-15 shows the asset-based threat tree for the category of other problems for PIDS. A comparison of that tree with the generic tree in Figure 6-4 shows that the team modified the tree in the following ways:

- The team removed the following threat actors from the PIDS threat profile: *third-party problems or unavailability of third-party systems* and *telecommunications problems or unavailability*.

- The team added the following threat actors to the PIDS threat profile: *lack of control over hardware and software* and *lack of trained maintenance personnel*.

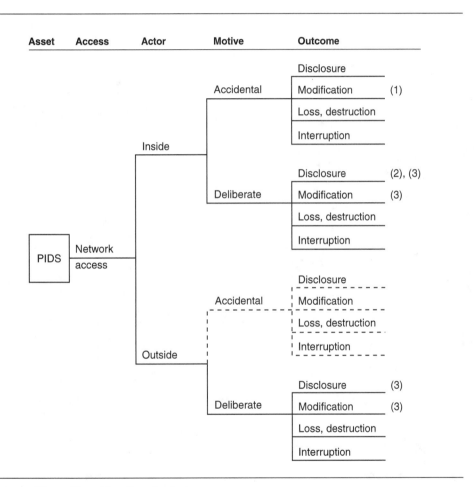

FIGURE 6-14 Threat Tree After Gap Analysis

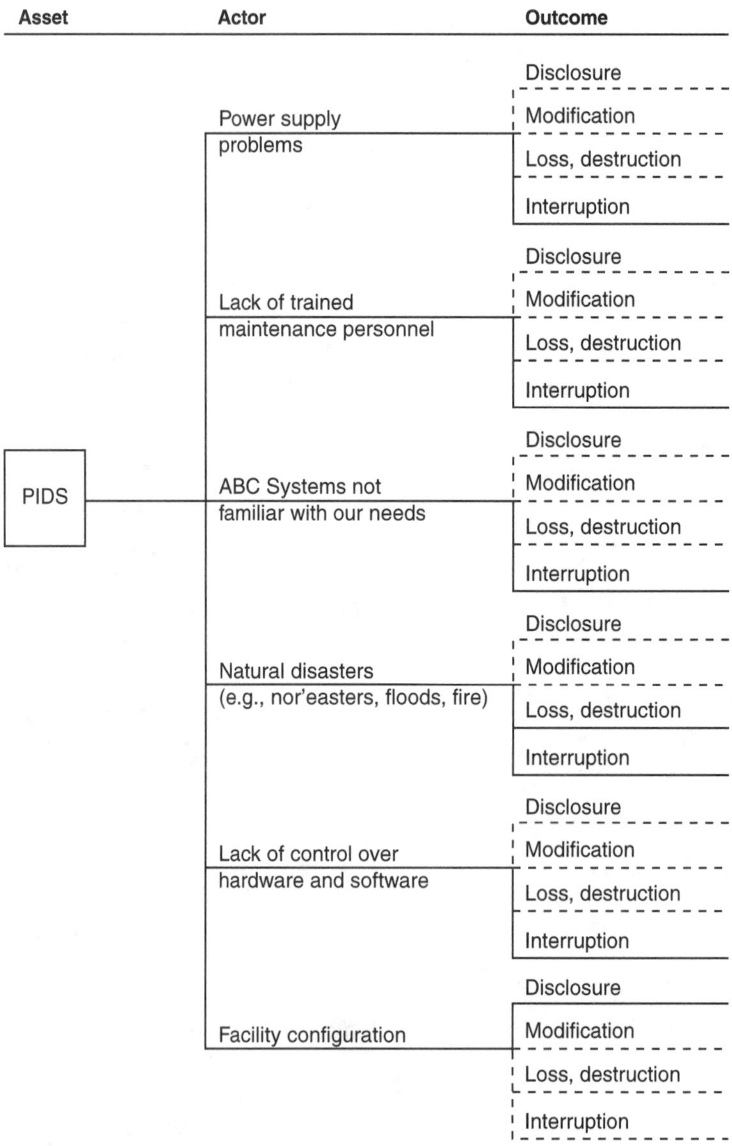

Asset	Actor	Outcome
		Disclosure
	Power supply problems	Modification
		Loss, destruction
		Interruption
		Disclosure
	Lack of trained maintenance personnel	Modification
		Loss, destruction
		Interruption
		Disclosure
PIDS	ABC Systems not familiar with our needs	Modification
		Loss, destruction
		Interruption
		Disclosure
	Natural disasters (e.g., nor'easters, floods, fire)	Modification
		Loss, destruction
		Interruption
		Disclosure
	Lack of control over hardware and software	Modification
		Loss, destruction
		Interruption
		Disclosure
	Facility configuration	Modification
		Loss, destruction
		Interruption

FIGURE 6-15 Other Problems Threat Tree for PIDS

Step 3: Check Threat Profiles for Consistency and Completeness

After you have created a threat profile for each critical asset, look at the outcomes across the threat profile. Compare the outcomes with the security requirements to check for consistency and completeness.

When comparing threat trees and security requirements, you must understand the relationships among the outcomes and the security requirements, as shown in Table 6-4.

TABLE 6-4 Relationships Among Security Requirements and Outcomes

Security Requirement	Related Outcome
Confidentiality	Disclosure
Integrity	Modification
Availability	Loss, destruction, interruption

For example, if you have a security requirement for confidentiality but no threats with disclosure as an outcome, you need to interpret the meaning of this situation. Consider the following possibilities:

- Confidentiality is not really a security requirement.
- You might have missed threats that result in disclosure of the critical asset.
- There is no possibility or only a negligible possibility, of threats resulting in disclosure of the critical asset.
- The security requirement might be driven by law or regulation rather than by an existing threat.

Threat Profiles and Asset Categories

You should note that the category of asset dictates which threat categories you should consider for a critical asset. Complete the threat trees for these categories, using the following information as a guide:

- For *information assets,* you need to determine whether the asset is represented electronically (on a systems asset), physically, or both. For electronic information, the following threat categories apply: human actors using network access, human actors using physical access, systems problems, and other problems.

- For information that is represented physically (for example, on paper only), the following threat categories apply: human actors using physical access and other problems.

- *Systems assets* generally represent groupings of information, software, and hardware assets. The following threat categories apply to systems assets: human actors using network access, human actors using physical access, systems problems, and other problems.

- *Software assets* focus on software applications or services. The following threat categories apply to software assets: human actors using network access, human actors using physical access, systems problems, and other problems.

- *Hardware assets* focus only on the physical information technology hardware. The following threat categories apply to hardware assets: human actors using physical access and other problems.

- *People assets* focus on either a special skill that the people have or a service that they provide. The only threat category that applies to people assets is other problems.

Looking Across Critical Assets

You should also consider checking for consistency across critical assets. For example, the analysis team at MedSite identified three systems assets as being critical (PIDS, ECDS, and personal computers). When mapping areas of concern to the PIDS threat profile, team members identified two unique threat actors for PIDS (*lack of control over hardware and software* and *lack of trained maintenance personnel*). As a consistency check, the team examined the threat profiles for ECDS and personal computers to see if either of the unique threat actors for PIDS affects those systems as well.

This completes our presentation of process 4. Chapter 7 looks at process 5, in which you identify the key components of your organization's computing infrastructure. These components are used to store, transmit, and process your organization's critical information, and they are evaluated for technological weaknesses during phase 2 of the OCTAVE Method.

7

Identifying Key Components
(Process 5)

Recall that security includes both organizational and technological aspects. The security-related practices of the people in the organization are important, as is the state of an organization's computing infrastructure. OCTAVE requires the examination of both organizational and technological issues during the evaluation.

Process 5, Identify Infrastructure Vulnerabilities, marks the beginning of phase 2 of OCTAVE. It requires the organization to examine its computing infrastructure in relation to phase 1's organizational information, setting the scope for a technological evaluation of the infrastructure. At this point in the evaluation, a transition occurs from the organizational view to the technological view. Phase 2 reflects what the majority of people think of when they hear the term "security evaluation": an assessment of the computing infrastructure. The difference here is that by positioning the assessment of the infrastructure within the larger context of OCTAVE, you can focus on the parts of the infrastructure that are important to the critical assets and thus help the business succeed. OCTAVE increases the effectiveness of traditional, technology-focused vulnerability assessments.

7.1 Overview of Process 5

Upon completion of process 4 you identified your organization's critical assets and examined the threats to those assets. In process 5 you use this information to determine how to evaluate your organization's computing infrastructure for technology vulnerabilities.

You need to focus on the vulnerability evaluation to complete it in an efficient *and* effective manner. To understand your risk, you need to collect vulnerability information only on key components relative to the critical assets. Process 5 enables you to identify those key components.

Process 5 Workshop

Process 5 is implemented using the core analysis team members as well as any supplemental personnel that this team decides to include. Since this workshop also marks the beginning of the technology-intensive activities of the evaluation, you might include additional information technology personnel in the workshop.

The workshop should take an experienced analysis team two to four hours to conduct. Remember to review all activities for process 5 and decide whether your team collectively has the required knowledge and skills to complete all tasks successfully. We suggest that your team members have the following skills:

- Understanding of the organization's business environment and how business staff legitimately use information technology in the organization
- Understanding of the organization's information technology environment and knowledge of its network topology
- Good communication skills

- Good analytical skills
- Understanding of common exploits of technology vulnerabilities and the types of tools used to check for technology vulnerabilities

Table 7-1 summarizes the workshop activities for process 5.

Before looking at process 5 in detail, let's examine technology vulnerabilities and the supporting information you'll need to conduct this process.

Technology Vulnerabilities

Ultimately, your goal during phase 2 of OCTAVE is to identify technological weaknesses in the computing infrastructure. *Technology vulnerabilities* are weaknesses in systems, devices, and components that can directly lead to unauthorized action [NSTISSC 98]. Technology vulnerabilities are present in and apply to network services, architecture, operating systems, and applications. They are often grouped into three categories [Howard 98]:

- *Design vulnerabilities*—a vulnerability inherent in the design or specification of hardware or software whereby even a perfect implementation will result in a vulnerability
- *Implementation vulnerabilities*—a vulnerability resulting from an error made in implementing software or hardware of a satisfactory design
- *Configuration vulnerabilities*—a vulnerability resulting from an error in the configuration and administration of a system or component

Consider a case in which designers specify a weak authentication mechanism for a system that will store classified information. This can be considered a

TABLE 7-1 Process 5 Activities

Activity	Description
Identify key classes of components	The analysis team establishes the system(s) of interest for each critical asset. The team then identifies the classes of components that are related to the system(s) of interest.
Identify infrastructure components to examine	The analysis team selects specific components to evaluate. The team selects one or more infrastructure components from each key class to evaluate. In addition, the team also selects an approach and specific tools for evaluating vulnerabilities.

design vulnerability. If system developers implement the requirement as specified, the resulting authentication mechanism will allow attackers to break into the system easily.

Now let's look at a common implementation vulnerability, the buffer overflow. A buffer overflow exploit takes advantage of programs that improperly parse data and inadvertently attempt to store too much data in a storage (memory) area that is too small, causing an overflow. One possible result of a buffer overflow is that an attacker can execute whatever command is desired, thus potentially affecting the confidentiality, integrity, or availability of the data on that system. Buffer overflows can also force a system to abort because it is trying to perform illegal instructions, compromising the availability of that system.

Or consider the following examples of configuration vulnerabilities:

- A system contains accounts with default passwords, allowing an attacker to gain access to the system by using a commonly known password.
- File permissions on a system are set up to allow "world write" permission for new files, meaning that anyone with access to the system can read or change information on that system.
- Services that are known to be vulnerable are running on a system, allowing attackers to exploit the vulnerability and gain access to the system.

Each of the above examples of configuration vulnerabilities stems from systems not being securely configured by administrators. You should also note that once design and implementation vulnerabilities become known (often because someone has exploited them and gained access to a system), vendors typically work to address the vulnerabilities and make software patches containing the fix available to their customers. It is then the responsibility of system and network administrators to apply the patches to the appropriate systems. Thus, you can see how design and implementation vulnerabilities can eventually be transformed into related configuration vulnerabilities.

In an operational information security risk evaluation, you primarily focus on configuration vulnerabilities. You check systems for known technological weaknesses, looking for indications of errors in the configuration of your organization's systems and networks. This information complements some of the information that you collected in process 3, whereby information technology staff members discussed current security practices related to configuring and maintaining the organization's computing infrastructure. Figure 7-1 highlights those

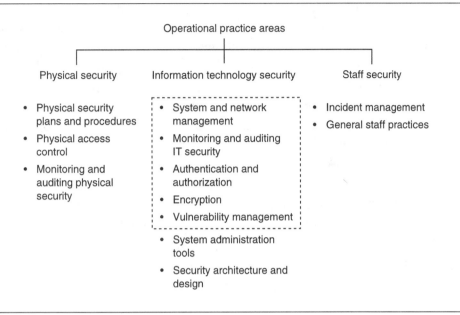

FIGURE 7-1 What Vulnerability Tools Identify

areas from the catalog of practices that focus on configuring and maintaining systems and networks. Technology vulnerabilities that are identified during phase 2 of OCTAVE can provide objective data that you can use to refine your understanding of the organization's current information technology practices.

Mapping the Computing Infrastructure

During process 5 you select components from your computing infrastructure to examine for technology vulnerabilities. As you do this, you will most likely refer to information about your computing infrastructure. For this, you will need a network topology, or map, that represents the layout of the computing infrastructure, including all access points to the organization's networks. You can also use a listing of the systems in the organization. It is important that one member of your team be able to read and interpret the network topology. The following list highlights three potential sources of information about your computing infrastructure that you can use:

- Network topology diagrams—electronic or paper documents used to display the logical or physical mapping of a network. These documents identify the connectivity of systems and networking components. They usually contain less detail than that provided by network mapping tools.
- Network mapping tools—software used to search a network, identifying the physical connectivity of systems and networking components. The software also displays detailed information about the interconnectivity of networks and devices (routers, switches, bridges, hosts).
- Computer prioritization listings—a listing of the computer inventory owned by an organization. This listing typically depicts a prioritized ordering of systems or networking components based on their importance to the organization (e.g., mission-critical systems, high/medium/low-priority systems, administrative systems, support systems, etc).

Any of the above sources of information can be used. You need to decide how much and what type of information you need to select the key classes of components. Typically, a network topology diagram is sufficient for the activities in process 5.

Next we look at the first activity of process 5, in which you identify key classes, or types, of components in your computing infrastructure.

7.2 Identify Key Classes of Components

In this activity you look at critical assets and threats from phase 1 in relation to your computing infrastructure. You examine network access paths (how information or services can be accessed via your organization's network) in the context of threat scenarios to identify the important classes of components for your critical assets.

You focus on the threat tree for *human actors using network access,* because that tree defines the range of scenarios that threaten the critical asset due to deliberate exploitation of technology vulnerabilities by people. Thus, this activity is limited to identifying information technology components that could be used as part of network attacks against critical assets. Figure 7-2 illustrates the relationship among a threat tree and infrastructure components.

Note that you could also use a similar approach to examine threat scenarios for *human actors using physical access.* By examining the physical threat

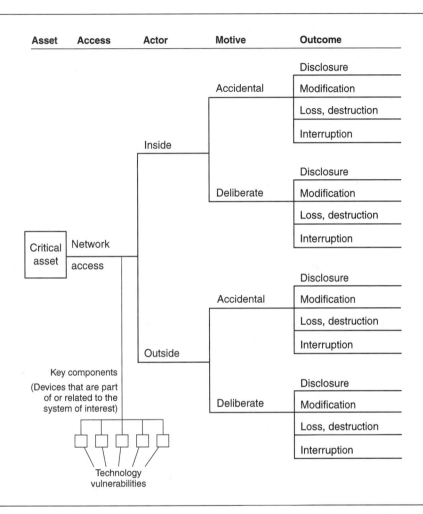

FIGURE 7-2 Relationship Between a Threat Tree and Infrastructure Components

scenarios, you could identify important components from your physical infra-structure that could be used during attacks.

Step 1: Identify the System of Interest

In this step you identify the system that is most closely linked to the critical asset. This is the *system of interest*. We define a *system* as a logical grouping of compo-nents designed to perform a defined function(s) or meet a defined objective(s).

The *system of interest* is a system that gives a threat actor access to a critical asset. It is also the system that gives legitimate users access to a critical asset. Consider the following guidelines as you identify the system of interest for different types of assets:

- For *systems assets,* the system of interest is the asset.
- For *information assets,* the system of interest is the one most closely linked to the information. It can be where the critical information asset is stored and processed. It can also be where the critical information asset moves outside the network (backup systems, off-site storage, other storage devices).
- For *software assets,* the system of interest is the system that is most closely linked to the software application or service. It can be the system from which the critical software asset is served or where it is stored.

To conduct step 1, select a critical asset. Remember, you will examine only the threat tree for *human actors using network access* during this activity. Review the scenarios represented by that threat tree. If the tree has no threats marked, you will not need to complete this activity for the critical asset, and you should move on to the next critical asset.

If threats for *human actors using network access* do exist for the critical asset, consider the following questions:

- Which system(s) is most closely linked to the critical asset? In which system(s) is the critical asset stored and processed?
- Where outside of the system of interest do critical information assets move? Backup system? Off-site storage? Other?
- Based on the critical asset, which system(s) would be the target of a threat actor acting deliberately?

Refer to your network topology diagrams as needed. Identify systems of interest for all applicable critical assets and record this information.

Multiple Systems of Interest

You may have multiple systems of interest for a critical asset, for example in the following situations:

- A group of interrelated systems collectively performs a unique function or meets a unique objective.

- A group of interrelated systems has common or overlapping functions.
- A critical asset is closely linked to multiple systems.

For example, you might identify multiple systems of interest for information and software assets because those types of assets are often closely linked to multiple systems. Distributed assets, such as the network, might also comprise multiple systems of interest. For distributed critical assets, you have a couple of options when identifying the system(s) of interest. If you realize that the critical asset is defined too broadly, you could then define it more narrowly or break it down into smaller critical assets. Alternatively, you can accept how the critical asset is defined and identify multiple systems of interest for it.

Let's consider the sample scenario. For process 5, the analysis team members augmented their skills by including two additional people from MedSite's information technology department as well as one member from the information technology staff at ABC Systems. They all reviewed their organization's network topology diagram and selected systems of interest for each of their critical assets, shown in Figure 7-3.

Systems of Interest

PIDS

Patient Information Data System (PIDS) is its own system of interest.

ECDS

ECDS is its own system of interest.

Personal Computers

Personal computers are themselves the system of interest (they are also a subsystem of the other systems such as PIDS and ECDS).

FIGURE 7-3 Systems of Interest

Note that the analysis team did not identify systems of interest for paper medical records and ABC Systems. Since the paper medical records are not electronic, there are no threats from network attacks on the paper medical records. ABC Systems refers to a group of people, and people assets are not subject to network attacks. The systems used by the staff at ABC Systems are subject to network attacks. However, those systems are outside the scope of MedSite's risk evaluation.

This situation emphasizes an interdependency issue for MedSite. If threats to the systems used by ABC Systems existed and then materialized, the service provided to MedSite by ABC Systems could be affected. The analysis team checked their threat trees for their systems assets (PIDS, ECDS, and personal computers) to make sure that a threat to ABC Systems was identified as an interdependency threat on the *other problems* threat trees.

Note that the results from process 5 caused the analysis team to go back and review information that they completed during process 4. This process shows the iterative nature of risk evaluations. Remember, the results of certain analysis activities will cause you to revisit decisions or review information from previous activities.

Step 2: Identify Key Classes of Components

In this step you identify the classes (or types) of components that are part of or are related to each system of interest. When legitimate users access a critical asset, they also access devices and components from these classes, as indeed threat actors do when they deliberately target a critical asset. Thus, in this step you are examining both how staff members legitimately access a system of interest via the network and how human threat actors use unauthorized access to reach the system of interest. Table 7-2 highlights the key classes of components that you will consider. This is a basic set of key component classes, and the classes that you consider in this activity are contextual. You may need to refine this list in order to conduct a meaningful evaluation.

To conduct step 2, consider the following questions for each critical asset for which you identified a system of interest:

- Which types of components are part of the system of interest? Consider servers, networking components, security components, desktop workstations, home machines, laptops, storage devices, wireless components, and others.

TABLE 7-2 Key Classes of Components

Component Class	Description
Servers	Hosts within your information technology infrastructure that provide information technology services to your organization
Networking components	Devices important to your organization's networks (e.g., routers, switches, and modems)
Security components	Devices that have security as their primary function (e.g., a firewall)
Desktop workstations	Hosts on your networks that staff members use to conduct business
Home computers	Home PCs that staff members use to access information remotely via your organization's networks
Laptops	Portable PCs that staff members use to access information remotely via your organization's networks
Storage devices	Devices where information is stored, often for backup purposes
Wireless components	Devices, such as cell phones and wireless access points, that staff members may use to access information (e.g., email)
Others	Any other type of device that could be part of your threat scenarios but does not fall into the above classes

- Which types of components are related to the system of interest? From which types of hosts can the system of interest be legitimately accessed? Desktop machines? Home machines? Laptops? Cellular phones? Handheld devices? Others?

- How could threat actors access the system of interest? Via the Internet? Via the internal network? Shared external networks? Wireless devices? Others?

- Which types of components could a threat actor use to access the system of interest? Which could serve as intermediate access points? Consider physical and network access to servers, networking components, security components, desktop workstations, home machines, laptops, storage devices, wireless components, and others.

- What other systems could a threat actor use to access the system of interest?

- Based on your answers to the above questions, which classes of components could be part of the threat scenarios?

By answering these questions, you are reviewing access paths for each system of interest. Remember to refer to your network topology as needed. When you identify which classes of components could be part of the threat scenarios, record this information and the rationale for selecting each key component class.

In our example, the analysis team selected key classes of components for each system of interest. In performing this step, the members of the analysis team from the administrative and clinical parts of the organization described how they used the systems to access information. The members of the team with information technology skills (remember that the team included three additional people with information technology skills for this workshop) reviewed the information about how systems are accessed in relation to the organization's network topology to identify the key classes of components. Figure 7-4 shows the key classes of components for PIDS and their rationale for selection; Figure 7-5 shows the network topology map used to identify the component classes. A check mark by a class in Figure 7-4 indicates that the team selected it as a key component class for PIDS. The team also recorded its reasons for selecting each class for PIDS.

Key Classes of Components for PIDS	
Class of Component	**Rationale for Selection**
✓ Servers	Patient information maintained on these
✓ Networking components	Routers and switches—on the main access route for all internal access
✓ Security components	Firewall—key part of security for external access from home PCs
✓ Desktop workstations	Used for all internal access
✓ Home computers	Used by physicians to access patient records and make updates
❒ Laptops	
❒ Storage devices	
❒ Wireless components	

FIGURE 7-4 Key Classes of Components

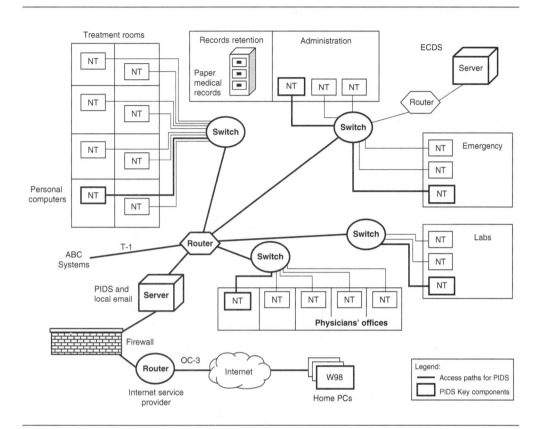

FIGURE 7-5 Access Paths and Key Classes of Components for PIDS

As the analysis team was reviewing the access paths for PIDS using the network topology (see Figure 7-5), the team members made some interesting observations. They noticed that several access paths relied upon components that were controlled by other organizations or by individuals, for example:

- ABC Systems had access to MedSite's internal network via a connection that bypassed the firewall.
- Staff with home machines could gain remote access to PIDS via the Internet and MedSite's Internet Service Provider.

Equipment used by ABC Systems, the Internet service provider, and home users could not be examined for technology vulnerabilities during the risk evaluation, because those components are not owned by MedSite. However, if any of those components have technology vulnerabilities, information belonging to MedSite could be at risk. The analysis team checked to see if this presented any threats that had not been recorded on the *human actors using network access* threat trees for applicable critical assets. They also recorded these observations as contextual notes on the appropriate threat trees. As they talked among themselves, the team members agreed that these were broad issues that had policy implications for the organization. The team members agreed to revisit the issues during process 8 when they develop risk mitigation plans and a protection strategy.

This concludes the first activity of process 5. In the next activity you select specific components from each key class to evaluate for technology vulnerabilities.

7.3 Identify Infrastructure Components to Examine

Recall that *focus on the critical few* is a guiding principle of this evaluation process. In this activity you follow that principle when you select specific components from each key class to examine for technology vulnerabilities.

One point that needs to be emphasized here is the difference between performing a vulnerability evaluation in the context of a risk evaluation and doing so in the context of an ongoing vulnerability management practice. During this activity your goal is to select enough components from each key class to enable you to gain an understanding of how vulnerable your computing infrastructure currently is.

By contrast, when you form your risk mitigation plans in process 8, you may decide that vulnerability management is a practice that your organization should undertake to mitigate your risks. (The catalog of practices in Appendix C presents more information about vulnerability management.) As part of that ongoing vulnerability management practice, you periodically examine *all* components of your infrastructure. Your goal in vulnerability management is continually to identify and then eliminate technology vulnerabilities in your computing infrastructure. In this activity you target your collection of vulnerability information.

Step 1: Select Specific Components

In this step you answer the following two questions:

- Which specific component(s) in this class will we evaluate for vulnerabilities?
- What is our rationale for selecting this specific component(s)?

Look at the key classes of components you identified for your critical assets. Review your organization's network topology diagram in relation to each key class of component for that critical asset. You must determine how many infrastructure components to evaluate from each class. You need to evaluate enough components from each class to get a sufficient understanding of the vulnerability status of a "typical" component from the class. As you select specific components to evaluate, consider the following questions:

- Is the infrastructure component typical of its class?
- How accessible is the infrastructure component? Is it "owned" by another organization? Is it a home machine?
- How critical is the infrastructure component to business operations? Will you be interrupting business operations when you evaluate the component?
- Will special permission or scheduling be required to evaluate the component?

When you select a specific component, you also need the Internet Protocol (IP) address and the host/domain name system (DNS) name (fully qualified domain name) for the device. Remember to select one or more components in each key class. Once you have chosen components from a class, you need some consistent way of identifying them. We suggest using components' IP addresses and host/DNS names. In larger organizations, IP addresses can change on a daily basis for many components, although this is not likely for servers, routers, and firewalls. Recording the fully qualified domain name of the component helps to identify it more reliably than the IP address alone because of services like DHCP (dynamic host configuration protocol), which change the IP address each time a machine boots. Record the IP addresses or fully qualified domain names as well as the rationale for selecting those devices.

You'll need to select infrastructure components from each key class for all critical assets. Keep in mind that some components will be important to more than one critical asset. As you select components to evaluate, look for any overlaps and redundancy across critical assets.

Comprehensiveness versus Effort

In selecting specific components to include in a vulnerability evaluation, you need to balance the comprehensiveness of the evaluation with the effort required to evaluate the components. For example, if you have selected desktop workstations as a key class of components, you need to select one or more workstations to include in your vulnerability evaluation. If you have a thousand desktop workstations in your organization, you need to decide how many to include in the technology evaluation. Since your goal is just to get a feel for the vulnerability status of a typical workstation, you probably need to evaluate only a handful of workstations.

In general, you want to make sure that you have enough information to understand the vulnerability status of the key class, but you don't want to select so many components that you have trouble sorting through all of the data. You need to determine when you have enough information to move forward in the process. No universal guideline can tell you how many devices you should select from a given class. You have to use your best judgment.

Figure 7-6 shows which components the analysis team at MedSite selected for evaluation, as well as information about how the analysis team intends to con-

Key Component	IP Addresses[1]	Vulnerability Evaluation Approach	Tool(s)[2]	Rationale
Office PCs	- - - - - - - - - - - - - - - - - - - - - - - - - - - - - - - - - - - - - - - -	ABC Systems personnel will be responsible for running all of the tools. MedSite's IT personnel will be present and will also get some on-the-job training.	Vulnerability scanner-Vulnerabilities-R-Found, version 6.73	These are common tools used at ABC Systems. Our IT personnel do not have the knowledge to run them but want to learn.
Home PCs	- - - - - - - - - - - - - - - - - - - -			
Firewall	- - - - - - - - - -		Network/Internet-level tool-Improve-UR-Network, version 4.8	
PIDS server	- - - - - - - - - -			
ECDS server	- - - - - - - - - -			
Routers	- - - - - - - - - - - - - - - - - - - -			

FIGURE 7-6 Infrastructure Components to Examine

---

1. Real IP addresses are not supplied in this figure.

2. These are fictitious tools.

duct the vulnerability evaluation. You identify this information during the next step of this activity, when you develop a plan for conducting vulnerability evaluation.

Step 2: Select Evaluation Approach

In this step you answer the following question: What approach will we use to evaluate each selected component?

When you select an approach for evaluating an infrastructure component, you determine how the evaluation will be performed. You decide whether your information technology staff will perform the evaluation or whether you intend to outsource the evaluation to external experts. If you already run vulnerability tools, check to see if you have recent results that can be used.

If you decide that your organization will perform the evaluation, you need to identify the software tool(s) you will use. You also need to identify who will perform the evaluation and interpret the results. Always make sure that you have permission to run any tools on your site's infrastructure. There may be legal implications or personal liability issues. Also make sure that you set a specific schedule for running the tools and that you let all stakeholders know what you intend to do and when you intend to do it. You should determine if there are any potential side effects from running the tools and notify stakeholders accordingly.

If you decide to outsource, think about how you will communicate your needs and requirements to the external experts and how you intend to verify whether they have sufficiently addressed those needs and requirements. Also make sure that the external experts set a specific schedule for running any tools on your networks and that they let all stakeholders know what they intend to do and when they intend to do it.

Some organizations use contractors or managed service providers to maintain their systems and networks. If contractors or personnel from managed service providers are going to participate in the vulnerability evaluation, you need to decide whether to include them on the analysis team, or treat them as external experts. It depends on the nature of the working relationship that your organization has with them.

Either you or your external experts must also decide which tool(s) you will use. Tools include software, checklists, and scripts. You need to decide whether to automate the process of evaluating technology vulnerabilities (by using software) or whether to use checklists or scripts. Checklists, for example, might be needed for components that are not currently supported by tools (e.g., mainframes). Once you have made this decision, you need to select the specific tools,

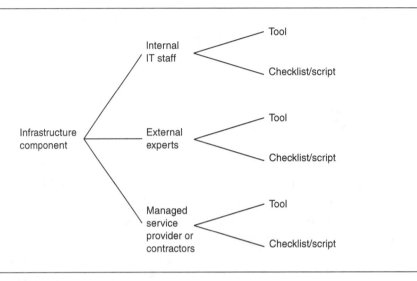

FIGURE 7-7 Vulnerability Evaluation Approaches

checklists, or scripts. Figure 7-7 illustrates your choices in creating an approach for evaluating an infrastructure component for technology vulnerabilities. The next section examines the topic of vulnerability evaluation tools in more depth.

Let's review these concepts in the context of our example. The analysis team at MedSite decided to contract with ABC Systems for the vulnerability evaluation. ABC Systems maintains the systems and networks at MedSite and is contractually obligated to scan MedSite's computing infrastructure periodically for technology vulnerabilities. Analysis team members scheduled a meeting with their contacts at ABC Systems to convey MedSite's requirements for performing a vulnerability evaluation of MedSite's infrastructure. They also included staff from MedSite's contracting office to ensure that any contractual issues with ABC Systems could be addressed. Figure 7-6 highlighted the information recorded by the analysis team for this activity.

Vulnerability Evaluation Tools

Before you run any vulnerability evaluation tools on your organization's networks, you will need to obtain appropriate management approval. In addition, you may decide that you need to research available vulnerability evaluation tools in order to choose the right tools. You may also need to acquire the selected tools and/or undergo training in their use. You should recognize that this process may significantly delay the overall evaluation schedule.

Cost estimates may also be required, particularly if tools need to be purchased or upgraded, or if someone needs to be trained to run them. You must also consider the cost of personnel time to coordinate and run the tools, as well as time lost by staff members who might not be able to perform their duties efficiently when testing occurs.

Let's examine the topic of software tools used to evaluate vulnerabilities. These software tools assess devices or components, identifying known weaknesses (exploits) and misconfigurations. They also provide information about the potential for success if a threat actor were to attempt an intrusion. These types of tools are often used by threat actors attacking an organization's systems and networks. An actor will commonly scan systems remotely from the Internet to find vulnerabilities. The scans can provide the actor with the means to access (read, modify, or destroy) and interrupt (deny availability of) your systems and networks.

Types of Tools

The following list highlights types of vulnerability evaluation tools that you should consider:

- Operating system scanners—these target specific operating systems such as Windows NT/2000, Sun Solaris, Red Hat Linux, or Apple Mac OS.
- Network infrastructure scanners—these focus on the components of the network infrastructure, such as routers and intelligent switches, DNS (domain name system) servers, firewall systems, and intrusion detection systems.
- Specialty, targeted, or hybrid scanners—these target a range of services, applications, and operating system functions, such as Web servers (CGI, JAVA), database applications, registry information (e.g., Windows NT/2000), and weak password storage and authentication services.
- Checklists—these provide the same functionality as automated tools. However, unlike automated tools, checklists are manual, not automated. They also require a consistent review of the items being checked and must be routinely updated. However, checklists may be all you can find or use.
- Scripts—these provide the same functionality as automated tools, but they usually have a singular function. The more items you test, the more scripts

you'll need. As with checklists, scripts require a consistent review of the items being checked and must be routinely updated.

The reports generated by software tools provide a wide range of content and format. First you need to determine what information you require, and then you need to match your requirements to the report(s) provided by the tool(s). You should also consider how much information each tool provides and whether it provides any means to filter or interpret the information. The reports that are generated by software tools can be quite long (300+ pages), especially when a large number of systems are scanned.

Limitations

Vulnerability tools do have limitations. They will not indicate when some system administration procedures are being improperly or incorrectly performed. For example, a tool will not be able to determine whether users are being given access to more information or services than they need. The information technology staff needs to follow good practices for defining required security levels, setting up and managing accounts, and configuring infrastructure components. In addition, vulnerability tools check only for known vulnerabilities; the tools will not identify unknown vulnerabilities or new vulnerabilities. Thus, you need to ensure that you keep your vulnerability tools current with the latest vulnerability information provided by vendors and other sources (i.e., a catalog of vulnerabilities) and that you run them properly.

Finally, vulnerability tools may not indicate whether staff members are following good practices (e.g., if staff members have shared passwords or ignored physical security procedures) or whether implemented security rules are in line with your business objectives. This is why the surveys and protection strategy discussion from processes 1 to 3 are so important; they evaluate aspects of security that tools can't examine.

Some automated tools have the potential to cause interruptions in service or other problems when they are run, depending upon your particular systems and the way in which they are configured. The analysis team and any supplemental members need to discuss these possibilities and determine who would be affected should anything happen.

This concludes process 5. You have now selected components from your organization's computing infrastructure to evaluate for technology vulnerabilities. In process 6 you conduct the vulnerability evaluation and interpret the results.

8

Evaluating Selected Components (Process 6)

An information security risk evaluation is a lot like solving a puzzle. Prior to process 6, you don't quite have enough information to start developing solutions. You are missing a key piece of the puzzle, namely, the current state of your organization's computing infrastructure. The data that you must collect are the technological weaknesses present in the infrastructure.

Process 6 completes phase 2 of OCTAVE. You execute the vulnerability evaluation approach that you outlined in process 5, completing the data gathering for the evaluation and setting you up for subsequent analysis and planning activities.

8.1 Overview of Process 6

Process 6 is a data collection and analysis task. When you started the evaluation, your objective was to understand your organization's information security risks. To examine your risk, you needed to focus on the individual components of risk: asset, threat, vulnerability, and impact.

Prior to this point in the evaluation, you have identified your critical assets, the threats to the assets, current security practices used by your organization, and organizational vulnerabilities present in your organization. It is now time to take another step toward completing the picture of risk by setting your sights on the infrastructure.

Process 6 Workshop

Process 6 is unique because it requires the completion of a major technical task prior to the workshop. The task involves running vulnerability evaluation tools on the key infrastructure components that you identified in process 5. Depending on the approach that you selected during process 5, either your managed service provider, members of your organization's information technology staff, or external experts conduct the vulnerability evaluation. In any case the people who run the tools must also review and analyze the results and prepare a preliminary summary of technology vulnerabilities prior to the process 6 workshop. Running vulnerability evaluation tools and preparing the preliminary summary can take up to several days to complete. Table 8-1 summarizes what must be accomplished prior to the workshop.

The process 6 workshop includes the core analysis team members, selected members of the information technology staff, and the people who performed the vulnerability evaluation. It can be conducted in about two to three hours. For process 6, the leader must also make sure that the technology evaluation task is

TABLE 8-1 Preparation Activities for Process 6

Activity	Description
Run vulnerability evaluation tools on selected infrastructure components	The IT staff or external experts conduct the vulnerability evaluation. They are responsible for running the vulnerability evaluation tools and creating a vulnerability summary for each critical asset prior to the workshop.

completed prior to the workshop and that the people who conducted the evaluation are ready to present the preliminary summary.

You conduct only one activity during the process 6 workshop. Before you start the workshop, review the activity and decide whether your team collectively has the required knowledge and skills to complete all tasks successfully. We suggest that your team members have the following skills:

- Understanding of the organization's information technology environment and knowledge of its topology
- Understanding of common exploits of technology vulnerabilities
- Knowledge of how to use and interpret the results of vulnerability evaluation tools
- Good communication skills
- Good analytical skills

Table 8-2 highlights the process 6 workshop activity.

Catalog of Vulnerabilities

During process 6, you run vulnerability evaluation tools on your organization's systems and networks to identify the technological weaknesses in selected infrastructure components. The tools examine each component for known weaknesses (exploits) and misconfigurations, also known as technology vulnerabilities. Technology vulnerabilities change constantly. To effectively evaluate your systems and networks for technology vulnerabilities, you need to make sure that your tools are examining components for the latest set of known weaknesses.

To ensure that you are evaluating components for all currently known technology vulnerabilities, you must select tools that are designed to examine specific components and are aligned with an established catalog or collection of

TABLE 8-2 Process 6 Activities

Activity	Description
Review technology vulnerabilities and summarize results	The information technology staff members or external experts who ran the vulnerability tool(s) present a vulnerability summary for each critical asset and interpret it for the analysis team. Each vulnerability summary is reviewed by the team and refined if appropriate.

vulnerabilities. A catalog of vulnerabilities contains a listing of known technological weaknesses, based on platform and application. At the time of writing this book, the one broadly recognized catalog of vulnerabilities was MITRE's Common Vulnerabilities and Exposures (CVE)[1], collaboratively developed by representatives across the community and maintained by the MITRE Corporation.

"CVE is a list of standardized names for vulnerabilities and other information security exposures—CVE aims to standardize the names of all publicly known vulnerabilities and security exposures."[2]

CVE is not considered to be a database; rather, it is a list or dictionary that provides common names for publicly known vulnerabilities [Merkow 00]. A common naming convention enables effective communication about vulnerabilities, their potential impact, and approaches for addressing them. Thus, CVE enables open and shared information among vulnerability databases and tools without any distribution restrictions.

Individual vulnerability tool providers generally use their own vulnerability databases, which are often consistent with CVE. The CVE Web site provides considerable information on the contents of the CVE list, how it was developed, and how it continues to be updated. CVE information can be downloaded free or searched online.

The CERT© Coordination Center's (CERT/CC) Vulnerability Notes Database[3] also provides a source of vulnerability information based on an analysis of the reports CERT/CC receives. The Vulnerability Notes Database is a Web-based, searchable collection of the CERT Vulnerability Notes. The database can be searched by several fields (including the CVE name) and supports customized queries. It is also fully CVE compatible.

This chapter addresses software-based vulnerability evaluation tools rather than checklists and scripts. Most organizations rely on commercial or freeware tools to perform vulnerability evaluations, rather than more time-consuming checklists and scripts. You need to make sure that any software tool you use is consistent with a catalog of vulnerabilities, such as CVE. Check with your vendor or examine the tools for yourself.

---

1. http://www.cve.mitre.org/
2. These works were taken from MITRE's CVE Web page dated 12/10/2001.
3. http://www.kb.cert.org/vuls/

8.2 Before the Workshop: Run Vulnerability Evaluation Tools on Selected Infrastructure Components

The focus of this activity rests squarely on the computing infrastructure. You goal is to make sure that each component you selected during process 5 is evaluated against known technological weaknesses to see which are present in that component.

Staff members from your information technology department, or possibly external experts, take lead roles in process 6. Remember, it takes specialized information technology and security knowledge to run the tools and interpret the results. You need to make sure that you have the right people engaged in this part of the evaluation.

Step 1: Run Vulnerability Evaluation Tools

In this step you conduct the vulnerability evaluation by running the vulnerability evaluation tools you selected during process 5. Before you use the tools, you must verify that

- The correct tool(s) is being used
- The latest version of the tool(s) is being used
- All necessary approvals have been obtained and all affected personnel have been notified

You should always make sure that you have proper permission and management approval prior to running vulnerability evaluation tools on your networks. Your organization's information technology department should have procedures for obtaining approval to use the tools. You should notify personnel who may use or rely on the systems and networks being evaluated in case something unexpected happens and they lose access to the asset(s).

Run the tools on the selected components. Remember, designated people with information technology skills lead this activity. Members of the analysis team can be present to observe the evaluation or participate in it directly, if appropriate.

In our sample scenario, three members from ABC Systems led the vulnerability evaluation for MedSite. The analysis team member with information technology skills participated in the evaluation, as did two other information technology staff members from MedSite who wanted to learn more about vulnerability tools. They used a suite of commercial and freeware tools that were approved for use according to ABC Systems' policies and procedures. The staff members from ABC Systems knew how to run the tools, which they used on a regular basis. The staff members helped the members from MedSite to become familiar with the tools and how they are used.

Prior to running the tools on MedSite's networks, the analysis team and the staff from ABC Systems made sure to obtain approval from MedSite's management. Everyone agreed that the tools should be run after standard working hours at MedSite to minimize any problems that might occur. At that point, they ran the tools. Figure 8-1 shows the components at MedSite on which the vulnerability evaluation tools were run. Note that despite their efforts to gain approval, they were blocked from looking at home machines due to corporate policy.

Component	IP Addresses[4]	Scanned (Y/N)
Office PCs	---------------- ---------------- ---------------- ----------------	y
Home PCs	---------------- ----------------	N—company policy does not allow access to home equipment owned by staff members.
Firewall	----------------	y
PIDS server	----------------	y
ECDS server	----------------	y
Routers	---------------- ----------------	y

FIGURE 8-1 Components Examined for Technology Vulnerabilities

4. Real IP addresses are not supplied in this figure.

Step 2: Prepare Preliminary Vulnerability Summary

After you have completed step 1, you have to review the reports generated by the tools. Software vulnerability evaluation tools typically produce the following types of information for each component:

- Vulnerability name
- Description of the vulnerability
- Severity level of the vulnerability
- Actions required to repair the vulnerability

During step 2, you review the detailed vulnerability reports, interpret the results, and create a preliminary summary of the technology vulnerabilities for each key component. A vulnerability summary should state how many vulnerabilities should be fixed immediately (high-severity vulnerabilities), how many should be fixed soon (medium-severity vulnerabilities), and how many should be fixed later (low-severity vulnerabilities).

Note that the severity levels defined above are a basic set used to indicate how soon action should be taken to address vulnerabilities. The levels are contextual for any organization, and you should tailor them to meet your organization's needs. Some tools identify severity levels for vulnerabilities but interpret high, medium, and low severity differently.

The need for a preliminary summary is based on the assumption that the vulnerability evaluation is not conducted by all of the analysis team members. Software vulnerability evaluation tools produce very detailed reports that are not easily understood by personnel who do not have information technology *and* security backgrounds. Remember that the analysis team includes business staff members who probably do not configure and manage systems on a day-to-day basis.

If additional information technology staff members or external experts conduct the evaluation, a preliminary vulnerability summary is necessary to communicate vulnerability information to the core analysis team members. The summary should be presented to the analysis team during the process 6 workshop. However, if all core analysis team members are able to participate actively in the vulnerability evaluation, you can wait until the workshop to analyze and interpret the results.

Let's go back to our example. The staff members from ABC Systems and MedSite first established severity levels for technology vulnerabilities, shown in Figure 8-2.

Vulnerability Serverity Level	Definition
High-severity vulnerabilities	Must be fixed immediately (within the next 24 hours)
Medium-severity vulnerabilities	Must be fixed soon (within 1 month)
Low-severity vulnerabilities	May be fixed later

FIGURE 8-2 Vulnerability Severity Levels

Next, they analyzed the reports generated by the tool and interpreted the results, creating a preliminary summary for the key components. That summary is shown in Figure 8-3.

Component	IP Addresses	Tool(s)	Vulnerability Summary
Office PCs	- - - - - - - - - - -	Vulnerabilities-R-Found, v. 6.73	3 medium 20 low
	- - - - - - - - - - -	Vulnerabilities-R-Found, v. 6.73	3 medium 22 low
	- - - - - - - - - - -	Vulnerabilities-R-Found, v. 6.73	3 medium 22 low
Firewall	- - - - - - - - - - -	Improve-UR-Network, v.4.8	1 medium 5 low
PIDS server	- - - - - - - - - - -	Improve-UR-Network, v.4.8	3 high 21 medium 43 low
ECDS server	- - - - - - - - - - -	Improve-UR-Network, v.4.8	9 medium 15 low
Routers	- - - - - - - - - - -	Improve-UR-Network, v.4.8	3 low
	- - - - - - - - - - -	Improve-UR-Network, v.4.8	3 low

FIGURE 8-3 Preliminary Summary

8.3 Review Technology Vulnerabilities and Summarize Results

The previous activity required specialized information technology and security knowledge to complete. Before you can move to the risk analysis activities of phase 3, you need to make sure that all analysis team members have an appreciation of the results of the infrastructure examination. Thus, part of this activity requires communicating technological issues effectively to people who may not have technology backgrounds.

A second part of this activity requires you to think about the technology information in the context of your organization. You refine the picture of current security practices and organizational vulnerabilities. You also revisit the threat profile for each critical asset to see if the vulnerability evaluation has exposed any new threats.

Step 1: Review and Refine the Preliminary Summary

In this step the entire analysis team reviews the preliminary summary of vulnerabilities. The information technology staff or external experts who conducted the evaluation lead the review. During this step you must make sure that you understand the following information for each critical asset:

- The types of vulnerabilities found and when they need to be addressed
- The potential effects on the critical assets
- How the technology vulnerabilities might be addressed (applying a patch, hardening a component, etc.)

You can make changes to the summary during the discussion, if appropriate. For example, you might decide to change the definitions of severity levels. Once the summary is reviewed and refined for each component, make sure that you document it. You should also keep the detailed reports generated by the tools. You might need to reference them after the evaluation when you fix specific vulnerabilities.

In our sample scenario, one member of ABC Systems presented the results of the vulnerability evaluation to the analysis team. The presenter highlighted the types of vulnerabilities that were found on the key components and illustrated how those weaknesses could enable attackers to access PIDS, ECDS, and desktop computers (the critical assets that can be accessed using the network). This activity helped all members of the analysis team to appreciate the relationship between technology vulnerabilities and their business processes. No changes were made to the vulnerability summary shown in Figure 8-3.

Step 2: Identify Actions and Recommendations

As you review and refine the summary of vulnerabilities, you may identify specific actions or recommendations for addressing the technology vulnerabilities. If you need to address any technology vulnerabilities immediately, make sure that you assign an action item and designate responsibility for it.

Remember to look at the technology vulnerabilities across components and critical assets for patterns that can help you better understand the security issues. Patterns of technology vulnerabilities can indicate problems with the current security practices in your organization. (See the catalog of practices in Appendix C for a list of Information Technology Security practices.) For example, staff members may indicate that they perform a practice, but the pattern of technology vulnerabilities might show evidence to the contrary. You also need to be careful when establishing vulnerability patterns. Make sure that you don't jump to conclusions based solely on one (or a few) technology vulnerabilities. Review patterns of technology vulnerabilities that affect a critical asset as well as patterns of technology vulnerabilities across critical assets.

Record all actions and recommendations. This information will be useful during process 8, when you create a protection strategy, risk mitigation plans, and an action list.

At MedSite the workshop group, which included three staff members from ABC Systems and the analysis team, performed this step in conjunction with step 1. As the presenter from ABC Systems discussed the vulnerability summary and illustrated how attackers could exploit technology vulnerabilities to access critical information and systems, the group identified a number of actions that they needed to take, including a review of the policy that prevents assessment of home PCs. These actions are shown in Figure 8-4.

Step 3: Perform a Gap Analysis

Remember from our discussion in Chapter 7 that technology vulnerabilities define the access paths that human threat actors can use to access a critical asset. Thus, when you identify a technology vulnerability on a key infrastructure component, you have identified a weakness that can directly lead to unauthorized action by a human threat actor. You now need to review the threats you identified

**Actions and Recommendations for Addressing
Technology Vulnerabilities**

- Determine how and where PDAs are linking into the systems. Coordinate with ABC Systems and the physicians who have begun using PDAs. Handle after completion of OCTAVE.

- Only a few of the vulnerabilities were of high severity. These will be fixed immediately by ABC Systems. However, all of the high-severity vulnerabilities were on the PIDS server, and that is some cause for concern, given the criticality of PIDS.

- Most of the vulnerabilities were considered to be of medium severity, but many of them in combination could result in either extensive interruption of access to PIDS or the loss/destruction of data on PIDS. This problem should be considered when the risks and mitigation plans are looked at in processes 7 and 8. The analysis team needs to consider the cumulative effects of the medium-severity vulnerabilities on the key components for PIDS, which is also the email server. Use as input to mitigation/ protection strategy planning.

- The same vulnerabilities show up on all of the PCs, which may mean a common configuration problem. It could also mean that the MedSite IT personnel and ABC Systems are not able to keep up with the latest revisions. Further investigation into the process IT uses to set up and maintain PCs is needed to determine whether the different configurations are a legacy or whether unapproved changes are being made.

- The analysis team and ABC Systems also came to the conclusion that vulnerability management isn't really being done well, due to the high-severity vulnerabilities found on the PIDS server. ABC Systems personnel admitted they were not always able to run vulnerability scanners, but they were surprised by the number of high- and medium-severity vulnerabilities that were found. They thought the MedSite IT staff members were fixing these as soon as they were found. IT staff admitted that they had no knowledge of what to do with the vulnerability reports. Vulnerability management must be investigated and the weaknesses in procedure corrected. A plan will be needed to increase IT knowledge and skills and to improve the formality of ABC Systems' procedures.

- Review policy for assessing home PCs.

FIGURE 8-4 Actions and Recommendations

in process 4 in light of your understanding of how vulnerable your infrastructure is. Your view of threats may have changed.

After you have reviewed and discussed the vulnerability summary, perform a gap analysis of the threat profile for each critical asset you created during process 4. During the gap analysis, you reexamine the unmarked branches of the threat tree for *human actors using network access*.

Consider the following question when you review the unmarked branches of a threat tree: Do the technology vulnerabilities associated with the critical asset's key infrastructure components indicate that there is a more than negligible possibility of additional threats to the asset? Make sure that you mark any new threats on the appropriate branches of the threat tree and document any important contextual comments or notes (e.g., refer to the vulnerability summary).

The workshop group at MedSite reviewed the *human actors using network access* threat trees for PIDS, ECDS, and personal computers and determined that there were no threats in addition to those already marked. (See the complete example in Appendix A for the complete threat profiles for each critical asset in the example.)

This completes the process 6 workshop. By this point in the process you have gathered a lot of asset, threat, and vulnerability information. It is time for you to start making sense of the data by identifying and analyzing your organization's risks. Process 7 kicks off OCTAVE's risk identification and analysis activities.

9

Conducting the Risk Analysis (Process 7)

OCTAVE is focused on building an organizationwide view of information security risks. Up to this point in the evaluation you have collected data about three of the components of risk—threat, asset, and vulnerability. Your analysis activities have focused on critical assets, how they are threatened, and how they are technologically vulnerable. Now you broaden your view by considering the organization. You examine how threats to your organization's critical assets can affect its business objectives and its mission.

Process 7 begins phase 3 of the OCTAVE Method, Develop Security Strategy and Plans. This process creates the link between critical assets and what is important to your organization, putting your organization in a better position to manage the uncertainty that it faces.

9.1 Overview of Process 7

One of the evaluation attributes presented in Chapter 2 was the *focus on risk*. This attribute requires you to look beyond the immediate results (outcome) of the threat to a critical asset and place it in the context of what is important to your organization (impact). Up to this point in OCTAVE, you have collected data that will help you examine the security threats that affect your organization's mission and business objectives. In process 7 the focus shifts to risk identification and analysis.

Process 7 Workshop

The workshop for process 7 includes the core analysis team members as well as supplemental personnel, if needed. Your team, including supplemental members, should have the following skills:

- Understanding of the organization's business environment
- Understanding of the organization's information technology environment
- Good communication skills
- Good analytical skills

If you decide to supplement the skills of your analysis team, you should consider including people who understand the specific context of your business environment (e.g., people from the legal department, strategic planners, people from the business continuity office, policy managers). Your team needs these skills, because process 7 requires you to examine how threats to critical assets affect the business objectives and mission of your organization.

An experienced analysis team can complete the activities in about 4½ to 6 hours. The activities of process 7 are summarized in Table 9-1.

TABLE 9-1 Process 7 Activities

Activity	Description
Identify the impact of threats to critical assets	The analysis team defines impact descriptions for threat outcomes (disclosure, modification, loss, destruction, interruption). The impact description is a narrative statement that describes how a threat ultimately affects the organization's mission.
Create risk evaluation criteria	The analysis team creates evaluation criteria that will be used to evaluate the risks to the organization. Evaluation criteria define what constitutes a high, medium, and low impact.
Evaluate the impact of threats to critical assets	The combination of a threat and the resulting impact to the organization defines the risk to the organization. The analysis team reviews each risk and assigns it an impact value (high, medium, or low).

Risk

Risk is the possibility of suffering harm or loss. It is the potential for realizing unwanted negative consequences of an event [Rowe 88]. It refers to a situation in which a person could do something undesirable or a natural occurrence could cause an undesirable outcome, resulting in a negative impact or consequence.

A risk comprises an event, uncertainty, and a consequence. In information security, the basic event in which we are interested is a threat. Uncertainty is embodied in much of the information you have gathered during the evaluation. The uncertainty concerns whether a threat will develop as well as whether your organization is sufficiently protected against the threat actor. In many risk methodologies, uncertainty is represented using likelihood of occurrence, or probability. As Section 9.3 explains, there is a lack of objective data for certain types of information security threats, making it difficult to use a forecasting approach based on probability. To handle the uncertainty inherent in risk, we propose an analysis technique based on scenario planning.

Finally, the consequence that ultimately matters in information security risk is the resulting impact on the organization due to a threat. Impact describes how the organization would be affected based on the following threat outcomes:

- Disclosure of a critical asset
- Modification of a critical asset
- Loss/destruction of a critical asset
- Interruption of access to a critical asset

The outcomes listed above are directly related to assets and describe the effect of the threat on an asset. However, the impact is focused on the organization; it is the direct link back to the organization's mission and business objectives. This chapter shows you how to explicitly identify the risks to your organization's critical assets. We begin looking at risk in the next section, as we present an approach for describing the organizational impact of threats to critical assets.

9.2 Identify the Impact of Threats to Critical Assets

Risk broadens the view of threat by considering how threats ultimately affect an organization. In this activity, you create and record narrative descriptions of potential impacts that can result from threats to your critical assets. As you do this, you establish the link among assets, threats, and what is important to your organization (i.e., your business objectives), providing you with a basis on which you can analyze your risk.

Step 1: Review Information

Before you work though the steps in this activity, you need to review information about your critical assets. This is important, because you are building on information from process 4, which you probably completed a while ago. Specifically, we suggest that you look at the following for each critical asset:

- Security requirements
- Threat profiles
- Areas of concern

These data indicate what is important about each critical asset (security requirements) and how they are threatened (threat profile and areas of concern). You need to make sure that this information is fresh in your mind as you move on to step 2.

Step 2: Create Narrative Impact Descriptions

Your objective in this step is to record a narrative description of the potential impact on your organization of threats to your critical assets. Note the difference in the use of the terms "outcome" and "impact." An outcome is the immediate result of a threat; it centers on what happens to an *asset*. There are four possible threat outcomes: disclosure, modification, loss/destruction, and interruption. The impact, on the other hand, is broader, describing the effect of a threat on an organization's *mission and business objectives*. Consider the following example.

> *Someone inside the organization uses network access to deliberately modify the medical records database. This could result in patient death, improper treatment delivered to patients, lawsuits, and additional staff time to correct the records.*

In this example the threat outcome is modification. Notice that modification is tied to an asset, namely, the medical records database. Now consider how modification of the medical records database can affect the organization. The potential impact on the organization includes the following: patient death, improper treatment delivered to patients, lawsuits, and additional staff time to correct the records. Again, an outcome is the immediate result of the threat actor and centers on assets, whereas the impact considers the resulting effect on the operations and people in the organization.

We ask you to consider impact in the following areas during this activity:

- Reputation/customer confidence
- Safety/health issues
- Fines/legal penalties
- Financial
- Productivity

These impact areas are contextual and should be tailored to meet the needs of your organization. Before you conduct an evaluation, you should determine which areas of impact to consider. One way to determine unique areas for your organization is to consider its business objectives and make sure that impact areas are linked to your key business objectives. For example, a military organization may add combat readiness as an area of impact.

To conduct step 2, select one of your critical assets. Review the threat pro-file for that critical asset. Make sure that you note which of the threat outcomes (disclosure, modification, loss/destruction, interruption) are part of the scenarios in the profile. Next, answer the following questions for each outcome that appears in at least one of the scenarios:

- What is the potential impact on the organization's reputation?
- What is the potential impact on customer confidence?
- What is the potential impact on customers' health or safety?
- What is the potential impact on staff members' health or safety?
- What fines or legal penalties could be imposed on the organization?
- What is the potential financial impact on the organization?
- What is the potential impact on the organization's or customers' productivity?
- What other types of impact could occur?

Continue with this activity until you have described the impact in relation to all critical assets. Make sure that you document your results.

Let's looks at our example to see how MedSite's analysis team completed this activity, specifically, how they created impact descriptions for PIDS. The team members reviewed the information that they had recorded for PIDS. They reviewed the threat profile, the security requirements, and areas of concern. (See Appendix A for a summary of this information for PIDS.)

The team members noted that at least one threat resulted in disclosure of PIDS information. Likewise, at least one threat resulted in modification, loss/destruction, and interruption of access to PIDS information. Thus, all threat outcomes were possible. As a result, the team would have to consider impacts in relation to all four outcomes. They discussed the key questions for each outcome and documented the resulting types of impact on MedSite. These are shown in Figure 9-1.

We have just shown you how to begin expanding threats into risks by considering the impact on the organization. Next, we present an approach for setting qualitative risk levels for your organization.

Outcome	Impact Description
Disclosure	• Failure to safeguard privacy would result in loss of credibility of medical treatment facility/organization.
Modification	• Incorrect modifications could affect appointments and productivity.
	• Work could be affected if modifications were made and we were unable to determine the extent easily. Verification of patient information would be tedious.
	• Patients' lives and health could be affected due to improper changes to treatment plans or medical records.
	• Medical treatment facility could lose credibility, causing patients to seek care from another source.
Loss/destruction	• The information in PIDS would be nearly impossible to reconstruct in a timely manner. Just trying to verify and reenter what was lost between the last backup and the present would take all our time and resources.
Interruption	• An interruption could have a direct impact on our role in this community. We are rendered virtually helpless without PIDS capability. We have become computer-dependent in order to function.
	• Our organization cannot deliver effective or efficient health care without PIDS.

FIGURE 9-1 Impact Descriptions for PIDS

9.3 Create Risk Evaluation Criteria

During this activity you define your organization's tolerance for risk by creating evaluation criteria. These criteria are measures against which you evaluate the types of impact you described during the previous activity. An organization must explicitly prioritize known risks, because it cannot mitigate all of them. Funding, staff, and schedule constraints limit how many and to what extent risks can be addressed. This activity provides decision makers with additional information that they can use when establishing mitigation priorities.

Step 1: Review Information

You need to review relevant background information to help you define evaluation criteria. Such information includes the following:

- Strategic and/or operational plans that outline the major business objectives of your organization
- Legal requirements, regulations, and standards of due care with which your organization must comply
- Insurance information related to information security and information protection
- Results from other risk management processes used by your organization

You can also use the narrative impact information that you documented during the previous activity. Your goal is to develop an understanding of any existing organizational risk limits based on strategic and operational plans, liability, and insurance-related issues. These data are important in shaping evaluation criteria.

Evaluation criteria are highly contextual. For example, while $1 million may represent a high impact for one organization, it might signify only a medium or low impact for another. Also, some organizations will have risks that could result in a loss of life, but others will not. The contextual nature of evaluation criteria is the reason every organization must define its own criteria and why you need to review relevant background information.

Step 2: Define Evaluation Criteria

In this step you define your organization's evaluation criteria. Discuss the following questions for each area of impact (see previous activity for a discussion of areas of impact):

- What defines a "high" impact on the organization?
- What defines a "medium" impact on the organization?
- What defines a "low" impact on the organization?

You are trying to define specific measures that constitute high, medium, and low risks for your organization in each case. For example, a low impact on productivity might be three lost days, whereas a high impact might be three weeks. As always, make sure that you record this information.

Now let's look at evaluation criteria in the context of an example. The analysis team at MedSite included a member from the risk management department to help them construct evaluation criteria. Prior to the process 7 workshop, the staff member from the risk management department worked with one of the analysis team members to collect background information. They gathered the organization's operational plan and information about legal requirements and regulations.

Prior to the workshop, all members of the team reviewed the information. They selected the following areas of impact for which to create evaluation criteria:

- Reputation/customer confidence
- Life/health of customers
- Productivity
- Fines/legal penalties
- Finances
- Facilities

The team discussed what constitutes a high, medium, and low impact on the organization for each of the relevant areas and recorded the information. Figure 9-2 highlights the evaluation criteria for reputation/customer confidence. You will find a complete set of criteria for the example in Appendix A of this book.

Scenario Planning and Probability

You might have noticed that we are focusing only on impact at this point. A second commonly used risk measure is probability. For information security risks, probability is a more complex and imprecise variable than is normally found in other risk management domains, because risk factors are constantly changing. Probability is highly subjective in the absence of objective data and must be used carefully during risk analysis.

Because objective data for certain types of information security threats (i.e., human actors exploiting known vulnerabilities) are lacking, it is difficult to use a forecasting approach based on probability. Without objective data, it is impossible to develop a reliable forecast of the future [HBR 99]. What you can

Evaluation Criteria			
Area of Impact	High	Medium	Low
Reputation/ customer confidence	• Reputation irrevocably destroyed or damaged • Loss of rating or accreditation by review organizations • More than 30 percent drop in customers due to loss of confidence	• Reputation damaged; some effort and expense required to recover • Reduction or warning of reduction of rating or accreditation by authorizing organizations • 10 to 30 percent drop in customers due to loss of confidence • Public violations of Privacy Act: disclosure to (1) personnel within the medical treatment facility without the need to know; (2) anyone who violates the Privacy Act and reveals sensitive medical information • Patient driven to seek care from another source	• Reputation minimally affected; little or no effort or expense required to recover • No change in rating or accreditation by authorizing organizations • Less than 10 percent drop in customers due to loss of confidence • Nonpublic violation of Privacy Act (disclosure to personnel within the medical treatment facility with a need to know—trusted agent)

FIGURE 9-2 Evaluation Criteria

do, however, is carefully analyze threats to limit the range of potential options, so that you become able to manage your risk. In information security, you can define a range of threats that could affect a critical asset, but you cannot reliably predict which scenario(s) will occur. However, by broadly defining the range of threats that your organization faces, you can make fairly certain that those that develop do so within the defined bounds.

The analysis approach that we are describing here is derived from a technique called scenario planning. A range of threat scenarios, or a threat profile, is constructed for each critical asset. The scenarios in each threat profile represent those in the probable range of outcomes, not necessarily the entire range. Because data with respect to threat probability are limited for the scenarios, they are assumed to be equally likely [Van der Heijden 97]. Thus, priorities are based on the qualitative impact values assigned to the scenarios.

Probability values can be factored into prioritization, but you must take care when doing so. Remember, probability is a forecasting technique based on the premise that you can forecast threat probability with reliable precision. Thus, in many cases you may be forcing decisions based on probability forecasts that are nothing more than guesswork. Nonetheless, incorporating probability into a risk analysis continues to be a popular topic. Section 9.5 considers an approach for incorporating subjective probability in OCTAVE.

When Should You Create Evaluation Criteria?

Note the following two conditions governing risk evaluation criteria:

- There is one set of evaluation criteria for all assets; the criteria are not unique to an asset.
- Evaluation criteria are created for predefined areas of impact, which are related to the organization's key business objectives.

Because evaluation criteria are asset-independent and address broad organizational issues, you could create them earlier in the evaluation process. Some organizations decide to add this activity to process 1, the senior management workshop. By doing so, these organizations are able to gather input from senior managers with a broad perspective on organizational issues. Another idea is to create evaluation criteria when preparing to conduct the OCTAVE Method, as part of your tailoring activities.

If you have previously conducted the OCTAVE Method in your organization, you could use the set of criteria that you already created. If you decide to use evaluation criteria from a previous evaluation, remember to review them and adjust them as appropriate before using them in the current evaluation.

No matter when you create evaluation criteria, it can be a long process. You will probably find that it is also an iterative process. An organization will often revisit its evaluation criteria and adjust them after trying to use them. However, once you are satisfied with your criteria, you have a useful tool for interpreting risk. In the next activity we show how you use this tool.

9.4 Evaluate the Impact of Threats to Critical Assets

This activity builds upon the first two. You use the evaluation criteria that you created previously to evaluate the impact descriptions that you developed earlier during the first activity of process 7. By doing this, you are able to estimate the impact on the organization for each threat to a critical asset. The ultimate result is that you can now establish priorities to guide your risk mitigation activities during process 8.

Step 1: Review Information

Before you evaluate your risks, you need to review the information gathered so far from earlier processes. Specifically, we suggest that you look at the evaluation criteria and the following for each critical asset:

- Threat profiles
- Impact descriptions

These data provide you with scenarios that threaten your critical assets (threat profiles), the resulting impact (impact descriptions), and risk measures for your organization (evaluation criteria). Together, they provide you with a picture of the information security risks that your organization is facing.

Step 2: Evaluate Risk Impact

For each critical asset, first review the impact descriptions for each threat outcome (disclosure, modification, destruction/loss, interruption). Some outcomes will have more than one impact description associated with them. Next evaluate each impact description by assigning it an impact measure (high, medium, or low). Using the qualitative evaluation criteria that you created during the previous activity as a guide, continue evaluating impacts until you have evaluated all of the impacts for each critical asset. Make sure you record your results.

Finally, when you add impact values to the threat profile, you create a risk profile. Essentially, you have created a set of risk scenarios for a critical asset.

Let's see how the team at MedSite evaluated impacts. The analysis team and the representative from MedSite's risk management department started with

PIDS. They reviewed its threat profiles and impact descriptions, as well as the evaluation criteria, and evaluated each impact that they recorded for PIDS.

Let's specifically look at how the team evaluated the impact of modification of PIDS information. In reviewing the PIDS threat profile, they found the following threats with an outcome of modification in the profile:

- People inside MedSite can use network access to modify PIDS information accidentally.
- People inside MedSite can use network access to modify PIDS information deliberately.
- Outsiders (i.e., attackers) can use network access to modify PIDS information deliberately.
- People inside MedSite can use physical access to modify PIDS information deliberately.
- People outside MedSite can use physical access to modify PIDS information deliberately.
- A virus can modify PIDS information.

Note that the above threats are textual versions of PIDS threat profile branches. Next, the team reviewed the various types of impact. Consider the following impact from Figure 9-1:

Medical treatment facility could lose credibility, causing patients to seek care from another source.

This impact is related to the area of reputation/customer confidence, for which the evaluation criteria are shown in Figure 9-1. After the team discussed this impact and examined it in relation to these criteria, they felt that MedSite's reputation would be damaged, but that it could be recovered with some effort and expense. Thus, the team assigned the value of "medium" to this impact. Figure 9-3 shows the impact values for the levels of impact resulting from modification of PIDS information.

Notice that there are four levels of impact associated with modification of PIDS information. Each impact was evaluated, and its value recorded in the right column. Three were assigned a value of medium, while the fourth was judged to be high. The team evaluated all levels of impact for PIDS and the other critical assets. You will find the complete set of evaluation results in Appendix A.

Outcome	Impact Description	Impact Measure
Modification	• Incorrect modifications could affect appointments and productivity.	Medium
	• Work could be affected if modifications were made and we were unable to determine the extent easily. Verification of patient information would be tedious.	Medium
	• Patients' lives and health could be affected due to improper changes to treatment plans or medical records.	High
	• Medical treatment facility could lose credibility, causing patients to seek care from another source. We can recover our reputation.	Medium

FIGURE 9-3 Impact Values for Modification of PIDS Information

The final step is to create what we call a risk profile. To do this, you simply append the impact values to the trees in the threat profile and record the range on the risk profile—in this case, high to medium. Figure 9-4 shows the threat tree for human actors using network access for PIDS with all impact values added. Note that a solid line in Figure 9-4 indicates the existence of a risk, while a dashed line indicates no risk to the asset.

If you have difficulty using the evaluation criteria as you evaluate the impact descriptions, then one of the following might be occurring:

- The impact *description* might be too vague to enable you to match it to the evaluation criteria. If this is the case, you need to refine the impact descriptions by making them more specific.

- The evaluation *criteria* might not be specific enough to enable you to assign measures to impact descriptions. In this case you need to refine the evaluation criteria by making them more specific.

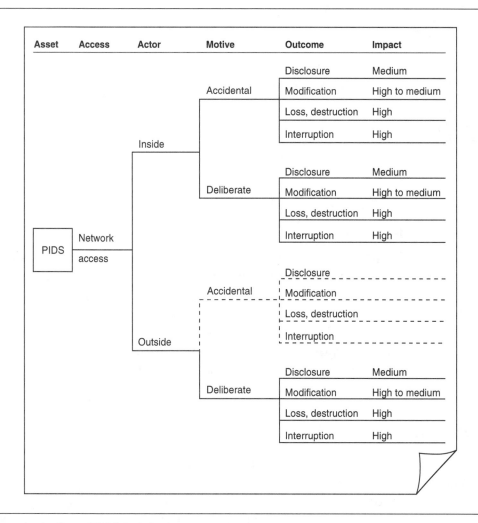

Asset	Access	Actor	Motive	Outcome	Impact
				Disclosure	Medium
			Accidental	Modification	High to medium
				Loss, destruction	High
		Inside		Interruption	High
				Disclosure	Medium
			Deliberate	Modification	High to medium
				Loss, destruction	High
PIDS	Network access			Interruption	High
				Disclosure	
			Accidental	Modification	
				Loss, destruction	
		Outside		Interruption	
				Disclosure	Medium
			Deliberate	Modification	High to medium
				Loss, destruction	High
				Interruption	High

FIGURE 9-4 Part of PIDS Risk Profile: Human Actors Using Network Access Tree

In the second case you might also want to check any impact values that were assigned using the first set of criteria to make sure that they are consistent with the refined criteria.

This completes the basic risk analysis activities for OCTAVE. The next section presents a special topic: incorporating probability into the risk analysis.

9.5 Incorporating Probability into the Risk Analysis

So far this chapter has focused on an analysis technique based on scenario planning. We incorporated this technique in OCTAVE, because the lack of objective data for certain types of information security threats makes it difficult to incorporate a forecasting approach based on probability. However, we have found that there is considerable interest in using probability during a more traditional risk analysis. This section presents some basic concepts of probability and shows how you can include probability in the activities of process 7.

9.5.1 What Is Probability?

We define probability as the likelihood that an event will occur. We first consider the *classical concept* of probability. This concept is the oldest historically and was originally developed in connection with games of chance [Bernstein 96]. For example, consider a die, which is simply a cube with six faces. Because of its symmetry, each face is as likely to come up as any other. Thus, you could easily determine the probability of one face coming up with a roll of the die as 1 in 6. The key for this concept of probability is that all possibilities must be equally likely to occur.

Frequency

Next, we consider the *frequency interpretation* of probability. This interpretation indicates that the probability of an event occurring (or a given outcome occurring) is the proportion of the time that similar events will occur over a long period of time. Note that when using the frequency interpretation of probability, you cannot guarantee what will happen on any particular occasion. Thus, you actually never really "know" the probability that an event will occur, because you will not be able to collect enough information to know precisely what will happen in the long run. Although you cannot know the exact value of a probability, you can estimate it by observing how often similar events have occurred in the past. Estimates of probability made after observing similar events are useful because of the *law of large numbers* [Freund 93]. This law states that as the number of times a situation is repeated becomes larger, the proportion of successes tends toward the actual probability of success. For example, consider multiple flips of a coin. If you flip a coin repeatedly and chart the accumulated proportion of time that you get heads, you will find that over time the proportion comes closer and closer to 1 in 2 (the probability of getting heads with each flip).

A common example that uses the frequency interpretation of probability is weather forecasting. If the forecast calls for a 60 percent chance of rain, it means that under the same weather conditions, it will rain in 60 percent of cases. Next, let's consider a variation of this case—how do you estimate the probability of something that occurs just once? Consider how doctors estimate the probability of how long it will take a patient to recover from an illness. A doctor can check medical records and discover that in the past, 50 percent of the patients recovered within two months under a specific treatment plan. By using this information from similar cases, the doctor can predict that there is a 50 percent probability that the patient will recover within two months.

You can probably see how complicated this can get. It is not always easy or straightforward to determine which cases are similar to the one that you are considering. In the case of the patient, the doctor might consider not just the treatment plan being prescribed but also the patient's age, gender, height, and weight, among other factors. This approach can be difficult and requires individual judgment, indicating how easy it is for two individuals to arrive at different probabilities for the same event.

Subjective Probability

The final type of probability that we will discuss is *subjective* probability. This approach is often used in situations where there is very little direct evidence. You might have only some indirect, or collateral, information, educated guesses, intuition, or other subjective factors to consider [Freund 93]. A person determines a probability based on what he or she *believes* to be the likelihood of occurrence. The key word here is "believes." Different people assess probabilities differently, based on their personal evaluation of a situation. One disadvantage of this approach is that it is often hard for people to estimate probability, and the same person can end up estimating different probabilities for the same event using different estimating techniques.

Probability and Information Security

In information security, you are interested in estimating the likelihood that a threat will actually materialize. For some types of security threats, you have information upon which you can draw. For example, you can use the frequency data to estimate the probability of natural disasters (e.g., floods, earthquakes) in your region. You might also be able to use the frequency of occurrence to estimate the probability of some systems problems, such as system crashes and susceptibility to viruses. However, for some other types of threats there are no frequency data.

How would you estimate the probability of an attacker viewing confidential customer data from your organization's customer database? How much company data do you have to estimate the probability of this attack? Most likely, your organization has not collected sufficient data about such attacks to enable an estimation of probability based on frequency of occurrence. If it has occurred, it has probably happened only once or twice. In addition, you cannot be sure how many times this attack has occurred but gone undetected. What about industry data? Is this the kind of information that companies readily disclose? Many attacks of this type go unreported, making it difficult to obtain sufficient data to derive probability based on frequency models. Finally, even if you had some industry data about these types of attacks, how do you establish which events are similar? For example, does information about past attacks in the banking sector apply to organizations in the manufacturing sector? All of these factors make a frequency-based estimation of probability difficult and time-consuming, if not impossible. That leaves us with subjective probability for threats resulting from human attackers.

Subjectively estimating probability for attacks by human threat actors is tricky. You need to consider the following factors:

- Motive—how motivated is the attacker? Is the attacker motivated by political concerns? Is the attacker a disgruntled employee? Is an asset an especially attractive target for attackers?

- Means—which attacks can affect your critical assets? How sophisticated are the attacks? Do likely attackers have the skills to execute the attacks?

- Opportunity—how vulnerable is your computing infrastructure? How vulnerable are specific critical assets? (Note that this question is linked to the vulnerability data that you gathered in process 6.)

When estimating the above factors, people typically rely upon their experience to make educated guesses about the likelihood of attacks occurring. You would need experience with networked systems security as well as an understanding of the industry sector in which an organization operates. Note that some people do not have sufficient experience to estimate probability using subjective techniques. In fact, probabilities estimated by inexperienced people can actually skew the results of a risk analysis.

In general, you must be careful when incorporating probability into your risk analysis. The next section explains how you can incorporate probability into the activities of process 7 using a combination of frequency data and subjective estimation.

9.5.2 Probability in the OCTAVE Method

We propose using a combination of frequency and subjective probability into the OCTAVE Method's risk analysis activities. There are three activities to add if you choose to do this:

1. Describe the probability of threats to critical assets.
2. Create probability evaluation criteria.
3. Evaluate the probability of threats to critical assets.

Step 1: Describe the Probability of Threats to Critical Assets

In addition to identifying the impacts of threats, you identify probability. You gather information related to the factors that contribute to determining probability. Consider the following questions for each threat profile:

- Which critical assets are likely targets of human threat actors?
- What are the motive, means, and opportunity of each human threat actor who might use network access to violate the security requirements of the critical asset?
- What are the motive, means, and opportunity of each human threat actor who might use physical access to violate the security requirements of the critical asset?
- What historical data for your company or domain are available for all threats in the threat profile? How often have threats of each type occurred in the past?
- What unusual current conditions or circumstances might affect the probability of the threats in the threat profile?

By answering the above questions, you gather both subjective and objective data about threats to your critical assets. You can then use them to estimate threat probability. Notice that the first three questions and the last question are subjective in nature, while the fourth question relates to any objective threat data you may have. You need to make sure that you record all subjective information and objective data for each type of threat to your critical assets.

Step 2: Create Probability Evaluation Criteria

In addition to developing evaluation criteria for impact, you also create evaluation criteria for probability. These criteria are measures against which you will evaluate each threat to establish a qualitative probability value for that threat. Evaluation criteria for probability indicate how often threats occur over a common period of time. When you create evaluation criteria for probability, you define measures for high, medium, and low likelihood of occurrence for your organization.

Review the probability information that that you gathered during the previous activity and answer the following questions:

- What defines a "high" likelihood of occurrence?
- What defines a "medium" likelihood of occurrence?
- What defines a "low" likelihood of occurrence?

Remember, your goal is to define probability measures using any objective data that you have in addition to your subjective experience and expertise. You also need to make sure that your criteria are meaningful to your organization. As always, record your results.

Let's examine what evaluation criteria might look like for our sample organization. At MedSite the analysis team supplemented their skills by including the following:

- A member of ABC Systems who had extensive information technology security experience. This individual understands the range of possible attacks in the medical domain and the degree of skill required to execute each attack.
- A member from MedSite's risk management department. This individual has background knowledge about many of the threat actors in the threat profile.

The expanded team reviewed background information. The people with information technology and risk management expertise provided valuable insight into creating frequency ranges for each probability level. Figure 9-5 shows the resulting probability evaluation criteria.

Notice that the criteria in Figure 9-5 use frequency of occurrence to define probability levels. Team members used the data that they had for certain sources of threat in conjunction with their subjective experience for those sources for which they had little or no objective data. Thus, despite the use of frequency in the criteria, this represents a highly subjective look at probability, and it should be noted as such.

Step 3: Evaluate the Probability of Threats to Critical Assets

Finally, in addition to evaluating the impact of each threat, you evaluate its probability. Review all relevant background information before you complete this activity. Make sure that you review threat profiles for each critical asset and the evaluation criteria for probability.

Select a critical asset. Assign each threat a qualitative probability value (high, medium, or low) based on (1) the probability information that you have gathered, (2) the probability evaluation criteria that you created, and (3) your team's collective experience and expertise.

If you find that your probabilities don't make intuitive sense—for example, if all of your threats are evaluated as "high probability"—you might want to go

Value	Frequency of Occurrence (subjective)
High	>12 times per year
Medium	1 time every year–11 times per year
Low	<1 time every year

FIGURE 9-5 MedSite's Probability Evaluation Criteria

back and adjust your probability criteria. Once you are satisfied with your evaluation results, the final step is to add probabilities to the risk profile.

At MedSite the expanded team (the analysis team plus supplemental personnel) assigned probability values to each threat in all threat profiles. Figure 9-6 shows part of the PIDS risk profile with probability added to the tree.

This concludes process 7. Chapter 10, which examines risk mitigation, revisits the topic of probability and looks at building risk mitigation plans for each critical asset and forming a protection strategy for organizational improvement.

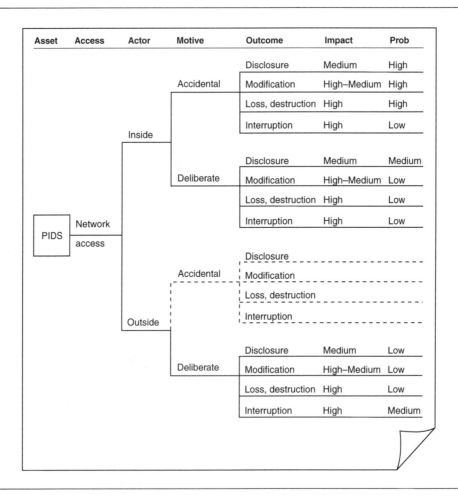

FIGURE 9-6 Part of the PIDS Risk Profile (Including Probability): Human Actors Using Network Access Tree

10

Developing a Protection Strategy—
Workshop A (Process 8A)

The stage is now set for you to address your most important security-related issues. The activities that you have completed to this point in the evaluation have enabled you to define your organization's unique information security risks and have laid a foundation for addressing those risks. You are ready to solve the puzzle.

The first workshop of process 8 marks the transition from identifying and characterizing risks to addressing them. In this workshop you develop both strategic and tactical solutions designed to manage the uncertainty your organization faces due to its information security risks. At the end of this workshop you will have produced a proposed protection strategy for organizational security improvement and risk mitigation plans to reduce the risks to your organization's critical assets.

10.1 Overview of Process 8A

Upon completing process 7, you identified the risks to your organization's critical assets and evaluated the potential impact on your organization of those risks. In the first workshop of process 8 (also referred to as process 8A), you analyze all the risk-related information that you gathered throughout the evaluation and decide how to improve your organization's security posture.

Process 8A Workshop

Process 8A is implemented using the core analysis team members and any supplemental personnel that they decide to include. It takes an experienced team about a day to complete the activities in this workshop. Review all activities for this process and decide whether your team collectively has the required knowledge and skills to complete all tasks successfully. We suggest that your team have the following mix of skills in this process:

- Understanding of the organization's business environment
- Understanding of the organization's information technology environment
- Understanding of the planning practices of the organization
- Ability to develop plans
- Good communication skills

Process 8A requires data consolidation prior to th
security practice information gathered during processe:
surveys and follow-on discussions). If you haven't alr
mation, you will need to do so prior to the workshop. Ta
data consolidation activities, while Table 10-2 summari:
analysis team must perform during the workshop.

TABLE 10-1 Preparation Activities for Process 8A

Activity	Description
Compile survey results	The survey results from processes 1 to 3 are compiled according to organizational level.
Consolidate protection strategy information	The contextual information (security practices and organizational vulnerabilities) from processes 1 to 3 is consolidated according to organizational level.

TABLE 10-2 Process 8A Activities

Activity	Description
Review risk information	The analysis team members individually review the following information that they have generated during the process: • Threats to critical assets • Areas of concern for the critical assets • Current security practices and organizational vulnerabilities • Potential impact on the organization of each threat and associated impact values • Technology vulnerabilities for selected components • Recommended actions resulting from the infrastructure vulnerability evaluation
Create protection strategy	The analysis team creates a proposed protection strategy for the organization. A protection strategy defines the strategies that an organization uses to enable, initiate, implement, and maintain its internal security.
Create mitigation plans	The analysis team creates risk mitigation plans for the organization's critical assets. A mitigation plan defines the activities required to mitigate the risks/threats to the critical assets.
Create action list	The analysis team creates an action list. An action list defines any actions that people in the organization can take in the near term without the need for specialized training, policy changes, etc.

xt, we look at how to prepare for the workshop by consolidating the sur-
and the security practice data that you collected during processes 1 to 3.

10.2 Before the Workshop: Consolidate Information from Processes 1 to 3

Before you can analyze the practice-related information that you collected during processes 1 to 3, you need to compile and format the data. The consolidation
activities for process 8 do require some interpretation of the data, so you want to
make sure that you involve a couple of members of your analysis team in those
activities.

This section outlines the following data consolidation steps:

- Compilation of survey results
- Consolidation of protection strategy information

Step 1: Compile Survey Results

In this activity, you compile the results of the surveys that you asked participants
to complete during the workshops in processes 1 to 3. Remember that the surveys
asked the respondents to consider whether certain security-related practices were
used by the organization. Specifically, respondents were asked to give one of
three possible answers for each practice:

1. They believe that the practice is used by their organization (a "yes"
   response).
2. They believe that the practice is not used by their organization (a "no"
   response).
3. They don't know whether the practice is used by their organization (a "don't
   know" response).

We suggest that you tabulate the survey results for each question according to
organizational level and then convert the results to percentages, based on the number of overall respondents from that organizational level for that question.

Let's look at how the results were compiled in our sample organization. The
analysis team at MedSite created a spreadsheet that automatically compiled the

survey results. Figure 10-1 shows the results for senior management responses to practices related to Security Awareness and Training.

Once you have calculated the percentages, you will need to interpret the numbers. We suggest that you use the following guidelines when examining the data:

- A strong majority of respondents from an organizational level believe that the practice is used by the organization. This is an indication of a current security practice that is most probably used by your organization.

- A strong majority of respondents from an organizational level believe that the practice is not used by the organization. This indicates that the practice is most probably not used by the organization. This is a strong indication of an organizational vulnerability.

Senior Managers			
Survey Statement	Yes	No	Don't Know
Security Awareness and Training			
Staff members understand their security roles and responsibilities. This is documented and verified.	5 100%	0 0%	0 0%
There is adequate in-house expertise for all supported services, mechanisms, and technologies (e.g., logging, monitoring, or encryption), including their secure operation. This is documented and verified.	2 40%	1 20%	2 40%
Security awareness, training, and periodic reminders are provided for all personnel. Staff understanding is documented, and compliance is periodically verified.	2 40%	3 60%	0 0%

FIGURE 10-1 Survey Results from Senior Managers for Security Awareness and Training

- The opinions of the respondents give no strong indication that a practice is used or not used by the organization. Thus, the practice may be used by some individuals but is not an organizationwide security practice. This is also an indication of an organizational vulnerability.

You are probably wondering how to define "a strong majority of respondents." You need to select a threshold that indicates a strong preference for a response. When we work with organizations, we usually recommend using 75 percent as a threshold. One word of caution is warranted here. Typically, you have only a few respondents from each organizational level. Thus, you will not have enough responses to be able to draw definitive conclusions, but you can use the numbers as indicators of preference. Compile the results for all organizational levels (senior management, operational area management, staff, and information technology staff).

At MedSite the analysis team decided to use the following guidelines when interpreting the survey results:

- *Yes*—75 percent or more of respondents replied "yes." The percentage of respondents stating that a practice was used by the organization was high enough to indicate that the practice is most likely used by the organization.
- *No*—75 percent or more of respondents replied "no." The percentage of respondents stating that a practice was not used by the organization was high enough to indicate that the practice is most likely not used by the organization.
- *Unclear*—Neither of the first two criteria was met. If the percentages of "yes" and "no" responses do not meet the 75 percent threshold, it is unclear whether the practice is present or not. It may be that some people use the practice while others don't.

The analysis team used these guidelines when interpreting the senior managers' survey results for security awareness and training (see Figure 10-1). The team decided that the first statement indicated that the senior managers believe that staff members understand their security roles and responsibilities. All of the managers indicated that this practice is currently used by MedSite. On the other hand, it was unclear whether the second and third statements indicated the presence of practices in the organization. The results show no strong indication whether the managers believe that the practices are or are not currently being used at MedSite. The analysis team interpreted the results for all of the organizational levels. Figure 10-2 shows the results for security awareness and training for all organizational levels.

Notice that there is little agreement among the organizational levels and that the number of "unclear" responses is high. Section 10.4 discusses how to use this type of information.

Step 2: Consolidate Protection Strategy Information

In this activity you compile contextual information about security practices that you recorded during the knowledge elicitation workshops of processes 1 to 3. Recall that you conducted a facilitated discussion about current security practices

Security Awareness and Training				
Survey Statement	Senior Managers	Op. Area Managers	Staff	IT Staff
Staff members understand their security roles and responsibilities. This is documented and verified.	Yes	No	No	Unclear
There is adequate in-house expertise for all supported services, mechanisms, and technologies (e.g., logging, monitoring, or encryption), including their secure operation. This is documented and verified.	Unclear	Yes	Unclear	Unclear
Security awareness, training, and periodic reminders are provided for all personnel. Staff understanding is documented, and compliance is periodically verified.	Unclear	Unclear	Unclear	Unclear

FIGURE 10-2 Survey Results for Security Awareness and Training

Security Awareness and Training				
Survey Statement	**Senior Managers**	**Op. Area Managers**	**Staff**	**IT Staff**
Staff members understand their security roles and responsibilities. This is documented and verified.	Yes	No	No	Unclear
There is adequate in-house expertise for all supported services, mechanisms, and technologies (e.g., logging, monitoring, or encryption), including their secure operation. This is documented and verified.	Unclear	Yes	Unclear	Unclear
Security awareness, training, and periodic reminders are provided for all personnel. Staff understanding is documented, and compliance is periodically verified.	Unclear	Unclear	Unclear	Unclear

Org. Level	Security Practice	Organizational Vulnerability
Senior Management	We have training, guidance, regulations, and policies.	Personnel understand systems but not incident management and/or recognizing and reporting anomalies.
Operational area management	Awareness training is required to gain account/access.	IT personnel are inadequately trained. Staff do not understand security issues.
Staff		Whom do you call with a problem? Who is responsible? The training is weak as it relates to PIDS, Medical Records, and other systems. I do not understand my role or responsibility for security.
IT staff	100 percent security awareness training is carried out.	Awareness training is inadequate.

FIGURE 10-3 Practice Information for Security Awareness and Training

in the organization after participants completed the surveys, using the surveys as a point of departure for a discussion about organizational security practices. The facilitated discussions produced information about current security practices and organizational vulnerabilities according to the perspectives of the participants. You recorded this information for each workshop group.

In this activity you group each security practice and organizational vulnerability identified during the knowledge elicitation workshops according to the practice area to which it is most related. As in the previous activity, we suggest that you compile the information by organizational level. Since you are transcribing information, be sure to record the information as it was originally documented.

Let's examine how the analysis team at MedSite consolidated this information. The team grouped each security practice and organizational vulnerability according to the security practice areas as defined in the catalog of practices. They then added this information to the survey results. Figure 10-3 shows the results for security awareness and training, and Appendix A presents the results for all of the practice areas.

This completes the data consolidation for process 8A. We now move on to the first activity of the process 8A workshop, Review Risk Information.

10.3 Review Risk Information

Up to this point in the OCTAVE Method, you have been setting the stage for problem-solving activities. If you are in a large organization, you probably scheduled the evaluation activities over many weeks. Thus, before you start to create solutions for your organization's security issues, you need to review the data that you have gathered.

In this activity you review the major pieces of data that you have collected and generated throughout the previous processes of the OCTAVE Method. You can either complete your review individually before the workshop, or you can review the information as a group as part of the first activity of the process 8A workshop.

Reviewing Information

You must review both organizational information as well as asset-specific information during this activity. First, review the compiled survey results and contextual information that you consolidated prior to the workshop. As you review these data, make sure that you keep both the global and asset perspectives in mind. Information about security practices used by your organization and organizational vulnerabilities present in your organization is vital to the development of your organization's protection strategy (using the global perspective) as well as each risk mitigations plan (using the asset perspective).

Next, review the following risk information for each critical asset:

- Threats to the critical assets
- Areas of concern for the critical assets
- Potential impact on the organization for each threat and associated impact values
- Technology vulnerabilities for selected components
- Recommended actions resulting from the infrastructure vulnerability evaluation

When you review asset-specific information, remember to look for common themes across assets as well as themes unique to an asset. Looking for themes across critical assets can help you to identify mitigation actions that are appropriate for more than one critical asset. In addition, consider looking at the security practice and organizational vulnerability information in relation to the asset-specific data. Think about how current security practices and organizational vulnerabilities might relate to potential mitigation actions.

Let's briefly look at how the organization in our example approached this activity. The analysis team at MedSite included a staff member from the Strategic Planning department in process 8A. The team wanted to supplement its skills by adding someone with an organizationwide perspective as well as someone with good planning skills. They found both in the representative from the Strategic Planning department.

The core team members decided to review the risk information as part of the process 8A workshop. One of the primary reasons for doing this was to help the additional team member become familiar with the data that had been collected. The team reviewed the consolidated security practice information as well as all asset-specific data. After about an hour and a half, the team was ready to move on to the next activity, creating a protection strategy for the organization.

10.4 Create Protection Strategy

Information security affects the entire organization. It is ultimately a business problem whose solution involves more than the deployment of information technology. Solution strategies need to balance the organization's long- and short-term needs by incorporating both strategic and tactical (or operational) views of risk. An organization can take strategic actions focused on organizational improvement (by implementing a protection strategy) as well as operational actions focused on protecting their critical assets (by implementing risk mitigation plans). In this activity you develop a protection strategy for organizational improvement, addressing the strategic view of risk.

Protection Strategy

A *protection strategy* defines the initiatives that an organization uses to enable, initiate, implement, and maintain its internal security. It tends to incorporate long-term organizationwide activities.

A protection strategy leads to a series of steps that an organization can take to raise or maintain its existing level of security. Its objective is to provide a direction for future information security efforts rather than to find an immediate solution to every security vulnerability and concern [Dempsey 97]. Since a protection strategy provides organizational direction with respect to information security activities, we suggest structuring it around the catalog of practices. A protection strategy contains approaches in each of the following practice areas:

- Security awareness and training
- Security strategy
- Security management
- Security policies and regulations
- Collaborative security management
- Contingency planning/disaster recovery
- Physical security
- Information technology security
- Staff security

During this activity, you define strategic initiatives in each of the above areas, defining the direction for information security efforts in your organization. However, practical considerations will prevent you from immediately implementing all of the initiatives after the evaluation. Your organization will likely have limited funds and staff members available to implement the protection strategy. After the evaluation, you must prioritize the activities in the protection strategy and then focus on implementing the highest-priority activities.

Using Security Practice Information from Processes 1 to 3

In this activity you use the practice information that you collected during processes 1 to 3. Specifically, you should consider the survey results across all organizational levels and contextual security practice information (protection strategy practices and organizational vulnerabilities across all organizational levels).

You will likely find discrepancies in the survey results across the different organizational levels. You may also find that the survey results from an organizational level contradict the contextual information from the same level. Your task is to make sense of the information. You should have been present for all of the workshops to allow you to hear a variety of perspectives on what is happening in the organization. Now you have to sort through everything that you have recorded and heard during the previous workshops.

The survey results may give indications about the organization's current security practices. You will be able to identify some security practices that a strong majority of respondents from an organizational level believe are currently used by the organization. You will also identify some security practices that a strong majority of respondents from an organizational level believe are *not* used by the organization. For the majority of the practices, there will be no strong indication in either direction.

Be careful when you use the survey results. Remember, this is not designed to be a scientific activity; your sample groups from each organizational level were not selected from a statistical perspective. Do not try to extrapolate too much from the results. Look for instances in which the vast majority of respondents from an organizational level responded in the same way. You should also look for inconsistencies across organizational levels. For example, perhaps the senior managers responded that the organization had a complete set of security policies, while the staff members indicated that the organization does not have security policies. Obviously, there is a discrepancy here, and it is up to you to interpret the information.

We believe that you will find the contextual information about current security practices and organizational vulnerabilities more useful to you than the survey results as you develop your organization's protection strategy. You will most likely find that participants have identified many instances of what is currently working well in your organization and where there is room for improvement.

Step 1: Develop a Protection Strategy for Strategic Practice Areas

You develop the strategy in two parts. First, you identify approaches in each strategic security practice area that could improve or maintain your organization's security posture. Then you explore what is required to enable good practice in the operational practice areas. In this step we focus on the strategic practice areas.

As you create a protection strategy, you must consider the following:

- The current practices in this area that your organization should continue to use
- The current practices in this area that your organization needs to improve
- New practices that your organization should adopt

To conduct step 1, you need to answer the questions about each strategic practice area presented in Table 10-3.

Remember to review the survey and contextual security practice information as you answer the questions in Table 10-3. Also, remember to review the actions and recommendations that you recorded during process 6. You might find that these recommendations help you to identify security-related strategies for your organization. Record the approaches that you identify for each strategic practice area.

As you develop your organization's protection strategy, you should also think about any near-term actions that could help you develop or implement the protection strategy. Make sure that you record these action items, which you should use as input to the final activity of process 8A, in which you formally document action items.

Let's look at how the analysis team at MedSite created the protection strategy. Remember that the overall team developing the protection strategy includes the core analysis team members and a staff member from MedSite's Strategic

TABLE 10-3 Key Questions for Strategic Practice Areas

Strategic Practice Area	Key Questions
Security awareness and training	What can you do to maintain or improve the level of information security training that all staff members receive (consider awareness training as well as technology-related training)?
	Does your organization have adequate in-house expertise for all supported technologies? What can you do to improve your staff's technology expertise?
	What can you do to ensure that all staff members understand their security roles and responsibilities?
Security strategy	Are security issues incorporated into your organization's business strategy? What can you do to improve the way in which security issues are integrated into your organization's business strategy?
	Are business issues incorporated into your organization's security strategy? What can you do to improve the way in which business issues are integrated into your organization's security strategy?
	What can you do to improve the way in which security strategies, goals, and objectives are documented and communicated to the organization?
Security management	Does management allocate sufficient funds and resources to information security activities? What level of funding for information security activities is appropriate for your organization?
	What can you do to ensure that security roles and responsibilities are defined for all staff in your organization?
	Do your organization's hiring and retention practices take information security issues into account (also applies to contractors and vendors)? What could you do to improve your organization's hiring and retention practices?
	What can you do to improve the way in which your organization manages its information security risk?
	What can you do to improve the way in which security-related information is communicated to your organization's management?
Security policies and regulations	What can you do to ensure that your organization has a comprehensive set of documented, current security policies?
	What can you do to improve the way in which your organization creates, updates, and communicates security policies?
	Does your organization have procedures to ensure compliance with laws and regulations affecting security? What can you do to improve how well your organization complies with laws and regulations affecting security?
	What can you do to ensure that your organization uniformly enforces its security policies?

TABLE 10-3 Key Questions for Strategic Practice Areas (*continued*)

Strategic Practice Area	Key Questions
Collaborative security management	Does your organization have policies and procedures for protecting information when working with external organizations (e.g., third parties, collaborators, subcontractors, or partners)? What can your organization do to improve the way in which it protects information when working with external organizations?
	What can your organization do to improve the way in which it verifies that external organizations are taking proper steps to protect critical information and systems?
	What can your organization do to improve the way in which it verifies that outsourced security services, mechanisms, and technologies meet its needs and requirements?
Contingency planning/disaster recovery	Does your organization have a defined business continuity plan? Has the business continuity plan been tested? What can you do to ensure that your organization has a defined and tested business continuity plan?
	Does your organization have a defined disaster recovery plan? Has the disaster recovery plan been tested? What can you do to ensure that your organization has a defined and tested disaster recovery plan?
	What can you do to ensure that staff members are aware of and understand your organization's business continuity and disaster recovery plans?

Planning department. The team considered the key questions for each strategic practice area. As team members discussed the questions in each area, they often referred to the surveys and contextual security practice information. Based on the information collected, the team felt that it needed to create a strategy to improve security awareness and training at MedSite. Figure 10-4 shows the strategies that the team selected. The team also reviewed the actions and recommendations that it recorded during process 6, but none of those actions and recommendations was related to security awareness and training. The analysis team identified initiatives related to all strategic practice areas. You can find the complete protection strategy for MedSite in Appendix A.

Step 2: Develop a Protection Strategy for Operational Practice Areas

Next, you develop the strategy for the operational security practice areas. Remember that in this step you are identifying strategies to enable operational practices in your organization. To conduct step 2, you need to answer the following key

Protection Strategy	
Security awareness and training	Security awareness and training are sporadic. Provide all newcomers with baseline training.
	Develop a long-range plan to upgrade training for all personnel, and provide periodic refresher training.
	Provide annual training in physical security for all staff (including staff in outlying clinics).
	Enhance training for IT staff to address all job requirements.
	• Reduce reliance on on-the-job-training.
	• Update training plan within six months to include formal training.
	• Find an easily obtained, inexpensive security training product (CD or take-home program).
	• Establish a baseline for security-related training and upgrades.
	Establish uniform procedures for systems training.
	Conduct joint training with ABC Systems.

FIGURE 10-4 Protection Strategy for Security Awareness and Training

questions for each main operational practice area (physical security, information technology security, staff security):

- What training and education initiatives could help your organization maintain or improve its practices in each area?
- What funding level is appropriate to support your organization's needs in each area?
- Are your policies and procedures sufficient for your organization's needs in each area? How could they be improved?
- Who has responsibility for each area? Should anyone else be involved?

- What other departments in your organization should be involved in each area?
- What external experts could help you with each area? How will you communicate your requirements? How will you verify that your requirements are met?

For example, consider information technology practices. The information technology practice area contains practices for securely configuring and maintaining an organization's systems and networks. What strategies could enable your organization's information technology security practices? Perhaps your organization's information technology staff members need to receive training in secure system administration. Or perhaps you need to better define roles and responsibilities for information technology security. These are examples of strategies designed to enable information technology security practices.

Remember to review the survey and contextual security practice information as you answer the key questions for this activity. Also, remember to review the actions and recommendations that you recorded during process 6. Record each strategy that you identify for each operational practice area. Finally, remember to record any near-term actions that you identify as you develop the strategy.

At MedSite the team considered the key questions for each operational practice area. Team members referred to relevant survey and contextual practice information as needed. They also reviewed the recommendations from process 6. They determined that the following recommendation from process 6 has strategic implications with respect to how MedSite approaches security:

> *The analysis team and ABC Systems also came to the conclusion that vulnerability management isn't really being done well. . . . Vulnerability management must be investigated and the weaknesses in procedure corrected. A plan will be needed to increase the knowledge and skills of IT and to improve the formality of ABC Systems' procedures.*

The team incorporated vulnerability management into the protection strategy along with other strategies that could improve MedSite's information technology security practices. Figure 10-5 illustrates the activities that the team recorded for the information technology security practice area. You can find the complete protection strategy for MedSite in Appendix A. After developing the protection strategy for MedSite, the analysis team was ready to develop risk mitigation plans.

Protection Strategy

Information technology security	Develop a long-range plan for modernization of security-related services. Recommend that this be assigned to the executive committee.
	Establish clear policies and procedures for information technology security services.
	Investigate the need for encryption on patient information that is emailed on unsecured lines.
	Assign a small task force to look into our use of PDAs.
	Ask ABC Systems to set up a review meeting for next quarter to discuss our security requirements and the current network design to see if there are ways to improve security without affecting work efficiency.
	Investigate the use of user profiles to restrict access to sensitive information during off-hours and weekends.
	Enforce user password policies (e.g., do not share passwords).
	Add time-outs to workstations in treatment rooms and open-access areas.
	Establish the vulnerability management practice and consider making this a joint effort with ABC Systems.

FIGURE 10-5 Protection Strategy for Information Technology Security

10.5 Create Risk Mitigation Plans

This activity marks a transition from the strategic view of risk to a more tactical, or operational, view. Rather than identifying long-term initiatives that result in organizational security improvement, you develop risk mitigation plans that directly reduce risks to your organization's critical assets. The focus shifts from the organization to critical assets.

Risk Mitigation Plans

Risk mitigation plans are intended to reduce the risks to critical assets. These plans tend to incorporate actions, or countermeasures, designed to overcome the threats to the assets. In some cases these mitigation actions can be directed toward reducing the impact on the organization, but most often you reduce the risk to a critical asset by addressing the underlying threat.

Mitigation plans are linked to business continuity, or enterprise survivability, because they are based on recognizing or detecting threats as they develop, resisting or preventing threats from developing, and recovering from threats after they develop.

There is no hierarchical relationship between the protection strategy and the mitigation plans. The mitigation plans are generally consistent with the protection strategy, since both are based on security practices (and there might be some overlap between them). However, mitigation plans are not plans to implement the protection strategy. A protection strategy is based on addressing organizational improvement and is strategic in nature, whereas mitigation plans are focused on protecting critical assets and are tactical.

Since a risk mitigation plan includes actions designed to counter the threats to a critical asset, we suggest structuring the mitigation plan for each critical asset according to threat categories that apply to that critical asset. Recall that there are four basic threat categories:

- Human actors using network access
- Human actors using physical access
- System problems
- Other problems

Step 1: Select Mitigation Approach

In this step you determine the mitigation approach for each risk. When you identify a *mitigation approach,* you decide which risks to accept and which to mitigate. When you *accept* a risk, you take no action to reduce the risks and accept the consequences should the risk materialize. When you *mitigate* a risk, you identify actions designed to counter the threat and thereby reduce the risk.

Remember to review the narrative impact descriptions and impact values before you decide whether to accept or mitigate a risk. Will your organization generally accept risks that have *low* impact values? Will your organization generally mitigate risks that have *high* impact values? What approach will you take for risks with *medium* impact values? Your answers to these questions will help you to select a mitigation approach for each risk. Make sure that you use your answers to support your decisions, not as absolute rules. Always remember to use your best judgment based on your review of all background information.

To conduct step 1, decide whether to accept or mitigate the risks to each critical asset. Make sure that you record your decisions in that asset's risk profile. It is also useful to record your rationale for accepting a risk. At the end of this step, you will have selected the risks for which you intend to identify mitigation actions in step 2. You should also record your rationale for any risk you chose to accept.

At MedSite the analysis team members (including the representative from the Strategic Planning department) reviewed the risk profiles and areas of concern for each critical asset. They also reviewed all the narrative impact descriptions they recorded during process 7. (See Appendix A for PIDS areas of concern and impact descriptions.) The team members then set general rules for selecting mitigation approaches. They would generally mitigate risks with *high* impact values while accepting those with *low* impact values. The team would make decisions for risks with *medium* impact values on a case-by-case basis.

Note that the team set general guidelines, not absolute rules, for high and low impact risks, and it made the decisions for medium-impact risks entirely contextual. Team members discussed each risk before selecting a mitigation approach.

Figure 10-6 shows part of the risk profile and associated mitigation plan for PIDS. (Figure 10-6 illustrates mitigation approaches and mitigation plans; we are exploring only mitigation approaches in this step.) The figure highlights the risks in the *human actors using network access* threat category. All of the risks were judged to have impact values of medium or high. The team quickly decided to mitigate all of the high-impact risks. After some discussion, team members decided to mitigate the medium-impact risks for PIDS, which were related to disclosure of medical information. Since medical organizations must comply with government privacy regulations, the team decided that the organization needed to take measures to prevent the disclosure of personal medical information. The scribe recorded each mitigation approach next to the impact value in Figure 10-6.

Part of the risk profile for ECDS is shown in Figure 10-7. Remember that ECDS contains mainly billing-related information for emergency cases. The figure shows ECDS's risks in the *other problems* threat category. One risk in this category had a medium-impact value, while all other risks had low-impact values. The team decided to accept all low risks and mitigate the medium risk.

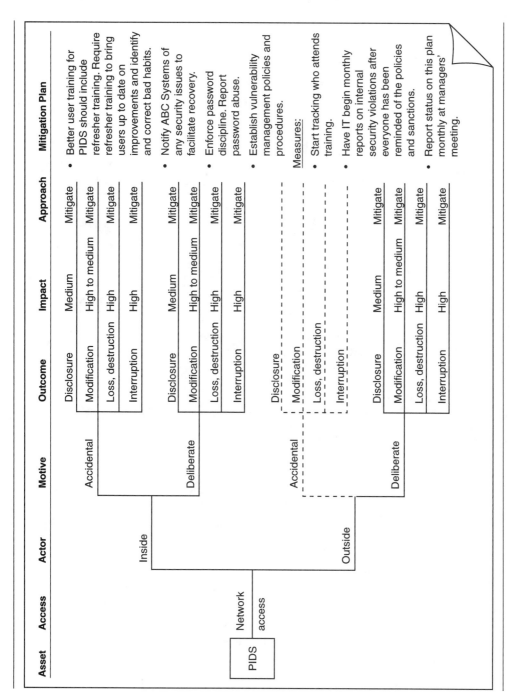

FIGURE 10-6 Part of PIDS Risk Profile (Human Actors Using Network Access) with Mitigation Plan

Asset	Actor	Outcome	Impact	Approach	Mitigation Plan
ECDS	Power supply problems	Disclosure			• Add security concerns to MedSite building committee meeting next quarter to see if anything can be done about reconfiguring workspace.
		Modification			
		Loss, destruction	Low	Accept	
		Interruption	Low	Accept	
	Telecommunications problems or unavailability	Disclosure			
		Modification			
		Loss, destruction	Low	Accept	Measures:
		Interruption	Low	Accept	• Report status on this plan monthly at managers' meeting.
	ABC Systems not familiar with our needs	Disclosure			
		Modification			
		Loss, destruction	Low	Accept	Acceptance rationale:
		Interruption	Low	Accept	• Impact is considered low enough to accept the risks.
	Natural disasters (e.g., nor'easters, floods, fire)	Disclosure			
		Modification			
		Loss, destruction	Low	Accept	
		Interruption	Low	Accept	
	Lack of control over hardware and software	Disclosure			
		Modification			
		Loss, destruction	Low	Accept	
		Interruption	Low	Accept	
	Facility configuration	Disclosure	Medium	Mitigate	
		Modification			
		Loss, destruction			
		Interruption			

FIGURE 10-7 Part of ECDS Risk Profile (Other Problems) with Mitigation Plan

Step 2: Select Mitigation Actions

In this step you select mitigation actions, or countermeasures, designed to over-come the threats to the critical assets. First, make sure that you review the survey results and contextual security practice information. By doing so, you will better understand what your organization is currently doing well and where it needs to improve, providing a basis for selecting mitigation actions. Also, remember to review the actions and recommendations you recorded during process 6. These can be incorporated into your mitigation plans.

You create risk mitigation plans for each critical asset. Recall that you struc-ture each mitigation plan around the threat categories that apply to that critical asset. If there are no risks in a given threat category, you will not need to develop a plan for that category. For each critical asset, answer the following questions as you identify mitigation actions for a threat category:

- What actions could you take to *recognize* or detect this type of threat as it is developing?
- What actions could you take to *resist* or prevent this type of threat from developing?
- What actions could you take to *recover* from this type of threat if it develops?
- What other actions could you take to address this type of threat?
- How will you test or verify that this mitigation plan works and is effective?

As you consider the questions for a given threat category, think about the administrative, physical, and technical practices that you could implement to reduce the risks to the critical asset. Complete and document mitigation plans for all critical assets.

During this activity, you identify a range of mitigation actions. After the eval-uation, you prioritize the mitigation actions by examining the costs and benefits of each action and by considering any organizational budget and staff constraints. You then focus on implementing the highest-priority mitigation actions.

When you develop risk mitigation plans, think about any near-term actions that could help you implement the plans. Make sure that you record these ac-tion items. You will use these as input for the final activity of process 8A, in which you formally record action items.

The analysis team at MedSite reviewed the survey results and contextual security practice information, as well as the actions and recommendations that it recorded during process 6. Team members considered these data when they created risk mitigation plans for MedSite's critical assets. Figure 10-6 shows part of the risk mitigation plan for PIDS. One of the recommendations from process 6 was to improve the way in which technology vulnerabilities were being managed. As you can see in Figure 10-6, the analysis team included a mitigation action to establish vulnerability management policies and procedures. Note that the team also included measures of success in the mitigation plans.

Figure 10-7 illustrates the risk mitigation plan for the *other problems* threat category for ECDS. Note that the mitigation action is related to the only risk in that category that is being mitigated.

Step 3: Review Mitigation Plans for Themes and Gaps

Next, look across mitigation plans for common themes and gaps. You want to ensure that the risk mitigation plans are consistent with each other. You must resolve any inconsistencies that you find. In addition, you should also note which mitigation actions might reduce risks to more than one critical asset. These mitigation actions should be high on your list for implementing after the evaluation.

MedSite's analysis team reviewed the mitigation plans for the organization's critical assets. One theme that was consistent across many of the plans was the need for enhanced training—both general security awareness training for users and enhanced training for MedSite's information technology staff—in how to configure and maintain systems and networks securely.

The team also noticed another interesting point when they reviewed mitigation plans across critical assets. Figure 10-8 shows the risks and mitigation plan for *other problems* threats for PIDS, whereas Figure 10-7 shows the risks and mitigation plan for *other problems* threats for ECDS. Notice that many of the risks result from the same threat sources. Most of the risks in the *other problems* category for ECDS were accepted, whereas all of the risks in this category for PIDS were mitigated. The analysis team noted that the following mitigation actions for PIDS also helped mitigate risks in the *other problems* category for ECDS that were accepted:

- Update contingency plans to include addressing power supply problems.
- Enhance training for IT staff in securely configuring and maintaining systems and networks.

Asset	Actor	Outcome	Impact	Approach	Mitigation Plan
PIDS	Power supply problems	Disclosure			• Update contingency plans to include addressing power supply problems.
		Modification			
		Loss, destruction			• Enhance training for IT staff in securely configuring and maintaining systems and networks.
		Interruption	High	Mitigate	
	Lack of trained maintenance personnel	Disclosure			• Invite ABC Systems representatives to review the results of this evaluation and open a dialog.
		Modification			
		Loss, destruction			
		Interruption	High	Mitigate	
	ABC Systems is not familiar with our needs	Disclosure			• Update hardware and software maintenance procedures.
		Modification			• Add security concerns to MedSite building committee meeting next quarter to see if anything can be done about reconfiguring workspace.
		Loss, destruction			
		Interruption	High	Mitigate	
	Natural disasters (e.g., nor'easters, floods, fire)	Disclosure			
		Modification			Measures:
		Loss, destruction	High	Mitigate	• Contingency plans are updated and tested.
		Interruption	High	Mitigate	• Enhanced IT training is available.
	Lack of control over hardware and software	Disclosure			• Meeting with ABC Systems is scheduled and held.
		Modification			• Hardware and software maintenance procedures are updated.
		Loss, destruction			
		Interruption	High	Mitigate	
	Facility configuration	Disclosure	Medium	Mitigate	• Security concerns have been addressed at next quarter's MedSite building committee meeting.
		Modification			
		Loss, destruction			• Report status on this plan monthly at managers' meeting.
		Interruption			

FIGURE 10-8 Part of PIDS Risk Profile (Other Problems) with Mitigation Plan

Remember that *focus on the critical few* is one of the principles of OCTAVE. The above example with ECDS and PIDS shows why it is effective. Think of the assets in your organization as forming a chain. When you identify critical assets, you identify the weakest links in the chain. If the weakest links are stressed too much, the chain could break apart. Likewise, if something happens to your organization's critical assets, your organization could suffer catastrophic consequences. Thus, the critical assets define the level of protection that you need in your organization. You will find that when you improve your organization's security practices based on the risks to critical assets, you improve the way in which you protect all similar assets.

Consider the ECDS and PIDS example above. When MedSite updates its contingency plans to include addressing power supply problems, it will address risks for all assets that are threatened as a result of problems with MedSite's power supply. Likewise, if information technology staff members receive enhanced training in how to configure and maintain systems and networks securely, they can apply that knowledge to all systems and networks. All risks to systems and networks resulting from mistakes and errors made by people who do not have adequate training will be reduced. The improved practice employed by the information technology staff members will thus be applied to both critical and noncritical systems.

Step 4: Incorporate Strategic Themes into Protection Strategy

This is the final step in creating risk mitigation plans. In step 3, you looked across mitigation plans for common themes and gaps to ensure that the risk mitigation plans were consistent with each other. In this step you determine whether any themes that emerged in step 3 need to be incorporated into the protection strategy. Make sure that you update your organization's protection strategy accordingly.

MedSite's analysis team did not find any new themes. However, they did note that security awareness and training was a common theme among the risk mitigation plans and the organization's protection strategy. In the protection strategy for security awareness and training (see Figure 10-4), the team documented the need for security awareness training for system users at MedSite, as well as enhanced training for the information technology staff, in how to configure systems and networks securely. Mitigation actions for PIDS (see Figures 10-6 and 10-8) emphasized the importance of improved security awareness and training as it relates to PIDS. This will likely be a high priority for MedSite after the evaluation.

Thus far, you have created a protection strategy and risk mitigation plans. In the final activity of process 8A, you document near-term action items that your organization needs to address.

10.6 Create Action List

In the previous two activities you developed a protection strategy for organizational improvement and risk mitigation plans to reduce the risks to your critical assets. In this activity you look for near-term actions that people in your organization can immediately start to implement. By employing a few simple actions, your organization can start to improve in a few areas. By taking these initial steps toward improvement, your organization can start to build the momentum needed to implement its protection strategy and risk mitigation plans.

Action List

An *action list* defines any action items that people in your organization can take in the near term without the need for specialized training, policy changes, etc. Because items on the action list have little cost associated with them, you can start implementing them immediately after the evaluation. Implementing action items is an easy way to start improving your organization's security posture. Here are two examples of action items that can be placed on the action list:

- Assign an IT staff member to fix the high-severity vulnerabilities that were identified during phase 2 of OCTAVE.
- Assign the analysis team and the organization's management an action to define the details of implementing the protection strategy.

An action list typically comprises the following information:

- Near-term actions that need to be taken
- The person responsible for completing each action item
- A completion date for each action item
- Any management support that is required to facilitate completion of each action item

Step 1: Identify Action Items

As you created the protection strategy and risk mitigation plans, you should have recorded any near-term actions that could help you implement the strategy and plans. Review your list of actions and decide if any are appropriate for the action list.

Think about any additional near-term actions that could help you implement your protection strategy and risk mitigation plans. What near-term actions need to be taken? Remember to document all action items.

Step 2: Assign Responsibility for Action Items

Now that you have identified specific action items for the action list, you need to assign responsibility for completing them as well as a completion date. Answer the following question for each action item on your list and record the results:

- Who will be responsible for each action item?
- By what date does the action item need to be addressed?
- What can management do to facilitate the completion of this action item?

At MedSite the analysis team members reviewed the action items that they recorded when they developed the protection strategy and the risk mitigation plans, as well as the actions and recommendations from process 6. MedSite's action list is shown in Figure 10-9.

When the team was developing the protection strategy, it recorded the following action item related to incident management:

Develop a card that tracks administrators and their capabilities. Also establish points of contact for incidents.

The team felt that this action should be included on the action list, and it is the second item in Figure 10-9. The third action item in Figure 10-9 is one of the recommendations from process 6. The last action item was documented during the development of the risk mitigation plan for paper medical records. The team believed that a physical security test within the next 90 days was important, because MedSite has encountered some problems with the physical security of medical records. For each action item that team members documented, they also assigned responsibility, established a completion date, and identified any management actions that would facilitate completing that action.

Action Item	Related Information
• Look for vulnerabilities in selected components of all the key classes of components. • Analyze the results of the new vulnerability evaluations and prioritize the vulnerabilities to determine immediate, mid-term, and long-range goals (e.g., standard policy for password changes for all systems). • Analyze proposed solutions from perspectives of both systems and operators.	Responsibility: IT and ABC Systems Completion date: Within the next 30 days Required management actions: To address budget and staffing concerns to complete actions
• Develop a pocket card for administrators to clearly identify other administrators and their capabilities, the points of contact, wiring diagram of administrators, and program oversight (e.g., "X controls virus management"). • Update and distribute annually. • Use as a part of administrators in-processing.	Responsibility: Management team Completion date: Within the next 90 days Required management actions: None
• Determine how and where PDAs are linking into the systems. Coordinate with ABC Systems and the physicians who have begun using PDAs.	Responsibility: Management team, IT, and ABC Systems Completion date: Within the next 120 days Required management actions: None
• Coordinate a physical security audit or test relative to the security of the paper medical records, particularly access to the Records Room during regular and off-hours.	Responsibility: Management team Completion date: Within the next 90 days Required management actions: None

FIGURE 10-9 Action Item List

Order of Process 8A Workshop Activities

Note that we present the three major development activities of process 8A in the following order:

1. Create protection strategy.
2. Create mitigation plans.
3. Create action list.

The order in which we present these activities is not mandatory. Different teams will address the activities in different orders, depending on their preferences. This particular sequence requires you to think strategically first. However, if strategic thinking is not one of your team's strengths, you might want to start by identifying near-term action items and then develop risk mitigation plans. You could then look across the action list and mitigation plans to see what strategic themes emerge, providing input for your protection strategy.

On the other hand, you might want to first examine the tactical view of risk by developing risk mitigation plans. Once you have identified tactical actions, you can identify strategic themes and near-term action items.

Make sure you think about how you want to approach the activities and address them in the order that makes most sense for you. However, remember that creating your strategy and plans is not a lockstep process. No matter what order you choose for the activities, you will likely need to iterate among the activities.

This completes the activities of the first workshop of process 8. You now have one more hurdle to complete before the evaluation is over. In the second workshop of process 8, you review the evaluation results with your organization's senior managers and allow the managers to refine the protection strategy, risk mitigation plans, and action list. Before we move on to Chapter 11, we need to complete our discussion of incorporating probability into the evaluation. The next section looks at how to incorporate probability into risk mitigation decisions.

10.7 Incorporating Probability into Risk Mitigation

Chapter 9 presented the concept of probability and showed how it could be incorporated into process 7 of OCTAVE. The chapter then focused on the problems of estimating probability in the absence of extensive data on threats. This section revisits the concept of probability, but this time focusing on using it when making risk mitigation decisions. Specifically, it addresses issues relating to expected value.

Setting Priorities Using Expected Value

The *expected value* (or expected loss) for a risk is the product of the potential loss that could occur (or impact value) multiplied by its projected frequency of occurrence (or probability). The expected value is often measured in *annualized loss expectancy* (ALE), that is, the monetary loss that can be expected in a year [Hutt 95].

Many common risk analysis approaches use expected value (also referred to as risk exposure) to set priorities. Higher expected values in a given year correspond to a higher-priority risk. In addition, conventional wisdom dictates that funds dedicated to mitigation activities in a year should not exceed the expected ALE.

Using expected value to set priorities is a straightforward way of setting priorities. However, there is one major problem with this approach. Extreme and catastrophic events have low probabilities and a very high impact on the organization. An analysis based solely on expected value equates catastrophic events with those that have a high probability but very low consequences [Haimes 98]. Thus, decision makers relying only on expected values when making decisions would put the same effort into mitigating a high-probability, low-impact event as a low-probability, high-impact (i.e., catastrophic) event.

Assigning Expected Values

Let's take a look at how you would assign expected values to risks. First, let's consider how to determine the expected value in a quantitative analysis. Since expected value is the product of a particular risk's impact value and probability, you simply multiply those two numbers to calculate the expected value for that risk.

Now, how would you determine the expected value in a qualitative analysis? Remember, we do not use numbers in a qualitative analysis; rather, we assign "high," "medium," and "low" values to the impact and probability of each risk. To look at the combination of impact and probability, use a table like the one in Figure 10-10 [Dorofee 96].

For example, for a risk that has an impact value of "medium" and a probability of "high," the expected value would be "high." The expected value for the

		Probability		
		High	Medium	Low
Impact	High	High	High	Medium
	Medium	High	Medium	Low
	Low	Medium	Low	Low

FIGURE 10-10 Expected Value Matrix

risk lies in the table cell where the individual probability and impact values for that risk intersect. See Figure 10-11 for a graphic representation of this example.

Tending Toward Medium

Let's take a look at expected value in the context of our running example (see Figure 9-6). Chapter 9 showed how the analysis team could have estimated probability using the risks to PIDS resulting from *human actors using network access*. Figure 10-12 presents the expected values for those risks determined using the matrix in Figure 10-10.

Notice as you look across the risks in the tree that there is a tendency toward "medium." Also note that any potential catastrophic event that has a

		Probability		
		High	Medium	Low
Impact	High	High	High	Medium
	Medium	*High*	Medium	Low
	Low	Medium	Low	Low

FIGURE 10-11 Expected Value Example

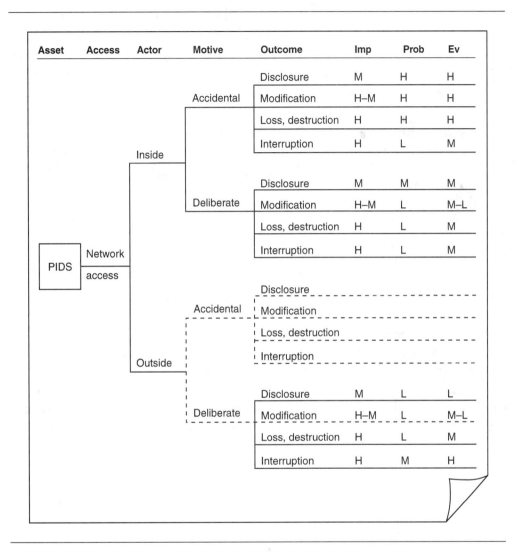

Asset	Access	Actor	Motive	Outcome	Imp	Prob	Ev
			Accidental	Disclosure	M	H	H
				Modification	H–M	H	H
				Loss, destruction	H	H	H
		Inside		Interruption	H	L	M
			Deliberate	Disclosure	M	M	M
				Modification	H–M	L	M–L
				Loss, destruction	H	L	M
PIDS	Network access			Interruption	H	L	M
			Accidental	Disclosure			
				Modification			
				Loss, destruction			
		Outside		Interruption			
			Deliberate	Disclosure	M	L	L
				Modification	H–M	L	M–L
				Loss, destruction	H	L	M
				Interruption	H	M	H

FIGURE 10-12 Expected Values (EV) for Part of PIDS Risk Profile: Human Actors Using Network Access Tree

"low" probability and "high" impact would be assigned a "medium" expected value. A high-probability, low-impact risk would also be assigned a "medium" expected value. But would you mitigate these two risks in the same way? The first risk might put you out of business, whereas the second might merely be a nuisance. Using expected values alone obscures the significant differences between these two cases.

Expected value in a qualitative risk analysis approach does separate the extremes and can be used to help guide decisions. However, you must not depend upon it completely, for the reasons mentioned above.

Assigning Numerical Values to Qualitative Data

As we finish our discussion about expected value, we want to warn you about a common mistake that we see in many risk analysis methods. These methods express "high," "medium," and "low" as numerical values. For example, a method might assign high a value of 3, medium a value of 2, and low a value of 1.

To determine expected value, the numbers are multiplied (as in a *quantitative* analysis). Figure 10-13 shows the resulting matrix.

A qualitative approach indicates only relative priority. If you assign numbers to those qualitative measures and then perform mathematical operations on the numbers, you are implying a *quantitative* relationship that you have not established. For example, it might be tempting to say that a high-impact, medium-probability risk has twice the expected value of a high-impact, low-probability risk, because their respective expected values using the numerical values in Figure 10-13 are 6 and 3. However, because we have looked only at relative ranking of impact and probability, we can merely conclude that we consider the first risk greater than the second. We cannot begin to say how much greater.

		Probability		
		High (3)	Medium (2)	Low (1)
Impact	High (3)	High (9)	High (6)	Medium (3)
	Medium (2)	High (6)	Medium (4)	Low (2)
	Low (1)	Medium (3)	Low (2)	Low (1)

FIGURE 10-13 Expected Value Matrix with Numerical Values

So beware of assigning too much meaning to relative rankings. We have seen some risk analyses that assign numerical values to relative rankings and then put those numbers in a "proprietary algorithm." The results can be meaningless and dangerous if people base their decisions solely on the resulting numbers.

Uncertainty

Finally, we offer one last caution about using expected values. Consider a quantitative risk analysis approach where impact values and probabilities are quantitatively estimated. In this case, expected values can be calculated using multiplication. Many approaches that incorporate quantitative estimates of impact and probability leave out one major concept, namely, the uncertainty associated with each numerical value. When you quantitatively estimate impact and probability, each estimate will have an uncertainty associated with it. The uncertainty depends on the data that you have gathered and the statistical approach that you use to estimate each value. The resulting expected value has an uncertainty that is a combination of the individual uncertainties of impact and probability. Many risk analysis approaches produce a number as the expected value but give no indication of the confidence level (or uncertainty range) associated with it. As a result, less sophisticated decision makers will have a false sense of security in the quantitative expected value produced by the tool. Therefore, you must also beware of assigning too much meaning to quantitative results of a risk analysis. Know how the values were estimated and calculate the resulting uncertainty associated with each number.

Thoughts About How to Use Probability

Our overall message is simple: be careful how you incorporate probability into your decision-making process. People who have less experience with risk evaluations will most likely have greater confidence in their estimates of impact than in their estimates of probability. Thus, you might want to use impact as the primary driver when you decide whether to mitigate or accept a risk. You could use probability to help determine which mitigation plans to implement first. For example, you might use scarce resources to address a medium-impact, high-probability risk in the near term. Later on, you might be able to free up enough resources to address a medium-impact, medium-probability risk. In this case you are using probability to refine your priorities by determining *when* to implement mitigation plans. You are not using probability to drive the decision of whether to accept or mitigate the risk.

Unfortunately, we cannot offer a silver bullet or a step-by-step process that applies in all circumstances. No matter which risk analysis method you decide to use, you need to understand the limitations of any information that you gather. Risk analysis methods support your decision making and help you to make reasonable decisions about information security; they do not replace your need to think. Just remember that you always have to use your best judgment when making decisions in any risk analysis approach.

Chapter 11 presents the final workshop of the OCTAVE Method, in which you take the results of the evaluation and present them to your organization's senior managers.

11

Developing a Protection Strategy— Workshop B (Process 8B)

One of the principles of OCTAVE is setting the *foundation for a continuous process*. This principle addresses the need to implement the results of an information security risk evaluation, providing the basis for security improvement. If an organization fails to implement the results of an evaluation, it will also fail to improve its security posture.

The second workshop of process 8 marks the end of the OCTAVE Method. Although the formal evaluation process comes to an end, the organization needs to consider what happens after the evaluation. This workshop sets up the transition from conducting the evaluation to implementing the results, to ensure that your organization is in a position to benefit from the whole process.

11.1 Overview of Process 8B

One of the most difficult tasks in any improvement activity is maintaining the momentum generated during an evaluation. As you conduct an evaluation, you spend concentrated time gathering information, analyzing it, and creating solutions. Because of the intensity of these activities and the well-defined goals of the process, you develop a momentum that culminates in creating solution strategies and plans. It's easy to think that the hard work is over when you finish the final activity, but actually it is just beginning. In this workshop your organization's senior managers must think about what happens after the evaluation, setting forth the direction for security improvement and establishing their sponsorship for ongoing security improvement.

Process 8B Workshop

Process 8B is a facilitated workshop led by the analysis team and attended by the organization's senior managers. In this workshop you incorporate the senior management perspective into the protection strategy, risk mitigation plans, and the action list. The workshop can be conducted in about two to three hours under the direction of an experienced facilitator. One member of the analysis team assumes the role of scribe and records any changes to the protection strategy, the risk mitigation plans, and the action list. Review all activities for process 8B and decide whether your team collectively has the skills to conduct all the activities success-fully. We suggest that your team have the following skills for this workshop:

- Facilitation skills
- Ability to present to and work with senior managers
- Good communication skills
- Good analytical skills

Before you meet with senior managers, you need to compile all information in a concise, meaningful format. Table 11-1 summarizes the preparation activity, while Table 11-2 highlights the activities that are performed during the workshop. The next section kicks off the presentation of process 8B by highlighting some ideas about what to include in a presentation to your organization's senior managers.

TABLE 11-1 Preparation Activity for Process 8B

Activity	Description
Prepare to meet with senior management	A briefing for senior managers is created. The briefing contains two parts. The first part sets the context for the managers by providing a summary of the risk information that was collected during the evaluation. The second part of the briefing highlights the results of the evaluation and features the protection strategy, risk mitigation plans, and action list.

TABLE 11-2 Process 8B Activities

Activity	Description
Present risk information	The following risk-related information that was generated during the OCTAVE process is presented to senior managers: • Current practices and organizational vulnerabilities • Asset information • Risk profiles for critical assets
Review and refine protection strategy, mitigation plans, and action list	The protection strategy, risk mitigation plans, and action list are presented to senior managers. The managers then refine each as necessary.
Create next steps	The senior managers decide how to implement the protection strategy, risk mitigation plans, and action list by determining (1) what steps will be taken after the evaluation, (2) who will be responsible for the next steps, and (3) when these steps will be completed. This is the starting point for long-term security improvement.

11.2 Before the Workshop: Prepare to Meet with Senior Management

You need to prepare thoroughly for your meeting with senior managers. This task is more difficult than it appears. Since most senior managers have a limited amount of time to spend on efforts such as this, you need to be able to set the context for the managers and get input from them in a span of an hour or two. You must help them understand which assets are critical to the organization, why they are critical, and how they are at risk. You also need to help managers understand what the organization is currently doing well to protect its critical assets and where its protection measures are missing or inadequate. Finally, you need to present solutions that you developed to improve how the organization is protecting its critical assets. In this activity you prepare for your meeting with your organization's senior managers by deciding how you will present the issues identified during the evaluation and the solutions that you developed to address those issues.

Prepare a Presentation for Senior Managers

Your presentation will likely be broken into the following two themes: (1) background risk information and (2) proposed solutions. Table 11-3 shows key elements that you should consider including in the presentation.

Remember to consider the requirements of your audience (the organization's senior managers) before you create your presentation, as well as the time constraints involved. Tailor your presentation to the needs of your managers and make sure that it is consistent with any requirements or conventions in your organization. You might consider providing senior mangers with a summary of the evaluation results in advance. Each organization and each set of senior managers are different, so there are no universal rules, but Table 11-3 provides some guidelines and ideas for you to consider. When preparing to meet with senior managers, you need to rely upon your experience in the organization and use your best judgment. Appendix A presents a sample final report from our case example.

Now that you have created a presentation for your organization's senior managers, you are ready to meet with them. The next section looks at the process 8B workshop.

TABLE 11-3 Key Elements of Presentation to Senior Managers

Presentation Theme	Information	Description
Background risk information	Asset information	Asset information includes a summary of all of the assets that were identified during the evaluation and those that were identified as important by each workshop group from processes 1 to 3.
	Critical assets and the rationale for their selection	This information indicates which of the assets you believe to be most critical to the organization. You also need to include your rationale for designating these assets as critical.
	Security practices and organizational vulnerabilities	This part of the presentation summarizes the results of the security practices surveys and follow-up discussions. This information conveys what the organization is doing well in addition to which practices are missing or inadequate.
	Risk profile for each critical asset	The risk profile for each critical asset includes the threats to that critical asset, potential impact on the organization (narrative descriptions and qualitative impact values), key infrastructure components, and a summary of the vulnerabilities that were discovered.
Solutions	Protection strategy	The protection strategy highlights the long-term initiatives you propose to improve the organization's security posture.
	Risk mitigation plan for each critical asset	These plans illustrate proposed actions that are intended to reduce the risks to critical assets.
	Action list	The action list is a set of proposed action items that need to be addressed in the near term.

11.3 Present Risk Information

In this activity you present background information to your organization's senior managers. Your goal is to set the context for the managers so that the protection strategy, risk mitigation plans, and action list make sense to them. You should explain any terms and concepts that may be new or different, for example, *asset, threats, risk,* and *risk profile*.

You might want to begin this activity by summarizing the OCTAVE process for the managers. Remember, they probably have not been involved in the evaluation since process 1. By reviewing the process for the managers, you can refresh their memories about the evaluation approach and provide additional context for the background information.

Review Risk Information with Senior Managers

One member of your analysis team should present risk information to the managers. Present the assets that were identified during the evaluation. Make sure that you focus the managers' attention on the critical assets that you identified during process 4. Review your rationale for selecting those critical assets.

Next, describe the basic structure of the catalog of practices and how it was used to construct the surveys used during processes 1, 2, and 3. Explain that you also used the catalog of practices to structure the organization's protection strategy and as a reference when selecting actions for risk mitigation plans. Present the following data to the senior managers:

- Composite, analyzed results of the surveys
- Protection strategy practices and organizational vulnerabilities grouped by practice area
- Threat, risk, and vulnerability information for each critical asset

Make sure that you summarize the above data in your presentation. You want to make sure that the managers understand the information, but you don't want to spend too much time on the details. After you have provided the background data, ask the managers if they have any questions. Let them know that they will next review the protection strategy and risk mitigation plans.

11.4 Review and Refine Protection Strategy, Mitigation Plans, and Action List

In the previous activity you set the context for the senior managers. In this activity you have the following two objectives:

- To present the protection strategy, risk mitigation plans, and action list that you developed in process 8A
- To allow the managers to refine each item as appropriate

Remember that your organization's senior managers have a broad, organizationwide perspective that you might not have. Senior managers understand the parameters within which the organization must operate. They have an appreciation for how many organizational resources can be applied to information security improvement efforts, as well as the constraints that must be factored into the protection strategy and risk mitigation plans.

Step 1: Present the Protection Strategy, Risk Mitigation Plans, and Action List

One member of your analysis team should present solutions while the other team members support the lead presenter as appropriate. First you need to establish ground rules for reviewing and refining strategies and plans. We suggest that you ask the managers to wait until they have seen all strategies and plans before they suggest changes. By waiting, they will be able to get a feel for the "big picture." If you think that the managers will nevertheless want to dive into the details of the strategy and plans immediately, you might try to define the big picture right away with a summary of the information. Alternatively, you can temporarily record any potential changes on flip charts and address them later in the workshop. Use your best judgment, be flexible, and manage the activities as best you can.

First, define what constitutes a protection strategy; next, present the one that you developed in process 8A; and then ask the managers if they have any questions about it. Try to postpone discussing any changes to this strategy until after you have also presented the risk mitigation plans and the action list. If the managers insist on making changes before seeing the other items, at most this might require some iteration when they see the mitigation plans or action list.

Now define the term risk mitigation plan, pointing out that there is no hierarchical relationship between the protection strategy and the mitigation plans. (The protection strategy defines long-term organizational initiatives, whereas risk mitigation plans define actions to reduce the risks to the organization's critical assets.) Present each risk mitigation plan to the managers, and ask them if they have any questions. Again, try to postpone discussing any changes to the plans until after you have presented the action list.

Finally, discuss what an action list involves and present the action list you have created. Ask the managers if they have any questions about the list. After this you are ready to ask the managers for their thoughts on refining the protection strategy, risk mitigation plans, and action list.

Step 2: Refine the Protection Strategy, Risk Mitigation Plans, and Action List

Ask the senior managers if they want to propose any refinements or modifications to the protection strategy, risk mitigation plans, and action list. Guide the discussion to cover all proposed changes, and make sure that the managers think about any implications or ripple effects that these might cause. Remember to record any changes to the protection strategy, risk mitigation plans, and action list.

Let's look at how this activity was implemented in the context of our sample scenario. At MedSite the following people were present for the meeting with MedSite's senior managers:

- All analysis team members
- The member of the strategic planning department who participated in process 8A
- The manager of MedSite's information technology department
- One member of MedSite's information technology staff who participated in processes 5 and 6
- One staff member from ABC Systems who led the process 6 vulnerability evaluation

The team used the following approach to present to MedSite's senior managers:

- One of the analysis team members presented the risk information to the managers.
- The staff member from MedSite's strategic planning department presented the strategy, risk mitigation plans, and action list.

The manager of MedSite's information technology department, the information technology staff member, and the representative from ABC Systems were present to participate in any technological discussions that might arise. MedSite's senior managers, upon reviewing the recommendations of the analysis team, made no major changes to the protection strategy, mitigation plans, and action list. Their primary concern was to determine a practical way to implement the recommendations with a limited budget and other resources.

After completing this activity, you have one last evaluation activity to conduct. Your organization's senior managers now need to decide what the organization will do to implement the results of the evaluation.

11.5 Create Next Steps

This activity marks the end of the evaluation process. In many ways it is one of the most critical steps; as you now ask your organization's senior managers to think about what happens after the evaluation, they determine the ultimate direction for security improvement efforts in the organization.

Identify Next Steps

Ask the senior managers the following questions:

- What will your organization do to build on the results of this evaluation?
- What will you do to ensure that your organization improves its information security?
- What can you do to support this security improvement initiative? What can other managers in your organization do?
- What are your plans for ongoing security evaluation activities?

Notice that the questions really focus on what the senior managers plan to do to enable and encourage implementation of the evaluation results as well as ongoing security improvement activities. Facilitate a discussion around each question, and make sure that you record all next steps.

At MedSite the senior managers determined a set of next steps that were intended to build on the results of the evaluation. Figure 11-1 shows the next steps for MedSite. The managers decided to get the strategic planning department involved in implementing the protection strategy and risk mitigation plans. They also decided to continue their discussion of how to manage implementation of the protection strategy and mitigation plans at the next management team meeting. This constitutes a first step in making security management a permanent part of their organizational processes.

> **Next Steps**
>
> - A representative from the strategic planning department will work with the analysis team to prioritize the security practices in the protection strategy and mitigation plans and to develop implementation details for the highest-priority items.
>
> - The manager of the information technology department will create a team to review all security polices and procedures and establish a schedule for updating, expanding, and communicating them as part of the protection strategy implementation.
>
> - The manager of the information technology department will designate IT staff members to meet with ABC Systems and the other network contractors to prioritize vulnerability fixes and set up a more coordinated, routine vulnerability evaluation and correction process. Vulnerability management policies and procedures must be developed jointly by ABC Systems and the IT staff.
>
> - One hour of the next management team meeting will be set aside to determine how to assign responsibility and oversight for implementing the protection strategy and mitigation plans.

FIGURE 11-1 Next Steps

After the Meeting with Senior Managers

The second workshop of process 8 is the final evaluation activity. After the workshop is completed, you formally document the results of the evaluation. The format for documenting all OCTAVE results should fit your organization's normal documentation guidelines and should be tailored to meet your organization's needs.

Remember from our discussion of OCTAVE attributes in Chapter 2 that it is important to establish a permanent record of evaluation results. The information that you record can serve as source material for subsequent evaluations and is also useful when tracking the status of plans and actions after the evaluation.

In addition, make sure that you ask the senior managers whether they would like a results briefing for the evaluation participants or other staff members in the organization. Encourage the managers to make the results of the evaluation known, in line with the key OCTAVE principle of *open communication.*

At MedSite the analysis team completed its documentation of the evaluation results. One week later, the team presented the results to all of the participants. ABC Systems sent two representatives to support the presentation. After the meeting, the representatives from ABC Systems met with MedSite's information technology manager and staff. They discussed how to prioritize vulnerabilities and set up a more coordinated, routine vulnerability evaluation and correction process.

You should note that your work is not finished when you complete OCTAVE. After the evaluation, you must identify high-priority activities in the protection strategy as well as high-priority mitigation actions. Doing so will focus your post-evaluation activities. Remember, organizational budget and staff constraints will prevent you from immediately addressing everything in the protection strategy and risk mitigation plans. Finally, to improve your organization's security posture, you need to manage your information security risks by implementing the results of the evaluation. We examine concepts related to managing risks in Chapter 14, which presents a framework for information security risk management.

11.6 Summary of Part II

This concludes our presentation of the OCTAVE Method and brings to a close Part II of this book. Part I defined the essential principles, attributes, and outputs of the OCTAVE approach. Part II presented the OCTAVE Method, an evaluation methodology consistent with the OCTAVE approach.

The OCTAVE Method has five main features:

- It uses a three-phase approach to examine organizational and technology issues, assembling a comprehensive picture of the organization's information security needs.

- It comprises a progressive series of workshops, each of which requires interaction among the people who participate in it.

- It comprises eight processes: four in phase 1, two in phase 2, and two in phase 3.

- It is led by an analysis team, a small, interdisciplinary group of the organization's personnel.

- It includes facilitated discussions with various members of the organization and self-directed workshops in which members of the analysis team conduct a series of activities on their own.

We designed the OCTAVE Method for large organizations. However, you can use it as a baseline or starting point from which to tailor the method for a variety of organizational sizes, operational environments, or industry segments. Part III examines tailoring options and considers how to adjust the OCTAVE Method to meet the needs of both small and complex organizations while remaining faithful to OCTAVE's principles, attributes, and outputs. It also lays the groundwork for managing your information security risks after OCTAVE.

PART III

Variations on the OCTAVE Approach

Parts I and II of this book focused on the OCTAVE approach and provided detailed guidance on how to conduct the OCTAVE Method. Part III broadens our view in two ways. First, it examines the contextual nature of information security risk evaluations by addressing how to tailor the OCTAVE approach for a variety of operational environments. Next, it looks at how to improve your organization's security posture by implementing the results of the evaluation and managing your information security risks.

Chapter 12 describes a number of ways in which you can tailor the processes, activities, and artifacts of the OCTAVE Method. Chapter 13 highlights examples of how OCTAVE is being applied in a range of operational environments. Finally, Chapter 14 presents a framework for managing information security risks.

12

An Introduction to Tailoring OCTAVE

ailoring is a rather generic term. Chapter 2 described the requirements of the OCTAVE approach as a set of principles, attributes, and outputs. The OCTAVE Method was designed to be consistent with those requirements. When we designed the OCTAVE Method, we realized that evaluating information security risk is so contextual that no single implementation of the requirements could be designed for universal use. For example, the needs of small organizations differ drastically from those of large organizations. The way in which organizations choose to implement the OCTAVE approach will vary, based on the characteristics of each organization. We designed the OCTAVE Method to be easily modified to meet the needs of many organizations.

So what do we mean by tailoring? Almost any option that doesn't violate the basic set of requirements of the OCTAVE approach qualifies, and that list is very long. This chapter describes a variety of tailoring options, and Chapter 13 presents several practical implementations based on these options.

Section	Page
12.1 The Range of Possibilities	242
12.2 Tailoring the OCTAVE Method to Your Organization	245

12.1 The Range of Possibilities

As an organization's analysis team is preparing to conduct an information security risk evaluation, it also needs to think about how to implement the evaluation in its organization. The team needs to ensure that the evaluation is tailored to the organization's unique operational environment.

To illustrate the possibilities, let's consider how to address the collective needs of companies from a specific domain, for example, medical or financial. These organizations might pool their resources to modify and extend the evaluation process for their domain. Tailoring an evaluation for a domain could mean modifying the catalog of practices to be consistent with an imposed standard of due care or extending the generic threat profile by adding sources of threat unique to that domain.

A very large, dispersed organization could tailor the evaluation to suit its particular geographic constraints. A government organization could create its own version of the evaluation and require its contractors to use that version in their organizations, providing common ground for communication. The options are endless, especially because evaluating and managing information security risk are highly contextual activities, and no single solution is suitable for all organizations.

So, What Is Tailoring?

Chapter 2 introduced the OCTAVE criteria: a set of principles, attributes, and outputs for information security risk evaluations. These criteria define the basic requirements for information security risk evaluations. Recall that many methods can be consistent with those criteria (see Figure 12-1). Part II of this book provided a detailed exploration of one such method, the OCTAVE Method. You can take the artifacts and activities presented for the OCTAVE Method and tailor them to any unique environment, as long as you remain consistent with the

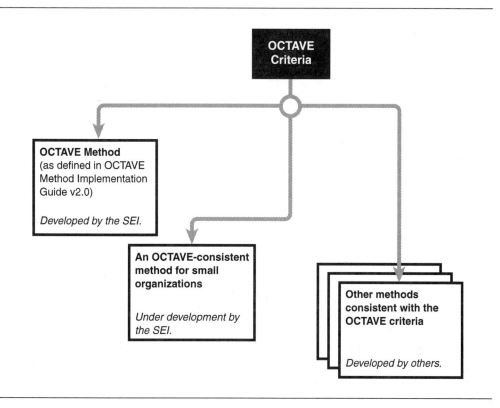

FIGURE 12-1 OCTAVE Approach

approach's principles, attributes, and outputs. Thus, a method for smaller organizations can be *tailored* from the OCTAVE Method. For example, you could
consolidate worksheets, change the order of some activities, or simplify how
information is presented and collected.

The following tailoring options help to frame the idea of tailoring OCTAVE:

- Creating an evaluation for small organizations
- Tailoring the OCTAVE Method for different domains
- Creating an evaluation led by consultants
- Tailoring the processes of the OCTAVE Method

How would you approach evaluating information security risks in a small
organization? You might begin with the following goal in mind: streamlining the

OCTAVE Method for efficient data collection and analysis activities. Consider the requirements of a small medical office consisting of five physicians, seven nurses, and four administrative staff members, where an external vendor maintains the systems and network for the office. The personnel in the office do not possess significant information technology expertise. Thus, they would work with their external vendor for the technological parts of the evaluation (phase 2). In addition, because of the small number of staff in the organization, only one knowledge elicitation workshop is really needed. Processes 1 to 3 would therefore be condensed into one self-directed (as opposed to facilitated) workshop, with only the analysis team participating. Chapter 13 explores the evaluation requirements of small organizations in more detail.

Next, let's look at the financial community, which must comply with a standard of due care and federal regulations [Gramm 01]. The community could replace the catalog of practices used during the OCTAVE Method with one specifically tailored to their standard of due care and regulations. The community could also revise the generic threat profile, adding threats to cover fraud, electronic banking transactions, money laundering, and international finance and accounting issues. The actual processes of the OCTAVE Method could remain largely untouched, with only the artifacts being modified.

Consider how consultants might use this approach. They could tailor the OCTAVE Method by providing a consultant to facilitate the evaluation. This facilitated version still requires an analysis team staffed by the client's personnel to play an integral role in making all decisions during the evaluation. The consultant's role is to facilitate the process and support activities after the evaluation to help institutionalize improved security practices. The activities during each process are modified to accommodate the use of an external facilitator.

Finally, each individual process of the OCTAVE Method can be tailored to meet the needs of any organization. If a company has extensive, secure, Web-based collaborative tools, the surveys used during processes 1 to 3 can be distributed, completed, and collected via the company's intranet.

As you can see, tailoring can cover a wide variety of issues. We can't address every permutation in this chapter. What we can do is focus on tailoring the processes and artifacts of the OCTAVE Method for an organization. The next section takes a closer look at what an organization might do to tailor the OCTAVE Method to suit its needs.

12.2   Tailoring the OCTAVE Method to Your Organization

The first step as you start preparing to conduct the OCTAVE Method is to decide where you need to modify the method for your organization. The ideas that we present in this section do not address all of the ways in which the method can be tailored. We have included ideas to help you think about your organization's unique needs and decide which aspects of the method you need to adjust to meet those needs. There are two major aspects of the OCTAVE Method that can be tailored: the evaluation activities and the artifacts used during the method. We start with how to tailor the evaluation.

12.2.1   Tailoring the Evaluation

The following list highlights some major areas in which you can modify the OCTAVE Method for your organization:

- Order of processes
- Policy reviews
- Schedule
- Number and format of workshops
- Physical security evaluations
- Outsourcing
- Risk probability
- Multiple impact values
- Automated tools
- Independent internal analysis teams

This section addresses each of these aspects, starting with the order in which you conduct processes 1 to 3.

Order of Processes

Strongly hierarchical organizations might prefer reversing the order of the knowledge elicitation workshops, interviewing senior managers last. If you hold the senior management workshop after the other knowledge elicitation workshops, you can provide the senior managers with the results of the other workshops and then ask them to address any gaps that they see. You need to be careful to ensure that senior managers contribute their perspectives and do not simply rubber-stamp the results presented to them. Remember that the point of processes 1 to 3 is to build a global perspective of organizational security knowledge. Thus you need everyone's input, especially that of senior managers. However, we acknowledge that some senior managers prefer to review results and then provide their input. They are often able to do this more quickly than if they participated in a full workshop. Your team should understand the needs of your senior managers and adjust the evaluation process to address any management constraints, while still obtaining the required input.

Policy Reviews

Policy reviews can be a useful addition to the beginning of an evaluation. Your analysis team gathers and reviews the policies, procedures, regulations, laws, and standards of due care that apply to your organization. For some companies, this task could be very long; others might be able to complete it quickly, depending on the nature of the policies that currently exist. You may find that you can use the results of this review to tailor the evaluation. For example, you can tailor the catalog of practices to meet a new or emerging standard of due care. Or you might be able to use this information when you develop your protection strategy and risk mitigation plans. Finally, finding out exactly how many security-related policies and regulations actually exist in your organization and domain could be an eye-opening experience.

Schedule

The time required to conduct the OCTAVE Method varies. Organizations that follow the process faithfully have taken anywhere from six weeks to six months to conduct the evaluation. One major reason for this variability is how much concentrated time the analysis team has available. Remember, many analysis team members have regular duties to perform in addition to their analysis team tasks. A part-time approach to staffing the analysis team increases the length of time it takes to complete an evaluation. While most organizations cannot afford a dedicated analysis team, they must also be careful not to allow the schedule to be stretched so far that the results of their evaluations are stale before they are completed. If you find yourself using an extended schedule, consider providing a mechanism for identifying and completing some critical, near-term action items as they arise, such as fixing high-severity vulnerabilities found during process 6.

Number and Format of Workshops

The number of knowledge elicitation workshops is flexible. Certainly, a larger organization may need more of these workshops than a small company with only two departments. In addition, some processes can be combined to save time (e.g., processes 7 and 8A). It is the results of the workshops that are important, not the specific number of workshops. Always remember that the OCTAVE Method is not a lockstep process. You have great latitude to change the processes that make sense for your organization, but make sure that whatever you do puts you in a position to make the best decisions about information security for your organization. For example, some of the knowledge elicitation activities, such as surveys, can be completed prior to the workshop. You also might want to consider conducting workshops over brown-bag lunches to deal with time constraints. Experiment a bit to determine what works best for your organization.

Physical Security Vulnerabilities

Phase 2 of OCTAVE requires you to examine your computing infrastructure for technology vulnerabilities. You can expand phase 2 by examining your organization's physical infrastructure for weaknesses, for example, by doing the following:

- Examining access routes into buildings
- Examining access paths into areas containing critical paper documents or infrastructure equipment
- Testing door locks
- Verifying proper use of badges or other identification mechanisms

Evaluating your organization's physical security will identify additional vulnerabilities and build upon some of the areas of concern elicited during the early discussions with organization personnel.

Outsourcing

Information technology outsourcing is becoming more and more popular. Many organizations cannot conduct a vulnerability evaluation of their computing infrastructures, because external service providers maintain their systems and networks. The organizations simply do not have the capability to evaluate their computing infrastructure. Typically, external organizations, or service providers, address the security needs for many of these organizations.

Organizations that rely upon such outsourcing as a business strategy need to determine how to work with their service providers during information security risk evaluations. An organization can identify its critical assets, the threats to those assets, and what its staff members are doing to protect the critical assets (the phase 1 activities of OCTAVE). However, that organization will have to work with the service provider to determine whether the provider is using due care in maintaining systems and networks. Often, this process demands a contracting mechanism, whereby the service provider is required to meet a level of due care. Verification of such contracting mechanisms is often difficult and costly. We will revisit this topic in Chapter 13.

Risk Probability

Chapters 9 and 10 explored how you can incorporate probability into the risk analysis. You should note that some standards of due care do require the estimation of probability. If you are required to use probability, do so with care. Some risk analysis techniques that incorporate probability can obscure the risk of extreme events that have a very low probability but produce disastrous results. See Chapters 9 and 10 for more information on probability.

Multiple Impact Values

The OCTAVE Method requires the analysis team to record the range of impact values as part of the risk profile. As you will recall from Chapter 7, you estimate impact values for the following types of impact areas: reputation, health and safety issues, productivity, and legal and financial information. Rather than recording the range of impact values for these areas, you might find it more useful to record the value of each area of impact separately. You can then review the value of each area of impact when you set mitigation priorities. For example, if your organization's reputation is more important than any other type of impact, a medium impact on your reputation might have a higher priority than a high impact on your productivity. Thus, by recording impact values for each area separately, you will be able to differentiate among different types of impacts and make more effective use of mitigation-related resources. Figure 12-2 illustrates a

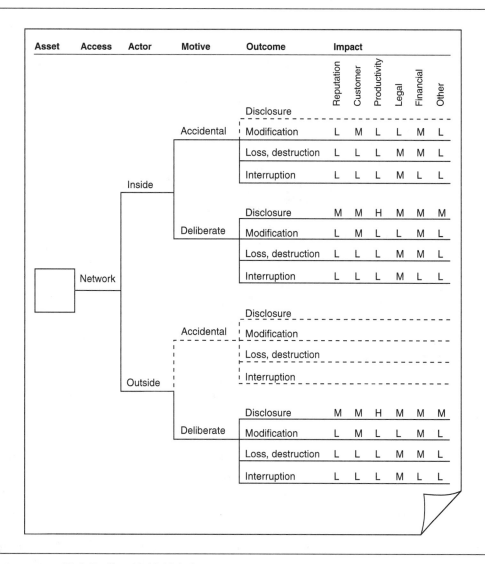

FIGURE 12-2 Risk Profile with Multiple Impacts

risk profile that includes multiple impact values based on area of impact. (A risk profile showing a range of impacts is shown in Figure 9-4.)

Automated Tools

Any evaluation will proceed more efficiently if tools are used, even if you only use a simple spreadsheet application. Custom-developed databases and analysis tools can improve the efficiency of your evaluation, but they aren't critical unless you are dealing with an extremely large set of information. Tools can also provide a more effective foundation for managing information security risks by allowing easy maintenance of data and tracking status changes of risks and mitigation plans.

Independent Internal Analysis Teams

Think about how the OCTAVE Method might be implemented throughout a large, geographically dispersed company. One approach involves using an internal independent analysis team. The team travels from site to site, or department to department. It facilitates information security risk evaluations in a department, while local personnel play an integral role in making all decisions during the evaluation. The internal team's main role is to facilitate the process and help sites and/or departments implement security improvement activities. This is a variation on the consulting model mentioned earlier in this chapter.

We hope that some of the ideas presented here help you think about how you might modify the process for your organization. The next section offers ideas about how to tailor specific artifacts used during the OCTAVE Method for your organization.

12.2.2 Tailoring Artifacts

The artifacts, particularly those found in the appendices of this book, can always be tailored to suit an organization or a particular domain.

Catalog of Practices

The catalog of practices (see Appendix C) is a general catalog of accepted security practices. If you must comply with a specific standard of due care (e.g., HIPAA), you can modify the catalog to ensure that it addresses the range of practices in the standard. You can add specific practices unique to your domain or remove practices that are not relevant. You can also modify the catalog to make it consistent with the terminology used in your domain. The goal is to *have* a catalog of generally accepted, good security practices against which you can evaluate your current security practices. The catalog must be meaningful to your organization.

Generic Threat Profile

Before you start OCTAVE, you can tailor the generic threat profile to meet your evaluation needs by doing the following:

- Adding a new threat category
- Adding new threats to an existing category
- Deleting inapplicable threats from a category
- "Decomposing" or adding depth to a threat category

For some organizations the standard categories are sufficient. Other organizations might require additional categories of threat. Threat categories are contextual and are based on the environment in which an organization must operate. The standard categories are a good starting place. As you implement the OCTAVE Method, you may start identifying unique threats that require the creation of new threat categories.

The following example addresses how to tailor the threat actors for the *human actors using network access* category. The basic threat tree for this category focuses on two types of threat actors: those inside the organization and those outside it. Depending on the evaluation needs of an organization, this classification of actors could be too broad. For example, an organization that deals with national security issues would probably want a more detailed classification of threat actors. The following list is an expanded classification of threat actors:[1]

- Nonmalicious employees—people within the organization who accidentally abuse or misuse computer systems and their information
- Disgruntled employees—people within the organization who deliberately abuse or misuse computer systems and their information

---

1. This list was created using [Howard 98], [Hutt 99], and [Parker 98].

- Attackers—people who attack computer systems for challenge, status, or thrill
- Spies—people who attack computer systems for political gain
- Terrorists—people who attack computer systems to cause fear and for destruction for political gain
- Competitors—people who attack computer systems for economic gain
- Criminals—people who attack computer systems for personal financial gain
- Vandals—people who attack computer systems to cause damage

The asset-based threat profile could be modified to include the above classifications and more detailed motives. In addition, other forms of tailoring can be applied to add detail to the access paths. Separate trees could be created for different means of network access or for different means of physical access. The trees do become more complicated with the additional detail and could make the subsequent analysis more complex. For many organizations, however, the standard generic set of trees will be sufficient. As a general guideline, make sure that your organization's threat profile addresses the range of threats known to affect your operational environment.

Worksheets

Any worksheet from Appendix B can be modified to suit the particular needs or standards of an organization or domain. Certainly the final report contained in Appendix A will look very different based on who writes it and the documentation requirements of the organization. Worksheets can be combined, split apart, and rearranged to be more efficient or to adapt them to a particular database or other automated tool. Figure 12-2 illustrates one modification of the risk profile. Figure 12-3 further modifies the risk profile to include vulnerability information, combining elements from two of the worksheets from processes 6 and 7.

Choose Wisely

In the end, every organization needs to tailor and adapt OCTAVE to suit its particular needs. The key is to maintain consistency with the principles, attributes, and outputs presented in Chapter 2. You need to choose an implementation that works in your environment and helps you to make sensible information protection decisions for your organization. There are, of course, many unwise choices

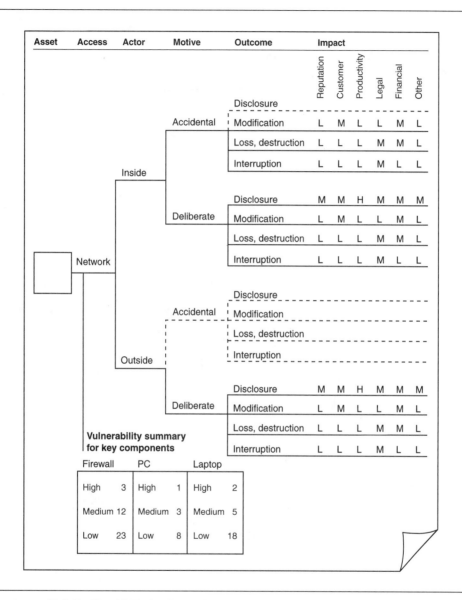

FIGURE 12-3 Risk Profile with Technological Vulnerabilities

that you can make when you tailor the OCTAVE approach. You could decide that your organization doesn't need to work collaboratively with your service provider and assume that the provider is keeping your organization's network and Web sites secure. In this case you will be omitting phase 2 from your evaluation. You could also choose to focus *only* on the computing infrastructure and skip the phase 1 activities. If you modify the evaluation in these ways, you are only getting part of the big picture, and your protection strategy and risk mitigation plans are not likely to keep critical assets secure.

Ultimately, it does not matter if you follow the OCTAVE Method religiously or adapt it. What does matter is that you gather the information you need to make informed decisions and improve your organization's security posture.

13

Practical Applications

We have designed the OCTAVE approach to be modular and flexible. Organizations ranging from the simplest to the most complex can benefit from implementing tailored versions of the OCTAVE approach. This chapter outlines practical scenarios that highlight how organizations are currently implementing OCTAVE.

13.1 Introduction

Before conducting an OCTAVE, you must decide how to set the scope of the evaluation. You must also tailor the evaluation to meet the needs of the organization and to complement your unique operational environment and business processes. So where do you start? The following questions will help you think about how to implement OCTAVE in your organization:

- How complex is your organization? What size is it? Is it national or international? How many business lines are in the organization? How many products does your organization produce? Is your organization geographically dispersed, or is it centralized? How diverse is the organizational culture?

- Who is within your organization's sphere of influence? Who will be affected by your organization's security practices and policies? Which other organizations' security practices and policies affect you? (Consider customers, partners, contractors, subcontractors, visitors, Web site visitors, etc.)

- Who can legitimately access your systems and assets? What assumptions are you making about the trustworthiness of those people and their organizations?

- How complex are your organization's systems and networks? How diverse are your organization's computing systems? How interconnected is your organization to external parties?

- What are the existing and pending laws and regulations with which your organization must comply? What are the domain-specific standards to which your organization must adhere? What political considerations might affect how your organization implements security?

- Are there other methods, processes, audits, or assessments conducted by your organization that overlap with or complement OCTAVE?

- How much of this evaluation will your organization conduct? How much will you depend upon third-party experts or service providers? Should you require external partners or contractors to conduct their own evaluations?

- If you need to share security-related information with other business units or organizations, will you need all parties to use a common or consistent process?

- What is the best way to implement the analysis team(s) in your organization? Will your organization require one team or many? How many teams will be needed per site? How many teams will be needed per division? If you require more than one analysis team in your organization, will there be personnel common to all teams? Will all teams require local personnel? Will your organization allow external representatives on analysis teams?

These questions focus on integrating OCTAVE with the way your organization conducts its business. We designed the OCTAVE Method to be flexible because a "one-size-fits-all" approach doesn't work for evaluating information security risks. A key requirement was to make the evaluation approach flexible, enabling it to be tailored to each organization's unique environment.

The remainder of this chapter focuses on the flexible nature of OCTAVE by presenting four scenarios based on how organizations are currently implementing the approach. As you will see, each organization adjusted OCTAVE to fit its operational environment. The following organizations are profiled in the scenarios:

- A small organization
- A very large, global organization
- A web service provider
- A professional society comprising a large central office and small member organizations

The chapter concludes with a few additional ideas that can be incorporated into OCTAVE.

13.2 The Small Organization

OCTAVE is a context-sensitive approach that is applicable to most organizations. This section examines some of the unique issues related to implementing the approach in a small organization.

13.2.1 Company S

Company S is a small manufacturing facility with 22 people in three departments: shop floor, management, and administrative. The company has one location and many longtime employees. It has used two interconnected computer systems to run its manufacturing equipment and administrative functions for seven years. A Web-based marketing and order-processing system has recently been added, enabling Company S to expand its customer base. The Web system is also connected to the administrative system to enable easy transfer of customer information.

The organization outsources configuration and maintenance of its systems and networks to two external vendors. One vendor maintains the computer systems for manufacturing and administration. These systems are used to access many important assets, including manufacturing control software, customer information, product information, insurance records, and personnel records. The second vendor maintains the Web site. Because Company S has implemented Web-based order processing, the Web server stores some customer information. Company S also relies on both vendors to address its information security needs. Role-based access has not been implemented at Company S; the company has always cross-trained its staff members and permits them to access whatever they need.

Recently, a competitor fell victim to the actions of a disgruntled employee, taking down that organization's systems for a week. Because of this incident, the managers at Company S decided that they need to pay closer attention to information security in their organization. In particular, they are worried about protecting the following items:

- Customer information
- Manufacturing control software
- Insurance records
- Personnel records

Senior managers decided to build an in-house capability to conduct information security risk evaluations. The managers also knew that they had two issues to overcome:

1. Staff members at Company S can perform some information security risk evaluation tasks, but they don't have a lot of experience with information security issues.

2. The organization needs to work with the vendors to ensure that they are using due care to protect the company's critical information and systems.

Company S is tightly run, with little margin in its schedule or resource loading. The organization needs to schedule the information security risk evaluation carefully. It also needs to negotiate with its vendors about providing Company S with information verifying that they are managing vulnerabilities in their computing infrastructures. Overall, Company S needs an evaluation process that is efficient, requiring a modest time investment (e.g., taking from two to five days); is easy to use; focuses on the entire organization, rather than one area; and helps it to define an approach for interacting with its vendors.

13.2.2 Implementing OCTAVE in Small Organizations

Most approaches for evaluating information security risks that we have seen generally focus on the needs of large organizations. A pragmatic approach designed for small organizations does not exist today, and most small organizations cannot afford the cost of outsourcing this function to external parties. Our intent is to provide those organizations with an efficient, inexpensive approach to begin identifying and managing their information security risks, enabling them to improve their security posture. The resulting evaluation will provide small organizations with an approach that is consistent with the OCTAVE principles, attributes, and outputs and is tailored to their unique environments. This section presents our current work in this area.

Different Organizational Characteristics

When we were developing the OCTAVE Method, we met with people from many types of organizations to understand their requirements as potential users of the method. People who indicated that they worked in small organizations typically liked the approach, but they needed an implementation consistent with their organization's business processes. These organizations generally contained 100 or fewer employees. (We'll use this as our working definition of a "small" organization.)

The requirements for implementing OCTAVE in small organizations are driven by the following organizational characteristics:

1. Structure of small organizations. Small organizations typically have a flat, nonhierarchical organizational structure and require breadth of skills among staff members.
2. Lack of core competency in information technology management, including secure systems and network management. Small organizations often outsource management of their computing infrastructures.

3. Scarce resources. Very small organizations are typically quite lean and have limited staff time available for security improvement initiatives.

Although these characteristics are typical of small organizations, we have seen organizations with fewer than 100 employees that are very hierarchical, manage their computing infrastructures, and implement process improvement efforts. Likewise, we have seen instances of organizations with more than 100 employees that have a flat organizational structure, outsource management of their computing infrastructures, and do not have staff available for process improvement activities. There is no absolute definition of a small organization. The approach described in this section addresses the "typical" small organization that is nonhierarchical, outsources management of its computing infrastructures, and has very limited staff time to conduct OCTAVE.

Let's examine each characteristic in more detail, starting with organizational structure. When we discuss approaches for implementing an evaluation process based on organizational structure, we often use the following analogy. Think of information security as trying to solve a puzzle. In large, hierarchical organizations, people can become very specialized in their job duties. Their understanding of the big picture related to the organization's business processes often becomes very narrow. Thus, each person in such an organization holds one piece of the information security puzzle.

By contrast, in small, nonhierarchical organizations people often acquire a range of skills and perform a variety of tasks. Each person in such an organization has greater insight into business processes and holds many pieces of the information security puzzle. In hierarchical organizations the evaluation process requires a series of knowledge elicitation workshops to build the big picture of security in the organization, with each person contributing his or her piece of the puzzle. In nonhierarchical organizations, only one workshop may be needed to build the global view of security, because analysis team members bring most of the puzzle with them.

Now, let's focus on outsourcing. Consider an organization whose management decides to build a core competency in information technology management. Managers will likely hire people with information technology backgrounds and provide educational opportunities for them to keep their skills up to date with current technology trends. People within the organization have the knowledge and skills to lead the technological aspects of an information security risk evaluation.

By contrast, consider an organization whose management decides to outsource information technology management. Contractors or managed service providers maintain the organization's systems and networks. In essence the organization has *transferred* responsibility for managing its computing infrastructure to contractors and service providers. People within the organization do not have the knowledge and skills to lead or interpret the technological aspects of an information security risk evaluation. They must work collaboratively with contractors and managed service providers to ensure that the technological aspects of the evaluation are addressed.

Finally, we look at how limited resources affect the evaluation process. Note that this characteristic applies to many organizations, but small organizations are especially constrained by limited staff time. Consider a large organization that has implemented many process improvement initiatives using a quality assurance department for oversight and guidance. The OCTAVE Method presented in Part II is probably a good fit for that organization. Personnel in the quality assurance department can become core analysis team members and lead the evaluation in the organization.

Now consider a small organization with only 40 employees. It does not have a quality assurance department and may not be experienced in implementing process improvement initiatives. This organization needs an evaluation process that doesn't take too much time and still provides sufficient information for the organization to characterize its risks.

A version of OCTAVE tailored for the typical small organization will have the following features:

- It will not require a series of knowledge elicitation workshops, because the analysis team has sufficient insight into the organization's operational environment.

- It will enable people without an information technology background to record their requirements for a technology vulnerability evaluation, which can then be communicated to the organization's contractors or service providers.

- It will be designed for efficient data collection, enabling the analysis team to characterize risks in a timely manner.

From Eight to Four Processes

Figure 13-1 shows what OCTAVE for small organizations might look like. Each process is a self-directed activity; there are no facilitated knowledge elicitation workshops. Also notice that process 3 is explicitly designed to incorporate outsourcing. The processes shown in Figure 13-1 are described below.

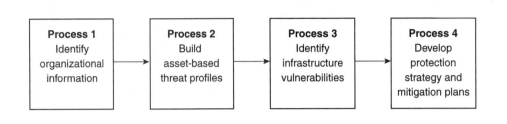

FIGURE 13-1 OCTAVE in a Small Organization

Process 1: Identify Organizational Information. In this process the analysis team identifies information-related assets and selects those that are most critical to the organization. The team then evaluates current security practices to identify what the organization is doing well (current security practices) and which practices are missing or inadequate (organizational vulnerabilities).

Process 2: Build Asset-Based Threat Profiles. The analysis team identifies security requirements for the organization's critical assets and threats to those assets. The first two processes together provide similar outputs to phase 1 of the OCTAVE Method described in Part II of this book.

Process 3: Identify Infrastructure Vulnerabilities. In this process the analysis team examines the organization's computing infrastructure to the extent that it can. Team members first set the strategy for process 3 by deciding to conduct the vulnerability evaluation or defer it until after OCTAVE. If the organization routinely performs vulnerability evaluations, then the analysis team identifies components to evaluate for technology vulnerabilities and conducts an evaluation of those components. If the organization does not routinely perform vulnerability evaluations, the team moves to process 4 and recommends that the organization develop a vulnerability management practice (this recommendation is considered during process 4). Note that OCTAVE is not the time to learn how to conduct vulnerability evaluations. The organization should stay within its current capabilities, or it will quickly become overwhelmed by information it cannot address in a reasonable timeframe. This process addresses phase 2 of OCTAVE.

Process 4: Develop Protection Strategy and Mitigation Plans. Finally, the analysis team identifies risks to the organization's critical assets and then evaluates the risks to establish a value for the resulting impact on the organization. The team decides whether to accept or mitigate each risk, and then selects mitigation strategies for the appropriate risks. The team analyzes risk mitigation strategies across the critical assets and selects the highest-priority actions. Finally, it develops a protection strategy for organizational security improvement. This process corresponds to phase 3 of the OCTAVE Method.

The basic premise for this approach is that information security requires knowledge of both business and information technology processes. We believe that staff members in most organizations have sufficient understanding of their business processes and how they *use* information technology on a day-to-day basis. Thus, most organizations can *characterize* their information security risks.

Small organizations, by our definition, often outsource information technology management. An information security risk evaluation must provide these organizations with a way to address the technological aspects of an information security risk evaluation. Process 3 in Figure 13-1 enables a small organization to tailor the vulnerability evaluation based on its current capability.

Efficient and Focused Data Collection

The evaluation process for small organizations must be highly efficient and focused. Information security knowledge and experience must be engineered directly into the evaluation's worksheets and artifacts, enabling an analysis team from a small organization to characterize their information security risks based on (1) team members' understanding of business processes and (2) the way in which information technology is used in those organizations.

Figure 13-2 shows an example of a worksheet used to record the risk profile for a critical asset, documenting relevant risk and mitigation information for that asset. Note that it combines aspects from several worksheets presented in Appendix B. Highly structured, streamlined worksheets such as this are essential for making the evaluation process efficient while still producing useful results. An evaluation tailored in this way may not provide the same level of detail as the OCTAVE Method. That method was designed to be an open-ended examination

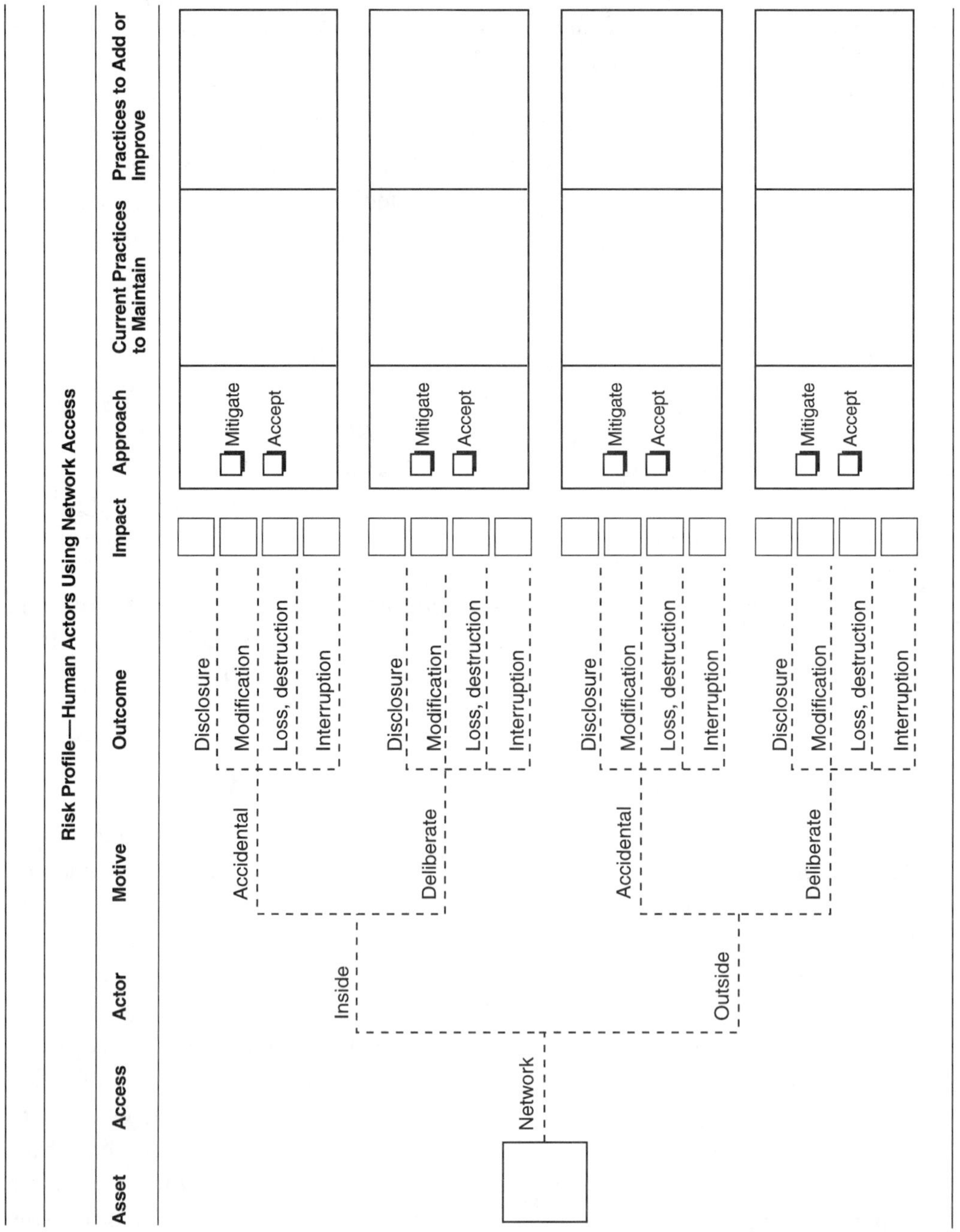

FIGURE 13-2 Critical Asset Risk Profile for OCTAVE Focused on Small Organizations

of information security issues, which is useful for exploring complex organizational issues often found in large, hierarchical organizations. Early testing of OCTAVE in small organizations indicates that a streamlined approach can help them characterize their information security risks without having a strong security background. More testing is required to determine if this approach for small organizations will scale to larger, more hierarchical organizations.

13.3 Very Large, Dispersed Organizations

As mentioned in Part I of this book, we designed the OCTAVE Method for large organizations. However, "large" is an imprecise and relative term. This section describes an organization that would fit almost anyone's definition of large. We turn our attention to implementing OCTAVE in a global organization that is distributed across multiple locations.

Company X

Figure 13-3 shows the organizational structure for Company X. Some sites in Company X are large facilities that use the latest technology; others are small, remote offices with small staffs. Company X is hierarchical in nature; it is organized according to geographic regions and has one director per region. The company has tens of thousands of employees and an extremely large, relatively stable customer base for its products and services. The corporate culture values diversity of skills in the company's workforce, and management encourages employees periodically to rotate across sites. This globally diversified organization has facilities on every major continent and uses local employees to staff those facilities. To conduct its business efficiently, the company uses large numbers of contractors and subcontractors to complement its in-house expertise.

Company X uses a few common systems across all of its sites. In addition, many local, independent systems are used and maintained by individual sites. Management has recently initiated a plan to standardize most of the major information systems across the company. A few regions are also being subjected to stringent new standards of due care in information security. Management has decided to use the new standards of due care as an opportunity to standardize and improve its information security practices across the organization.

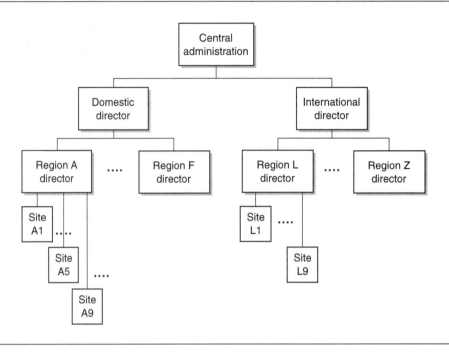

FIGURE 13-3 The Structure of Company X

At the center of its information security program is a common, systematic information security risk evaluation (OCTAVE) that will be implemented across the entire organization. Senior management wants everyone using the same process as a means of ensuring consistent quality. The organization is also creating a common database to collect site-specific information security data. The information in the database will be analyzed to identify common issues and solutions across the organization.

The organization's personnel will conduct OCTAVE. The director in each region is responsible for ensuring that all sites in the region conduct OCTAVE. Each medium and large-scale site (as defined in the company's policy) is required to create an analysis team to lead the evaluation. A team is also being formed in each region to coordinate the evaluations within the region and to provide specialized expertise when needed. At small sites, the analysis team will include local staff as well as members from the regional team.

Their Approach

The approach that Company X implemented for conducting OCTAVE involved the following steps:

- Requiring a uniform evaluation methodology
- Creating a basic catalog of practices for all regions and sites
- Acquiring an automated tool to be used by all sites
- Using an external, third-party trainer to rapidly train multiple analysis teams in the evaluation methodology
- Developing regional information security risk evaluation expertise
- Performing data analysis of the results reported from all site results to identify common issues and solutions
- Requiring all sites to conduct an OCTAVE within a specified time
- Requiring all sites to perform a policy review before starting their evaluations

13.4 Integrated Web Portal Service Providers

OCTAVE can help an organization establish the means to effectively communicate its information protection requirements with its service providers or system maintenance contractors. It can also provide a common framework for communicating with customers, partners, and contractors about information security issues. This section looks at a small company that consolidates access to the Web sites and services of many other organizations. This organization needs to coordinate its information security efforts with those of several organizations.

Company SP

Company SP provides an integrating service that consolidates access to Web sites and services provided by other organizations. Figure 13-4 shows how the company must work with several partners, service providers, and customers.

Company SP has approximately 40 staff members and is located at one site. It depends upon a prime contractor and a large number of subcontractors to build

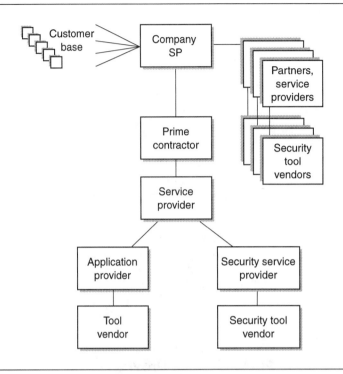

FIGURE 13-4 Company SP and Its Interrelationships

and maintain the integrating Web portal. The prime contractor is located in the same city as the company, but many of the subcontractors and vendors are based in other cities. Company SP provides only one service, but its customer base is solid.

One primary system provides the Web portal service and is linked to all customer Web sites. The system physically exists at the company's facilities but is managed remotely from the prime contractor's site. The company has a second system that it uses to manage its internal business processes.

The Web portal exists as a dynamic environment, because the customer Web sites to which it links change frequently. The dynamic environment coupled with number of organizations involved in maintaining the Web portal creates a complex situation for Company SP. Management at the company is worried that the complexity could lead to information security problems.

Senior managers at Company SP have decided to conduct a comprehensive information security risk evaluation. They understand the value of having their staff involved in the evaluation, but they did not want their staff to lead the evaluation process. Management contracted with an independent consultant to lead the evaluation. Two staff members from Company SP and one staff member from the prime contractor were members of the analysis team.

Their Approach

The approach that Company SP implemented for OCTAVE involved the following steps:

- Contracting with a consultant to lead the evaluation
- Keeping the scope narrow (evaluating only Company SP)
- Allowing the consultant to select and run vulnerability evaluation tools in cooperation with the prime contractor
- Continuing the relationship with the consultant after the evaluation, making the consultant responsible for revising security policies and procedures based on the results of the evaluation

Results of the Evaluation

The analysis team conducted knowledge elicitation workshops with personnel at Company SP, the prime contractor, and one subcontractor. From these workshops, an organizational vulnerability related to contracting was identified. Company SP had not explicitly communicated its security requirements to the prime contractor, and there was no mechanism in place to monitor what the contractor was doing with respect to information security. With the number of subcontractors and service providers involved, Company SP had no idea what was being done to secure its Web portal.

The analysis team suggested that Company SP use the information gathered during OCTAVE to generate security requirements. It further recommended that Company SP and its contractors establish a formal mechanism for communicating security requirements and verifying that they are being met.

OCTAVE highlighted a complex interorganizational problem for Company SP. The complex web of relationships among all parties created unique security issues related to the Web portal service. Company SP staff need to review all of these relationships in light of the organization's security requirements and then determine how they can work with multiple organizations to meet their business goals *and* their security requirements.

13.5 Large and Small Organizations

We now examine how a professional society comprising organizations of various sizes intends to implement OCTAVE. The central office of the society wants to use different implementations of OCTAVE to manage information security risks collaboratively among its members.

The Professional Society

Figure 13-5 depicts a professional society that is a loosely interconnected organization. The central organization is large, and it provides services to many small member companies. The professional society's central office has about 400

FIGURE 13-5 Professional Society—Large and Small Organizations

employees, including 40 information technology professionals. There are several thousand organizations affiliated with the society. The key objective of the central office is to provide benefits and services to its membership. It also acts as a central repository and distribution site for useful products and services. The central office provides member organizations with connectivity to several of its systems. Personnel can access the central office's systems from home computers, laptops, and wireless devices. Staff members at the central office are concerned about security issues related to unmonitored access to the office's systems and networks.

Impending data security regulations will affect all of the society's members as well as the central office. Senior managers at the central office have decided to use the OCTAVE Method to evaluate information security risks. For its member organizations, the central office is recommending a version of OCTAVE tailored to small organizations.

Using a consistent evaluation approach enables effective communication of security issues and requirements among all participating organizations. A common approach also facilitates sharing critical information among the organizations (e.g., recommended security practices, potential threats to consider). The society is planning to create a database to collect evaluation results from participating organizations. Managers at the society have requested that member organizations contribute sanitized, aggregate evaluation results that can be analyzed for trends. Senior managers at the society hope to identify common issues that member organizations can address collaboratively through the society's working groups.

Management wants to conduct the OCTAVE Method initially at the central office before it rolls out a tailored version to its membership. Staff members from the central office will provide OCTAVE training and consulting services related to the evaluation process for the society's members.

Their Approach

The approach that the professional society wants to implement for OCTAVE involves the following steps:

- Chartering an analysis team at the central office
- Encouraging member organizations to conduct evaluations
- Providing experts and consulting services to assist small organizations

- Tailoring the catalog of practices for consistency with impending data security requirements
- Acting as a focal point for using vulnerability assessment tools
- Disseminating unattributed results of data analysis to all member organizations

13.6 Other Considerations

Finally, we present a few additional issues that organizations are addressing when they implement OCTAVE.

Floating Analysis Team, Local Expertise

Section 13.3 illustrated issues related to implementing OCTAVE in a large, dispersed company. Recall that each medium and large site was required to create an analysis team to lead the evaluation. An alternative approach is to create and maintain independent, "floating" analysis teams, which could travel from site to site to lead the evaluations. The analysis team for a site would include the independent team members and a couple of local staff members. Local analysis team members could be given just-in-time training, and the independent team members could lead the evaluation process. This type of approach is often used in process improvement activities (e.g., software engineering process groups for software process improvement). Organizations with a large, centralized quality assurance or risk management department are good candidates for using this type of approach.

Consolidating Results from Multiple Evaluations

Many organizations are pursuing the idea of creating a database to collect evaluation results from multiple sites. While the results of each individual OCTAVE can help the organization that conducts it, larger organizations also see benefits in analyzing evaluation results across the organization for common issues and for trends. For example, each major division of an organization might identify similar issues that can be addressed only through changes to corporate-level policy or through the creation of corporate resources.

Managing Common Systems

Large, diverse organizations often have shared computing systems. For example, an organization might have a single financial system that is used by all business units. Managing the security of a common system will likely require cooperation across business units. Individual evaluations conducted by the business units will provide information about issues related to the system, but mitigation plans need to be coordinated across the business units to avoid conflicts. The resulting benefit is the identification of dependencies and interrelationships among all users, maintainers, and information technology staff members. Once all parties understand the issues related to common systems, the organization can work to ensure that security requirements for common assets are addressed.

Customers and Collaborators

Organizations need to consider security issues related to how customers and collaborators access their systems and networks. For example, collaborators might inadvertently compromise security when they access an organization's computing infrastructure. Do they understand the organization's security policies? Does the organization provide open access to its infrastructure that bypasses its firewall? A balance is needed between meeting customer needs and securing the computing infrastructures. In some cases an organization might include customers or collaborators as part of its knowledge elicitation activities.

Shared Facilities

Organizations must also consider how to manage physical security in shared facilities. Is an organization located in a building with other companies? Does the building's owner provide a central security service? After it conducts OCTAVE, an organization is in a better position to identify security requirements related to the facility. Someone from the organization can then meet with the building's facility management group to see which requirements that group is already meeting. For example, the building's facility management group might already be addressing some business continuity issues, such as uninterrupted power supply. An organization located in that building could leverage existing resources rather than duplicate them.

This chapter has identified a few practical scenarios to help you decide how to implement OCTAVE's flexible evaluation approach in your organization. OCTAVE is applicable to a variety of organizations, and the key to making it work in your organization is to consider how to tailor it for your unique environment. At this point we're ready to examine some ideas about managing information security risks on a continual basis, presented in Chapter 14.

14

Information Security Risk Management

Information security risk management is more than simply completing an evaluation. The results of an evaluation provide a direction for improving your organization's security posture. However, the evaluation merely provides a *direction;* it does not necessarily lead to meaningful improvement. Such improvement occurs only when your organization follows through by implementing the results of the evaluation. This final chapter introduces a framework for managing information security risks.

14.1 Introduction

As indicated in Chapter 1, an information security risk evaluation provides a snapshot, or baseline, of the organization's current risks. However, this baseline is not static or frozen in time. After an evaluation has been completed, an organization will implement its protection strategy and risk mitigation plans; new threats and vulnerabilities will emerge; and the organization will identify new critical assets. New risks will emerge and old risks may go away or change their nature.

To understand how its security risks change over time, an organization typically "resets" its baseline periodically by conducting another evaluation. The time between evaluations can be predetermined (e.g., yearly) or triggered by major events (e.g., corporate reorganization, redesign of an organization's computing infrastructure).

We also indicated in Chapter 1 that an organization improves its security posture only after it implements its protection strategy and risk mitigation plans. Figure 14-1 illustrates the framework for managing information security risks as

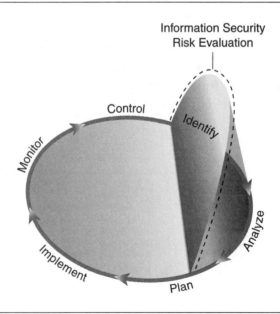

FIGURE 14-1 Information Security Risk Evaluation and Management

well as the "slice" provided by the evaluation. We derived the framework from previous work, in which we developed an approach to managing risks on software and system development projects [Dorofee 96].

Key Principles

Think back to the principles presented in Chapter 2 (see Figure 14-2). To be effective, information security risk management must be consistent with these principles. Our discussion will focus on two of the principles: *open communication* and *integrated management*. Recall that information security risk management cannot succeed without a reasonable degree of open communication of security-related issues.[1] A culture that supports open communication of risk

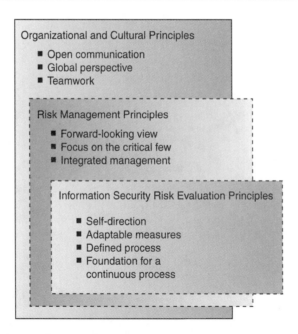

FIGURE 14-2 Information Security Risk Management Principles

---

1. Remember that information security risks constitute very sensitive information. While open communication among key decision makers and trusted personnel is important, you must use discretion when sharing this information with people with whom you have not established a level of trust.

information is the basis for effective information security risk management. A process for managing your information security risks must ensure that the right people get the right information in a timely manner.

Integrated management requires that security policies and strategies be consistent with organizational policies and strategies. The organization's management must strike a balance between business and security goals. To accomplish this, an organization should integrate its information security risk management processes with its business processes. Figure 14-3 illustrates this concept. Notice that the information security risk management practices in the organizations must fulfill three requirements:

1. Support organizational goals and objectives.
2. Be integrated with management practices and organizational policies.
3. Comply with laws and regulations within which the organization operates.

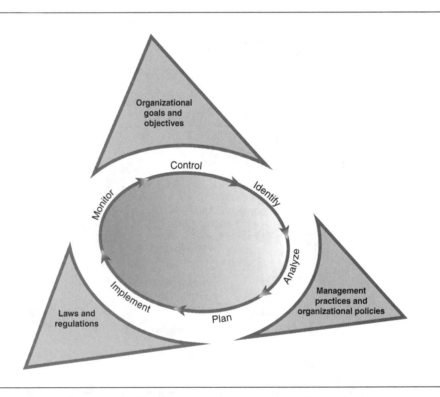

FIGURE 14-3 Information Security Risk Management Framework in Context

An information security risk management framework must complement and support the organization's current business practices, not conflict with it or exist in isolation. Most organizations focus their information security risk management efforts on an evaluation. Conducting an organizationwide information security risk evaluation enables an organization to create a global perspective of risks within the larger context of the organization's mission and business objectives. The organization must then determine how to address those risks and improve its security posture.

After OCTAVE

The key results of OCTAVE include a protection strategy for organizational improvement and mitigation plans to reduce the risks to the organization's critical assets. To manage information security risks effectively, you must develop detailed action plans and manage the implementation of those plans. The post-OCTAVE activities are nothing more than a *plan-do-check-act* cycle, ensuring that selected aspects of your organization's protection strategy and mitigation plans are implemented. To build on the results of OCTAVE, you must address the following operations from Figure 14-3:

- Plan for implementation by developing develop detailed action plans for key aspects of your organization's protection strategy and risk mitigation plans.
- Implement action plans as specified.
- Monitor the execution of action plans for schedule and effectiveness.
- Control any variations in action plans by implementing corrective measures.

The next section presents a framework for information security risk management—a "roadmap" for managing your risks. Following that, Section 14.3 examines an approach for implementing the framework.

14.2 A Framework for Managing Information Security Risks

Information security risk management is the ongoing process of identifying and addressing information security risks. This section explores the details of a structured approach for managing risks. Figure 14-4 illustrates the operations required

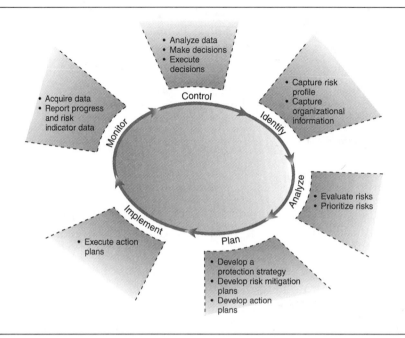

FIGURE 14-4 Operations and Tasks of the Information Security Risk Management Framework

by the information security risk management framework as well as the major tasks completed during each operation. This type of framework is common to risk management approaches in many domains, including information security [GAO 98].

Assigning Responsibility

To manage your information security risks effectively, you must clearly define roles and responsibilities for all of the operations and tasks in the framework. Effective risk management requires everyone in the organization to know his or her role in managing risks. During OCTAVE, an analysis team was responsible for identifying and analyzing risks and for completing high-level planning tasks. This team may not have a permanent existence in your organization, and new people might be assigned responsibility for managing the risks after the evaluation. As you consider the framework in this section and how it might apply to your organization, remember that you will eventually need to determine the appropriate set of roles and responsibilities and distribute them effectively. The remainder of this section examines each operation in Figure 14-4, starting with "Identify."

14.2.1 Identify

Identification is the process of transforming uncertainties and issues related to how well an organization's assets are being protected into distinct (tangible) risks. The objective of this activity is to anticipate risks before they become problems and to incorporate this information into the organization's information security risk management process. Table 14-1 illustrates the types of tasks that are conducted during risk identification and the key results produced by each task.

TABLE 14-1 Risk Identification Tasks

Task	Description	Key Results
Capture risk profile.	Capturing a risk profile requires gathering and recording information about the individual components of risk (asset, threat, vulnerability, and impact).	• Critical assets • Threats to critical assets • Security requirements for critical assets • Narrative description of the potential impact of the risks on the organization • Key infrastructure components related to critical assets
Capture organizational information.	Capturing organizational information calls for gathering and recording contextual information that supports the risk profile.	• Current security policies, practices, and procedures • Current technology vulnerabilities • Current organizational vulnerabilities

Overall, when implemented, risk identification should

- Enable staff members throughout the organization to identify and communicate risk-related information periodically or as needed
- Provide a means for documenting all risk-related information in a consistent format

At the end of identification, you will have documented a set of risks, including information about the organization's critical assets, the threats to those assets, and applicable vulnerabilities (both organizational and technological). You will also have collected sufficient supporting information, providing the overall organizational context for interpreting the organization's risks. In the next operation, you build on this information by setting priorities for addressing risks.

14.2.2 Analyze

Analysis is the process of projecting how extensive risks are and using those projections to set priorities. The objective of risk analysis is to gain a better understanding of risks by examining all risk-related data in relation to a set of organizational evaluation criteria. Table 14-2 illustrates the risk analysis tasks.

Risk analysis should include techniques for setting priorities based on established evaluation criteria. These criteria define those aspects of impact (and probability, if used) that are most important to the organization's business objectives. The analysis process should

- Enable staff members to evaluate or reevaluate risks for impact and probability (if used)
- Provide personnel who analyze risks with sufficient guidance to set or revise priorities

TABLE 14-2 Risk Analysis Tasks

Task	Description	Key Results
Evaluate risks.	Evaluating risks involves establishing the current values for impact and probability (if used).	• Values for risk measures (impact, probability)
Prioritize risks.	Prioritizing risks requires determining which risks need to be addressed based on the nature of the risk and the organization's general tolerance for risk.	• Mitigation approach (accept, mitigate)

When analyzing the risks to your critical assets, you establish the potential impact on the organization and review all risks in the context of organizational needs and objectives. You then use that information to determine which risks to mitigate actively and, after setting your priorities, to decide what your organization can do to address those risks.

14.2.3 Plan

Planning is the process of determining which actions to take to improve the organization's security posture and protect its critical assets. The objectives of planning are to develop and maintain the following three security enhancements:

1. A protection strategy to improve the organization's overall security posture
2. Mitigation plans designed to reduce risks to the organization's critical assets
3. Detailed action plans to implement key aspects of the protection strategy and risk mitigation plans

Table 14-3 highlights the risk planning tasks.

TABLE 14-3 Risk Planning Tasks

Task	Description	Key Results
Develop a protection strategy.	Developing a protection strategy requires defining (or updating) a protection strategy for improving an organization's security-related practices.	• Protection strategy
Develop risk mitigation plans.	Developing risk mitigation plans requires defining (or updating) plans to reduce risks to the organization's critical assets.	• Risk mitigation plans
Develop action plans.	Developing (or updating) action plans involves specifying a set of actions for implementing key aspects of the protection strategy and risk mitigation plans. Action plans are defined based on an assessment of available resources as well as any organizational constraints. Each action plan includes a completion date, success criteria, and funding requirements. In addition, measures for monitoring plans against their schedules and success criteria are selected. Finally, personnel must be assigned to implement the action plans.	• Action plans • Budget • Schedule • Success criteria • Measures to monitor action plans • Personnel assigned to implement action plans

Remember, during OCTAVE, the analysis team completes all high-level planning tasks (i.e., developing a protection strategy and risk mitigation plans). The task of developing detailed action plans occurs after the evaluation. The planning process should include the following specifications:

- Require planners to review existing plans and strategies for common actions.
- Provide planners with established methods for incorporating return on investment, dealing with limited resources, and prioritizing corrective actions.
- Enable the use of both technological and organizational solutions.
- Require planners to select measures for monitoring plans against their schedules and success criteria.
- Afford planners the authority to allocate or reallocate resources.
- Incorporate all necessary reviews and approvals.

During the planning process, you develop a protection strategy and risk mitigation plans. First you want to understand the range of available options and next you develop detailed action plans. This second step initially involves selecting key aspects of the protection strategy and risk mitigation plans to implement, based on a cost-benefit analysis. You then formulate an action plan for each key aspect that includes the following elements:

- The budget required to support implementation of the action plan
- A schedule that defines all key milestones
- Success criteria that define the objectives of the action plan
- Measures to monitor the progress of the action plan relative to its schedule and success criteria
- Responsibility for implementing the action plan

After you finish planning, you have defined the direction for improving your organization's security posture. In the next operation you execute the action plans as designed.

14.2.4 Implement

Implementation is the process of taking planned action to improve an organization's security posture. The objective of risk implementation is to execute all action plans according to the schedules and success criteria that were defined during risk planning. Implementation is tightly linked to risk monitoring and control, during which you follow and correct implementation progress. Table 14-4 illustrates the risk implementation task.

You assign responsibility for implementing action plans during the planning process. People who are assigned responsibility for implementing action plans must follow through by ensuring that those plans are completed according to the plan's defined schedules and success criteria.

The implementation process should

- Communicate to organizational personnel that staff members are authorized to implement their assigned action plans
- Enable staff members to reprioritize existing work tasks to incorporate their action plan activities
- Provide staff members with sufficient funds, equipment, and other required resources to complete the action plans

As you implement action plans, you also need to monitor them to ensure that they are being implemented according to schedule and are meeting their defined success criteria.

14.2.5 Monitor

The monitoring process tracks action plans to determine their current status and reviews organizational data for indications of new risks or changes to existing risks. The objectives of monitoring risks are to collect accurate, timely, and relevant information about the progress of action plans being implemented and any major changes to the organization's operational environment that could indicate the existence of new risks or significant changes to existing risks.

Table 14-5 illustrates the tasks completed as risks are monitored.

TABLE 14-4 Risk Implementation Task

Task	Description	Key Results
Execute action plans.	Executing action plans requires successfully completing all actions in those plans according to their documented schedules.	• Completed actions

TABLE 14-5 Tasks for Monitoring Risks

Task	Description	Key Results
Acquire data.	This task requires the collection of quantitative or information that • measures the status of action plans with respect to their schedules and success criteria • indicates the presence of new risks or significant changes to existing risks	• Data tracking the progress of action plans • Data about key risk indicators
Report progress and risk indicator data.	Reporting progress involves ensuring that key decision makers understand an action plan's current status. Reporting risk data requires passing on all indications of new risks to the appropriate personnel in the organization.	• Communicated progress reports • Communicated risk indicators

Typically, the people who are responsible for implementing action plans also monitor those plans. In addition, everyone in the organization needs to be empowered to look for and report information that might indicate the presence of new risks or significant changes to existing risks. For example, if there are major changes to the organization's operational environment (e.g., corporate reorganization, major redesign of the organization's computing infrastructure), management might decide to conduct another information security risk evaluation.

Risk monitoring should provide an organization with an efficient and effective way to track the progress of action plans, indications of new risks, and significant changes to existing risks. The monitoring process should both leverage current project management practices within the organization and enable effective and timely communication of status information and risk indicators.

As you monitor risks, you need to interpret the data that you collect. Controlling risks allows you to decide how to proceed with action plans, whether the organization needs to identify new risks, and how to address significant changes to existing risks.

14.2.6 Control

Controlling risks is a process whereby designated personnel adjust the course of action plans and determine whether changing organizational conditions indicate the presence of new risks. The objective of controlling risks is to make informed, timely, and effective decisions about corrective measures for action plans and about whether to identify new risks to the organization. Table 14-6 highlights the tasks required to control risks.

You can make two types of control decisions. The first type deals with adjusting the course of action plans. Part of the responsibility for making control decisions lies with the person who is monitoring an action plan. If action plans were being implemented according to their schedules and were meeting defined success criteria, the person monitoring the plans would simply continue tracking them. The decision in this case is to continue as planned. On the other hand, if the person monitoring the risk noticed a deviation or anomaly that was causing a delay in a plan's schedule or indicated that success criteria were not being met, that person would make sure that the issue was raised at the appropriate management level. It might be necessary to revise that action plan or execute predefined contingency actions.

The second type of control decision focuses on interpreting risk indicators. You are looking for major changes to the organization's operational environment, indicating the possible existence of new risks or significant changes to existing risks. As mentioned during our discussion about monitoring risks, anyone in the

TABLE 14-6 Tasks for Controlling Risks

Task	Description	Key Results
Analyze data.	Analyzing data involves examining reported data for trends, deviations, and anomalies. The following types of information are reviewed: • Data tracking the progress of action plans • Data about key risk indicators	• Analyzed progress reports • Analyzed risk indicators
Make decisions.	Making decisions requires designated personnel to determine • How to proceed with action plans • Whether to identify new risks to the organization	• Decisions about changes to action plans • Decisions about identifying new risks
Execute decisions.	Executing decisions involves putting control decisions into practice.	• Communicated decisions • Implemented changes to action plans • Start of risk identification activity

organization could look for and report information that might indicate the presence of new risks or changes to existing risks. Whoever believes that changes to the operational environment could significantly change the nature of the organization's information security risks should make sure that those issues are raised at the appropriate management level. If appropriate, new risks could be identified (e.g., by conducting another evaluation) or action plans could be revised based on changes to the underlying risks.

Continuous control of risks should be tightly integrated into the organization's management practices. The control process should

- Ensure that responsibility for making control decisions is formally assigned and accepted
- Provide personnel with guidance for weighing alternatives and making trade-offs
- Provide a mechanism for elevating sensitive issues to an appropriate organizational level
- Be integrated with general business risk planning, implementation, and identification activities in the organization

This concludes our presentation of the information security risk management framework. The next section looks at a common implementation of the framework.

14.3 Implementing Information Security Risk Management

The information security risk management framework provides guidance about the operations that organizations can implement to identify and address their information security risks. This section presents a common implementation of the framework. At the heart of this implementation is the information security risk evaluation.

Time Line Between Evaluations

Figure 14-5 illustrates a time line between two successive evaluations. Notice that after the organization completes Evaluation A, it has set its baseline with respect to its information security risks (i.e., the organization has taken its "snapshot" of its

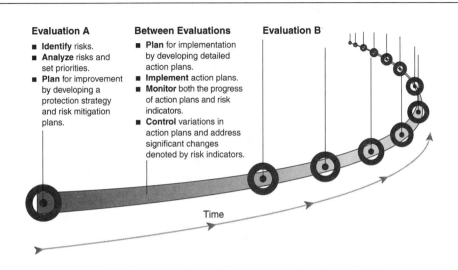

Evaluation A
- **Identify** risks.
- **Analyze** risks and set priorities.
- **Plan** for improvement by developing a protection strategy and risk mitigation plans.

Between Evaluations
- **Plan** for implementation by developing detailed action plans.
- **Implement** action plans.
- **Monitor** both the progress of action plans and risk indicators.
- **Control** variations in action plans and address significant changes denoted by risk indicators.

Evaluation B

Time

FIGURE 14-5 Evaluation-Based Information Security Risk Management

current risks). The organization must then address, or manage, the highest-priority risks that were identified during the evaluation, using these to galvanize mitigation and improvement activities. During the time between evaluations, people in the organization implement action plans designed to improve the organization's security posture. Assuming that those people effectively manage implementation of the action plans, the organization's security posture will indeed change.

Because the organization's security posture changes over time, it must periodically "reset" its baseline by conducting another evaluation. This creates another cycle of implementing and managing action plans from that evaluation, followed by another evaluation. The time between evaluations is generally predetermined (e.g., every one or two years). Therefore, it can take an organization a couple of years (or even longer) to complete each cycle.

Section 14.2.5 introduced the idea that an organization needs to monitor risk indicators for significant changes to its operational environment, indicating the existence of new risks or changes to existing risks. A "significant" change to an organization's operational environment would be one that alters the nature of the organization's information security risks and potentially affects its protection strategy and mitigation priorities. Because the organization's protection strategy and mitigation priorities may both be affected, the organization might decide to conduct another evaluation before its scheduled interval.

For example, a significant change to the organization's operational environment could be the acquisition of a former rival company. Such an acquisition might trigger an evaluation before the scheduled interval, setting a new baseline just before the acquisition. This step would establish an updated view of the organization's security posture going into the acquisition and could identify risks that must be addressed before the merger.

An organization's staff typically expends a lot of time and effort conducting an information security risk evaluation. Thus, an organization's management needs to be selective about which changes in its operational environment are significant enough to warrant another evaluation. The vast majority of changes do not meet this threshold.

Addressing Small Changes Between Evaluations

So how do organizations handle small changes between evaluations? Typically, they rely upon established security practices and procedures to address small changes. (Appendix C provides a catalog of security practices.) If there are no established procedures in place for a given situation, staff members are likely to handle it in an ad hoc fashion.

For example, consider how an organization handles a newly discovered vulnerability. New vulnerabilities are identified quite frequently and generally neither change the nature of the risks that the organization is managing nor affect the organization's mitigation priorities. The information technology staff could use established vulnerability management procedures to address the new vulnerability.

Likewise, if an organization acquires or develops a new business system, the nature of the risks to that system are likely to be *similar* to those affecting other systems and not affect the organization's mitigation priorities. The staff would apply existing security policies and procedures to designing, configuring, maintaining, and using the new system.

14.4 Summary

Much of this book has focused on the OCTAVE approach and the need for organizations to assess their information security risks. Recall from Chapter 2 that one of the information security risk evaluation principles is *foundation for a continuous process* (see Figure 14-2). This principle states that the results of an information security risk evaluation provide the foundation for improvement. To realize any improvement in its security posture, an organization must implement the results of information security risk evaluations.

This chapter presented a framework for managing information security risks. The framework provides basic requirements for an information security risk management approach. In defining this approach, we have merged the asset-driven, risk-based concepts from OCTAVE with general risk management concepts commonly used in other domains to create a comprehensive approach for managing information security risks in an organization. A risk-based approach enables organizations to develop solution strategies tailored to their unique environments.

We view using information security risk evaluations to improve an organization's security posture as a sound business practice. Since most organizations rely upon access to electronic data to conduct business, the data need to be adequately protected from misuse. The ability of an organization to achieve its mission and meet its business objectives is directly linked to the state of its computing infrastructure and the manner in which people interact with it. For an organization to be in the best position to achieve its mission, its people need to understand both which information-related assets are important and what they need to do to protect those assets. We believe that a self-directed, risk-based approach for managing information security can help put organizations in a better position to achieve their missions.

Glossary

Accept   a decision made during risk analysis to take no action to address a risk and to accept the consequences should the risk occur.

Access path   ways in which information or services can be accessed via an organization's network.

Action list   a list of actions that people in an organization can take in the near term without the need for specialized training, policy changes, etc. It is essentially a list of near-term action items.

Actor   a property of a threat that defines who or what may violate the security requirements (confidentiality, integrity, availability) of an asset.

Analysis team   an interdisciplinary team, comprising representatives of both the mission-related and information technology areas of the organization, which conducts the evaluation and analyzes the information. An analysis team generally consists of about three to five people, depending on the size of the overall organization and the scope of the evaluation.

Annualized loss expectancy (ALE)   the typical monetary loss that can be expected in a year resulting from a risk. Annualized loss expectancy is the product of the potential loss that could occur (impact value) multiplied by the projected frequency of occurrence of the risk in a given year (probability).

Area of concern   a situation or scenario in which someone is concerned about a threat to important assets. Typically, areas of concern have a source and an outcome—a causal action that has an effect on the organization.

Asset   something of value to the enterprise. Information technology assets are the combination of logical and physical assets and are grouped into the specific classes (information, systems, software, hardware, people).

Attributes   the distinctive qualities, or characteristics, of an information security risk evaluation.

Availability   the extent to which, or frequency with which, an asset must be present or ready for use.

Catalog of practices   a collection of good strategic and operational security practices that an organization can use to manage its security.

Catalog of vulnerabilities   a collection of vulnerabilities based on platform and application, used to evaluate an organization's computing infrastructure for technology vulnerabilities.

Champion   someone internal to an organization with an interest in conducting an information security risk evaluation. A champion generally does not have the authority to allocate resources to conduct the evaluation but must persuade someone in the organization who does have the authority to sponsor the activity.

Checklist   a vulnerability evaluation tool that functions the same as automated tools. However, unlike automated tools, checklists are manual, not automated. Checklists require a consistent review of the items being checked and must be routinely updated.

Classical concept of probability   the likelihood that an event will occur when all possibilities are known to be equally likely to occur. This concept of probability is the oldest historically and was originally developed in connection with games of chance.

Computer prioritization listing   a listing of the computer inventory owned by an organization. This listing typically depicts a prioritized ordering of systems or networking components based on their importance to the organization (e.g., mission-critical systems, high/medium/low-priority systems, administrative systems, support systems).

Confidentiality   the requirement of keeping proprietary, sensitive, or personal information private and inaccessible to anyone who is not authorized to see it.

Configuration vulnerability   a weakness resulting from an error in the configuration and administration of a system or component.

Critical assets an organization's most important assets. The organization will suffer a large adverse impact if something happens to critical assets.

Desktop workstation hosts on an organization's networks that staff members use to conduct business.

Design vulnerability a weakness inherent in the design or specification of hardware or software whereby even a perfect implementation will result in a vulnerability.

Destruction the irrevocable elimination of an asset.

Disclosure the viewing of confidential or proprietary information by someone who should not see the information.

Evaluation criteria a set of qualitative measures against which a risk is evaluated. Evaluation criteria define high, medium, and low impacts for an organization.

Expected value the product of the potential loss that could occur (impact value) multiplied by the projected frequency of occurrence of a risk (probability). Expected value is also known as expected loss or risk exposure.

Extreme event an event that has a low probability of occurrence but a potentially catastrophic impact on the organization.

Frequency interpretation of probability the likelihood that an event (or a given outcome) will occur, based on the proportion of the time that similar events have occurred over a long period of time.

Generic threat profile a catalog containing a range of all potential threats under consideration. The generic threat profile is a starting point for creating a unique threat profile for each critical asset.

Hardware asset information technology physical devices (workstations, servers, etc.). Normally, hardware assets focus solely on the replacement costs for physical devices.

Home computer home personal computers that staff members use to access information remotely via an organization's networks.

Hybrid scanner a vulnerability evaluation tool that targets a range of services, applications, and operating system functions. Hybrid scanners may address Web servers (CGI, JAVA), database applications, registry information (e.g., Windows NT/2000), and weak password storage and authentication services. These are also known as specialty and targeted scanners.

Impact   the effect of a threat on an organization's mission and business objectives.

Impact value   a qualitative measure of a risk's impact on the organization (high, medium, or low).

Implementation vulnerability   a weakness resulting from an error made in the software or hardware implementation of a satisfactory design.

Information asset   documented (paper or electronic) data or intellectual property used to meet the mission of an organization.

Integrity   the authenticity, accuracy, and completeness of an asset.

Interruption   the limiting of an asset's availability; interruption refers mainly to services.

Key classes of components   types of devices that are important in processing, storing, or transmitting critical information. They represent assets related to critical assets.

Laptop   portable personal computer used to access information remotely via an organization's networks.

Law of large numbers   the rule that as the number of times a situation is repeated becomes larger, the proportion of successes tends toward the actual probability of success.

Loss   the limiting of an asset's availability; the asset still exists but is temporarily unavailable.

Mitigate   addressing a risk by implementing actions designed to counter the underlying threat.

Mitigation approach   the way in which an organization intends to address a risk. An organization can either mitigate or accept a risk.

Modification   an unauthorized changing of an asset.

Motive   a property of a threat that defines whether the intentions of a human actor are deliberate or accidental. Motive is also sometimes referred to as the objective of a threat actor.

Networking component   devices important to an organization's networks. Routers, switches, and modems are all examples of this class of component.

Network infrastructure scanner   a vulnerability evaluation tool that focuses on the components of the network infrastructure, such as routers and intelligent switches, DNS (domain name system) servers, firewall systems, and intrusion detection systems.

Network mapping tools   software used to search a network by identifying the physical connectivity of systems and networking components. The software also displays detailed information about the interconnectivity of networks and devices (routers, switches, bridges, hosts).

Network topology diagrams   electronic or paper documents used to display the logical or physical mapping of a network. These documents identify the connectivity of systems and networking components. They usually contain less detail than that provided by network mapping tools.

Operating system scanner   a vulnerability evaluation tool that targets specific operating systems such as Windows NT/2000, Sun Solaris, Red Hat Linux, or Apple Mac OS.

Operational practice   security practices that focus on technology-related issues. They include issues related to how people use, interact with, and protect technology.

Organizational vulnerability   a weakness in organizational policy or practice that can result in the occurrence of unauthorized actions. Vulnerabilities are indications of missing or inadequate security practices.

Outcome   a property of a threat that defines the immediate outcome (disclosure, modification, destruction, loss, interruption) of violating the security requirements of an asset.

Outputs   the outcomes that an analysis team must achieve during an information security risk evaluation.

People asset   the people in an organization who possess unique skills, knowledge, and experience that are difficult to replace.

Principles   the fundamental concepts driving the nature of an information security risk evaluation.

Probability   the likelihood that an event will occur.

Protection strategy   the policy an organization develops to enable, initiate, implement, and maintain its internal security. It tends to incorporate long-term, organizationwide initiatives.

Protection strategy practice   an action that helps initiate, implement, and maintain security within an organization. A protection strategy practice is also called a security practice.

Risk   the possibility of suffering harm or loss; the potential for realizing unwanted negative consequences of an event. Risk refers to a situation in which either a person could do something undesirable or a natural occurrence could cause an undesirable outcome, resulting in a negative impact or consequence.

Risk evaluation   a process that generates an organizationwide view of information security risks. It provides a baseline that can be used to focus mitigation and improvement activities.

Risk management   the ongoing process of identifying risks and implementing plans to address them.

Risk measure   a qualitative value used to estimate some aspect of risk. There are two risk measures: impact value and probability.

Risk mitigation plan   a plan intended to reduce the risks to a critical asset. Risk mitigation plans tend to incorporate actions, or countermeasures, designed to counter the threats to the assets.

Risk profile   a definition of the range of risks that can affect an asset. Risk profiles contain categories grouped according to threat source (human actors using network access, human actors using physical access, system problems, other problems).

Script   a vulnerability evaluation tool that works as well as an automated tool except that it usually has a singular function. If a large number of items are being evaluated, a corresponding number of scripts will be required. Scripts require a consistent review of the items being checked and must be routinely updated.

Security component   devices that have security as their primary function (e.g., a firewall).

Security practice   actions that help initiate, implement, and maintain security within an organization. A security practice is also called a protection strategy practice.

Security requirements   requirements outlining the qualities of information assets that are important to an organization. Typical security requirements are confidentiality, integrity, and availability.

Self-direction   a policy whereby people manage and direct information security risk evaluations for their own organization. These people are responsible for directing risk evaluation activities and for making decisions about the organization's security efforts.

Server   host within the information technology infrastructure that provides information technology services to an organization.

Software assets   software applications and services (operating systems, database applications, networking software, office applications, custom applications, etc.) that process, store, or transmit information.

Storage device   device where information is stored, often for backup purposes.

Strategic practice   security practice that focuses on organizational issues at the policy level. They include business-related issues as well as issues that require organizationwide plans and participation.

Subjective probability   the likelihood that an event (or a given outcome) will occur, based on indirect or collateral information, educated guesses, intuition, or other subjective factors.

System   a logical grouping of components designed to perform a defined function(s) or meet a defined objective(s).

System of interest   the system that is most closely linked to a critical asset.

Systems assets   information systems that process and store information. Systems are a combination of information, software, and hardware assets. Any host, client, or server can be considered a system.

Technology vulnerability   a weakness in systems that can lead directly to unauthorized action. Technology vulnerabilities are present in and apply to network services, architecture, operating systems, and applications. Types of technology vulnerabilities include design, implementation, and configuration vulnerabilities.

Threat   an indication of a potential undesirable event; the existence of a situation in which either a person could do something undesirable (e.g., initiating a denial-of-service attack against an organization's email server) or a natural occurrence could cause an undesirable outcome (a fire damaging an organization's information technology hardware). Threats have defined properties (asset, actor, motive, access, outcome).

Threat profile   a definition of the range of threats that can affect an asset. Threat profiles contain categories grouped according to threat source (human actors using network access, human actors using physical access, system problems, other problems).

Vulnerability   a weakness in an information system, system security practices and procedures, administrative controls, internal controls, implementation, or physical layout that could be exploited by a threat to gain unauthorized access to information or to disrupt processing. There are two basic types of vulnerabilities: organizational and technology.

Vulnerability evaluation approach   method of evaluating each infrastructure component; this includes deciding who will perform the evaluation and selecting the appropriate tool(s).

Vulnerability summary   a summary of the technology vulnerabilities for each component that is evaluated. A vulnerability summary lists the types of technology vulnerabilities found, when they need to be addressed, their potential effect on the critical assets, and how they can be dealt with.

Wireless component   devices, such as cell phones and wireless access points, that staff members may use to access information (for example, email).

Bibliography

This bibliography contains references cited in the text as well as general sources of security and risk management information. References are grouped into the following categories:

- Risk management
- General security information
- Guides for managers and policymakers
- Security practices
- System survivability
- Network security guides
- Web security
- Handling intrusions and incidents

Risk Management

Alberts, Christopher; Behrens, Sandra; Pethia, Richard; and Wilson, William. *Operationally Critical Threat, Asset, and Vulnerability Evaluation (OCTAVE^{SM}) Framework, Version 1.0* (CMU/SEI-99-TR-017, ADA 367718). Pittsburgh, PA: Software Engineering Institute, Carnegie Mellon University, 1999. Available online: <http://www.sei.cmu.edu/publications/documents/99. reports/99tr017/99tr017abstract.html>.

Alberts, Christopher J. et al. "Health Information Risk Assessment and Management: Toolkit Section 4.5." *CPRI Toolkit: Managing Information Security in Health Care, Version 2*. Available online: <http://www.cpri-host.org/toolkit/4_5.html> (2000).

Alberts, Christopher J. and Dorofee, Audrey J. *OCTAVE^{SM} Method Implementation Guide, v2.0.* Pittsburgh, PA: Software Engineering Institute, Carnegie Mellon University, 2001. Can be downloaded at no cost: <http://www.cert.org/octave/>.

Alberts, Christopher and Dorofee, Audrey. *Operationally Critical Threat, Asset, and Vulnerability Evaluation (OCTAVE^{SM}) Criteria* (CMU/SEI-01-TR-016). Pittsburgh, PA: Software Engineering Institute, Carnegie Mellon University, 2001. Available online: <http://www.sei.cmu.edu/publications/documents/01.reports/01tr016/01tr016abstract.html>.

Bernstein, Peter L. *Against the Gods: The Remarkable Story of Risk.* New York: John Wiley & Sons, Inc., 1996.

Charette, Robert N. *Software Engineering Risk Analysis and Management.* New York: Intertext Publications/Multiscience Press, Inc., 1989.

Dorofee, A.; Walker, J.; Alberts, C.; Higuera, R.; Murphy, R.; and Williams, R. *Continuous Risk Management Guidebook.* Pittsburgh, PA: Software Engineering Institute, Carnegie Mellon University, 1996.

Freund, John E. *Introduction to Probability.* Mineola, NY: Dover Publications, Inc., 1993.

United States General Accounting Office. *Executive Guide: Information Security Management* (GAO/AIMD-98-68). Washington, DC: GAO, May 1998.

United States General Accounting Office. *Information Security Risk Assessment, Practices of Leading Organizations* (GAO/AIMD-00-33). Washington, DC: GAO, November 1999.

Haimes, Yacov Y. *Risk Modeling, Assessment, and Management.* New York: John Wiley & Sons, Inc., 1996.

Harvard Business Review. *Harvard Business Review on Managing Uncertainty.* Boston: Harvard Business School Press, 1999.

Institute of Electrical and Electronics Engineers. *IEEE Standard for Software Lifecycle Processes—Risk Management* (IEEE Std 1540-2001). New York: IEEE, Inc., 2001.

Lange, Scott K.; Davis, Julie K.; Jaye, Daniel; Erwin, Dan; Mullarney, James X.; Clarke, Leo L.; and Loesch, Martin C. *e-Risk: Liabilities in a Wired World.* Cincinnati, OH: National Underwriter Co., 2000.

Peltier, Thomas R. *Information Security Risk Analysis.* Boca Raton, FL: Auerbach Publications, 2001.

Rowe, William D. *An Anatomy of Risk.* Malibu, FL: Robert E. Crier, 1988.

Van der Heijden, Kees. *Scenarios: The Art of Strategic Conversation.* Chichester, England: John Wiley & Sons, Inc., 1997.

General Security Information

Abrams, Marshall D.; Podell, Harold J.; and Jajodia, Sushil. *Information Security: An Integrated Collection of Essays.* Los Alamitos, CA: IEEE Computer Society Press, 1995.

Allen, Julia et al. "Improving the Security of Networked Systems." *Crosstalk: The Journal of Defense Software Engineering 13,* 10 (October 2000). Available online: <http://www.stsc.hill.af.mil/crosstalk/>.

Ahuja, Vijay. *Network and Internet Security.* Boston, MA: AP Professional, 1996.

Atkinson, Randall J. "Toward a More Secure Internet." *IEEE Computer* 30, 1 (January 1997): 57–61.

Barrett, Daniel J. *Bandits on the Information Superhighway.* Sebastopol, CA: O'Reilly and Associates, 1996.

Bosselaers, Antoon and Preneel, Bart. "Integrity Primitives for Secure Information Systems: Final Report of RACE Integrity Primitives Evaluation RIPE-RACE 1040." *Lecture Notes in Computer Science: 1007.* Berlin: Springer, 1995.

Caelli, William; Longley, Dennis; and Shain, Michael. *Information Security Handbook.* New York: Stockton Press, 1991.

Cohen, Frederick B. *Protection and Security on the Information Superhighway.* New York: Wiley, 1995.

Comer, Douglas E. *Internetworking with TCP/IP, Volume 1: Principles, Protocols, and Architecture.* Third edition. New York: Prentice-Hall, 1995.

Computer Security Institute. "2000 CSI/FBI Computer Crime and Security Survey." *Computer Security Issues and Trends,* vol. VI, no. 1 (spring 2000).

Davis, Peter T., ed. *Securing Client/Server Computer Networks.* New York: McGraw-Hill, 1996.

Dempsey, Rob and Bruce, Glen. *Security in Distributed Computing.* Upper Saddle River, NJ: Prentice-Hall, Inc., 1997.

Denning, P. J. and Denning, D. E. *Internet Besieged: Countering Cyberspace Scofflaws.* New York: Addison-Wesley, 1998.

Denning, D. E. *Information Warfare and Security.* New York: Addison-Wesley, 1999.

Ellis, James et al. *Report to the President's Commission on Critical Infrastructure Protection.* Pittsburgh, PA: Software Engineering Institute, Carnegie Mellon University, 1997. Available online: <http://www.cert.org/pres_comm/cert.rpcci.abstract.html>. Also published as an SEI Special Report (CMU/SEI-97-SR-003, ADA 324232) Available online: <http://www.sei.cmu.edu/publications/documents/97.reports/97sr003/97sr003abstract.html>.

Ermann, D. M.; Williams, M. B.; and Shauf, M. S. *Computers, Ethics, and Society.* Second edition. New York: Oxford University Press, 1997.

Fites, P. E.; Kratz, M. P.; and Brebner, A. F. *Control and Security of Computer Information Systems.* Rockville, MD, Computer Science Press, Inc., 1989.

Ford, Warwick and Baum, Michael. *Secure Electronic Commerce.* New York: Prentice-Hall, 1997.

Gollmann, Dieter. *Computer Security.* Chichester, England: John Wiley & Sons, 1999.

Howard, John and Longstaff, Tom. *A Common Language for Computer Security Incidents.* (SAND98-8997). Albuquerque, NM: Sandia National Laboratories, 1998.

Hutt, Arthur E.; Bosworth, Seymour; and Hoyt, Douglas B. *Computer Security Handbook.* Third edition. New York: John Wiley & Sons, Inc. 1995.

Kaufman, C.; Perlman, R.; and Speciner, M. *Network Security: Private Communication in a Public World.* Englewood Cliffs, NJ: PTR Prentice-Hall, 1995.

Kessler, Gary C. "Web of Worries." *Information Security* (April 2000). Available online: <http://www.infosecuritymag.com/articles/april00/cover.shtml>.

King, Nathan. "Sweeping Changes for Modem Security." *Information Security* (June 2000). Available online: <http://www.infosecuritymag.com/articles/june00/features1.shtml> (2000).

Kyas, O. *Internet Security, Risk Analysis, Strategies and Firewalls.* Boston: Int'l Thompson, 1997.

Laswell, Barbara; Simmel, Derek; and Behrens, Sandra. *Information Assurance Curriculum and Certification: State of the Practice* (CMU/SEI-99-TR-021, ADA 367575). Pittsburgh, PA: Software Engineering Institute, Carnegie Mellon University, 1999. Available online: <http://www.sei.cmu.edu/publications/documents/99.reports/99tr021/99tr021abstract.html>.

Longstaff, Thomas et al. "Security of the Internet," 231–255. *The Froelich/Kent Encyclopedia of Telecommunications, vol. 15.* New York: Marcel Dekker, Inc., 1997. Also available online: <http://www.cert.org/encyc_article/tocencyc.html>.

McGraw, Gary and Felten, Edward W. *Java Security.* New York: John Wiley and Sons, Inc., 1996.

Merkow, M. S. and Breithaupt, J. *The Complete Guide to Internet Security,* New York: AMACOM, American Management Association, 2000: pp. 95–109.

NIST. *NIST Federal Information Processing Standards (FIPS) on Computer Security.* Available online: <http://csrc.nist.gov/publications/fips/index.html> (2001).

NCSC. *NCSC Glossary of Computer Security Terms.* Ft. George G. Meade, MD: National Computer Security Center: Washington, DC: For sale by the Supt. of Docs., U.S. Government Printing Office, 1989.

National Research Council. *Computers at Risk: Safe Computing in the Information Age.* Washington DC: National Academy Press, 1991.

National Security Telecommunications and Information Systems Security Committee. *Index of National Security Telecommunications Information Systems Security Issuances* (NSTISSI No. 4014). Ft. Mead, MD: NSTISSC Secretariat, January 1998.

Parker, Donn B. *Fighting Computer Crime.* New York: John Wiley & Sons, 1998.

Pethia, Richard. *Internet Security Issues: Testimony Before the U.S. Senate Judiciary Committee.* Carnegie Mellon University, Software Engineering Institute, May 25, 2000. Available online: <http://www.cert.org/congressional_testimony/Pethia_testimony25May00.html>.

Pfleeger, Charles P. *Security in Computing.* Second edition. Upper Saddle River, NJ: Prentice-Hall, 1997.

Power, Richard. "1999 CSI/FBI Computer Crime and Security Survey." *Computer Security Journal,* volume XV, 2. San Francisco, CA: Computer Security Institute, 1999.

Rogers, Lawrence R. *rlogin(1): The Untold Story* (CMU/SEI-98-TR-017, ADA 358797). Pittsburgh, PA: Software Engineering Institute, Carnegie Mellon University, 1998. Available online: <http://www.sei.cmu.edu/publications/documents/98.reports/98tr017/98tr017abstract.html>.

Ruiu, Dragos. *Cautionary Tales: Stealth Coordinated Attack HOWTO.* Available online: <http://www.nswc.navy.mil/ISSEC/CID/Stealth_Coordinated_Attack.html> (1999).

Russell, Deborah and Gemi, Sr., G. T. *Computer Security Basics.* Sebastopol, CA: O'Reilly & Associates, Inc., 1991.

Sams.net Publishing. *Maximum Security: A Hacker's Guide to Protecting Your Internet Site and Network.* Indianapolis, IN: Sams.net Publishing, 1997.

SANS Institute. *How to Eliminate the Ten Most Critical Internet Security Threats: The Experts' Consensus, Version 1.32.* Available online: <http://www.sans.org/topten.htm> (2001).

Schneider, Fred B., ed. *Trust in Cyberspace.* Washington, DC: National Academy Press, 1999.

Schwartau, Winn. *Time-Based Security.* Seminole, FL: Interpact Press, 1999.

Sellens, John. "System and Network Monitoring." *login:* 25, 3 (June 2000).

Simmel, Derek et al. *Securing Desktop Workstations* (CMU/SEI-SIM-004, ADA 361388). Pittsburgh, PA: Software Engineering Institute, Carnegie Mellon University, 1999. Available online: <http://www.cert.org/security-improvement/modules/m04.html>.

Stevens, W. Richard. *TCP/IP Illustrated, Volume 1: The Protocols.* Reading, MA: Addison-Wesley, 1994.

Stoll, Cliff. *The Cuckoo's Egg: Tracking a Spy Through the Maze of Computer Espionage.* New York: Doubleday, 1989.

Summers, Rita C. *Secure Computing.* New York: McGraw-Hill, 1997.

Wadlow, Thomas A. *The Process of Network Security.* Reading, MA: Addison-Wesley, 2000.

Guides for Managers and Policymakers

Allen, Julia et al. *Security for Information Technology Service Contracts* (CMU/SEI-SIM-003, ADA 336329). Pittsburgh, PA: Software Engineering Institute, Carnegie Mellon University, 1998. Available online: <http://www.cert.org/security-improvement/modules/m03.html>.

Best, Reba A. and Piquet, D. Cheryl. *Computer Law and Software Protection: A Bibliography of Crime, Liability, Abuse, and Security.* Jefferson, NC: McFarland, 1993.

Cappel, James J.; Vanecek, Michael T.; and Vedder, Richard G. "CEO and CIO Perspectives on Competitive Intelligence." *Communications of the ACM* (August 1999).

Dijker, Barbara L., ed. *Short Topics in System Administration. Vol. 2, A Guide to Developing Computing Policy Documents.* Berkeley, CA: The USENIX Association for SAGE, the System Administrators Guild, 1996.

Guttman, B. and Bagwill, R. *Internet Security Policy: A Technical Guide.* Gaithersburg, MD: NIST Special Publication 800-XX, 1997. Available online: <http://csrc.nist.gov/isptg/html/>.

Kimmins, John; Dinkel, Charles; and Walters, Dale. *Telecommunications Security Guidelines for Telecommunications Management Network* (NIST Special Publication: 800-13). Gaithersburg, MD: Dept. of Commerce, Technology Administration, National Institute of Standards and Technology, 1995.

Kuncicky, D. and Wynn, B. A. *Short Topics in System Administration, Vol. 4, Educating and Training System Administrators: A Survey.* Berkeley, CA: The USENIX Association for the System Administrators Guild (SAGE), 1998.

Oppenheimer, David L.; Wagner, David A.; and Crabb, Michele D. *Short Topics in System Administration, Vol. 3, System Security: A Management Perspective.* Berkeley, CA: The USENIX Association for the System Administrators Guild (SAGE), 1997.

Phillips, G. *Short Topics in System Administration, Vol. 5, Hiring System Administrators.* Berkeley, CA: The USENIX Association for the System Administrators Guild (SAGE), 1999.

Regan, Priscilla M. *Legislating Privacy: Technology, Social Values, and Public Policy.* Chapel Hill, NC: University of North Carolina Press, 1995.

Schweitzer, James A. *Protecting Business Information: A Manager's Guide.* Boston: Butterworth-Heinemann, 1996.

Sterling, Bruce. *The Hacker Crackdown: Law and Disorder on the Electronic Frontier.* New York: Bantam Books, 1992.

Wood, Charles Cresson. *Information Security Policies Made Easy Version 7.* Baseline Software, Inc., 2000.

Security Practices

Allen, Julia H. *The CERT® Guide to System and Network Security Practices.* Reading, MA: Addison-Wesley, 2001.

British Standards Institution. *Information Security Management, Part 1: Code of Practice for Information Security Management of Systems* (BS7799: Part 1 : 1995). London, England: British Standards Institution, February 1995.

"Interagency Guidelines Establishing Standards for Safeguarding Customer Information and Rescission of Year 2000 Standards for Safety and Soundness; Final Rule," *Federal Register,* vol. 66, no. 22 (February 1, 2001): 8616–8641.

"Security Standards and Electronic Signature Standards; Proposed Rule," *Federal Register,* vol. 63, no. 155 (August 1998): 43242–43280.

Swanson, Marianne and Guttman, Barbara, *Generally Accepted Principles and Practices for Securing Information Technology Systems,* (NIST SP 800-14). National Institute of Standards and Technology, Department of Commerce, Washington, DC: 1996.

System Survivability

Ellison, R. J. et al. *Survivable Network Systems: An Emerging Discipline* (CMU/SEI-97-TR-013, ADA 341963). Pittsburgh, PA: Software Engineering Institute, Carnegie Mellon University, 1997. Available online: <http://www.sei.cmu.edu/publications/documents/97.reports/97tr013/97tr013abstract.html>.

Ellison, Robert; Linger, Richard; and Mead, Nancy. *Case Study in Survivable Network System Analysis* (CMU/SEI-98-TR-014, ADA 355070). Pittsburgh, PA: Software Engineering Institute, Carnegie Mellon University, 1998. Available online: <http://www.sei.cmu.edu/publications/documents/98.reports/98tr014/98tr014abstract.html>.

Firth, Robert et al. *An Approach for Selecting and Specifying Tools for Information Survivability* (CMU/SEI-97-TR-009, ADA 350658). Pittsburgh, PA: Software Engineering Institute, Carnegie Mellon University, 1997. Available online: <http://www.sei.cmu.edu/publications/documents/97.reports/97tr009/97tr009abstract.html>.

Mead, Nancy R.; Ellison, Robert J.; Linger, Richard C.; Longstaff, Thomas; and McHugh, John. *Survivable Network Analysis Method* (CMU/SEI-2000-TR-013, ADA 383771). Pittsburgh, PA: Software Engineering Institute, Carnegie Mellon University, 2000. Available online: <http://www.sei.cmu.edu/publications/documents/00.reports/00tr013.html>.

Mead, N. R.; Lipson, H. F.; and Sledge, C. A. "Toward Survivable COTS-Based Systems," *Cutter IT Journal* 14, 2 (February 2001): 4–11.

Salter, Chris; Saydjari, O. Sami; Schneier, Bruce; and Wallner, Jim. "Toward a Secure System Engineering Methodology." New Security Paradigms Workshop, 1998. Available online: <http://www.counterpane.com/secure-methodology.html> (1998).

Network Security Guides

Allen, Julia and Kossakowski, Klaus-Peter. *Securing Network Servers* (CMU/SEI-SIM-010, ADA 379469). Pittsburgh, PA: Software Engineering Institute, Carnegie Mellon University, 2000. Available online: <http://www.cert.org/security-improvement/modules/m10.html>.

Ford, Gary et al. *Securing Network Servers* (CMU/SEI-SIM-007, ADA 361387). Pittsburgh, PA: Software Engineering Institute, Carnegie Mellon University, 1999. Available online: <http://www.cert.org/security-improvement/modules/m07.html>.

Internet Engineering Task Force, Network Working Group. *Guidelines for the Secure Operation of the Internet* (RFC 1281). Available online: <http://www.isi.edu/in-notes/rfc1281.txt> (1991).

Internet Engineering Task Force, Site Security Policy Handbook Working Group. *Site Security Handbook* (RFC 2196, FYI 8). Available online: <http://www.isi.edu/in-notes/rfc2196.txt> (1997).

National Institute of Standards and Technology. *Internet Security Policy: A Technical Guide.* Washington, DC: National Institute of Standards and Technology. Available online: <http://csrc.nist.gov/isptg> (1998).

Kabay, Michel E. *The NCSA Guide to Enterprise Security: Protecting Information Assets.* New York: McGraw-Hill, 1996.

Northcutt, Stephen. *Network Intrusion Detection: An Analyst's Handbook.* Indianapolis, IN: New Riders Publishing, Macmillan, 1999.

Web Security

How to Remove Meta-characters from User-Supplied Data in CGI Scripts. Available online: <http://www.cert.org/tech_tips/cgi_metacharacters.html> (1999).

Understanding Malicious Content Mitigation for Web Developers. Available online: <http://www.cert.org/tech_tips/malicious_code_mitigation.html> (2000).

Frequently Asked Questions About Malicious Web Scripts Redirected by Web Sites. Available online: <http://www.cert.org/tech_tips/malicious_code_FAQ.html> (2000).

Garfinkel, S. and Spafford, G. *Web Security and Commerce.* Sebastopol, CA: O'Reilly and Associates, Inc., 1997.

Kossakowski, Klaus-Peter and Allen, Julia. *Securing Public Web Servers* (CMU/SEI-SIM-011). Pittsburgh, PA: Software Engineering Institute, Carnegie Mellon University, 2000. Available online: <http://www.cert.org/security-improvement/modules/m11.html>.

Larson, Eric and Stephens, Brian. *Web Servers, Security and Maintenance.* Upper Saddle River, NJ: Prentice-Hall, 2000.

McCarthy, Vance. "Web Security: How Much Is Enough?" *Datamation* (January 1997).

Rubin, A. D.; Geer, D.; and Ranum, M. *Web Security Sourcebook.* New York: John Wiley and Sons, 1997.

Rubin, Aviel and Geer, Daniel. "A Survey of Web Security." *IEEE Computer* (September 1998).

Soriano, Ray and Bahadur, Gary. "Securing Your Web Server." *Sys Admin* (May 1999).

Spainhour, Stephen and Quercia, Valerie. *Webmaster in a Nutshell.* Sebastopol. CA: O'Reilly and Associates, 1996.

Stein, Lincoln. *Web Security: A Step-by-Step Reference Guide.* Reading, MA: Addison-Wesley, 1998.

Stein, Lincoln. *The World Wide Web Security FAQ.* Available online: <http://www.w3.org/Security/Faq> (1999).

World Wide Web Consortium. *W3C Security Resources.* Available online: <http://www.w3.org/Security/> (November 1999).

Handling Intrusions and Incidents

Allen, Julia et al. *State of the Practice of Intrusion Detection Technologies.* (CMU/SEI-99-TR-028, ADA 357846). Pittsburgh, PA: Software Engineering Institute, Carnegie Mellon University, 1999. Available online: <http://www.sei.cmu.edu/publications/documents/99.reports/99tr028/99tr028abstract.html>.

Allen, Julia and Stoner, Ed. *Detecting Signs of Intrusion* (CMU/SEI-SIM-009). Pittsburgh, PA: Software Engineering Institute, Carnegie Mellon University, 2000. Available online: <http://www.cert.org/security-improvement/modules/m09.html>.

Amoroso, Edward. *Intrusion Detection: An Introduction to Internet Surveillance, Correlation, Trace Back, Traps, and Response.* Sparta, NJ: Intrusion.Net Books, 1999.

Base, Rebecca Gurley. *Intrusion Detection.* Indianapolis, IN: Macmillan Technical Publishing, 2000.

CERT Coordination Center. *Results of the Distributed-Systems Intruder Tools Workshop.* Pittsburgh, PA: Software Engineering Institute, Carnegie Mellon University, 1999. Available online: <http://www.cert.org/reports/dsit_workshop-final.html>.

CERT Coordination Center. *Intruder Detection Checklist* (UNIX). Available online: <http://www.cert.org/tech_tips/intruder_detection_checklist.html> (1999).

CERT Coordination Center. *How the FBI Investigates Computer Crime.* Available online: <http://www.cert.org/tech_tips/FBI_investigates_crime.html> (2000).

Dunigan, Tom and Hinkel, Greg. "Intrusion Detection and Intrusion Prevention on a Large Network: A Case Study." *Proceedings of the 1st Workshop on Intrusion Detection and Network Monitoring.* Santa Clara, CA. April 9–12, 1999. Available online: <http://www.usenix.org/publications/library/proceedings/detection99/full_papers/dunigan/dunigan_html/index.html>.

Escamilla, Terry. *Intrusion Detection: Network Security Beyond the Firewall.* New York: Wiley Computer Publishing, 1998.

Howard, John. *An Analysis of Security Incidents on the Internet: 1989–1995.* Pittsburgh, PA: Carnegie Mellon University, 1997. Available online: <http://www.cert.org/research/JHThesis/Start.html>.

Kossakowski, Klaus-Peter et al. *Responding to Intrusions* (CMU/SEI-SIM-006, ADA 360500). Pittsburgh, PA: Software Engineering Institute, Carnegie Mellon University, 1999. Available online: <http://www.cert.org/security-improvement/modules/m06.html>.

Maiwald, Eric. "Automating Response to Intrusions," *Proceedings of the Fourth Annual UNIX and NT Network Security Conference.* Orlando, FL, October 24–31, 1998. Bethesda, MD: The SANS Institute, 1998.

Marchany, Randy. "Incident Response: Scenarios and Tactics." *Proceedings of the Fourth Annual UNIX and NT Network Security Conference.* Orlando, FL, October 24–31, 1998. Bethesda, MD: The SANS Institute, 1998.

Newsham, Tim and Ptacek, Tom. *Insertion, Evasion, and Denial of Service: Eluding Network Intrusion Detection.* Available online: <http://www.snort.org> under Security Info (1998).

Northcutt, Stephen. "Computer Security Incident Handling: Step-by-Step." *Proceedings of the Fourth Annual UNIX and NT Network Security Conference.* Orlando, FL, October 24–31, 1998. Bethesda, MD: The SANS Institute, 1998.

Northcutt, Stephen. *Network Intrusion Detection: An Analyst's Handbook.* Indianapolis, IN: New Riders Publishing, 1999.

Ranum, Marcus. "Some Tips on Network Forensics." *Computer Security Institute* 198 (September 1999): 1–8.

Reavis, Jim. "Do You Have an Intrusion Detection Response Plan?" *Network World Fusion* (September 13, 1999). Available online: <http://www.nwfusion.com/newsletters/sec/0913sec1.html>

SANS Institute. *Computer Security Incident Handling Step by Step Guide, vol. 5.* Bethesda, MD: The SANS Institute. May 1998.

Schultz, Eugene. "Effective Incident Response." *Proceedings of the Fourth Annual UNIX and NT Network Security Conference.* Orlando, FL, October 24–31, 1998: Bethesda, MD: The SANS Institute, 1998.

Toigo, Jon William. *Disaster Recovery Planning for Computers and Communication Resources.* New York: John Wiley, 1996.

West-Brown, Moira J.; Stikvoort, Don; and Kossakowski, Klaus-Peter. *Handbook for Computer Security Incident Response Teams (CSIRTs)* (CMU/SEI-98-HB-001). Pittsburgh, PA: Software Engineering Institute, Carnegie Mellon University, 1998. Available online: <http://www.sei.cmu.edu/publications/documents/98.reports/98hb001/98hb001abstract.html>.

Appendix A
Case Scenario for
the OCTAVE Method

Part II of this book looked at some brief examples of the outputs resulting from processes and activities of the OCTAVE Method. This appendix provides the final report produced by the analysis team at MedSite. The OCTAVE Method produces a wealth of information in considerable detail. Rather than show all the interim stages of data consolidation, we instead provide the complete set of results in a format that could be used to brief and inform senior managers.

Finally, you should remember that the results you achieve from any information security risk evaluation are meaningful only if you use them. The final strategy and plans resulting from the data acquired and analyzed during processes 1 through 7 will have meaning only if they are implemented and tracked to completion.

A.1 MedSite OCTAVE Final Report: Introduction

This report is the final result of applying the OCTAVE Method within MedSite. It was written by the analysis team and provides our recommendations for an organizationwide protection strategy, mitigation plans for risks to our critical assets, and short-term action items. Section 4 of this report also contains a considerable amount of additional information gathered during the course of OCTAVE. As a reminder, the analysis team comprised the following members:

- L. Pierce
- J. Cutter
- S. Nolan (alternate R. Green)
- K. Brown

This information is organized as follows:

A.2 Protection Strategy for MedSite

A.3 Risks and Mitigation Plans for Critical Assets

A.4 Technology Vulnerability Evaluation Results and Recommended Actions

A.5 Additional Information

A.2 Protection Strategy for MedSite

The protection strategy outlined in Table A-1 focuses on improving the security posture of the entire MedSite organization. We developed the protection strategy after analyzing the results of the surveys completed by senior and operational area managers as well as general and information technology staff members during processes 1 to 3 of the OCTAVE Method. We also considered the risks identified during OCTAVE when developing the strategy. The protection strategy is organized according to the structure of the OCTAVE catalog of practices. The results of the security practice surveys are contained in Section 4 of this report.

TABLE A.1 Protection Strategy for MedSite

Organization Protection Strategy Strategy Area	
Strategy Area	*Strategy*
Security awareness and training	Security awareness and training is sporadic. Provide all newcomers with baseline training.
	Develop a long-range plan to upgrade training for all personnel and provide periodic refresher training.
	Provide annual training in physical security for all staff (including staff in outlying clinics).
	Enhance training for IT staff to address all job requirements.
	• Reduce reliance on on-the-job-training.
	• Update training plan in next six months to include formal training.
	• Find an easily obtained, inexpensive security training product (CD or take-home program).
	• Establish a baseline for security-related training and upgrades.
	Establish uniform procedures for systems training.
	Conduct joint training with ABC Systems.
Security strategy	Incorporate results from this analysis team into the MedSite strategic plan, upon approval of the executive committee.
	Determine overall time line for implementing these security improvement measures at the strategic planning level.
Security management	Allocate greater funds for system security. Annual budgeting should weigh expenditures to forecast future needs adequately.
	Reexamine results from this analysis team in one year.
	Clearly define staff roles and responsibilities and communicate to all personnel.
	Meet with human resources to determine what security-related issues need to be included in hiring/firing procedures and criteria.
	Begin a review of security status reports from IT at biweekly managers' meeting.
Security policies and regulations	Disseminate revised policies and procedures at all levels and actively enforce them.
	Document, publish, and disseminate specifications to all personnel outlining sanctions for security violations.
	Currently, security policies and procedures are neither clearly understood nor consistently enforced at all levels of the organization. Review all policies and procedures, compare them to other medical treatment facilities considered to have best practices, and revise them.

(continued)

TABLE A.1 Protection Strategy for MedSite (*continued*)

Organization Protection Strategy Strategy Area	
Strategy Area	*Strategy*
Security policies and regulations (*continued*)	Ensure that laws and regulations are understood at all levels of the organization and that they are incorporated into revised policies, procedures, and training.
Collaborative security management	Review and update the current policies and procedures for working with third parties, especially service providers.
	Develop a set of checklists and tools to set up contracts with third parties with clear instructions concerning disclosures, restrictions, and verification of compliance.
	Establish/enhance dialogue with ABC Systems.
	Invite ABC Systems to attend joint management meetings.
Contingency planning/ disaster recovery	Review contingency plans and procedures annually and brief all personnel during medical readiness training.
	Coordinate contingency plans with the network service provider and ABC Systems.
	Update business continuity plan to include electronic/network access.
Physical security	Enforce the security badge policy with spot checks.
	Continue joint exercises to challenge our physical security measures.
	Continue security challenges to outlying clinics.
	Identify the outlying clinics' physical security measures to the appropriate custodians.
	Review, update, and enforce our policies on workstation use.
	Review the physical security requirements for computers in free-flow areas in conjunction with their usage requirements. Institute adjustments in usage, physical location, or other measures to maintain physical security.
	Identify key system components' locations and verify the physical security of the components on a recurring basis (from both internal staff and external organizations).
	Enforce software installation security procedures at all levels and ensure they are adhered to both internally and externally.
	Establish a mechanism for the safety committee to verify that each section is aware of identified physical vulnerabilities. Include a member of IT on the committee to help it deal with computer systems' physical security requirements.
	Clearly establish and communicate that both internal and external personnel are responsible for physical security.

TABLE A.1 Protection Strategy for MedSite (*continued*)

Organization Protection Strategy Strategy Area	
Strategy Area	*Strategy*
Information technology security	Develop a long-range plan for modernization of security-related services. Recommend assigning this to the executive committee.
	Establish clear policies and procedures for information technology security services.
	Investigate the need for encryption on patient information that is emailed on unsecured lines.
	Assign a small task force to look into our use of PDAs.
	Ask ABC Systems to set up a review meeting for next quarter to discuss whether our security requirements and the current network design allow for ways to improve security without affecting work efficiency.
	Investigate the use of user profiles to restrict access to sensitive information during off-hours and weekends.
	Enforce user password policies (e.g., do not share passwords).
	Add time-outs to workstations in treatment rooms and open-access areas.
	Establish the vulnerability management practice and consider making this a joint effort with ABC Systems.
Staff security	Document clear procedures and reporting mechanisms for incident identification and reporting.
	Immediately provide a "call list" of whom to contact and under what circumstances.
	Ensure dissemination of procedures and "call list" to lowest operator level, and conduct periodic incident exercises to verify compliance.
	Incident management is not currently defined. Address this high-vulnerability area immediately. Establish clear policy and guidance for the authority to terminate use, seize equipment, and notify chain of command and law enforcement agencies, and for the authority to disable accounts.
Issues	While the management team is a logical first place for all of these strategies to be considered, it may not be the best group to actually accomplish these tasks. Some consideration is needed to determine the best way to distribute responsibility without losing sight of the overall plan.

A.2.1 Near-Term Action Items

In addition to the protection strategy, we also recommend several short-term action items. Table A-2 summarizes the action items identified during the evaluation.

TABLE A-2 Action List for MedSite

Action List	
Action Item	*Information*
• Look for vulnerabilities in selected components of all the key classes of components. • Analyze the results of the new vulnerability evaluations and prioritize the vulnerabilities to determine immediate, mid-term, and long-range goals (e.g., standard policy for password changes for all systems). • Analyze proposed solutions from both systems and operators' perspectives.	*Responsibility:* IT and ABC Systems *Completion date:* within the next 30 days *Required management actions:* Address budget and staffing concerns to complete actions
• Develop a pocket card for administrators to clearly identify other administrators and their capabilities, the points of contact, wiring diagram of administrators, and program oversight (e.g., "X controls virus management"). • Update and distribute annually. • Use as a part of administrators in-processing.	*Responsibility:* management team *Completion date:* within the next 90 days *Required management actions:* none
• Determine how and where PDAs are linking into the systems. Coordinate with ABC Systems and the physicians who have begun using PDAs.	*Responsibility:* management team, IT, and ABC Systems *Completion date:* within the next 120 days *Required management actions:* none
• Coordinate a physical security audit or test relative to the security of the paper medical records, particularly access to the Records Room during regular and off-hours.	*Responsibility:* management team *Completion date:* within the next 90 days *Required management actions:* none

A.3 Risks and Mitigation Plans for Critical Assets

As a result of conducting the OCTAVE Method, we identified five assets that are critical to the survival and success of MedSite. We then defined the risks to these assets and developed mitigation plans to address these risks. The assets we identified as being the most critical, and our rationale for selecting them, are listed in Table A-3.

For each critical asset, we provide the following information in this report:

• Security requirements
• Areas of concern

TABLE A-3 MedSite's Critical Assets

Critical Asset	Rationale for Selection
Paper medical records	Number one documentation source
Personal computers	Almost complete worker dependency on PCs, the workstations everyone uses to access the information assets that are considered critical: PIDS and the other databases, email, the Internet, and so on
PIDS: Patient Information Data System	98 percent dependency for delivering patient care
ABC Systems	Almost complete dependency on them for PIDS, because they control the network
ECDS: Emergency Care Data System	Case history, encounter, and billing information (selected as a representative of the other 32 or 33 other systems used by MedSite)

- Risk impact descriptions
- Risk profile and mitigation plans

A.3.1 Paper Medical Records

Paper medical records are the official record of MedSite's patients' medical histories. While MedSite now stores and maintains much of its medical-related information on PIDS and other systems, providers still rely on paper medical records during all patient encounters. The security requirements for the paper medical records are defined in Table A-4. Integrity and availability are considered to be the most important security requirements for paper medical records.

Table A-5 summarizes the areas of concern for medical records organized by threat type.

TABLE A-4 Security Requirements for Paper Medical Records

Paper Medical Records: Security Requirements
Integrity: Records must be kept accurate and complete and should be modified only by those with the appropriate authority.
Availability: Access to records is required 24/7. They must be available for patient encounters.
Confidentiality: Information should be kept confidential (restricted to those with "need to know"); Privacy Act.

TABLE A-5 Areas of Concern for Paper Medical Records

Threat Type	Area of Concern for Paper Medical Records	Outcome of Concern
Human actors using physical access	Medical records are left where they shouldn't be (in offices and labs).	Disclosure
	Data in medical records (e.g., physician SSN, credentials) could be used by someone to "forge" a prescription.	Disclosure
	Misfiling paperwork could allow unauthorized personnel to view another's records.	Disclosure
	Too many people are entering the wrong data, resulting in incorrect records, and/or there may be multiple files and records for an individual.	Disclosure
	Staff personnel could view medical records in an unauthorized or inappropriate manner.	Disclosure
	Information is deliberately released to outside personnel.	Disclosure
	Medical reports are signed out to patients, so anyone can potentially view, alter, or lose records.	Disclosure Loss/destruction Modification
	Medical records could be signed out to the wrong person.	Disclosure
	Accidental problems with data entry can affect the integrity of information.	Modification
	Accidental mishandling by staff can lead to the destruction of physical medical records.	Destruction/loss
	Records are under "loose" control. There is no process to stop the patient from taking or modifying them and no mechanism to copy and release just what's needed. Integrity of record is compromised.	Loss/destruction Modification
	Patients could get poor-quality care or die if contradictory medications are prescribed or allergies are not accounted for.	Modification Loss/destruction Interruption
	Loss of paper record can mean permanent loss of critical information.	Loss/destruction
Other problems	Configuration of facilities/layout allows inappropriate viewing of medical records.	Disclosure
	Roof leaks, water, fire, etc., could destroy the physical medical records.	Loss/destruction
	Hurricane evacuation procedures require movement of assets off the first floor of all facilities due to flooding concerns.	Interruption

We defined the specific impact on the organization of disclosure, modification, loss or destruction, and unavailability of paper medical records. We then evaluated these various impacts against a set of evaluation criteria (defined in Section 4) that define what constitutes a high, medium, and low impact for MedSite. The types of impact related to paper medical records are shown in Table A-6.

The risk profile for paper medical records is shown in Figures A-1 and A-2. There are two trees in the risk profile for paper medical records, each with a specific mitigation plan. Because network access and system problems do not affect

TABLE A-6 Types of Impact and Impact Values for Paper Medical Records

Outcome	Impact Description	Impact Values
Disclosure	Loss of official accreditation.	High
	Health of patients could be affected by lack of continuity of care with PCM (primary care manager).	High
	Erratic visits to ER could result in incomplete diagnosis/prognosis and improper treatment.	High
	Patient with cancer and misfiled/nonfiled pathology report and no notification could file lawsuit against MedSite.	High
	Loss of credibility from our patients could ultimately result in patients seeking care from another source.	Medium
	Patient could maintain medical record at home due to lack of trust, and medical treatment could be incomplete in MedSite.	Medium
	Privacy violations can result in disclosure of medical treatment to unwanted sources, which could have negative results on patients, for example, divorce, loss of job, etc.	Medium
Modification	Deliberate modification could result in wrong diagnosis/treatment or death.	High
	Patients will seek care from another source.	Medium
	Loss of credibility with patients and the public.	Low
Loss/destruction	Loss of medical records would result in repeat of medical evaluations (lab, x-ray, etc.) for treatment, undue burden on patient, increased spending by MedSite, and decreased credibility.	Medium
Interruption	Lack of preplanning for known natural disasters would result in inability to provide services and a lack of faith in MedSite.	Medium

the paper records, trees for these threat categories are not included in the risk profile.

1. Human actors using physical access (Figure A-1)
2. Other problems (Figure A-2)

A.3.2 Personal Computers

Personal computers are used to access PIDS and other systems. Our definition of personal computers includes all office, treatment room, and lab computers, as well as the laptops used by some physicians. The security requirements for personal computers are defined in the Table A-7. Availability is considered to be the most important security requirement.

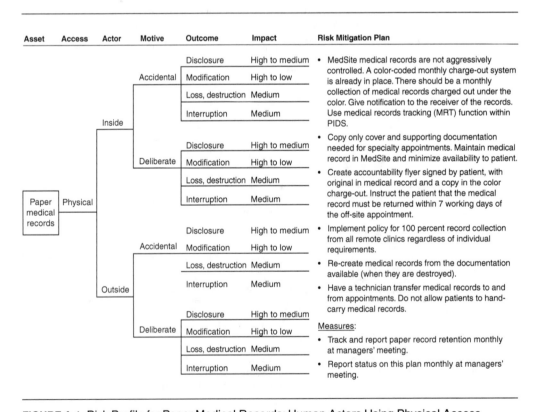

FIGURE A-1 Risk Profile for Paper Medical Records: Human Actors Using Physical Access

Asset	Actor	Outcome	Impact	Risk Mitigation Plan
Paper medical records	natural disasters (nor'easters, floods, fire)	Disclosure		• Update medical record disaster recovery plan. Specify removal procedures during nor'easters or inclement weather for outlying buildings as well as the main hospital.
		Modification	High to low	
		Loss, destruction	Medium	
		Interruption	Medium	
	facility configuration	Disclosure	High to medium	• As with PIDS, add security concerns to MedSite building committee meeting next quarter to see if anything can be done about reconfiguring workspace.
		Modification		
		Loss, destruction		Measures:
		Interruption		• Track and report paper record retention monthly at managers' meeting.
				• Report status on this plan monthly at managers' meeting.

FIGURE A-2 Risk Profile for Paper Medical Records: Other Problems

Evaluation participants did not consider personal computers to be an important asset. Thus, no areas of concern were recorded for personal computers. (Note: After reviewing all information, the analysis team concluded that personal computers were a critical asset to MedSite.)

We defined specific types of impact on the organization resulting from disclosure, modification, loss or destruction, and unavailability of information on personal computers. We then evaluated these against a set of evaluation criteria (defined in Section 4) that define what constitutes a high, medium, and low impact for MedSite. The types of impact related to personal computers are shown in Table A-8.

TABLE A-7 Security Requirements for Personal Computers

Personal Computers: Security Requirements
Availability: Computer assets should be available 24/7.
Confidentiality: Patient information and Privacy Act information stored on PCs should be confidential.
Integrity: Software should be uniform and current. Information should be complete and accurate.
Other: All PCs should be password protected. Incident reporting procedures should be established.

TABLE A-8 Types of Impact and Impact Values for Personal Computers

Outcome	Impact Description	Impact Values
Disclosure	Personal computers left unattended offer a huge potential for violation of Privacy Act. Access, either deliberate or unintentional, is readily available. Patients who feel their privacy is not protected will seek care from other sources. It depends on what information is violated and to whom it is disclosed.	Medium
Modification	Modification of software could result in lost staff time, lost information, incorrect patient information, lost billing, etc.	High
Loss/destruction	Destruction or loss of the PCs results in failure to support our business.	High
Interruption	Any lengthy interruption of access to PCs results in our inability to perform our work.	High

The risk profile for personal computers is shown in Figures A-3 through A-6. There are four trees in the risk profile, each with a specific mitigation plan.

- Human actors using network access (Figure A-3)
- Human actors using physical access (Figure A-4)
- System problems (Figure A-5)
- Other problems (Figure A-6)

A.3.3 PIDS

PIDS is essential to the operation of MedSite. MedSite's operations are dependent on the information provided by this system. The security requirements for PIDS are defined in Table A-9. Availability is considered the most important security requirement.

TABLE A-9 Security Requirements for PIDS

PIDS: Security Requirements
Availability: Access to information is required 24/7; it must be available for patient encounters. We need to have an adequate number of terminals for data entry operators.
Confidentiality: Information should be kept confidential (restricted to those with "need to know"). Information is subject to the Privacy Act.
Integrity: Records must be kept accurate and complete. All information should be available for the patient encounter. Only authorized users should be allowed to modify information.

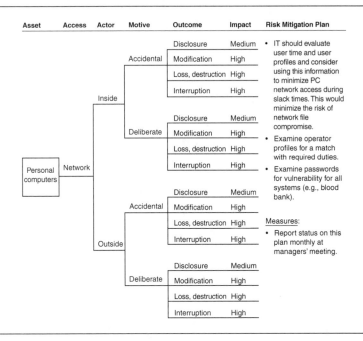

FIGURE A-3 Risk Profile for Personal Computers: Human Actors Using Network Access

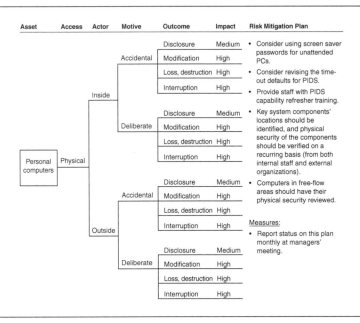

FIGURE A-4 Risk Profile for Personal Computers: Human Actors Using Physical Access

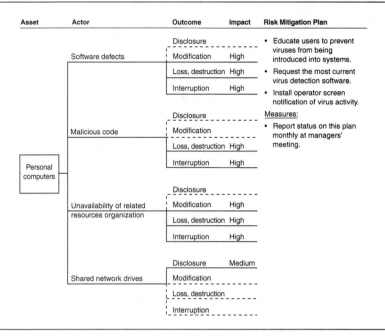

Asset	Actor	Outcome	Impact	Risk Mitigation Plan
	Software defects	Disclosure		• Educate users to prevent viruses from being introduced into systems.
		Modification	High	
		Loss, destruction	High	• Request the most current virus detection software.
		Interruption	High	• Install operator screen notification of virus activity.
	Malicious code	Disclosure		Measures:
		Modification		• Report status on this plan monthly at managers' meeting.
		Loss, destruction	High	
		Interruption	High	
Personal computers	Unavailability of related resources organization	Disclosure		
		Modification	High	
		Loss, destruction	High	
		Interruption	High	
	Shared network drives	Disclosure	Medium	
		Modification		
		Loss, destruction		
		Interruption		

FIGURE A-5 Risk Profile for Personal Computers: System Problems

Asset	Actor	Outcome	Impact	Risk Mitigation Plan
	Power supply problems	Disclosure		• Update PC disaster recovery plan (for nor'easters, lightning strikes, etc.). Include outlying buildings in the plan.
		Modification		
		Loss, destruction	High	
		Interruption	High	
	Telecommunications problems or unavailability	Disclosure		Measures:
		Modification		• Report status on this plan monthly at managers' meeting.
		Loss, destruction	High	
		Interruption	High	
Personal computers	ABC Systems support not available	Disclosure		
		Modification		
		Loss, destruction	High	
		Interruption	High	
	Misuse of Internet bogging down system	Disclosure		
		Modification		
		Loss, destruction	High	
		Interruption	High	
	Natural disasters (e.g., nor'easters, floods fire)	Disclosure		
		Modification		
		Loss, destruction	High	
		Interruption	High	

Note: Staff members use massive mailing lists or misuse the Internet and bog down the systems. The network has crashed a few times from this behavior.

FIGURE A-6 Risk Profile for Personal Computers: Other Problems

Table A-10 summarizes the areas of concern for PIDS organized by threat type.

We defined specific types of impact on the organization resulting from disclosure, modification, loss or destruction, and unavailability of information on

TABLE A-10 Areas of Concern for PIDS

Threat Type	Area of Concern for PIDS	Outcome
Human actors using network access	Personnel access information that they are not authorized to use; access is used inappropriately, or legitimately accessed information is distributed inappropriately.	Disclosure
	Too many people have access to too much information. Role-based access builds over time and replacements inherit all of those access privileges.	Disclosure
	Too many people are entering the wrong data, resulting in incorrect records, and/or multiple files and records for an individual.	Disclosure
	Staff could intentionally enter erroneous data into PIDS.	Disclosure Modification
	The risk of an outside intrusion into PIDS is much higher than newer systems because of the need to bypass the firewall.	Disclosure Modification
	Accidental loss of any patient information is a concern.	Loss/destruction
	Patient could get poor-quality care or die if contradictory medications are prescribed or allergies are not accounted for.	Modification Loss/destruction Interruption
	Doctors and staff email sensitive patient information on an insecure LAN.	Disclosure
	PIDS can be attacked from outside.	Disclosure Modification
	Shared network drives contain sensitive patient and personnel information.	Disclosure
	Inherent flaws and vulnerabilities in critical applications could exploited.	Modification Destruction/loss
Human actors using physical access	Doctors leave PIDS screens on after they have left treatment rooms. Patients and others could gain access. Passwords, logout, time-out, and screen savers are inconsistently used.	Disclosure
	Doctors and staff often leave terminals/PCs unattended in exam rooms, introducing the possibility of unauthorized access.	Disclosure

(continued)

TABLE A-10 Areas of Concern for PIDS (*continued*)

Threat Type	Area of Concern for PIDS	Outcome
System problems	PIDS is not compatible with newer systems, leading to system crashes.	Interruption
	Connectivity is an issue, including problems with availability of and access to PIDS. The uptime requirement in the contract is for the servers, not for our connectivity.	Interruption
	There are networking/connectivity issues. Access to PIDS is often restricted due to system crashes.	Interruption
	Instability of the local area network affects access to numerous systems and creates a backlog.	Interruption
Other problems	It's difficult to find and retain qualified personnel to help maintain PIDS.	Interruption
	Access to the majority of systems is supported by ABC Systems. They are responsible for hardware and software maintenance. We're concerned about our lack of control.	Interruption
	ABC Systems fails to recognize the importance of the Internet to the medical staff to access current best practice information.	Interruption
	Power outages, floods, and other external events can lead to a denial of access to PIDS. This essentially shuts the hospital down.	Interruption
	ABC Systems has many customers. They do not recognize the importance of the hospital. Priorities of the hospital are not understood.	Interruption
	The configuration of facilities/layout allows inappropriate viewing of systems and medical records by patients and visitors.	Disclosure
	Doctors and staff discuss patient issues and information in public areas.	Disclosure
	Hurricane evacuation procedures require removal of assets from the first floor of all facilities due to flooding concerns.	Interruption

PIDS. We then evaluated these against a set of evaluation criteria (defined in Section 4) that define what constitutes a high, medium, and low impact for MedSite. The types of impact related to PIDS are shown in Table A-11.

The risk profile for PIDS is shown in Figures A-7 through A-10. There are four trees in the risk profile, each with a specific mitigation plan.

TABLE A-11 Types of Impact and Impact Values for PIDS

Outcome	Impact Description	Impact Values
Disclosure	Failure to safeguard privacy would result in loss of credibility of medical treatment facility/organization.	Medium
Modification	Incorrect modifications could affect appointments and productivity.	Medium
	Work could be affected if modifications were made and we were unable to determine the extent easily. Verification of patient information would be tedious.	Medium
	Patient's life and health could be affected due to improper changes to treatment plans or medical records.	High
	Medical treatment facility could lose credibility. Loss of credibility could cause patients to seek care from another source.	Medium
Loss/destruction	The information in PIDS would be nearly impossible to reconstruct in a timely manner. Just trying to verify and reenter what was lost between the last backup and the present would take all our time and resources.	High
Interruption	An interruption could have a direct impact on our role in this community. We are rendered virtually helpless without PIDS capability. We have become computer-dependent in order to function.	High
	Our organization cannot deliver effective or efficient health care without PIDS.	High

- Human actors using network access (Figure A-7)
- Human actors using physical access (Figure A-8)
- System problems (Figure A-9)
- Other problems (Figure A-10)

A.3.4 ABC Systems

ABC Systems is responsible for the maintenance of PIDS and some of the other systems we have at MedSite. We rely on them to keep PIDS up and running. Because we depend on PIDS, we also depend on the services provided by ABC Systems. The security requirements at ABC Systems are defined in Table A-12. Availability is the most important security requirement. Note that confidentiality does not apply.

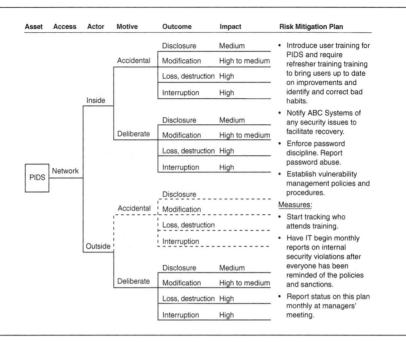

FIGURE A-7 Risk Profile for PIDS: Human Actors Using Network Access

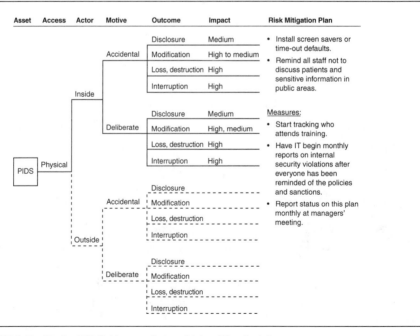

FIGURE A-8 Risk Profile for PIDS: Human Actors Using Physical Access

Asset	Actor	Outcome	Impact	Risk Mitigation Plan
PIDS	Software defects	Disclosure		• Systems continue to have connectivity problems. We cannot aggressively narrow down the problem source with erratic reporting. Revise policies to have daily report from our help desk/maintenance personnel to ABC Systems either to indicate that there are no problems or to list specific problems. Work out resolution in conjunction with ABC Systems using hard data.
		Modification		
		Loss, destruction	High	
		Interruption	High	
	Viruses	Disclosure		
		Modification	High to medium	• Upgrade system hardware and software components. Reconfigure for optimum user support.
		Loss, destruction	High	
		Interruption	High	• Update contingency plans.
	System crashes	Disclosure		Measures:
		Modification		• Start tracking who attends training.
		Loss, destruction		• Have IT begin monthly reports on internal security violations after everyone has been reminded of the policies and sanctions.
		Interruption	High	
	Telecommunications problems or unavailability	Disclosure		
		Modification		
		Loss, destruction		• Report status on this plan monthly at managers' meeting.
		Interruption	High	

FIGURE A-9 Risk Profile for PIDS: System Problems

Asset	Actor	Outcome	Impact	Risk Mitigation Plan
PIDS	Power supply problems	Disclosure		• Update contingency plans to include addressing power supply problems.
		Modification		
		Loss, destruction		• Enhance IT staff training in secure configuration and maintenance of systems and networks.
		Interruption	High	
	Lack of trained maintenance personnel	Disclosure		• Invite ABC Systems representatives to review the results of this evaluation and open a dialog.
		Modification		
		Loss, destruction		
		Interruption	High	• Update hardware and software maintenance procedures.
	ABC Systems is not familiar with our needs	Disclosure		• Add security concerns to MedSite building committee meeting next quarter to see if anything can be done about reconfiguring workspace.
		Modification		
		Loss, destruction		
		Interruption	High	Measures:
	Natural disasters (e.g., nor'easters, flood, fire)	Disclosure		• Contingency plans are updated and tested.
		Modification		• Enhanced IT training is available.
		Loss, destruction	High	
		Interruption	High	• Meeting with ABC systems is scheduled and held.
	Lack of control over hardware and software	Disclosure		• Hardware and software maintenance procedures are updated.
		Modification		
		Loss, destruction		• Security concerns have been addressed at next quarter's MedSite building committee meeting.
		Interruption	High	
	Facility configuration	Disclosure	Medium	• Report status on this plan monthly at managers' meeting.
		Modification		
		Loss, destruction		
		Interruption		

FIGURE A-10 Risk Profile for PIDS: Other Problems

Evaluation participants did not identify specific areas of concern for ABC Systems. The analysis team constructed the threat profile during the process 4 workshop.

We defined the specific types of impact on the organization resulting from modification and unavailability of the service provided by ABC Systems. We then evaluated these against a set of evaluation criteria (defined in Section 4) that define what constitutes a high, medium, and low impact for MedSite. The types of impact related to PIDS are shown in Table A-13.

The risk profile for ABC Systems is shown in Figure A-11. There is only one tree in the risk profile:

- Other problems (Figure A-11)

A.3.5 ECDS

The Emergency Care Data System (ECDS) is essential to the efficient operation of emergency rooms. It is also representative of systems we have that are linked to PIDS but are maintained by the local staff. ECDS is used to maintain and update

TABLE A-12 Security Requirements for ABC Systems

ABC Systems: Security Requirements
Availability: They must be available 24/7 to ensure that we are operational 24/7.
Integrity: We require a consistent level of competence and training from ABC Systems personnel.
Confidentiality: N/A

TABLE A-13 Types of Impact and Impact Values for ABC Systems

Outcome	Impact Description	Impact Values
Loss/destruction	Destruction at ABC Systems' site would directly impact our effectiveness.	High
	Loss of knowledgeable personnel at ABC Systems would severely affect their quality of service to us.	High
Interruption	Lengthy interruption of support from ABC Systems could lead to the system being down or inaccessible for a long time, resulting in a direct impact on our day-to-day operations.	Medium

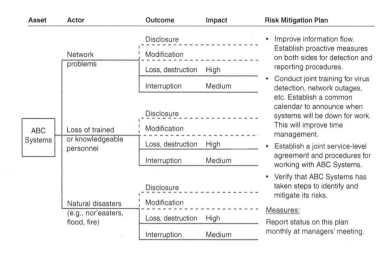

FIGURE A-11 Risk Profile for ABC Systems: Other Problems

patient records and billing for emergency cases, but it is not used during actual emergencies. The security requirements for ECDS are defined in Table A-14. Integrity and confidentiality are considered the most important security requirements.

Table A-15 summarizes the areas of concern for PIDS organized by threat type.

We defined specific impacts on the organization resulting from disclosure, modification, loss or destruction, and unavailability of information on ECDS. We then evaluated these impacts against a set of evaluation criteria (defined in Section 4) that define what constitutes a high, medium, and low impact for MedSite. The types of impact related to PIDS are shown in Table A-16.

TABLE A-14 Security Requirements for ECDS

ECDS: Security Requirements
Integrity: All information should be accurate and complete; this is essential for trend analysis and accounting.
Confidentiality: Information should be kept confidential (restricted to those with "need to know"); Privacy Act.
Availability: It must be available at the end of the day of the patient encounter.

TABLE A-15 Areas of Concern for ECDS

Threat Type	Area of Concern for ECDS	Outcome
Human actors using network access	Too many people are entering the wrong data, resulting in incorrect records, and/or there may be multiple files and records for an individual.	Disclosure
	Internet connectivity is lost.	Interruption
	Systems are susceptible to malicious code and virus activity (in part due to the location/configuration of the firewall).	Modification Loss/destruction Interruption
	Ultimate impact is on the quality of care. Patient could die if contradictory medications are prescribed or allergies are not accounted for.	Modification Loss/destruction Interruption
Other problems	ABC Systems does not recognize the importance of the hospital/health care organization. Priorities of the hospital are not understood.	Interruption

The risk profile for ECDS is shown in Figures A-12 through A-15. There are four trees in the risk profile, each with a specific mitigation plan. We also checked for consistency between the risk profiles for PIDS and ECDS and identified several threats previously not identified for ECDS.

- Human actors using network access (Figure A-12)
- Human actors using physical access (Figure A-13)
- System problems (Figure A-14)
- Other problems (Figure A-15)

TABLE A-16 Types of Impact and Impact Values for ECDS

Outcome	Impact Description	Impact Values
Disclosure	Privacy Act violation would occur if information were disclosed.	Medium
	Customer confidence would be affected by disclosure.	Medium
Modification	Heavy workload in facility leads to inadvertent modification and inaccurate data. Need to correct data affects manpower, resources, and budgeting.	Low
Interruption	Data entry delays following interruption of access would not be difficult to overcome, but doing so would take some clerical support time.	Low
Loss/destruction	Loss of information would result in duplication of effort to capture the data.	Low

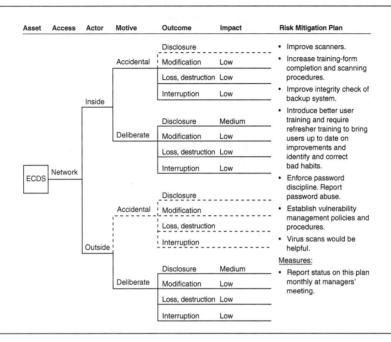

FIGURE A-12 Risk Profile for ECDS: Human Actors Using Network Access

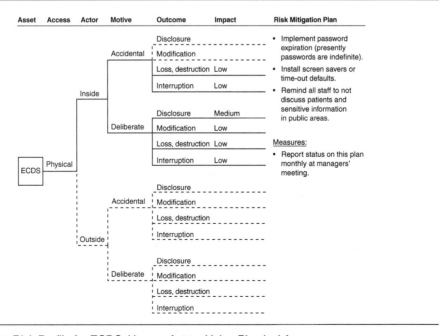

FIGURE A-13 Risk Profile for ECDS: Human Actors Using Physical Access

Asset	Actor	Outcome	Impact	Risk Mitigation Plan
ECDS	Software defects	Disclosure		• Update contingency plans.
		Modification		
		Loss, destruction	Low	Measures:
		Interruption	Low	• Report status on this plan monthly at managers' meeting.
	Malicious code	Disclosure		
		Modification	Low	
		Loss, destruction	Low	
		Interruption	Low	
	System crashes	Disclosure		
		Modification		
		Loss, destruction	Low	
		Interruption	Low	
	LAN instability	Disclosure		
		Modification		
		Loss, destruction	Low	
		Interruption	Low	

FIGURE A-14 Risk Profile for ECDS: System Problems

Asset	Actor	Outcome	Impact	Risk Mitigation Plan
ECDS	Power supply problems	Disclosure		• Add security concerns to MedSite building committee meeting next quarter to see if anything can be done about reconfiguring workspace.
		Modification		
		Loss, destruction	Low	
		Interruption	Low	
	Telecommunications problems or unavailability	Disclosure		
		Modification		Measures:
		Loss, destruction	Low	• Report status on this plan monthly at managers' meeting.
		Interruption	Low	
	ABC Systems not familiar with our needs	Disclosure		
		Modification		
		Loss, destruction	Low	
		Interruption	Low	
	Natural disasters (e.g., nor'easters, flood, fire)	Disclosure		
		Modification		
		Loss, destruction	Low	
		Interruption	Low	
	Lack of control over hardware and software	Disclosure		
		Modification		
		Loss, destruction	Low	
		Interruption	Low	
	Facility configuration	Disclosure	Medium	
		Modification		
		Loss, destruction		
		Interruption		

FIGURE A-15 Risk Profile for ECDS: Other Problems

A.4 Technology Vulnerability Evaluation Results and Recommended Actions

Once we identified the critical assets and the threats to those assets, we identified key infrastructure components to evaluate for technology vulnerabilities as part of phase 2 of the OCTAVE Method. This section summarizes our results and specific recommendations based on the results of phase 2. The summary provides a snapshot of how MedSite is managing its technology vulnerabilities.

Figure A-16 shows a high-level map of our computing infrastructure. As a part of the OCTAVE Method, we identified systems of interest for each critical asset and looked at access paths to identify key classes of components. From this, we selected specific instances of the key classes to evaluate for technology vulnerabilities.

We examined network access paths for PIDS, ECDS, and personal computers. Figure A-17 shows the main access routes for accessing PIDS and highlights the key components we selected for the vulnerability evaluation. The network access paths for ECDS are similar; however, ECDS is not accessible from home PCs.

Although paper records do not have a network access path, printed email is sometimes included in paper records, as are printouts from systems such as PIDS. We wanted to evaluate the PDAs and the local email server, but at this point we could not determine how the PDAs used by the physicians were linking into the system. A representative from ABC Systems was not available to help, so this action should be dealt with as soon as possible.

Note that we did not conduct a physical vulnerability evaluation of Med-Site; that was considered outside our scope of responsibility. However, we do recommend that a physical security audit or evaluation be conducted to verify that access to physical records is sufficient. Information that we gathered during the OCTAVE Method leads us to believe that paper medical records (stored in the Records Retention room) are physically vulnerable.

Key Components Per Asset

Table A-17 illustrates the system(s) of interest and key classes of components for each of the critical assets. There was some commonality among the key classes of components to be evaluated.

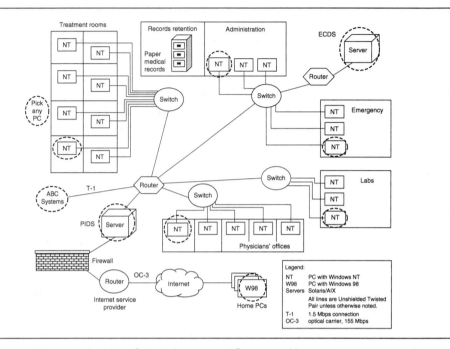

FIGURE A-16 Infrastructure Map, Critical Assets, and Systems of Interest

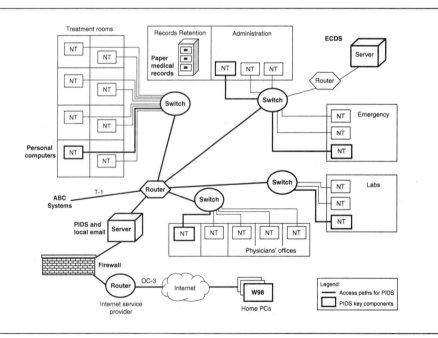

FIGURE A-17 Access Paths and Key Classes of Components for PIDS

TABLE A-17 Systems of Interest and Key Classes of Components

Critical Asset	System(s) of Interest	Key Classes of Components
PIDS	PIDS is its own system of interest.	• Servers • Networking components • Security components • Desktop workstations • Home computers
ECDS	ECDS is its own system of interest.	• Servers • Networking components • Security components • Desktop workstations
Personal Computers	Personal computers are themselves the system of interest. (They are also a subsystem of the other systems such as PIDS and ECDS.)	• Servers • Networking components • Security components • Desktop workstations • Home computers

Vulnerability Evaluation Approaches and Tools

Table A-18 shows specific components that were selected for the technology vulnerability evaluation, as well as the vulnerability evaluation approach for each component.

Evaluation Tools Results

Table A-19 summarizes the results of the technology vulnerability evaluation. Table A-20 provides the definitions for severity levels used in Table A-19.

Actions and Recommendations

During phase 2, we recorded recommendations and actions to consider based on the results of the technology vulnerability evaluation. Table A-21 shows those recommendations.

TABLE A-18 Infrastructure Components Examined

Key Component	IP Addresses[1]	Vulnerability Evaluation Approach	Tool(s)[2]	Rationale
Office PCs	----------------------- ----------------------- -----------------------	ABC Systems personnel will be responsible for running all of the tools. MedSite's IT personnel will be present and will also get some on-the-job training	Vulnerability scanner— Vulnerabilities-R-Found, version 6.73	These are common tools used at ABC Systems. Our IT personnel do not have the knowledge to run them but want to learn.
Home PCs	-----------------------			
Firewall	---------------------		Network/Internet level tool— Improve-UR-Network, version 4.8	
PIDS server	-----------------------			
ECDS server	-----------------------			
Routers	----------------------- -----------------------			

---

1. Real IP addresses are not supplied in this table.
2. These are fictitious tools.

TABLE A-19 Technology Vulnerability Evaluation Results

Identified Components	Selected Component/ IP Address(es)	Tool/Method/ Approach	Vulnerability Summary
PIDS client PCs— Windows 98	----------------------	Vulnerabilities-R-Found, v. 6.73	3 medium 20 low
	----------------------	Vulnerabilities-R-Found, v. 6.73	3 medium 22 low
	----------------------	Vulnerabilities-R-Found, v. 6.73	3 medium 22 low
Home PCs			N—could not identify one whose owner was willing to allow the scan
Firewall	----------------------	Improve-UR-Network, v.4.8	1 medium 5 low
PIDS and mail server	----------------------	Improve-UR-Network, v.4.8	3 high 21 medium 43 low
ECDS server	----------------------	Improve-UR-Network, v.4.8	9 medium 15 low
Router 1	----------------------	Improve-UR-Network, v.4.8	3 low
Router 2	----------------------	Improve-UR-Network, v.4.8	3 low

TABLE A-20 Severity Levels

Vulnerability Severity Level	Meaning
High-severity vulnerabilities	Must be fixed immediately (within the next week)
Medium-severity vulnerabilities	Must be fixed soon (within 1 month)
Low-severity vulnerabilities	May be fixed later

TABLE A-21 Phase 2 Recommendations

Actions and Recommendations for Addressing Technology Vulnerabilities
Determine how and where PDAs are linking into the systems. Coordinate with ABC Systems and the physicians who have begun using PDAs. Handle after completion of OCTAVE.
Only a few of the vulnerabilities were of high severity. These will be fixed immediately by ABC Systems. However, all of the high-severity vulnerabilities were on the PIDS server, and that is some cause for concern, given the criticality of PIDS.
Most of the vulnerabilities were considered to be of medium severity. But the combination of many of them could result in either extensive interruption of access to PIDS or the loss/destruction of data on PIDS. This possibility should be considered when the risks and mitigation plans are being looked at in processes 7 and 8. The analysis team needs to consider the combined effects of the medium-severity vulnerabilities on the key components for PIDS, which is also the email server. Use as input to mitigation/protection strategy planning.
The same vulnerabilities show up on all of the PCs, which may mean a common configuration problem. It could also mean that the MedSite IT personnel and ABC Systems are not able to keep up with the latest revisions. Further investigation into the process IT uses to set up and maintain PCs is needed to determine whether the different configurations are a legacy or whether unapproved changes are being made.
The analysis team and ABC Systems also came to the conclusion that vulnerability management isn't being well executed, due to the high-severity vulnerabilities found on the PIDS server. ABC Systems personnel admitted they were not always able to run vulnerability scanners, but they were surprised at the number of high- and medium-severity vulnerabilities that were found. They thought the MedSite IT staff members were fixing these as soon as they were found. IT staff admitted that they did not know what to do with the vulnerability reports. Vulnerability management must be investigated and the weaknesses in procedure corrected. A plan will be needed to increase the knowledge and skills of IT and to improve the formality of ABC Systems' procedures.
Review policies for assessing home PCs.

A.5 Additional Information

Additional information is provided in the following sections:

5.1 Risk Impact Evaluation Criteria. These are the criteria we used to evaluate the impact of risks on critical assets.

5.2 Other Assets. This list includes all of the assets identified as important during processes 1 to 3 of the OCTAVE Method.

5.3 Security Practice Survey Results. These are a complete set of results from the security practice surveys and follow-up discussions completed during processes 1 to 3 of the OCTAVE Method.

A.5.1 Risk Impact Evaluation Criteria

We defined the impact evaluation criteria and then evaluated each impact against those criteria. We recommend that these evaluation criteria, shown in Table A-22, become a standard for MedSite. We include criteria for the following areas:

- Reputation/customer confidence
- Life/health of customers
- Productivity
- Fines/legal penalties
- Finances
- Other (facilities)

TABLE A-22 Evaluation Criteria

Criteria for Evaluating Risk Impacts			
Impact Area	**High**	**Medium**	**Low**
Reputation/ customer confidence	• Reputation irrevocably destroyed or damaged • Loss of rating or accreditation by review organizations • More than 30 percent drop in customers due to loss of confidence	• Reputation damaged; some effort and expense required to recover • Reduction or warning of reduction of rating or accreditation by authorizing organizations • Drop in customers of 10 to 30 percent due to loss of confidence • Public violations of Privacy Act: (1) disclosure to personnel within the medical treatment facility without the need to know; (2) anyone who violates the Privacy Act and reveals sensitive medical information • Patient driven to seek care from another source	• Reputation minimally affected; little or no effort or expense required to recover • No change in rating or accreditation by authorizing organizations • Less than 10 percent drop in customers due to loss of confidence • Nonpublic violation of Privacy Act (disclosure to personnel within the medical treatment facility with a need to know— trusted agent)

(continued)

TABLE A-22 Evaluation Criteria (*continued*)

Criteria for Evaluating Risk Impacts			
Impact Area	**High**	**Medium**	**Low**
Life/health of customers	• Loss of customer life • Permanent impairment of one or more significant aspects of customer's health (e.g., loss of use of one or more limbs, blindness, brain damage) • Inability to provide patient care for more than a week • Safety violated	• Customer life threatened but recoverable with additional treatment • Temporary or recoverable impairment of customer's health (e.g., recovering use of limbs through physical therapy) • Inability to provide patient care for one to two days • Safety affected	• No loss or significant threat to customer life • Minimal, immediately treatable degradation in customer health with recovery within four days • Continuity of care requiring increased communication between providers at different facilities • Safety questioned
Productivity	• Physicians and/or nursing staff unable to perform critical job aspects for two or more days (e.g., no surgery, physical therapy, specialized patient care) • Increase in work hours of 40 percent or more required of at least 10 percent of general staff for >two days (e.g., manual re-creation of treatment records or manual correlation of lab results and plans) • Irrecoverable loss of patient records/information	• Physicians and/or nursing staff work increased by 10 to 40 percent for one day (e.g., locating paper records, verifying all decisions verbally); inability to access test or lab results • Increases in general staff work of 10 to 40 percent for one day (e.g., duplicating written records, re-creating patient billing records, retrieving and verifying backup data) • Inefficient continuity of care; delays while recovering misplaced information	• Physicians and/or nursing staff inconvenienced for less than a day but no measurable increase in work effort required (e.g., appointments delayed by hours, lab to be called for results) • General staff inconvenienced for less than a day but no measurable increase in work effort required
Fines/legal penalties	• Fines of greater than $100,000 levied • One or more nonfrivolous lawsuits of more than $3 million filed by customers	• Fines of $10,000 to $100,000 levied • One or more nonfrivolous lawsuits between $250,000 and $3 million filed by customers	• No fine or a fine of less than $10,000 levied • Lawsuits of less than $250,000 or frivolous lawsuit (95 percent probability of defeat) filed by customer

(*continued*)

TABLE A-22 Evaluation Criteria (*continued*)

Criteria for Evaluating Risk Impacts			
Impact Area	High	Medium	Low
Fines/legal penalties (*continued*)	• High-profile, in-depth investigation into organizational practices initiated by government or other investigative organization	• Information or records (low-profile) requested by government or other investigative organization	• No queries from government or other investigative organizations
Finances	• Yearly operational costs up 15 percent (e.g., using temps for records recovery, adding software to deter further intrusions) • Revenue loss of 20 percent yearly (e.g., relocating 20 percent of patients to other sites due to power loss) • Onetime financial cost >$1 million (e.g., replacing system damaged by water, hiring 25 temps to reenter records) • Irredeemable errors in funding and personnel	• Yearly operational costs up 2 to 15 percent (e.g., hiring temps for three months to hand-carry labor results several times a day) • Revenue loss of 5 to 20 percent yearly (e.g., delaying profitable surgeries due to file loss and recovery) • Onetime financial cost of $25,000 to $1 million (e.g., adding a server and reallocating assets) • Partially redeemable errors in funding and personnel	• Increase of less than 2 percent in operating costs (e.g., one week of overtime for four staff members to document changes in treatment plans) • Revenue loss of <5 percent yearly (e.g., $50,000 research funds if no remote university access) • Onetime financial cost of <$25,000 (e.g., retraining 20 staff members) • Inconvenient but redeemable errors in funding and personnel
Other (facilities)	• Loss of an entire facility or building due to fire • Patients harmed by falsely credentialed providers or medical staff	• Damage to a facility or building requiring temporary relocation of patients • Inability to verify credentials of providers or medical staff • Inability to track performance of facilities or providers accurately	• Loss of air conditioning for two weeks • Negligible impact on daily operations

A.5.2 Other Assets

The complete list of assets identified by personnel during processes 1 to 3 is shown in Table A-23. This list of assets highlights differences in opinion about what is important to MedSite. We recommend that any additional work with

TABLE A-23 Assets Grouped by Organizational Level

Organizational Level	Important Assets	Other Assets
Senior managers (process 1)	• Patient Information Data System (PIDS) • Paper medical records • Financial Record-Keeping System (FRKS) • Providers' credentials	• Emergency Care Data System (ECDS) • Email • Personnel management system • Internet connectivity • Medical Logistics System (MLS)
Operational area managers (process 2)	• Paper medical records • PIDS • ECDS	• Pharmacy system • Medical logistics system • Providers' credentials
Staff members (process 3)	• Paper medical records • PIDS • External relations • Email (PIDS and general)	• MLS • Internet access
IT staff members (process 3)	• ABC Systems • Internet connectivity • MedSite help desk • All servers	• Mr. Smith (a senior IT staff member) • Personal computers • 30+ functional systems

respect to documenting MedSite's information-related assets should start with this list.

A.5.3 Consolidated Survey Results

Tables A-24 through A-41 contain the following information:

- Security practice survey results
- Contextual security practices and organizational vulnerabilities

We organized all results according to strategic and organizational practice areas contained in the OCTAVE catalog of practices. The following list describes how to interpret the survey results:

- **Yes:** 75 percent or more of respondents answered that the practice is most likely used by the organization.
- **No:** 75 percent or more of respondents answered that the practice is most likely not used by the organization.
- **Unclear:** Based on the respondents' answers, it is not clear whether the practice is used by the organization.

Current Strategic Practices of MedSite

TABLE A-24 Security Awareness and Training

Security Awareness and Training: Survey Results				
Survey Statement	Senior Managers	Operational Area Managers	Staff	IT Staff
Staff members understand their security roles and responsibilities. This is documented and verified.	Yes	No	No	Unclear
There is adequate in-house expertise for all supported services, mechanisms, and technologies (e.g., logging, monitoring, or encryption), including their secure operation. This is documented and verified.	Unclear	Yes	Unclear	Unclear
Security awareness, training, and periodic reminders are provided for all personnel. Staff understanding is documented and conformance is periodically verified.	Unclear	Unclear	Unclear	Unclear
Comments				
Organizational Level	Protection Strategy Practices		Organizational Vulnerabilities	
Senior management	We have training, guidance, regulations, and policies.		Personnel understand systems, but not incident management and/or recognizing and reporting anomalies.	
Operational area management	Awareness training is required to gain account/access.		IT personnel are inadequately trained. Staff do not understand security issues.	

(continued)

TABLE A-24 Security Awareness and Training (*continued*)

Comments		
Organizational Level	*Protection Strategy Practices*	*Organizational Vulnerabilities*
Staff		Whom do you call with a problem? Who is responsible? There is weakness in the training as it relates to PIDS, medical records, and other systems. I do not understand my role or responsibility for security.
IT staff	Security awareness training is carried out 100 percent.	Awareness training is inadequate.

TABLE A-25 Security Strategy

Security Strategy: Survey Results				
Survey Statement	*Senior Managers*	*Operational Area Managers*	*Staff*	*IT Staff*
The organization's business strategies routinely incorporate security considerations.	No	Unclear		No
Security strategies and policies take into consideration the organization's business strategies and goals.	Unclear	Unclear		No
Security strategies, goals, and objectives are documented and are routinely reviewed, updated, and communicated to the organization.	Yes	Unclear		No
Comments				
Organizational Level	*Protection Strategy Practices*		*Organizational Vulnerabilities*	
Senior managers			We lack business sense, and do not have a proactive philosophy.	
Operational area managers			Current protection strategy ineffective.	
Staff				
IT staff			There is a lack of exposure to end-user activity.	

TABLE A-26 Security Management

Security Management: Survey Results				
Survey Statement	*Senior Managers*	*Operational Area Managers*	*Staff*	*IT Staff*
Management allocates sufficient funds and resources to information security activities.	Yes	Yes	Unclear	No
Security roles and responsibilities are defined for all staff in the organization.	Yes	Yes	Unclear	Unclear
The organization's hiring and termination practices for staff take information security issues into account.	Unclear	Yes	Unclear	Unclear
The organization manages information security risks by (1) assessing existing risks to information security and (2) taking steps to mitigate information security risks	No	No	Unclear	Unclear
Management receives and acts upon routine reports summarizing security-related information (e.g., audits, logs, risk and vulnerability assessments).	No	Unclear		No
Comments				
Organizational Level	*Protection Strategy Practices*		*Organizational Vulnerabilities*	
Senior management	We are doing this risk evaluation, so that's a start.		I don't think we actually get those kind of reports; maybe we should.	
Operational area management			I'm concerned about complacency—we've been very lucky so far.	
Staff				
IT staff			Budget and staff are inadequate. Equipment and software are out of date.	

TABLE A-27 Security Policies and Regulations

Security Policies and Regulations: Survey Results				
Survey Statement	Senior Managers	Operational Area Managers	Staff	IT Staff
The organization has a comprehensive set of documented, current policies that are periodically reviewed and updated.	Yes	Yes	Unclear	Yes
There is a documented process for management of security policies: 1. Creation 2. Administration (including periodic reviews and updates) 3. Communication	Yes	Yes	Unclear	Unclear
The organization has a documented process for evaluating and ensuring compliance with information security policies, applicable laws and regulations, and insurance requirements.	Yes	Yes		No
The organization uniformly enforces its security policies.	Unclear	No	No	No

Comments		
Organizational Level	Protection Strategy Practices	Organizational Vulnerabilities
Senior management	Policies and procedures exist. Training guidance and regulations exist.	Consequences, or lack thereof, for violating policies and procedures are not well known; we're not enforcing our own policies.
Operational area management	People know whom to call when a security incident occurs.	People don't always read or follow policies and procedures.
Staff		Policies are poorly communicated.
IT Staff	There are established incident-handling policies and procedures.	Follow-up on reported violations of security procedures is lacking. IT staff are unable to enforce procedures.

TABLE A-28 Collaborative Security Management

Collaborative Security Management: Survey Results				
Survey Statement	*Senior Managers*	*Operational Area Managers*	*Staff*	*IT Staff*
The organization has policies and procedures for protecting information when working with external organizations (e.g., third parties, collaborators, subcontractors, or partners): 1. Protecting information belonging to other organizations 2. Understanding the security policies and procedures of external organizations 3. Ending access to information by terminated external personnel	Yes	Yes	Unclear	Yes
The organization has verified that outsourced security services, mechanisms, and technologies meet its needs and requirements.	Unclear	Unclear		No

Comments		
Organizational Level	*Protection Strategy Practices*	*Organizational Vulnerabilities*
Senior management		There is distributed management of PIDS, and lack of centralized control.
Operational area management		We rely on multiple organizations to support our networks.
Staff		
IT staff	ABC Systems is responsible for security on its systems and networks; their staff are using good security practices (have a firewall, running Crack, etc.)	There is no single focal point for connectivity. Things get confused sometimes.

TABLE A-29 Contingency Planning/Disaster Recovery

Contingency Planning/Disaster Recovery: Survey Results				
Survey Statement	Senior Managers	Operational Area Managers	Staff	IT Staff
An analysis of operations, applications, and data criticality has been performed.	Yes	Unclear		Unclear
The organization has documented, reviewed, and tested business continuity or emergency operation plans, disaster recovery plan(s), and contingency plan(s) for responding to emergencies.	No	Unclear		Unclear
The contingency, disaster recovery, and business continuity plans consider physical and electronic access requirements and controls.	No	No		No
All staff are aware of the contingency, disaster recovery, and business continuity plans and understand and are able to carry out their responsibilities.	Yes	Unclear	No	Unclear
Comments				
Organizational Level	Protection Strategy Practices		Organizational Vulnerabilities	
Senior management	We do have a disaster recovery plans for natural disasters and some emergencies.		We don't have a business continuity plan.	
Operational area management			Business continuity and disaster recovery plans are lacking.	
Staff			I'm sure we have them, but I've never seen them and I'm not sure what I'm supposed to do.	
IT staff			Contingency plans if the network stays down or we lose the servers are lacking.	

Current Operational Practices of MedSite

TABLE A-30 Physical Security Plans and Procedures

Physical Security Plans and Procedures: Survey Results				
Survey Statement	*Senior Managers*	*Operational Area Managers*	*Staff*	*IT Staff*
Facility security plans and procedures for safeguarding the premises, buildings, and any restricted areas are documented and tested.	Unclear	Unclear	Unclear	No
There are documented policies and procedures for managing visitors.	Yes	Yes	Unclear	Yes
There are documented policies and procedures for physical control of hardware and software.	Yes	Yes	Unclear	Yes
Comments				
Organizational Level	*Protection Strategy Practices*		*Organizational Vulnerabilities*	
Senior management			I'm not sure how often the plans are tested.	
Operational area management			There is little challenging of people after hours. Once sensitive data are printed and distributed, they are not properly controlled or handled.	
Staff			If someone enters through the emergency room entrance, he or she can get anywhere. Storage space for sensitive information is insufficient.	
IT staff	Hardware security is very good.			

TABLE A-31 Physical Access Control

<table>
<tr><th colspan="5">Physical Access Control: Survey Results</th></tr>
<tr><th>Survey Statement</th><th>Senior Managers</th><th>Operational Area Managers</th><th>Staff</th><th>IT Staff</th></tr>
<tr><td>There are documented policies and procedures for controlling physical access to work areas and hardware (computers, communication devices, etc.) and software media.</td><td>Yes</td><td>Yes</td><td>Unclear</td><td>Unclear</td></tr>
<tr><td>Workstations and other components that allow access to sensitive information are physically safeguarded to prevent unauthorized access.</td><td>Yes</td><td>Yes</td><td>No</td><td>Yes</td></tr>
<tr><th colspan="5">Comments</th></tr>
<tr><th>Organizational Level</th><th colspan="2">Protection Strategy Practices</th><th colspan="2">Organizational Vulnerabilities</th></tr>
<tr><td>Senior management</td><td colspan="2"></td><td colspan="2"></td></tr>
<tr><td>Operational area management</td><td colspan="2"></td><td colspan="2"></td></tr>
<tr><td>Staff</td><td colspan="2">We are required to lock up our offices at the end of the day.</td><td colspan="2">Physical security is hampered by
• Location/distribution of terminals
• The need to share terminals
• Shared office space
• Shared codes to cipher locks
• Multiple access points to rooms</td></tr>
<tr><td>IT staff</td><td colspan="2">Hardware security is very good.</td><td colspan="2"></td></tr>
</table>

TABLE A-32 Monitoring and Auditing Physical Security

<table>
<tr><th colspan="5">Monitoring and Auditing Physical Security: Survey Results</th></tr>
<tr><th>Survey Statement</th><th>Senior Managers</th><th>Operational Area Managers</th><th>Staff</th><th>IT Staff</th></tr>
<tr><td>Maintenance records are kept to document the repairs and modifications of a facility's physical components.</td><td></td><td></td><td></td><td>Yes</td></tr>
<tr><td>An individual's or group's actions can be accounted for with respect to all physically controlled media.</td><td></td><td></td><td></td><td>No</td></tr>
<tr><td>Audit and monitoring records are routinely examined for anomalies, and corrective action is taken as needed.</td><td></td><td>Unclear</td><td></td><td>No

(continued)</td></tr>
</table>

TABLE A-32 Monitoring and Auditing Physical Security (*continued*)

Comments		
Organizational Level	*Protection Strategy Practices*	*Organizational Vulnerabilities*
Senior management		
Operational area management		I have never actually seen an overall audit report on maintenance and repairs.
Staff		
IT staff		We track repairs and modifications. Audit records are spotty. I'm not sure we ever review them.

TABLE A-33 System and Network Management

System and Network Management: Survey Results				
Survey Statement	*Senior Managers*	*Operational Area Managers*	*Staff*	*IT Staff*
There are documented and tested security plan(s) for safeguarding the systems and networks.	Yes	Unclear		No
Sensitive information is protected by secure storage (e.g., backups stored off-site, discard process for sensitive information).				Yes
The integrity of installed software is regularly verified.				Yes
All systems are up to date with respect to revisions, patches, and recommendations in security advisories.				Unclear
There is a documented and tested data backup plan for backups of both software and data. All staff understand their responsibilities under the backup plans.	Yes	Unclear	No	Yes
Changes to IT hardware and software are planned, controlled, and documented.				Yes
				(continued)

TABLE A-33 System and Network Management (*continued*)

System and Network Management: Survey Results				
Survey Statement	*Senior Managers*	*Operational Area Managers*	*Staff*	*IT Staff*
IT staff members follow procedures when issuing, changing, and terminating users' passwords, accounts, and privileges. • Unique user identification is required for all information system users, including third-party users. • Default accounts and default passwords have been removed from systems.				Yes
Only necessary services are running on systems; all unnecessary services have been removed.				Unclear
Comments				
Organizational Level	*Protection Strategy Practices*		*Organizational Vulnerabilities*	
Senior management	There is a security plan. ABC Systems has one.			
Operational area management			I'm not sure the people outside IT understand they have responsibilities.	
Staff				
IT staff	We know what we're supposed to do. ABC Systems does all of the virus and vulnerability checking. Their people send us the results. Systems are well protected with passwords, authorizations, etc. We force users to change passwords regularly. ABC Systems has reported very few intrusions.		There's no documented plan. ABC Systems must keep up to date with security notices, but I'm not sure. I don't think we clean up inherited access rights very well. One of the managers brought a database system down last week with access rights he should not have had. We are looking into that.	

TABLE A-34 System Administration Tools

System Administration Tools: Survey Results				
Survey Statement	*Senior Managers*	*Operational Area Managers*	*Staff*	*IT Staff*
Tools and mechanisms for secure system and network administration are used, and they are routinely reviewed and updated or replaced.				Unclear
Comments				
Organizational Level	*Protection Strategy Practices*		*Organizational Vulnerabilities*	
Senior management				
Operational area management				
Staff				
IT staff	ABC Systems is supposed to run most of these tools from its site.		We run some of them and are supposed to get updated versions and training, but that hasn't happened lately.	

TABLE A-35 Monitoring and Auditing IT Security

Monitoring and Auditing IT Security: Survey Results				
Survey Statement	Senior Managers	Operational Area Managers	Staff	IT Staff
System and network monitoring and auditing tools are routinely used by the organization. Unusual activity is dealt with according to the appropriate policy or procedure.				Unclear
Firewall and other security components are periodically audited for compliance with policy.				Yes
Comments				
Organizational Level	Protection Strategy Practices		Organizational Vulnerabilities	
Senior management				
Operational are management				
Staff				
IT staff	ABC Systems does all of the audits and runs monitoring tools.		I don't think ABC Systems reports unusual activity to anyone here, and I'm not sure if the response is according to our policy or ABC's.	

TABLE A-36 Authentication and Authorization

Authentication and Authorization: Survey Results				
Survey Statement	*Senior Managers*	*Operational Area Managers*	*Staff*	*IT Staff*
Appropriate access controls and user authentication (e.g., file permissions, network configuration) consistent with policy are used to restrict user access to information, sensitive systems, specific applications and services, and network connections.		Unclear		Yes
There are documented policies and procedures to establish and terminate the right of access to information for both individuals and groups.	Yes	Yes		Yes
Methods or mechanisms are in place to ensure that sensitive information has not been accessed, altered, or destroyed in an unauthorized manner. Methods or mechanisms are periodically reviewed and verified.				Yes

Comments		
Organizational Level	*Protection Strategy Practices*	*Organizational Vulnerabilities*
Senior management		
Operational area management	There are policies for access control and permissions.	But we're not using role-based management of accounts, and people inherit far too many privileges.
Staff		
IT staff	Systems are well protected with passwords, authorizations, etc.	

TABLE A-37 Vulnerability Management

<table>
<tr><th colspan="5">Vulnerability Management: Survey Results</th></tr>
<tr><th>Survey Statement</th><th>Senior Managers</th><th>Operational Area Managers</th><th>Staff</th><th>IT Staff</th></tr>
<tr>
<td>There is a documented set of procedures for managing vulnerabilities:

- Selecting vulnerability evaluation tools, checklists, and scripts
- Keeping up to date with known vulnerability types and attack methods
- Reviewing sources of information on vulnerability announcements, security alerts, and notices
- Identifying infrastructure components to be evaluated
- Scheduling vulnerability evaluations
- Interpreting and responding to the results
- Maintaining secure storage and disposition of vulnerability data</td>
<td></td><td></td><td></td><td>Unclear</td>
</tr>
<tr>
<td>Vulnerability management procedures are followed and are periodically reviewed and updated.</td>
<td></td><td></td><td></td><td>Unclear</td>
</tr>
<tr>
<td>Technology vulnerability assessments are performed on a periodic basis, and vulnerabilities are addressed when they are identified.</td>
<td></td><td></td><td></td><td>Unclear</td>
</tr>
<tr><th colspan="5">Comments</th></tr>
<tr><th>Organizational Level</th><th colspan="2">Protection Strategy Practices</th><th colspan="2">Organizational Vulnerabilities</th></tr>
<tr><td>Senior management</td><td colspan="2"></td><td colspan="2"></td></tr>
<tr><td>Operational area management</td><td colspan="2"></td><td colspan="2"></td></tr>
<tr><td>Staff</td><td colspan="2"></td><td colspan="2"></td></tr>
<tr><td>IT staff</td><td colspan="2">ABC Systems does all of the vulnerability management and assessment activities. They do a good job.</td><td colspan="2">We haven't been trained in what to do with those vulnerability reports. We usually file them in a drawer.</td></tr>
</table>

TABLE A-38 Encryption

Encryption: Survey Results				
Survey Statement	Senior Managers	Operational Area Managers	Staff	IT Staff
Appropriate security controls are used to protect sensitive information while in storage and during transmission (e.g., data encryption, public key infrastructure, virtual private network technology).				Yes
Encrypted protocols are used for remote management of systems, routers, and firewalls.				Yes
Comments				
None Provided				

TABLE A-39 Security Architecture and Design

Security Architecture and Design				
Survey Statement	Senior Managers	Operational Area Managers	Staff	IT Staff
System architecture and design for new and revised systems include considerations for: • Security strategies, policies, and procedures • History of security compromises • Results of security risk assessments				Unclear
The organization has up-to-date diagrams that show the enterprisewide security architecture and network topology.				Yes
Comments				

Organizational Level	Protection Strategy Practices	Organizational Vulnerabilities
Senior management		
Operational area management		
Staff		
IT staff		They're already building PIDS II, but no one ever talked to us about its security needs. Maybe ABC Systems already knows.

TABLE A-40 Incident Management

Incident Management: Survey Results				
Survey Statement	Senior Managers	Operational Area Managers	Staff	IT Staff
Documented procedures exist for identifying, reporting, and responding to suspected security incidents and violations.	Yes	Unclear	Unclear	Yes
Incident management procedures are periodically tested, verified, and updated.	Unclear	No	Unclear	No
There are documented policies and procedures for working with law enforcement agencies.	No	No	No	Unclear

Comments		
Organizational Level	Protection Strategy Practices	Organizational Vulnerabilities
Senior management		I never even considered dealing with law enforcement for security problems until just now.
Operational area management	Procedures exist for incident response.	Not everyone is aware of the procedures.
Staff		I don't know if I'm supposed to do anything or what to look for. Whom do we call?
IT staff		I suppose we should call law enforcement if the system really gets attacked. But do we call, or does ABC Systems?

TABLE A-41 General Staff Practices

General Staff Practices: Survey Results				
Survey Statement	Senior Managers	Operational Area Managers	Staff	IT Staff
Staff members follow good security practice as by doing the following: • Securing information for which they are responsible • Not divulging sensitive information to others (resistance to social engineering) • Ensuring they have adequate ability to use information technology hardware and software • Using good password practices • Understanding and following security policies and regulations • Recognizing and reporting incidents	Unclear	Unclear	No	Yes
All staff at all levels of responsibility implement their assigned roles and take responsibility for information security.	Unclear	No	Unclear	Yes
There are documented procedures for authorizing and overseeing all staff (including personnel from third-party organizations) who work with sensitive information or in locations where the information resides.	Yes	Unclear	No	Yes

Comments		
Organizational Level	Protection Strategy Practices	Organizational Vulnerabilities
Senior management		I'm fairly certain people share passwords and accounts.
Operational area management		They have so much trouble logging in and out and moving between machines that they just don't bother.
Staff	We get "don't share passwords" type of training.	Physical layouts, insufficient equipment, and cramped space all lead to sharing of passwords, accounts, machines, whatever. We all trust each other.
IT staff	All staff are trained on passwords.	

Appendix B
Worksheets

This appendix contains a set of worksheets that are used during the OCTAVE Method. We have classified the worksheets into the following types:

1. Knowledge elicitation worksheets. These are used during processes 1 through 3. There is one set of worksheets to be used for all three processes.

2. Asset profile. This profile is a set of worksheets that includes all of the information gathered or created for a critical asset. You will complete an asset profile for each critical asset.

3. Strategies and actions. These worksheets are used when developing the organizationwide protection strategy and the action list in process 8A.

All of the worksheets include a basic set of instructions derived from the *OCTAVE Method Implementation Guide, v2.0* [Alberts 01].

B.1 Knowledge Elicitation Worksheets

Processes 1 to 3 elicit knowledge from senior managers, operational area managers, general staff members, and information technology staff members. Participants in processes 1 to 3 provide their perspectives on assets that are important to the success of the organization, the way in which important assets are threatened, and security requirements for important assets.

The worksheets used when you elicit the above information are identical for all participants; we provide only one set. During the last activity of processes 1 to 3, you elicit information about security practices currently used by the organization and the organizational vulnerabilities that are present in the organization. There is a different survey for each organizational level, and all of the surveys are included in this appendix. The final worksheet in processes 1 to 3 is for a follow-up discussion after participants complete their surveys and is the same for all participants. The following worksheets are provided in this section of Appendix B:

- Asset Worksheet
- Areas of Concern Worksheet
- Security Requirements Worksheet
- Practice Surveys
  - Senior management survey
  - Operational area management survey
  - General staff survey
  - IT staff survey
- Protection Strategy Worksheet

You normally use these worksheets (except for the surveys) to prompt the participants and stimulate a discussion among them. However, you could ask them to complete the worksheets in advance and be prepared to discuss their answers. The workshop's scribe records the official results of each workshop. The scribe can record data on flip charts, copies of these worksheets, or in some other, more abbreviated, electronic form.

B.1.1 Asset Worksheet

Instructions	
Processes 1 to 3	*Activity: Identify Assets and Relative Priorities (Section 5.2)*
Purpose	To identify assets that are important to participants (senior managers, operational area managers, general staff, or information technology staff)
Instructions	1. Participants brainstorm a list of assets and then select those assets considered to be most important. Use the following questions to guide your discussions: • What are your important assets? • Are there any other assets that you are required to protect (e.g., by law or regulation)? • What related assets are important? • From the assets that you have identified, which are the most important? What is your rationale for selecting these assets as important?
	2. Hand out the Asset Worksheet to participants and discuss each question. Use the questions as prompts to guide the discussion.
	3. Record all assets identified during the workshop and note which ones were identified as most important by the participants.

Asset Worksheet
1. What are your important assets? Consider the following: • Information • Systems • Software • Hardware • People   *(continued)*

Asset Worksheet (*continued*)
2. Are there any other assets that you are required to protect (e.g., by law or regulation)?

3. What related assets are important?
 	
Consider the following:
 	
   • Information
 	
   • Systems
 	
   • Software
 	
   • Hardware
 	
   • People

(*continued*)

Asset Worksheet *(continued)*
4. From the assets that you have identified, which are the most important? What is your rationale for selecting these assets as important?

B.1.2 Areas of Concern Worksheet

Instructions	
Process 1 to 3	*Activity: Identify Areas of Concern (Section 5.3)*
Purpose	To identify areas of concern for each important asset previously identified by the participants
Instructions	1. Participants brainstorm scenarios that could threaten their most important assets. Use the following question to guide your discussions: What scenarios threaten your important assets?
	2. Hand out the Areas of Concern Worksheet to participants and ask them to use the sources and outcomes as prompts when considering scenarios that threaten important assets.
	3. Record all areas of concern identified during the workshop.

Areas of Concern Worksheet
What scenarios threaten your important assets?

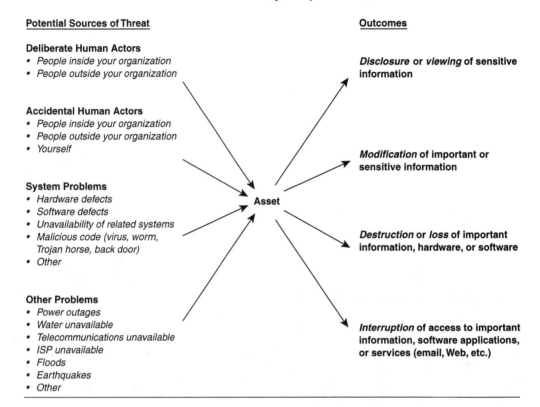

Potential Sources of Threat

Deliberate Human Actors
- *People inside your organization*
- *People outside your organization*

Accidental Human Actors
- *People inside your organization*
- *People outside your organization*
- *Yourself*

System Problems
- *Hardware defects*
- *Software defects*
- *Unavailability of related systems*
- *Malicious code (virus, worm, Trojan horse, back door)*
- *Other*

Other Problems
- *Power outages*
- *Water unavailable*
- *Telecommunications unavailable*
- *ISP unavailable*
- *Floods*
- *Earthquakes*
- *Other*

Asset

Outcomes

Disclosure or ***viewing*** **of sensitive information**

Modification **of important or sensitive information**

Destruction or ***loss*** **of important information, hardware, or software**

Interruption **of access to important information, software applications, or services (email, Web, etc.)**

B.1.3 Security Requirements Worksheet

Instructions	
Processes 1 to 3	*Activity: Identify Security Requirements for Most Important Assets (Section 5.4)*
Purpose	To identify security requirements for each important asset previously identified by the participants
Instructions	1. Participants brainstorm a list of security requirements for their important assets and then select which requirement is considered most important for each asset. Use the following questions to guide your discussions: • What are the important security requirements for each information asset? • What is the relative ranking of the security requirements for each information asset? Which security requirement is the most important?
	2. Hand out the Security Requirements Worksheet to participants and discuss each question. Use the questions as prompts to guide the discussion.
	3. Record security requirements identified for each important asset and note which requirement was identified as most important for each asset.

Security Requirements Worksheet

1. What are the important security requirements for each information asset?

   Consider the following:

   • Confidentiality

   • Integrity

   • Availability

   • Other

(continued)

Security Requirements Worksheet (*continued*)
2. What is the relative ranking of the security requirements for each information asset? Which security requirement is the most important?

B.1.4 Practice Surveys

Instructions	
Processes 1 to 3	*Activity: Capture Knowledge of Current Protection Strategy Practices and Organizational Vulnerabilities (Section 5.5)*
Purpose	To gather survey information about security practices currently used by the organization
Instructions	1. Hand out surveys and ask participants to complete them. Note that there are four types of surveys, each one tailored for a particular group of personnel: • Senior Management Survey • Operational Area Management Survey • General Staff Survey • Information Technology Staff Survey
	2. Have participants answer each question to the best of their knowledge in terms of how the practice is used in their organization by giving the following instructions: • If the practice is always or nearly always used, circle "Yes." • If the practice is not used or not used very much, circle "No." • If you're not sure or don't really know, circle "Don't Know."
	3. After participants complete their surveys, hold a follow-up discussion about current security practices and organization vulnerabilities. See Section B.1.5 of this appendix for more information about that discussion.

B.1.4.1 Senior Management Survey

Name (optional): _____

Position: _____

Senior Management Survey			
Practice	Is this practice used by your organization?		
Security Awareness and Training			
Staff members understand their security roles and responsibilities. This is documented and verified.	Yes	No	Don't know
There is adequate in-house expertise for all supported services, mechanisms, and technologies (e.g., logging, monitoring, or encryption), including their secure operation. This is documented and verified.	Yes	No	Don't know
Security awareness, training, and periodic reminders are provided for all personnel. Staff understanding is documented and conformance is periodically verified.	Yes	No	Don't know
Security Strategy			
The organization's business strategies routinely incorporate security considerations.	Yes	No	Don't know
Security strategies and policies take into consideration the organization's business strategies and goals.	Yes	No	Don't know
Security strategies, goals, and objectives are documented and are routinely reviewed, updated, and communicated to the organization.	Yes	No	Don't know
Security Management			
Management allocates sufficient funds and resources to information security activities.	Yes	No	Don't know
Security roles and responsibilities are defined for all staff in the organization.	Yes	No	Don't know
The organization's hiring and termination practices for staff take information security issues into account.	Yes	No	Don't know
The organization manages information security risks by assessing existing risks to information security and taking steps to mitigate information security risks.	Yes	No	Don't know
Management receives and acts upon routine reports summarizing security-related information (e.g., audits, logs, risk and vulnerability assessments).	Yes	No	Don't know

(continued)

Senior Management Survey *(continued)*			
Practice	*Is this practice used by your organization?*		
Security Policies and Regulations			
The organization has a comprehensive set of documented, current policies that are periodically reviewed and updated.	Yes	No	Don't know
There is a documented process for management of security policies: 1. Creation 2. Administration (including periodic reviews and updates) 3. Communication	Yes	No	Don't know
The organization has a documented process for evaluating and ensuring compliance with information security policies, applicable laws and regulations, and insurance requirements.	Yes	No	Don't know
The organization uniformly enforces its security policies.	Yes	No	Don't know
Collaborative Security Management			
The organization has policies and procedures for protecting information when working with external organizations (e.g., third parties, collaborators, subcontractors, or partners): 1. Protecting information belonging to other organizations 2. Understanding the security policies and procedures of external organizations 3. Ending access to information by terminated external personnel	Yes	No	Don't know
The organization has verified that outsourced security services, mechanisms, and technologies meet its needs and requirements.	Yes	No	Don't know
Contingency Planning/Disaster Recovery			
An analysis of operations, applications, and data criticality has been performed.	Yes	No	Don't know
The organization has documented, reviewed, and tested business continuity or emergency operation plans, disaster recovery plan(s), and contingency plan(s) for responding to emergencies.	Yes	No	Don't know
The contingency, disaster recovery, and business continuity plans consider physical and electronic access requirements and controls.	Yes	No	Don't know
All staff are aware of the contingency, disaster recovery, and business continuity plans and understand and are able to carry out their responsibilities.	Yes	No	Don't know

Senior Management Survey *(continued)*			
Practice	*Is this practice used by your organization?*		
Physical Security Plans and Procedures			
Facility security plans and procedures for safeguarding the premises, buildings, and any restricted areas are documented and tested.	Yes	No	Don't know
There are documented policies and procedures for managing visitors.	Yes	No	Don't know
There are documented policies and procedures for physical control of hardware and software.	Yes	No	Don't know
Physical Access Control			
There are documented policies and procedures for controlling physical access to work areas and hardware (computers, communication devices, etc.) and software media.	Yes	No	Don't know
Workstations and other components that allow access to sensitive information are physically safeguarded to prevent unauthorized access.	Yes	No	Don't know
System and Network Management			
There are documented and tested security plan(s) for safeguarding the systems and networks.	Yes	No	Don't know
There is a documented and tested data backup plan for backups of both software and data. All staff understand their responsibilities under the backup plans.	Yes	No	Don't know
Authentication and Authorization			
There are documented policies and procedures to establish and terminate the right of access to information for both individuals and groups.	Yes	No	Don't know
Incident Management			
Documented procedures exist for identifying, reporting, and responding to suspected security incidents and violations.	Yes	No	Don't know
Incident management procedures are periodically tested, verified, and updated.	Yes	No	Don't know
There are documented policies and procedures for working with law enforcement agencies.	Yes	No	Don't know

(continued)

Senior Management Survey (continued)			
Practice	Is this practice used by your organization?		
General Staff Practices			
Staff members follow good security practice, for example: • Securing information for which they are responsible • Not divulging sensitive information to others (resistance to social engineering) • Ensuring they have adequate ability to use information technology hardware and software • Using good password practices • Understanding and following security policies and regulations • Recognizing and reporting incidents	Yes	No	Don't know
All staff at all levels of responsibility implement their assigned roles and responsibility for information security.	Yes	No	Don't know
There are documented procedures for authorizing and overseeing all staff (including personnel from third-party organizations) who work with sensitive information or who work in locations where the information resides.	Yes	No	Don't know

B.1.4.2 Operational Area Management Survey

Name (optional): _____

Position: _____

Operational Area Management Survey			
Practice	Is this practice used by your organization?		
Security Awareness and Training			
Staff members understand their security roles and responsibilities. This is documented and verified.	Yes	No	Don't know
There is adequate in-house expertise for all supported services, mechanisms, and technologies (e.g., logging, monitoring, or encryption), including their secure operation. This is documented and verified.	Yes	No	Don't know
Security awareness, training, and periodic reminders are provided for all personnel. Staff understanding is documented and conformance is periodically verified.	Yes	No	Don't know (continued)

Operational Area Management Survey *(continued)*			
Practice	*Is this practice used by your organization?*		
Security Strategy			
The organization's business strategies routinely incorporate security considerations.	Yes	No	Don't know
Security strategies and policies take into consideration the organization's business strategies and goals.	Yes	No	Don't know
Security strategies, goals, and objectives are documented and are routinely reviewed, updated, and communicated to the organization.	Yes	No	Don't know
Security Management			
Management allocates sufficient funds and resources to information security activities.	Yes	No	Don't know
Security roles and responsibilities are defined for all staff in the organization.	Yes	No	Don't know
The organization's hiring and termination practices for staff take information security issues into account.	Yes	No	Don't know
The organization manages information security risks by assessing risks to information security and taking steps to mitigate information security risks.	Yes	No	Don't know
Management receives and acts upon routine reports summarizing security-related information (e.g., audits, logs, risk and vulnerability assessments).	Yes	No	Don't know
Security Policies and Regulations			
The organization has a comprehensive set of documented, current policies that are periodically reviewed and updated.	Yes	No	Don't know
There is a documented process for management of security policies: 1. Creation 2. Administration (including periodic reviews and updates) 3. Communication	Yes	No	Don't know
The organization has a documented process for evaluating and ensuring compliance with information security policies, applicable laws and regulations, and insurance requirements.	Yes	No	Don't know
The organization uniformly enforces its security policies.	Yes	No	Don't know

(continued)

Operational Area Management Survey *(continued)*			
Practice	*Is this practice used by your organization?*		
Collaborative Security Management			
The organization has policies and procedures for protecting information when working with external organizations (e.g., third parties, collaborators, subcontractors, or partners): 1. Protecting information belonging to other organizations 2. Understanding the security policies and procedures of external organizations 3. Ending access to information by terminated external personnel	Yes	No	Don't know
The organization has verified that outsourced security services, mechanisms, and technologies meet its needs and requirements.	Yes	No	Don't know
Contingency Planning/Disaster Recovery			
An analysis of operations, applications, and data criticality has been performed.	Yes	No	Don't know
The organization has documented, reviewed, and tested business continuity or emergency operation plans, disaster recovery plan(s), and contingency plan(s) for responding to emergencies.	Yes	No	Don't know
The contingency, disaster recovery, and business continuity plans consider physical and electronic access requirements and controls.	Yes	No	Don't know
All staff are aware of the contingency, disaster recovery, and business continuity plans and understand and are able to carry out their responsibilities.	Yes	No	Don't know
Physical Security Plans and Procedures			
Facility security plans and procedures for safeguarding the premises, buildings, and any restricted areas are documented and tested.	Yes	No	Don't know
There are documented policies and procedures for managing visitors.	Yes	No	Don't know
There are documented policies and procedures for physical control of hardware and software.	Yes	No	Don't know
Physical Access Control			
There are documented policies and procedures for controlling physical access to work areas and hardware (computers, communication devices, etc.) and software media.	Yes	No	Don't know
Workstations and other components that allow access to sensitive information are physically safeguarded to prevent unauthorized access.	Yes	No	Don't know

Operational Area Management Survey (*continued*)			
Practice	*Is this practice used by your organization?*		
Monitoring and Auditing Physical Security			
Audit and monitoring records are routinely examined for anomalies, and corrective action is taken as needed.	Yes	No	Don't know
System and Network Management			
There are documented and tested security plan(s) for safeguarding the systems and networks.	Yes	No	Don't know
There is a documented and tested data backup plan for backups of both software and data. All staff understand their responsibilities under the backup plans.	Yes	No	Don't know
Authentication and Authorization			
There are documented policies and procedures to establish and terminate the right of access to information for both individuals and groups.	Yes	No	Don't know
Incident Management			
Documented procedures exist for identifying, reporting, and responding to suspected security incidents and violations.	Yes	No	Don't know
Incident management procedures are periodically tested, verified, and updated.	Yes	No	Don't know
There are documented policies and procedures for working with law enforcement agencies.	Yes	No	Don't know
General Staff Practices			
Staff members follow good security practice, for example: • Securing information for which they are responsible • Not divulging sensitive information to others (resistance to social engineering) • Ensuring they have adequate ability to use information technology hardware and software • Using good password practices • Understanding and following security policies and regulations • Recognizing and reporting incidents	Yes	No	Don't know
All staff at all levels of responsibility implement their assigned roles and responsibility for information security.	Yes	No	Don't know

(*continued*)

Operational Area Management Survey (*continued*)			
Practice	*Is this practice used by your organization?*		
General Staff Practices (*continued*)			
There are documented procedures for authorizing and overseeing all staff (including personnel from third-party organizations) who work with sensitive information or who work in locations where the information resides.	Yes	No	Don't know

B.1.4.3 General Staff Survey

Name (optional): _____

Position: _____

Staff Survey			
Practice	*Is this practice used by your organization?*		
Security Awareness and Training			
Staff members understand their security roles and responsibilities. This is documented and verified.	Yes	No	Don't know
There is adequate in-house expertise for all supported services, mechanisms, and technologies (e.g., logging, monitoring, or encryption), including their secure operation. This is documented and verified.	Yes	No	Don't know
Security awareness, training, and periodic reminders are provided for all personnel. Staff understanding is documented and conformance is periodically verified.	Yes	No	Don't know
Security Management			
Management allocates sufficient funds and resources to information security activities.	Yes	No	Don't know
Security roles and responsibilities are defined for all staff in the organization.	Yes	No	Don't know
The organization's hiring and termination practices for staff take information security issues into account.	Yes	No	Don't know
The organization manages information security risks by assessing risks to information security and taking steps to mitigate information security risks.	Yes	No	Don't know

Staff Survey *(continued)*			
Practice	*Is this practice used by your organization?*		
Security Policies and Regulations			
The organization has a comprehensive set of documented, current policies that are periodically reviewed and updated.	Yes	No	Don't know
There is a documented process for management of security policies: 1. Creation 2. Administration (including periodic reviews and updates) 3. Communication	Yes	No	Don't know
The organization uniformly enforces its security policies.	Yes	No	Don't know
Collaborative Security Management			
The organization has policies and procedures for protecting information when working with external organizations (e.g., third parties, collaborators, subcontractors, or partners); 1. Protecting information belonging to other organizations 2. Understanding the security policies and procedures of external organizations 3. Ending access to information by terminated external personnel	Yes	No	Don't know
Contingency Planning/Disaster Recovery			
All staff are aware of the contingency, disaster recovery, and business continuity plans and understand and are able to carry out their responsibilities.	Yes	No	Don't know
Physical Security Plans and Procedures			
Facility security plans and procedures for safeguarding the premises, buildings, and any restricted areas are documented and tested.	Yes	No	Don't know
There are documented policies and procedures for managing visitors.	Yes	No	Don't know
There are documented policies and procedures for physical control of hardware and software.	Yes	No	Don't know
Physical Access Control			
There are documented policies and procedures for controlling physical access to work areas and hardware (computers, communication devices, etc.) and software media.	Yes	No	Don't know
Workstations and other components that allow access to sensitive information are physically safeguarded to prevent unauthorized access.	Yes	No	Don't know

(continued)

Staff Survey (*continued*)			
Practice	*Is this practice used by your organization?*		
System and Network Management			
There is a documented and tested data backup plan for backups of both software and data. All staff understand their responsibilities under the backup plans.	Yes	No	Don't know
Incident Management			
Documented procedures exist for identifying, reporting, and responding to suspected security incidents and violations.	Yes	No	Don't know
Incident management procedures are periodically tested, verified, and updated.	Yes	No	Don't know
There are documented policies and procedures for working with law enforcement agencies.	Yes	No	Don't know
General Staff Practices			
Staff members follow good security practice, for example: • Securing information for which they are responsible • Not divulging sensitive information to others (resistance to social engineering) • Ensuring they have adequate ability to use information technology hardware and software • Using good password practices • Understanding and following security policies and regulations • Recognizing and reporting incidents	Yes	No	Don't know
All staff at all levels of responsibility implement their assigned roles and responsibility for information security.	Yes	No	Don't know
There are documented procedures for authorizing and overseeing all staff (including personnel from third-party organizations) who work with sensitive information or who work in locations where the information resides.	Yes	No	Don't know

B.1.4.4 IT Staff Survey

Name (optional): _____

Position: _____

IT Staff Survey			
Practice	*Is this practice used by your organization?*		
Security Awareness and Training			
Staff members understand their security roles and responsibilities. This is documented and verified.	Yes	No	Don't know
There is adequate in-house expertise for all supported services, mechanisms, and technologies (e.g., logging, monitoring, or encryption), including their secure operation. This is documented and verified.	Yes	No	Don't know
Security awareness, training, and periodic reminders are provided for all personnel. Staff understanding is documented and conformance is periodically verified.	Yes	No	Don't know
Security Strategy			
The organization's business strategies routinely incorporate security considerations.	Yes	No	Don't know
Security strategies and policies take into consideration the organization's business strategies and goals.	Yes	No	Don't know
Security strategies, goals, and objectives are documented and are routinely reviewed, updated, and communicated to the organization.	Yes	No	Don't know
Security Management			
Management allocates sufficient funds and resources to information security activities.	Yes	No	Don't know
Security roles and responsibilities are defined for all staff in the organization.	Yes	No	Don't know
The organization's hiring and termination practices for staff take information security issues into account.	Yes	No	Don't know
The organization manages information security risks by assessing risks to information security and taking steps to mitigate information security risks.	Yes	No	Don't know
Management receives and acts upon routine reports summarizing security-related information (e.g., audits, logs, risk and vulnerability assessments).	Yes	No	Don't know

(continued)

IT Staff Survey *(continued)*			
Practice	*Is this practice used by your organization?*		
Security Policies and Regulations			
The organization has a comprehensive set of documented, current policies that are periodically reviewed and updated.	Yes	No	Don't know
There is a documented process for management of security policies: 1. Creation 2. Administration (including periodic reviews and updates) 3. Communication	Yes	No	Don't know
The organization has a documented process for evaluating and ensuring compliance with information security policies, applicable laws and regulations, and insurance requirements.	Yes	No	Don't know
The organization uniformly enforces its security policies.	Yes	No	Don't know
Collaborative Security Management			
The organization has policies and procedures for protecting information when working with external organizations (e.g., third parties, collaborators, subcontractors, or partners): 1. Protecting information belonging to other organizations 2. Understanding the security polices and procedures of external organizations 3. Ending access to information by terminated external personnel	Yes	No	Don't know
The organization has verified that outsourced security services, mechanisms, and technologies meet its needs and requirements.	Yes	No	Don't know
Contingency Planning/Disaster Recovery			
An analysis of operations, applications, and data criticality has been performed.	Yes	No	Don't know
The organization has documented, reviewed, and tested business continuity or emergency operation plans, disaster recovery plan(s), and contingency plan(s) for responding to emergencies.	Yes	No	Don't know
The contingency, disaster recovery, and business continuity plans consider physical and electronic access requirements and controls.	Yes	No	Don't know
All staff are aware of the contingency, disaster recovery, and business continuity plans and understand and are able to carry out their responsibilities.	Yes	No	Don't know

IT Staff Survey (continued)	
Practice	Is this practice used by your organization?
Physical Security Plans and Procedures	
Facility security plans and procedures for safeguarding the premises, buildings, and any restricted areas are documented and tested.	Yes No Don't know
There are documented policies and procedures for managing visitors.	Yes No Don't know
There are documented policies and procedures for physical control of hardware and software.	Yes No Don't know
Physical Access Control	
There are documented policies and procedures for controlling physical access to work areas and hardware (computers, communication devices, etc.) and software media.	Yes No Don't know
Workstations and other components that allow access to sensitive information are physically safeguarded to prevent unauthorized access.	Yes No Don't know
Monitoring and Auditing Physical Security	
Maintenance records are kept to document the repairs and modifications of a facility's physical components.	Yes No Don't know
An individual's or group's actions with respect to all physically controlled media can be accounted for.	Yes No Don't know
Audit and monitoring records are routinely examined for anomalies, and corrective action is taken as needed.	Yes No Don't know
System and Network Management	
There are documented and tested security plan(s) for safeguarding the systems and networks.	Yes No Don't know
Sensitive information is protected by secure storage (e.g., backups stored off-site, discard process for sensitive information).	Yes No Don't know
The integrity of installed software is regularly verified.	Yes No Don't know
All systems are up to date with respect to revisions, patches, and recommendations in security advisories.	Yes No Don't know
There is a documented and tested data backup plan for backups of both software and data. All staff understand their responsibilities under the backup plans.	Yes No Don't know

(continued)

IT Staff Survey *(continued)*			
Practice	*Is this practice used by your organization?*		
System and Network Management *(continued)*			
Changes to IT hardware and software are planned, controlled, and documented.	Yes	No	Don't know
IT staff members follow procedures when issuing, changing, and terminating users' passwords, accounts, and privileges: • Unique user identification is required for all information system users, including third-party users. • Default accounts and default passwords have been removed from systems.	Yes	No	Don't know
Only necessary services are running on systems; all unnecessary services have been removed.	Yes	No	Don't know
System Administration Tools			
Tools and mechanisms for secure system and network administration are used, and they are routinely reviewed and updated or replaced.	Yes	No	Don't know
Monitoring and Auditing IT Security			
System and network monitoring and auditing tools are routinely used by the organization. Unusual activity is dealt with according to the appropriate policy or procedure.	Yes	No	Don't know
Firewall and other security components are periodically audited for compliance with policy.	Yes	No	Don't know
Authentication and Authorization			
Appropriate access controls and user authentication (e.g., file permissions, network configuration) consistent with policy are used to restrict user access to information, sensitive systems, specific applications and services, and network connections.	Yes	No	Don't know
There are documented policies and procedures to establish and terminate the right of access to information for both individuals and groups.	Yes	No	Don't know
Methods or mechanisms are provided to ensure that sensitive information has not been accessed, altered, or destroyed in an unauthorized manner. Methods or mechanisms are periodically reviewed and verified.	Yes	No	Don't know

IT Staff Survey (continued)			
Practice	*Is this practice used by your organization?*		
Vulnerability Management			
There is a documented set of procedures for managing vulnerabilities: • Selecting vulnerability evaluation tools, checklists, and scripts • Keeping up to date with known vulnerability types and attack methods • Reviewing sources of information on vulnerability announcements, security alerts, and notices • Identifying infrastructure components to be evaluated • Scheduling of vulnerability evaluations • Interpreting and responding to the results • Maintaining secure storage and disposition of vulnerability data	Yes	No	Don't know
Vulnerability management procedures are followed and are periodically reviewed and updated.	Yes	No	Don't know
Technology vulnerability assessments are performed on a periodic basis, and vulnerabilities are addressed when they are identified.	Yes	No	Don't know
Encryption			
Appropriate security controls are used to protect sensitive information while in storage and during transmission (e.g., data encryption, public key infrastructure, virtual private network technology).	Yes	No	Don't know
Encrypted protocols are used for remote management of systems, routers, and firewalls.	Yes	No	Don't know
Security Architecture and Design			
System architecture and design for new and revised systems include considerations for • Security strategies, policies, and procedures • History of security compromises • Results of security risk assessments	Yes	No	Don't know
The organization has up-to-date diagrams that show the enterprisewide security architecture and network topology.	Yes	No	Don't know

(continued)

IT Staff Survey *(continued)*			
Practice	*Is this practice used by your organization?*		
Incident Management			
Documented procedures exist for identifying, reporting, and responding to suspected security incidents and violations.	Yes	No	Don't know
Incident management procedures are periodically tested, verified, and updated.	Yes	No	Don't know
There are documented policies and procedures for working with law enforcement agencies.	Yes	No	Don't know
General Staff Practices			
Staff members follow good security practice, for example: • Securing information for which they are responsible • Not divulging sensitive information to others (resistance to social engineering) • Ensuring they have adequate ability to use information technology hardware and software • Using good password practices • Understanding and following security policies and regulations • Recognizing and reporting incidents	Yes	No	Don't know
All staff at all levels of responsibility implement their assigned roles and responsibility for information security.	Yes	No	Don't know
There are documented procedures for authorizing and overseeing all staff (including personnel from third-party organizations) who work with sensitive information or who work in locations where the information resides.	Yes	No	Don't know

B.1.5 Protection Strategy Worksheet

Instructions	
Processes 1 to 3	*Activity: Capture Knowledge of Current Security Practices and Organizational Vulnerabilities (Section 5.5)*
Purpose	To build on the survey information by identifying specific security practices used by the organization and organizational vulnerabilities present in the organization

Instructions	
Processes 1 to 3	*Activity: Capture Knowledge of Current Security Practices and Organizational Vulnerabilities (Section 5.5)*
Instructions	1. Participants brainstorm a list of security practices and organizational vulnerabilities. Use the following questions to guide your discussions: • Which issues from the survey would you like to discuss in more detail? • What important issues did the survey not cover? • Are there specific security policies, procedures, and practices unique to certain assets? What are they? • Do you think that your organization's protection strategy is effective? How do you know?
	2. Hand out the Protection Strategy Worksheet to participants and discuss each question. Use the questions as prompts to guide the discussion.
	3. Record comments from the participants. Designate items that are security practices with a "+" and items that are organizational vulnerabilities with a "−".

Protection Strategy Worksheet
1. Which issues from the survey would you like to discuss in more detail?

(*continued*)

Protection Strategy Worksheet (*continued*)
2. What important issues did the survey not cover?
3. Are there specific security policies, procedures, and practices unique to certain assets? What are they?

Protection Strategy Worksheet *(continued)*
4. • Do you think that your organization's protection strategy is effective? How do you know?

B.2 Asset Profile Worksheets

Use the worksheets in this section to document the analysis results during processes 4 through 8A for each critical asset. Collectively, these worksheets are called an asset profile; you should develop one asset profile for each critical asset.

The worksheets in this section generally appear in the order in which they are used. Any exceptions are specifically noted in the instructions for a section. The following asset profile worksheets are presented in this section:

- Process 4
  - Critical Asset Information
  - Security Requirements
  - Threat Profile

- Process 5
  - System(s) of Interest
  - Key Classes of Components
  - Infrastructure Components to Examine
- Process 6
  - Technological Vulnerability Summary
  - Actions and Recommendations
- Process 7
  - Risk Impact Descriptions
  - Risk Evaluation Criteria
- Process 8
  - Risk Mitigation Plans

B.2.1 Critical Asset Information

Instructions	
Process 4	*Activity: Select Critical Assets (Section 6.3)*
Purpose	To document information pertaining to the selection of a critical asset
Instructions	Record the following information for the critical asset on the Critical Asset Information Worksheet: • The name of the asset and your rationale for selecting it • A brief description of the critical asset, including who controls it, who is responsible for it, who uses it, and how it is used

Critical Asset Information Worksheet
Asset
Rationale for selection as a critical asset
Brief description

B.2.2 Security Requirements

Instructions	
Process 4	*Activity: Refine Security Requirements for Critical Assets (Section 6.4)*
Purpose	To refine security requirements for the critical asset
Instructions	1. Review any security requirements and areas of concern for the critical asset that were identified during processes 1 to 3. Also review any areas of concern.

	2. Document the security requirements for the critical asset in the third column of the Security Requirements Worksheet. Use the following questions as prompts:
	
	 • Confidentiality
	
	     – Is this asset proprietary or sensitive?
	
	     – Does it contain personal information?
	
	     – Should it be inaccessible to anyone who is not authorized to see it?
	
	     – If the answer to any of these questions is yes, define the specific confidentiality requirement in the third column of the following table.
	
	 • Integrity
	
	     – Are authenticity, accuracy, and completeness important to this asset? If yes, define the specific integrity in the third column of the following table.
	
	 • Availability
	
	     – Is accessibility of the asset important? If yes, define the specific availability requirement in the third column of the following table.
	
	 • Other
	
	     – Are there any other security-related requirements that are important to this asset? If so, define them in the third column of the following table.

	3. Determine the most important security requirement by examining trade-offs among the security requirements. Consider what would happen if confidentiality, integrity, or availability of the asset were violated. Document the most important security requirement in the "priority" column of the Security Requirements Worksheet.

Security Requirements Worksheet		
Security Requirement Type	*Priority*	*Specific Requirement*
Confidentiality		
Integrity		
Availability		
Other		

B.2.3 Process 4: Threat Profile for Critical Asset

NOTE: You do not complete the entire worksheet during one activity. First complete the threat profile for the critical asset (all fields in the Threat Profile Worksheet with the exception of the impact field). Record impact values on the Threat Profile Worksheet after evaluating impacts in Section B.2.11.

Instructions	
Process 4	*Activity: Identify Threats to Critical Assets (Section 6.5)*
Purpose	To identify the range of threats that affect the critical assets, creating a threat profile for the critical asset
Instructions	1. Review the security requirements (Section B.2.2) and critical asset information (Section B.2.1). Also review any areas of concern for the critical asset identified during processes 1 to 3.
	2. Answer the following question: Which branches correspond to an expressed area of concern? Mark these branches on the appropriate tree.
	3. Review the remaining, unmarked branches (gaps) for threats that were not identified by the participants during processes 1 to 3. Consider the following questions: • For which of the remaining branches is there a more than negligible possibility of a threat to the asset? Mark these branches on the tree. • For which of the remaining branches is there a negligible possibility or no possibility at all of a threat to the asset? Do not mark these branches.
	4. Record notes to clarify threats as appropriate (i.e., branches that do not map to an existing area of concern).
	5. A blank tree entitled "Other Problems (cont.)" is provided for you to record any unique threat actors not addressed in the threat profile. Complete the tree for any unique threats that apply to the critical asset.

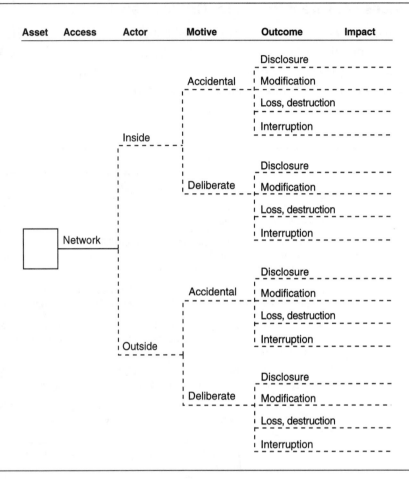

Threat Profile Worksheet: Human Actors Using Network Access

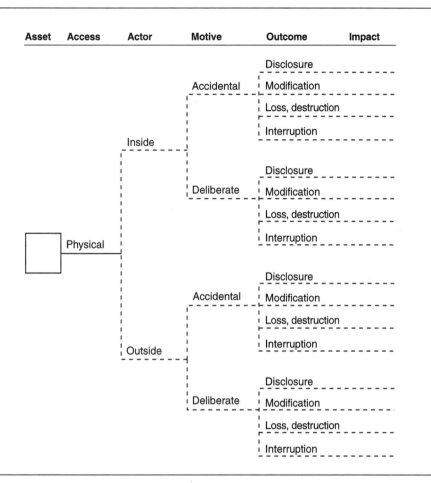

Threat Profile Worksheet: Human Actors Using Physical Access

Asset	Actor	Outcome	Impact
	Software defects	Disclosure	
		Modification	
		Loss, destruction	
		Interruption	
	Malicious code	Disclosure	
		Modification	
		Loss, destruction	
		Interruption	
	System crashes	Disclosure	
		Modification	
		Loss, destruction	
		Interruption	
	Hardware defects	Disclosure	
		Modification	
		Loss, destruction	
		Interruption	

Threat Profile Worksheet: System Problems

Asset	Actor	Outcome	Impact
		Disclosure	
	Power supply problems	Modification	
		Loss, destruction	
		Interruption	
		Disclosure	
	Telecommunications problems or unavailability	Modification	
		Loss, destruction	
		Interruption	
		Disclosure	
	Third-party problems or unavailability of third-party systems	Modification	
		Loss, destruction	
		Interruption	
		Disclosure	
	Natural disasters (e.g., flood, fire, tornado)	Modification	
		Loss, destruction	
		Interruption	
		Disclosure	
	Physical configuration or arrangement of buildings, offices, or equipment	Modification	
		Loss, destruction	
		Interruption	

Threat Profile Worksheet: Other Problems

Asset	Actor	Outcome	Impact
		Disclosure	
		Modification	
		Loss, destruction	
		Interruption	
		Disclosure	
		Modification	
		Loss, destruction	
		Interruption	
		Disclosure	
		Modification	
		Loss, destruction	
		Interruption	
		Disclosure	
		Modification	
		Loss, destruction	
		Interruption	
		Disclosure	
		Modification	
		Loss, destruction	
		Interruption	

Threat Profile Worksheet: Other Problems (*continued*)

B.2.4 Process 5: System(s) of Interest

Instructions	
Process 5	*Activity: Identify Key Classes of Components (Section 7.2)*
Purpose	To identify the system most associated with the critical asset
Instructions	Review the threat tree for *human actors using network access* in Section B.2.4. Use the following questions to guide your selection of the system(s) of interest. • Which system(s) is most closely linked to the critical asset? In which system(s) is the critical asset stored and processed? • Where outside the system of interest do critical information assets move? Backup system? Off-site storage? Other? • Based on the critical asset, which system(s) would be the target of a threat actor acting deliberately? Record the system(s) of interest for the critical asset on the System(s) of Interest Worksheet.

System(s) of Interest Worksheet

B.2.5 Process 5: Key Classes of Components

Instructions	
Process 5	*Activity: Identify Key Classes of Components (Section 7.2)*
Purpose	To identify key classes of components associated with the critical asset
Instructions	1. Consider key classes of components that are part of or related to the system of interest. Use the following questions to guide your selection of the key classes of components. • Which types of components are part of the system of interest? Consider servers, networking components, security components, desktop workstations, home machines, laptops, storage devices, wireless components, and others. • Which types of components are related to the system of interest? From which types of hosts can the system of interest be legitimately accessed? Desktop machines? Home machines? Laptops? Cellular phones? Handheld devices? Others? • How could threat actors access the system of interest? Via the Internet? Via the internal network? Shared external networks? Wireless devices? Others? • Which types of components could a threat actor use to access the system of interest? Which could serve as intermediate access points? Consider physical and network access to servers, networking components, security components, desktop workstations, home machines, laptops, storage devices, wireless components, and others. • What other systems could a threat actor use to access the system of interest? • Based on your answers to the above questions, which classes of components could be part of the threat scenarios? Based on the answers to the questions, decide which key classes of components could be part of the threat scenarios. Mark an *x* in the box by each applicable class on the Key Components Worksheet.
	2. Record your rationale for selecting each key class on the Key Components Worksheet.

Key Components Worksheet	
Class of Component	*Rationale for Selection*
❑ Servers	
❑ Networking components	
❑ Security components	
❑ Desktop workstations	
❑ Home computers	
❑ Laptops	
❑ Storage devices	
❑ Wireless components	
❑ Others (list) _____ _____ _____ _____	

B.2.6 Process 5: Infrastructure Components to Examine

Instructions	
Process 5	*Activity: Identify Infrastructure Components to Examine (Section 7.3)*
Purpose	To select specific components from each key class to evaluate for technology vulnerabilities
Instructions	1. From the key classes of components documented on the Key Components Worksheet, select specific components from each key class to evaluate for technology vulnerabilities. Use the following questions to guide your selection of infrastructure components. • Is the infrastructure component typical of its class? • How accessible is the infrastructure component? Is it "owned" by another organization? Is it a home machine? • How critical is the infrastructure component to business operations? Will you be interrupting business operations when you evaluate the component? • Will special permission or scheduling be required to evaluate the component? Record the selected components, including their IP addresses and host/DNS names, on the Infrastructure Components to Examine Worksheet.
	2. Record the rationale for selecting each infrastructure component on the Infrastructure Components to Examine Worksheet.
	3. Record the approach for evaluating each infrastructure component on the Infrastructure Components to Examine Worksheet. The approach should include the following information: • Who will perform the evaluation (e.g., IT staff, external experts) • The selected tools (e.g., software, checklists, scripts)

Infrastructure Components to Examine Worksheet			
Class of Component	*Selected Component/ IP Addresses/Host Names*	*Rationale*	*Approach*
System of interest			
Systems/servers			
Networking components			
Security components			
Desktop workstations			
Home computers			
Laptops			
Storage devices			
Wireless components			
Others			

B.2.7 Process 6: Summarize Technology Vulnerabilities

Instructions	
Process 6	*Activity: Review Technology Vulnerabilities and Summarize Results (Section 8.3)*
Purpose	To document a summary of the technology vulnerability evaluation
Instructions	1. For each evaluated component, review the proposed summary of the vulnerability evaluation. All analysis team members must understand • The types of vulnerabilities found and when they need to be addressed • The potential effect on the critical assets • How the technology vulnerabilities could be addressed (applying a patch, hardening a component, etc.) Make any necessary changes to the preliminary summary, and record the results on the Technology Vulnerabilities Summary Worksheet. (You can record the information after the workshop.) The vulnerability summary contains the following information for each component that was evaluated: • The number of vulnerabilities to fix immediately (high-severity vulnerabilities) • The number of vulnerabilities to fix soon (medium-severity vulnerabilities) • The number of vulnerabilities to fix later (low-severity vulnerabilities)
	2. Perform a gap analysis of the threat profile that you created during process 4. Turn to Section B.2.3, process 4: Threat Profile for Critical Asset. Reexamine the unmarked branches of the threat three for human actors using network access. Consider the following question: Do the technology vulnerabilities associated with the critical asset's key infrastructure components indicate that there is a more than negligible possibility of any additional threats to the asset? Mark any additional branches on the appropriate trees in Section B.2.3.

Technology Vulnerabilities Summary Worksheet		
Class	Selected Component/IP Address/Host Name	Vulnerability Summary

B.2.8 Process 6: Record Action Items

Instructions	
Process 6	*Activity: Review Technology Vulnerabilities and Summarize Results (Section 8.3)*
Purpose	To document any immediate or short-term actions or recommendations resulting from the technology vulnerability evaluation
Instructions	Review the vulnerability summary that you documented in Section B.2.7. Record any immediate or short-term actions or recommendations on the Actions and Recommendations for Addressing Technology Vulnerabilities Worksheet. Actions and recommendations are typically related to the technology vulnerabilities that were identified and the steps the organization needs to take to address those vulnerabilities.

Actions and Recommendations for Addressing Technology Vulnerabilities

B.2.9 Process 7: Risk Impact Descriptions

NOTE: Do not complete the entire worksheet during one activity. First complete the create narrative description of the potential impacts on the organization (the "Impact Description" field in the Impacts on the Organization Worksheet). Record impact values on the Impacts on the Organization Worksheet after evaluating impacts in Section B.2.11.

Instructions	
Process 7	*Activity: Identify the Impact of Threats to Critical Assets (Section 9.2)*
Purpose	To create narrative descriptions of impacts on the organization based on threat outcomes
Instructions	Potential impacts on your organization resulting from threats to your critical assets are generated according to threat outcome. Note that the second column in the Impacts on the Organization Worksheet contains questions to guide your creation of impact descriptions. Record descriptions of the impacts on the organization for each outcome on the Impacts on the Organization Worksheet. In general, the impact(s) on an organization for a given outcome will be the same regardless of the branch of the threat tree leading to that outcome. However, if there is a unique impact for a specific threat tree branch, note it in the description.

Impacts on the Organization			
Outcome	*Consider*	*Impact Descriptions*	*Values*
Disclosure	• How could the organization's reputation be affected if this asset were disclosed? • How could customer confidence be affected if this asset were disclosed? • How could the health of customers be affected if this asset were disclosed? • How could employee productivity be affected if this asset were disclosed? • How could other users of this asset be affected if this asset were disclosed? • What fines or legal penalties could be imposed as a result of disclosure of this asset?		*(continued)*

Impacts on the Organization (*continued*)			
Outcome	*Consider*	*Impact Descriptions*	*Values*
Disclosure (*continued*)	• What lawsuits could be filed against the organization if this asset were disclosed?		
	• How could the organization be affected financially if this asset were disclosed?		
	• What other impacts could occur if this asset were disclosed (for example, ethical considerations, other legal/financial impacts)?		
Modification	• How could the organization's reputation be affected if this asset were modified?		
	• How could customer confidence be affected if this asset were modified?		
	• How could the health of customers be affected if this asset were modified?		
	• How could employee productivity be affected if this asset were modified?		
	• How would other users of this asset be affected if this asset were modified?		
	• What fines or legal penalties could be imposed if this asset were modified?		
	• What lawsuits could be filed against the organization if this asset were modified?		
	• How could the organization be affected financially if this asset were modified?		
	• What other impacts could occur if this asset were modified (for example, ethical considerations, other legal/financial impacts)?		
Destruction/ Loss	• How could the organization's reputation be affected if this asset were destroyed, lost, or unavailable?		
	• How could customer confidence be affected if this asset were destroyed, lost, or unavailable?		
	• How could the health of customers be affected if this asset were destroyed, lost, or unavailable?		
	• How could employee productivity be affected if this asset were destroyed, lost, or unavailable?		
	• How would other users of this asset be affected if this asset were destroyed, lost, or unavailable?		

Impacts on the Organization (continued)			
Outcome	Consider	Impact Descriptions	Values
Destruction/ Loss (continued)	• What fines or legal penalties could be imposed as a result of destruction, loss, or unavailability of this asset?		
	• What lawsuits could be filed against the organization if this asset were destroyed, lost, or unavailable?		
	• How could the organization be affected financially if this asset were destroyed, lost, or unavailable?		
	• What other impacts could occur if this asset were destroyed, lost, or unavailable (for example, ethical considerations, other legal/financial impacts)?		
Interruption	• How could the organization's reputation be affected if access to this asset were unavailable?		
	• How could customer confidence be affected if access to this asset were unavailable?		
	• How could the health of customers be affected if access to this asset were unavailable?		
	• How could employee productivity be affected if access to this asset were unavailable?		
	• How would other users of this asset be affected if access to this asset were unavailable?		
	• What fines or legal penalties could be imposed as a result of unavailability of this asset?		
	• What lawsuits could be filed against the organization if access to this asset were unavailable?		
	• How could the organization be affected financially if access to this asset were unavailable?		
	• What other impacts could occur if access to this asset were unavailable (for example, ethical considerations, other legal/financial impacts)?		

B.2.10 Process 7: Risk Evaluation Criteria Worksheet

Instructions	
Process 7	*Activity: Create Risk Evaluation Criteria (Section 9.3)*
Purpose	To develop criteria to evaluate the impact descriptions that you created in Section B.2.9
Instructions	For each area of impact, define specific measures that define high, medium, and low risks for your organization. Use the following questions to guide your creation of impact values: • What defines a "high" impact on the organization? • What defines a "medium" impact on the organization? • What defines a "low" impact on the organization? Record the criteria on the Evaluation Criteria Worksheet. Note: You can use the evaluation criteria in Appendix A (Section 4) as an example. If you use the example as a guide, make sure that you modify it appropriately to make it meaningful and specific to you and your organization.

Evaluation Criteria			
Impact Area	*High*	*Medium*	*Low*
Reputation/ customer confidence			
Life/health of customers			

Evaluation Criteria (continued)			
Impact Area	High	Medium	Low
Productivity			
Fines/legal penalties			
Financial			
Other			

B.2.11 Process 7: Risk Profile Worksheet

NOTE: The tables and diagrams associated with the threat profiles and impact values already exist in this appendix. Only the instructions for completing them are listed here. See Section B.2.7 for threat profiles and Section B.2.9 for impact values.

Instructions	
Process 7	*Activity: Evaluate the Impact of Threats to Critical Assets (Section 9.4)*
Purpose	To evaluate the impact descriptions in Section B.2.9 against the evaluation criteria in Section B.2.10
Instructions	1. Evaluate the impact descriptions in Section B.2.9 against the evaluation criteria in Section B.2.10. Record the impact values for each impact description in the "Values" column on the Impacts on the Organization Worksheet (Section B.2.9).
	2. Also record the impact values in the "Impact" column of the Threat Profile Worksheet (Section B.2.3). If more than one value is associated with any outcome, record all of them in the "Impact" column. For example, if disclosure has three statements describing the impact on the organization, one with a value of "high" and two with values of "medium," record "medium, high" in the "Impact" column.

B.2.12 Process 8: Risk Mitigation Plans

Instructions	
Process 8	*Activity: Create Risk Mitigation Plans (Section 10.5)*
Purpose	To identify actions, or countermeasures, designed to counter the threats to the critical asset
Instructions	1. Decide whether to accept or mitigate the risks to each critical asset. Typically, when you decide whether to accept or mitigate a risk, you base your decision on whether you want to take action to counteract the underlying threat. Make sure that you record your decisions on the Threat Profile Worksheet in Section B.2.3.
	Note that you must make a decision for each risk in the risk profile, which includes the following categories:
	• Human actors using network access
	• Human actors using physical access
	• System problems
	• Other problems

Instructions *(continued)*	
Process 8	*Activity: Create Risk Mitigation Plans (Section 10.5)*
Instructions *(continued)*	2. For each risk that you decide to mitigate, create risk mitigation plans for the critical asset by selecting mitigation actions, or countermeasures, designed to counter the threats to the critical assets. Make sure that you review the survey results and contextual security practice information from processes 1 to 3 before creating mitigation plans. Use the following questions to guide your creation of risk mitigation plans: • What actions could you take to *recognize* or detect this threat type as it is occurring? • What actions could you take to *resist* or prevent this threat type from occurring? • What actions could you take to *recover* from this threat type if it occurs? • What other actions could you take to address this threat type? • How will you test or verify that this mitigation plan works and is effective?

Mitigation Plan for Human Actors Using Network Access	
Questions	*Actions*
What actions could you take to recognize or detect this threat type as it is occurring? What actions could you take to resist or prevent this threat type from occurring? What actions could you take to recover from this threat type if it occurs? What other actions could you take to address this threat type? How will you test or verify that this mitigation plan works and is effective?	*Consider administrative, physical, and technical actions that you could take.*

Mitigation Plan for Human Actors Using Physical Access	
Questions	*Actions*
What actions could you take to recognize or detect this threat type as it is occurring? What actions could you take to resist or prevent this threat type from occurring? What actions could you take to recover from this threat type if it occurs? What other actions could you take to address this threat type? How will you test or verify that this mitigation plan works and is effective?	*Consider administrative, physical, and technical actions that you could take.*

Mitigation Plan for System Problems	
Questions	*Actions*
What actions could you take to recognize or detect this threat type as it is occurring? What actions could you take to resist or prevent this threat type from occurring? What actions could you take to recover from this threat type if it occurs? What other actions could you take to address this threat type? How will you test or verify that this mitigation plan works and is effective?	*Consider administrative, physical, and technical actions that you could take.*

Mitigation Plan for Other Problems	
Questions	*Actions*
What actions could you take to recognize or detect this threat type as it is occurring? What actions could you take to resist or prevent this threat type from occurring? What actions could you take to recover from this threat type if it occurs? What other actions could you take to address this threat type? How will you test or verify that this mitigation plan works and is effective?	*Consider administrative, physical, and technical actions that you could take.*

B.3 Strategies and Actions

Use the worksheets in this section when you define and document the organizationwide protection strategy and near-term action items during process 8A. The following worksheets are contained in this section:

- Current Security Practices Worksheet
- Protection Strategy Worksheet
- Action List Worksheet

B.3.1 Current Security Practices Worksheets

Instructions	
Process 8	*Activity: Before the Workshop: Consolidate Information from processes 1 to 3 (Section 10.2)*
Purpose	To compile current security practice and organizational vulnerability information from processes 1 to 3.
Instructions	1. Note that there are two tables for each practice area in the Current Security Practices Worksheet. The first table summarizes the results of the surveys that were completed during processes 1 to 3. The second table consolidates contextual information (protection strategy practices and organizational vulnerabilities) that was identified during the protection strategy discussion from processes 1 to 3. Compile the results of the surveys that you asked participants to complete during processes 1 to 3. Consider the following guidelines when compiling survey data: • If 75 percent or more of respondents replied "yes," mark the result as **Yes**. The percentage of respondents stating that a practice was used by the organization was high enough that the practice is most likely used by the organization. • If 75 percent or more of respondents replied "no," mark the result as **No**. The percentage of respondents stating that a practice was not used by the organization was high enough that the practice is most likely not used by the organization. • If 75 percent or more of respondents replied "Don't Know," mark the result as **Unclear**. Neither the yes nor no criteria were met. Since the percentages of "yes" and "no" responses do not meet the 75 percent threshold, indicate that it is unclear whether the practice is present or not. This result could mean that some people use the practice while others don't, or that the practice is present to some degree but is not effective enough. *(continued)*

Instructions *(continued)*	
Process 8	*Activity: Before the Workshop: Consolidate Information from processes 1 to 3 (Section 10.2)*
Instructions *(continued)*	2. Compile contextual information about security practices and organizational vulnerabilities that you recorded during processes 1 to 3. Recall that you conducted a facilitated discussion about current security practices in the organization after participants completed the surveys.

Current Security Practices Worksheet

Security Awareness and Training (SP1): Survey Results				
Survey Statement	*Senior Managers*	*Operational Area Managers*	*Staff*	*IT Staff*
Staff members understand their security roles and responsibilities. This is documented and verified.				
There is adequate in-house expertise for all supported services, mechanisms, and technologies (e.g., logging, monitoring, or encryption), including their secure operation. This is documented and verified.				
Security awareness, training, and periodic reminders are provided for all personnel. Staff understanding is documented, and compliance is periodically verified.				

Security Awareness and Training (SP1): Contextual Information		
Organizational Level	*Protection Strategy Practices*	*Organizational Vulnerabilities*
Senior management		
Operational area management		

Security Awareness and Training (SP1): Contextual Information *(continued)*		
Organizational Level	*Protection Strategy Practices*	*Organizational Vulnerabilities*
Staff		
IT staff		

Security Strategy (SP2): Survey Results				
Survey Statement	*Senior Managers*	*Operational Area Managers*	*Staff*	*IT Staff*
The organization's business strategies routinely incorporate security considerations.				
Security strategies and policies take into consideration the organization's business strategies and goals.				
Security strategies, goals, and objectives are documented and are routinely reviewed, updated, and communicated to the organization.				

Security Strategy (SP2): Contextual Information		
Organizational Level	*Protection Strategy Practices*	*Organizational Vulnerabilities*
Senior management		
Operational area management		
Staff		
IT staff		

Security Management (SP3): Survey Results				
Survey Statement	Senior Managers	Operational Area Managers	Staff	IT Staff
Management allocates sufficient funds and resources to information security activities.				
Security roles and responsibilities are defined for all staff in the organization.				
The organization's hiring and termination practices for staff take information security issues into account.				
The organization manages information security risks by assessing risks to information security and taking steps to mitigate information security risks.				
Management receives and acts upon routine reports summarizing security-related information (e.g., audits, logs, risk and vulnerability assessments).				

Security Management (SP3): Contextual Information		
Organizational Level	Protection Strategy Practices	Organizational Vulnerabilities
Senior management		
Operational area management		
Staff		
IT staff		

Security Policies and Regulations (SP4): Survey Results				
Survey Statement	*Senior Managers*	*Operational Area Managers*	*Staff*	*IT Staff*
The organization has a comprehensive set of documented, current policies that are periodically reviewed and updated.				
There is a documented process for management of security policies: 1. Creation 2. Administration (including periodic reviews and updates) 3. Communication				
The organization has a documented process for evaluating and ensuring compliance with information security policies, applicable laws and regulations, and insurance requirements.				
The organization uniformly enforces its security policies.				

Security Policies and Regulations (SP4): Contextual Information		
Organizational Level	*Protection Strategy Practices*	*Organizational Vulnerabilities*
Senior management		
Operational area management		
Staff		
IT staff		

Collaborative Security Management (SP5): Survey Results				
Survey Statement	*Senior Managers*	*Operational Area Managers*	*Staff*	*IT Staff*
The organization has policies and procedures for protecting information when working with external organizations (e.g., third parties, collaborators, subcontractors, or partners): 1. Protecting information belonging to other organizations 2. Understanding the security policies and procedures of external organizations 3. Ending access to information by terminated external personnel				
The organization has verified that outsourced security services, mechanisms, and technologies meet its needs and requirements.				

Collaborative Security Management (S5): Contextual Information		
Organizational Level	*Protection Strategy Practices*	*Organizational Vulnerabilities*
Senior management		
Operational area management		
Staff		
IT staff		

Contingency Planning/Disaster Recovery (SP6): Survey Results				
Survey Statement	Senior Managers	Operational Area Managers	Staff	IT Staff
An analysis of operations, applications, and data criticality has been performed.				
The organization has documented, reviewed, and tested business continuity or emergency operation plans, disaster recovery plan(s), and contingency plan(s) for responding to emergencies.				
The contingency, disaster recovery, and business continuity plans consider physical and electronic access requirements and controls.				
All staff are aware of the contingency, disaster recovery, and business continuity plans and understand and are able to carry out their responsibilities.				

Contingency Planning/Disaster Recovery (SP6): Contextual Information		
Organizational Level	Protection Strategy Practices	Organizational Vulnerabilities
Senior management		
Operational area management		
Staff		
IT staff		

Physical Security Plans and Procedures (OP1.1): Survey Results				
Survey Statement	Senior Managers	Operational Area Managers	Staff	IT Staff
Facility security plans and procedures for safeguarding the premises, buildings, and any restricted areas are documented and tested.				
There are documented policies and procedures for managing visitors.				
There are documented policies and procedures for physical control of hardware and software.				

Physical Security Plans and Procedures (OP1.1): Contextual Information		
Organizational Level	Protection Strategy Practices	Organizational Vulnerabilities
Senior management		
Operational area management		
Staff		
IT staff		

Physical Access Control (OP1.2): Survey Results				
Survey Statement	*Senior Managers*	*Operational Area Managers*	*Staff*	*IT Staff*
There are documented policies and procedures for controlling physical access to work areas and hardware (computers, communication devices, etc.) and software media.				
Workstations and other components that allow access to sensitive information are physically safeguarded to prevent unauthorized access.				

Physical Access Control (OP1.2): Contextual Information		
Organizational Level	*Protection Strategy Practices*	*Organizational Vulnerabilities*
Senior management		
Operational area management		
Staff		
IT staff		

Monitoring and Auditing Physical Security (OP1.3): Survey Results				
Survey Statement	Senior Managers	Operational Area Managers	Staff	IT Staff
Maintenance records are kept to document the repairs and modifications of a facility's physical components.				
An individual's or group's actions can be accounted for with respect to all physically controlled media.				
Audit and monitoring records are routinely examined for anomalies, and corrective action is taken as needed.				

Monitoring and Auditing Physical Security (OP1.3): Contextual Information		
Organizational Level	Protection Strategy Practices	Organizational Vulnerabilities
Senior management		
Operational area management		
Staff		
IT staff		

System and Network Management (OP2.1): Survey Results				
Survey Statement	Senior Managers	Operational Area Managers	Staff	IT Staff
There are documented and tested security plan(s) for safeguarding the systems and networks.				
Sensitive information is protected by secure storage (e.g., backups stored off-site, discard process for sensitive information).				
The integrity of installed software is regularly verified.				
All systems are up to date with respect to revisions, patches, and recommendations in security advisories.				
There is a documented and tested data backup plan for backups of both software and data. All staff understand their responsibilities under the backup plans.				
Changes to IT hardware and software are planned, controlled, and documented.				
IT staff members follow procedures when issuing, changing, and terminating users' passwords, accounts, and privileges: • Unique user identification is required for all information system users, including third-party users. • Default accounts and default passwords have been removed from systems.				
Only necessary services are running on systems; all unnecessary services have been removed.				

System and Network Management (OP2.1): Contextual Information		
Organizational Level	Protection Strategy Practices	Organizational Vulnerabilities
Senior management		

(continued)

System and Network Management (OP2.1): Contextual Information (*continued*)		
Organizational Level	*Protection Strategy Practices*	*Organizational Vulnerabilities*
Operational area management		
Staff		
IT staff		

System Administration Tools (OP2.2): Survey Results				
Survey Statement	*Senior Managers*	*Operational Area Managers*	*Staff*	*IT Staff*
Tools and mechanisms for secure system and network administration are used, and they are routinely reviewed and updated or replaced.				

System Administration Tools (OP2.2): Contextual Information		
Organizational Level	*Protection Strategy Practices*	*Organizational Vulnerabilities*
Senior management		
Operational area management		

(*continued*)

System Administration Tools (OP2.2): Contextual Information *(continued)*		
Organizational Level	Protection Strategy Practices	Organizational Vulnerabilities
Staff		
IT staff		

Monitoring and Auditing IT Security (OP2.3): Survey Results				
Survey Statement	Senior Managers	Operational Area Managers	Staff	IT Staff
System and network monitoring and auditing tools are routinely used by the organization. Unusual activity is dealt with according to the appropriate policy or procedure.				
Firewall and other security components are periodically audited for compliance with policy.				

Monitoring and Auditing IT Security (OP2.3): Contextual Information		
Organizational Level	Protection Strategy Practices	Organizational Vulnerabilities
Senior management		
Operational area management		

(continued)

Monitoring and Auditing IT Security (OP2.3): Contextual Information *(continued)*		
Organizational Level	*Protection Strategy Practices*	*Organizational Vulnerabilities*
Staff		
IT staff		

Authentication and Authorization (OP2.4): Survey Results				
Survey Statement	*Senior Managers*	*Operational Area Managers*	*Staff*	*IT Staff*
Appropriate access controls and user authentication (e.g., file permissions, network configuration) consistent with policy are used to restrict user access to information, sensitive systems, specific applications and services, and network connections.				
There are documented policies and procedures to establish and terminate the right of access to information for both individuals and groups.				
Methods or mechanisms are provided to ensure that sensitive information has not been accessed, altered, or destroyed in an unauthorized manner. Methods or mechanisms are periodically reviewed and verified.				

Authentication and Authorization (OP2.4): Contextual Information		
Organizational Level	*Protection Strategy Practices*	*Organizational Vulnerabilities*
Senior management		

Authentication and Authorization (OP2.4): Contextual Information *(continued)*		
Organizational Level	*Protection Strategy Practices*	*Organizational Vulnerabilities*
Operational area management		
Staff		
IT staff		

Vulnerability Management (OP2.5): Survey Results				
Survey Statement	*Senior Managers*	*Operational Area Managers*	*Staff*	*IT Staff*
There is a documented set of procedures for managing vulnerabilities: • Selecting vulnerability evaluation tools, checklists, and scripts • Keeping up to date with known vulnerability types and attack methods • Reviewing sources of information on vulnerability announcements, security alerts, and notices • Identifying infrastructure components to be evaluated • Scheduling vulnerability evaluations • Interpreting and responding to the results • Maintaining secure storage and disposition of vulnerability data				
Vulnerability management procedures are followed and are periodically reviewed and updated.				

(continued)

Vulnerability Management (OP2.5): Survey Results *(continued)*				
Survey Statement	*Senior Managers*	*Operational Area Managers*	*Staff*	*IT Staff*
Technology vulnerability assessments are performed on a periodic basis, and vulnerabilities are addressed when they are identified.				

Vulnerability Management (OP2.5): Contextual Information		
Organizational Level	*Protection Strategy Practices*	*Organizational Vulnerabilities*
Senior management		
Operational area management		
Staff		
IT staff		

Encryption (OP2.6): Survey Results				
Survey Statement	Senior Managers	Operational Area Managers	Staff	IT Staff
Appropriate security controls are used to protect sensitive information while in storage and during transmission (e.g., data encryption, public key infrastructure, virtual private network technology).				
Encrypted protocols are used for remote management of systems, routers, and firewalls.				

Encryption (OP2.6): Contextual Information		
Organizational Level	Protection Strategy Practices	Organizational Vulnerabilities
Senior management		
Operational area management		
Staff		
IT staff		

Security Architecture and Design (OP2.7): Survey Results				
Survey Statement	*Senior Managers*	*Operational Area Managers*	*Staff*	*IT Staff*
System architecture and design for new and revised systems include the following considerations: • Security strategies, policies, and procedures • History of security compromises • Results of security risk assessments				
The organization has up-to-date diagrams that show the enterprisewide security architecture and network topology.				

Security Architecture and Design (OP2.7): Contextual Information		
Organizational Level	*Protection Strategy Practices*	*Organizational Vulnerabilities*
Senior management		
Operational area management		
Staff		
IT staff		

Incident Management (OP3.1): Survey Results				
Survey Statement	Senior Managers	Operational Area Managers	Staff	IT Staff
Documented procedures exist for identifying, reporting, and responding to suspected security incidents and violations.				
Incident management procedures are periodically tested, verified, and updated.				
There are documented policies and procedures for working with law enforcement agencies.				

Incident Management (OP3.1): Contextual Information		
Organizational Level	Protection Strategy Practices	Organizational Vulnerabilities
Senior management		
Operational area management		
Staff		
IT staff		

General Staff Practices (OP3.2): Survey Results				
Survey Statement	Senior Managers	Operational Area Managers	Staff	IT Staff
Staff members follow good security practice: • Securing information for which they are responsible • Not divulging sensitive information to others (resistance to social engineering) • Having adequate ability to use information technology hardware and software • Using good password practices • Understanding and following security policies and regulations • Recognizing and reporting incidents				
All staff at all levels of responsibility implement their assigned roles and responsibility for information security.				
There are documented procedures for authorizing and overseeing all staff (including personnel from third-party organizations) who work with sensitive information or who work in locations where the information resides.				

General Staff Practices (OP3.2): Contextual Information		
Organizational Level	Protection Strategy Practices	Organizational Vulnerabilities
Senior management		
Operational area management		

(continued)

General Staff Practices (OP3.2): Contextual Information *(continued)*		
Organizational Level	*Protection Strategy Practices*	*Organizational Vulnerabilities*
Staff		
IT staff		

B.3.2 Protection Strategy Worksheets

Instructions	
Process 8	*Activity: Create Protection Strategy (Section 10.3)*
Purpose	To create an organizationwide strategy for enabling security activities
Instructions	1. Review the survey results and contextual security practice information from processes 1 to 3 before creating the protection strategy.
	2. For each security practice area, select strategies to enable security practices in your organization. When selecting strategies, consider the following: • The current strategies in this area that your organization should continue to use or improve • New strategies that your organization should adopt Note that the Protection Strategy Worksheet contains questions to guide your selection of strategies.
	3. Finally, consider what issues related to each security practice area cannot be addressed by your organization. Record any such issues that you identify.

Protection Strategy Worksheet

<table>
<tr>
<td colspan="2">Protection Strategy for Strategic Practices
Security Awareness and Training (SP1)</td>
</tr>
<tr>
<td>Questions to Consider</td>
<td>Strategies</td>
</tr>
<tr>
<td>
<ul>
<li>What can you do to maintain or improve the level of information security training that all staff members receive (consider awareness training as well as technology-related training)?</li>
<li>Does your organization have adequate in-house expertise for all supported technologies? What can you do to improve your staff's technology expertise?</li>
<li>What can you do to ensure that all staff members understand their security roles and responsibilities?</li>
</ul>
</td>
<td>
Consider the following:
<ul>
<li>The current strategies in this area that your organization should continue to use</li>
<li>New strategies that your organization should adopt</li>
</ul>
</td>
</tr>
<tr>
<td colspan="2">Issues: What issues related to security awareness and training cannot be addressed by your organization?</td>
</tr>
</table>

<table>
<tr>
<td colspan="2">Protection Strategy for Strategic Practices
Security Strategy (SP2)</td>
</tr>
<tr>
<td>Questions to Consider</td>
<td>Strategies</td>
</tr>
<tr>
<td>
<ul>
<li>Are security issues incorporated into your organization's business strategy? What can you do to improve the way in which security issues are integrated with your organization's business strategy?</li>
<li>Are business issues incorporated into your organization's security strategy? What can you do to improve the way in which business issues are integrated with your organization's security strategy?</li>
<li>What can you do to improve the way in which security strategies, goals, and objectives are documented and communicated to the organization?</li>
</ul>
</td>
<td>
Consider the following:
<ul>
<li>The current strategies in this area that your organization should continue to use</li>
<li>New strategies that your organization should adopt</li>
</ul>
</td>
</tr>
<tr>
<td colspan="2">Issues: What issues related to security strategy cannot be addressed by your organization?</td>
</tr>
</table>

Protection Strategy for Strategic Practices Security Management (SP3)	
Questions to Consider	*Strategies*
• Does management allocate sufficient funds and resources to information security activities? What level of funding for information security activities is appropriate for your organization? • What can you do to ensure that security roles and responsibilities are defined for all staff in your organization? • Do your organization's hiring and retention practices take information security issues into account (also applies to contractors and vendors)? What could you do to improve your organization's hiring and retention practices? • What can you do to improve the way in which your organization manages its information security risk? • What can you do to improve the way in which security-related information is communicated to your organization's management?	Consider the following: • The current strategies in this area that your organization should continue to use • New strategies that your organization should adopt
Issues: What issues related to security management cannot be addressed by your organization?	

Protection Strategy for Strategic Practices Security Policies and Regulations (SP4)	
Questions to Consider	*Strategies*
• What can you do to ensure that your organization has a comprehensive set of documented, current security policies? • What can you do to improve the way in which your organization creates, updates, and communicates security policies? • Does your organization have procedures to ensure compliance with laws and regulations affecting security? What can you do to improve how well your organization complies with laws and regulations affecting security? • What can you do to ensure that your organization uniformly enforces its security policies?	Consider the following: • The current strategies in this area that your organization should continue to use • New strategies that your organization should adopt
Issues: What issues related to security policies and regulations cannot be addressed by your organization?	

Protection Strategy for Strategic Practices Collaborative Security Management (SP5)	
Questions to Consider	*Strategies*
• Does your organization have policies and procedures for protecting information when working with external organizations (e.g., third parties, collaborators, subcontractors, or partners)? What can your organization do to improve the way in which it protects information when working with external organizations? • What can your organization do to improve the way in which it verifies that external organizations are taking proper steps to protect critical information and systems? • What can your organization do to improve the way in which it verifies that outsourced security services, mechanisms, and technologies meet its needs and requirements?	Consider the following: • The current strategies in this area that your organization should continue to use • New strategies that your organization should adopt
Issues: What issues related to collaborative security management cannot be addressed by your organization?	

Protection Strategy for Strategic Practices Contingency Planning/Disaster Recovery (SP6)	
Questions to Consider	*Strategies*
• Does your organization have a defined business continuity plan? Has the business continuity plan been tested? What can you do to ensure that your organization has a defined and tested business continuity plan? • Does your organization have a defined disaster recovery plan? Has the disaster recovery plan been tested? What can you do to ensure that your organization has a defined and tested disaster recovery plan? • What can you do to ensure that staff members are aware of and understand your organization's business continuity and disaster recovery plans?	Consider the following: • The current strategies in this area that your organization should continue to use • New strategies that your organization should adopt
Issues: What issues related to contingency planning and disaster recovery cannot be addressed by your organization?	

Protection Strategy for Operational Practices Physical Security (OP1)	
Questions to Consider	*Strategies*
• What training and education initiatives could help your organization maintain or improve its physical security practices? • What funding level is appropriate to support your organization's physical security needs? • Are your policies and procedures sufficient for your organization's physical security needs? How could they be improved? • Who has responsibility for physical security? Should anyone else be involved? • What other departments in your organization should be involved with physical security? • What external experts could help you with physical security? How will you communicate your requirements? How will you verify that your requirements were met?	
Issues: What issues related to physical security cannot be addressed by your organization?	

Protection Strategy for Operational Practices Information Technology Security (OP2)	
Questions to Consider	*Strategies*
• What training and education initiatives could help your organization maintain or improve its information technology security practices? • What funding level is appropriate to support your organization's information technology security needs? • Are your policies and procedures sufficient for your organization's information technology security needs? How could they be improved? • Who has responsibility for information technology security? Should anyone else be involved? • What other departments in your organization should be involved with information technology security?	

Protection Strategy for Operational Practices Information Technology Security (OP2) *(continued)*	
Questions to Consider	*Strategies*
• What external experts could help you with information technology security? How will you communicate your requirements? How will you verify that your requirements were met?	
Issues: What issues related to information technology security cannot be addressed by your organization?	

Protection Strategy for Operational Practices Staff Security (OP3)	
Questions to Consider	*Strategies*
• What training and education initiatives could help your organization maintain or improve its staff security practices? • What funding level is appropriate to support your staff security needs? • Are your policies and procedures sufficient for your staff security needs? How could they be improved? • Who has responsibility for staff security? Should anyone else be involved? • What other departments in your organization should be involved with staff security? • What external experts could help you with staff security? How will you communicate your requirements? How will you verify that your requirements were met?	
Issues: What issues related to staff security cannot be addressed by your organization?	

B.3.3 Action List Worksheet

Instructions	
Process 8	*Activity: Create Action List (Section 10.6)*
Purpose	To define action items that people in your organization can take in the near term without the need for specialized training, policy changes, etc.
Instructions	1. As you created the protection strategy and risk mitigation plans, you should have recorded any near-term actions that could help you implement the strategy and plans. Review your list of actions and decide if any are appropriate for the action list. Record the action items on the Action List Worksheet.
	2. Think about any additional near-term actions that could help you implement your protection strategy and risk mitigation plans. Answer the following question: What near-term actions need to be taken? Remember to review the actions and recommendations that you recorded in Section B.2.8. Record the action items on the Action List Worksheet.
	3. Now that you have identified specific action items for the action list, you need to assign responsibility for completing them as well as a completion date. Answer the following question for each action item on your list and record the results on the Action List Worksheet: • Who will be responsible for each action item? • By when does the action item need to be addressed? • What can management do to facilitate the completion of this action item?

Action List Worksheet	
Action Item	*Information*
	Responsibility: Completion date: *(continued)*

Action List Worksheet *(continued)*	
Action Item	*Information*
	Required management actions:
	Responsibility: Completion date: Required management actions:

Appendix C
Catalog of Practices

This appendix contains the catalog of practices used in the OCTAVE approach. The catalog of practices comprises a collection of good strategic and operational security practices. An organization that is conducting an information security risk evaluation measures itself against this catalog of practices. The catalog is used as a measurement for what the organization is currently doing well with respect to security (its current security practices) and what it is not doing well (its organizational vulnerabilities). During each knowledge elicitation workshop, participants fill out a survey and then discuss any issues from the survey that they feel are important. The catalog of practices is also used during the creation of a new or revised protection strategy for the organization and risk mitigation plans.

The catalog of practices is deliberately divided into two types of practices: strategic and operational. Strategic practices focus on organizational issues at the policy level and provide good general management practices. Strategic practices include issues that are business-related as well as those that require organization-wide planning and participation. Operational practices focus on technology-related concerns. They include issues related to how people use, interact with, and protect technology. Since strategic practices are based on good management practice, they should be fairly stable over time. Operational practices are more subject to changes as technology advances and new practices arise to deal with those changes.

The catalog of practices is a general catalog; it is not specific to any domain, organization, or set of regulations. It can be modified to suit a particular domain's standard of due care or set of regulations (e.g., the medical community and HIPPA security regulations). It can also be extended to add organization-specific standards, or it can be modified to reflect the terminology of a specific domain.

Figure C-1 depicts the structure of the catalog of practices; the details can be found on the following pages. This catalog was developed using several sources, which are referenced on the last page of this appendix. In addition to these security-related references, we also used our experience developing, delivering, and analyzing the results of the Information Security Evaluation (ISE), a vulnerability assessment technique developed by the Software Engineering Institute and delivered to a variety of organization over the past six years.

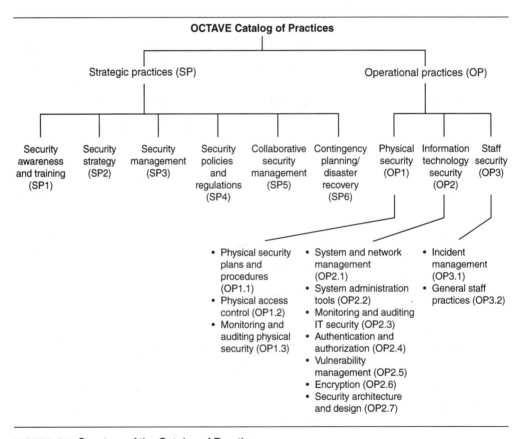

FIGURE C-1 Structure of the Catalog of Practices

	Strategic Practices **Security Awareness and Training (SP1)**
SP1.1	Staff members understand their security roles and responsibilities. This is documented and verified.
SP1.2	There is adequate in-house expertise for all supported services, mechanisms, and technologies (e.g., logging, monitoring, or encryption), including their secure operation. This is documented and verified.

SP1.3	Security awareness, training, and periodic reminders are provided for all personnel. Staff understanding is documented and conformance is periodically verified.
	Training includes these topics:
	• Security strategies, goals, and objectives
	• Security regulations, policies, and procedures
	• Policies and procedures for working with third parties
	• Contingency and disaster recovery plans
	• Physical security requirements
	• Users' perspective on
	   — system and network management
	   — system administration tools
	   — monitoring and auditing for physical and information technology security
	   — authentication and authorization
	   — vulnerability management
	   — encryption
	   — architecture and design
	• Incident management
	• General staff practices
	• Enforcement, sanctions, and disciplinary actions for security violations
	• How to properly access sensitive information or work in areas where sensitive information is accessible
	• Termination policies and procedures relative to security

	Strategic Practices **Security Strategy (SP2)**
SP2.1	The organization's business strategies routinely incorporate security considerations.
SP2.2	Security strategies and policies take into consideration the organization's business strategies and goals.
SP2.3	Security strategies, goals, and objectives are documented and are routinely reviewed, updated, and communicated to the organization.

	Strategic Practices **Security Management (SP3)**
SP3.1	Management allocates sufficient funds and resources to information security activities.
SP3.2	Security roles and responsibilities are defined for all staff in the organization.
SP3.3	The organization's hiring and termination practices for staff take information security issues into account.
SP3.4	The required levels of information security and how they are applied to individuals and groups are documented and enforced.
SP3.5	The organization manages information security risks, including • Assessing risks to information security both periodically and in response to major changes in technology, internal/external threats, or the organization's systems and operations • Taking steps to mitigate risks to an acceptable level • Maintaining an acceptable level of risk • Using information security risk assessments to help select cost-effective security/control measures, balancing implementation costs against potential losses
SP3.6	Management receives and acts upon routine reports summarizing the results of • Review of system logs • Review of audit trails • Technology vulnerability assessments • Security incidents and the responses to them • Risk assessments • Physical security reviews • Security improvement plans and recommendations

	Strategic Practices **Security Policies and Regulations (SP4)**
SP4.1	The organization has a comprehensive set of documented, current policies that are periodically reviewed and updated. These policies address key security topic areas, including • Security strategy and management • Security risk management • Physical security • System and network management • System administration tools • Monitoring and auditing • Authentication and authorization • Vulnerability management

	Strategic Practices **Security Policies and Regulations (SP4)** *(continued)*
SP4.1 *(continued)*	• Encryption • Security architecture and design • Incident management • Staff security practices • Applicable laws and regulations • Awareness and training • Collaborative information security • Contingency planning and disaster recovery
SP4.2	There is a documented process for management of security policies, including • Creation • Administration (including periodic reviews and updates) • Communication
SP4.3	The organization has a documented process for periodic evaluation (technical and nontechnical) of compliance with information security policies, applicable laws and regulations, and insurance requirements.
SP4.4	The organization has a documented process to ensure compliance with information security policies, applicable laws and regulations, and insurance requirements.
SP4.5	The organization uniformly enforces its security policies.
SP4.6	Testing and revision of security policies and procedures are restricted to authorized personnel.

	Strategic Practices **Collaborative Security Management (SP5)**
SP5.1	The organization has documented, monitored, and enforced procedures for protecting its information when working with external organizations (e.g., third parties, collaborators, subcontractors, or partners).
SP5.2	The organization has verified that outsourced security services, mechanisms, and technologies meet its needs and requirements.
SP5.3	The organization documents, monitors, and enforces protection strategies for information belonging to external organizations that is accessed from its own infrastructure components or is used by its own personnel.
SP5.4	The organization provides and verifies awareness and training on applicable external organizations' security policies and procedures for personnel who are involved with those external organizations.
SP5.5	There are documented procedures for terminated external personnel specifying appropriate security measures for ending their access. These procedures are communicated and coordinated with the external organization.

	Strategic Practices **Contingency Planning/Disaster Recovery (SP6)**
SP6.1	An analysis of operations, applications, and data criticality has been performed.
SP6.2	The organization has documented • Business continuity or emergency operation plans • Disaster recovery plan(s) • Contingency plan(s) for responding to emergencies
SP6.3	The contingency, disaster recovery, and business continuity plans consider physical and electronic access requirements and controls.
SP6.4	The contingency, disaster recovery, and business continuity plans are periodically reviewed, tested, and revised.
SP6.5	All staff • Are aware of the contingency, disaster recovery, and business continuity plans • Understand and are able to carry out their responsibilities

	Operational Practices **Physical Security (OP1)** **Physical Security Plans and Procedures (OP1.1)**
OP1.1.1	There are documented facility security plan(s) for safeguarding the premises, buildings, and any restricted areas.
OP1.1.2	These plans are periodically reviewed, tested, and updated.
OP1.1.3	Physical security procedures and mechanisms are routinely tested and revised.
OP1.1.4	There are documented policies and procedures for managing visitors, including • Sign in • Escort • Access logs • Reception and hosting
OP1.1.5	There are documented policies and procedures for physical control of hardware and software, including • Workstations, laptops, modems, wireless components, and all other components used to access information • Access, storage, and retrieval of data backups • Storage of sensitive information on physical and electronic media • Disposal of sensitive information or the media on which it is stored • Reuse and recycling of paper and electronic media

	Operational Practices **Physical Security (OP1)** **Physical Access Control (OP1.2)**
OP1.2.1	There are documented policies and procedures for individual and group access covering • The rules for granting the appropriate level of physical access • The rules for setting an initial right of access • Modifying the right of access • Terminating the right of access • Periodically reviewing and verifying the rights of access
OP1.2.2	There are documented policies, procedures, and mechanisms for controlling physical access to defined entities. This includes • Work areas • Hardware (computers, communication devices, etc.) and software media
OP1.2.3	There are documented procedures for verifying access authorization prior to granting physical access.
OP1.2.4	Workstations and other components that allow access to sensitive information are physically safeguarded to prevent unauthorized access.

	Operational Practices **Physical Security (OP1)** **Monitoring and Auditing Physical Security (OP1.3)**
OP1.3.1	Maintenance records are kept to document the repairs and modifications of a facility's physical components.
OP1.3.2	An individual's or group's actions, with respect to all physically controlled media, can be accounted for.
OP1.3.3	Audit and monitoring records are routinely examined for anomalies, and corrective action is taken as needed.

	Operational Practices **Information Technology Security (OP2)** **System and Network Management (OP2.1)**
OP2.1.1	There are documented security plan(s) for safeguarding the systems and networks.
OP2.1.2	Security plan(s) are periodically reviewed, tested, and updated.
OP2.1.3	Sensitive information is protected by secure storage, such as • Defined chains of custody • Backups stored off-site

(continued)

	Operational Practices **Information Technology Security (OP2)** **System and Network Management (OP2.1)** *(continued)*
OP2.1.3 *(continued)*	• Removable storage media • Discard process for sensitive information or its storage media
OP2.1.4	The integrity of installed software is regularly verified.
OP2.1.5	All systems are up to date with respect to revisions, patches, and recommendations in security advisories.
OP2.1.6	There is a documented data backup plan that • Is routinely updated • Is periodically tested • Calls for regularly scheduled backups of both software and data • Requires periodic testing and verification of the ability to restore from backups
OP2.1.7	All staff understand and are able to carry out their responsibilities under the backup plans.
OP2.1.8	Changes to IT hardware and software are planned, controlled, and documented.
OP2.1.9	IT staff members follow procedures when issuing, changing, and terminating users' passwords, accounts, and privileges. • Unique user identification is required for all information system users, including third-party users. • Default accounts and default passwords have been removed from systems.
OP2.1.10	Only necessary services are running on systems; all unnecessary services have been removed.

	Operational Practices **Information Technology Security (OP2)** **System Administration Tools (OP2.2)**
OP2.2.1	New security tools, procedures, and mechanisms are routinely reviewed for applicability in meeting the organization's security strategies.
OP2.2.2	Tools and mechanisms for secure system and network administration are used, and are routinely reviewed and updated or replaced. Examples are • Data integrity checkers • Cryptographic tools • Vulnerability scanners • Password quality-checking tools • Virus scanners

	Operational Practices **Information Technology Security (OP2)** **System Administration Tools (OP2.2)** (*continued*)
OP2.2.2 (*continued*)	• Process management tools • Intrusion detection systems • Secure remote administrations • Network service tools • Traffic analyzers • Incident response tools • Forensic tools for data analysis

	Operational Practices **Information Technology Security (OP2)** **Monitoring and Auditing IT Security (OP2.3)**
OP2.3.1	System and network monitoring and auditing tools are routinely used by the organization. • Activity is monitored by the IT staff. • System and network activity is logged/recorded. • Logs are reviewed on a regular basis. • Unusual activity is dealt with according to the appropriate policy or procedure. • Tools are periodically reviewed and updated.
OP2.3.2	Firewall and other security components are periodically audited for compliance with policy.

	Operational Practices **Information Technology Security (OP2)** **Authentication and Authorization (OP2.4)**
OP2.4.1	Appropriate access controls and user authentication (e.g., file permissions, network configuration) consistent with policy are used to restrict user access to • Information • Systems utilities • Program source code • Sensitive systems • Specific applications and services • Network connections within the organization • Network connections from outside the organization

(*continued*)

	Operational Practices **Information Technology Security (OP2)** **Authentication and Authorization (OP2.4)** (*continued*)
OP2.4.2	There are documented information-use policies and procedures for individual and group access to • Establish the rules for granting the appropriate level of access • Establish an initial right of access • Modify the right of access • Terminate the right of access • Periodically review and verify the rights of access
OP2.4.3	Access control methods/mechanisms restrict access to resources according to the access rights determined by policies and procedures.
OP2.4.4	Access control methods/mechanisms are periodically reviewed and verified.
OP2.4.5	Methods or mechanisms are provided to ensure that sensitive information has not been accessed, altered, or destroyed in an unauthorized manner.
OP2.4.6	Authentication mechanisms are used to protect availability, integrity, and confidentiality of sensitive information. Examples are • Digital signatures • Biometrics

	Operational Practices **Information Technology Security (OP2)** **Vulnerability Management (OP2.5)**
OP2.5.1	There is a documented set of procedures for managing vulnerabilities, including • Selecting vulnerability evaluation tools, checklists, and scripts • Keeping up to date with known vulnerability types and attack methods • Reviewing sources of information on vulnerability announcements, security alerts, and notices • Identifying infrastructure components to be evaluated • Scheduling of vulnerability evaluations • Interpreting and responding to the results • Maintaining secure storage and disposition of vulnerability data
OP2.5.2	Vulnerability management procedures are followed and are periodically reviewed and updated.
OP2.5.3	Technology vulnerability assessments are performed on a periodic basis, and vulnerabilities are addressed when they are identified.

	Operational Practices **Information Technology Security (OP2)** **Encryption (OP2.6)**
OP2.6.1	Appropriate security controls are used to protect sensitive information while in storage and during transmission, including • Data encryption during transmission • Data encryption when writing to disk • Use of public key infrastructure • Virtual private network technology • Encryption for all Internet-based transmission
OP2.6.2	Encrypted protocols are used when remotely managing systems, routers, and firewalls.
OP2.6.3	Encryption controls and protocols are routinely reviewed, verified, and revised.

	Operational Practices **Information Technology Security (OP2)** **Security Architecture and Design (OP2.7)**
OP2.7.1	System architecture and design for new and revised systems include considerations for • Security strategies, policies, and procedures • History of security compromises • Results of security risk assessments
OP2.7.2	The organization has up-to-date diagrams that show the enterprisewide security architecture and network topology.

	Operational Practices **Staff Security (OP3)** **Incident Management (OP3.1)**
OP3.1.1	Documented procedures exist for identifying, reporting, and responding to suspected security incidents and violations, including • Network-based incidents • Physical access incidents • Social engineering incidents
OP3.1.2	Incident management procedures are periodically tested, verified, and updated.
OP3.1.3	There are documented policies and procedures for working with law enforcement agencies.

	Operational Practices **Staff Security (OP3)** **General Staff Practices (OP3.2)**
OP3.2.1	Staff members follow good security practice, such as • Securing information for which they are responsible • Not divulging sensitive information to others (resistance to social engineering) • Having adequate ability to use information technology hardware and software • Using good password practices • Understanding and following security policies and regulations • Recognizing and reporting incidents
OP3.2.2	All staff at all levels of responsibility implement their assigned roles and responsibility for information security.
OP3.2.3	There are documented procedures for authorizing and overseeing those who work with sensitive information or who work in locations where the information resides. This includes • Employees • Contractors, partners, collaborators, and personnel from third-party organizations • Systems maintenance personnel • Facilities maintenance personnel

References

The following references were used as references for the catalog of practices:

CERT/CC

Julia H. Allen. *The CERT Guide to System and Network Security Practice.* New York: Addison-Wesley, 2001.

British Standards

British Standards Institution. *Information Security Management, Part 1: Code of Practice for Information Security Management of Systems* (BS7799: Part 1: 1995). London: British Standards Institution, February 1995.

Gramm-Leach-Bliley Act of 1999

"Interagency Guidelines Establishing Standards for Safeguarding Customer Information and Rescission of Year 2000 Standards for Safety and Soundness; Proposed Rule." *Federal Register,* vol. 65, no. 123. (June 2000), 39471–39489.

Health Insurance Portability and Accountability Act (HIPAA) of 1996

"Security Standards and Electronic Signature Standards; Proposed Rule." *Federal Register,* vol. 63, no. 155. (August 1998), 43242–43280.

NIST Principles and Practices

Marianne Swanson and Barbara Guttman, "Generally Accepted Principles and Practices for Securing Information Technology Systems" (NIST SP 800-14). National Institute of Standards and Technology, Department of Commerce, Washington, DC, 1996.

About the Authors

Christopher Alberts

Christopher Alberts is a senior member of the technical staff in the Networked Systems Survivability Program at the Software Engineering Institute (SEI). He is responsible for developing information security risk management methods, tools, and techniques. Alberts is currently the team leader for OCTAVE[SM], a risk assessment technique designed for self-directed use by organizations. Prior to his work in networked systems security, Alberts focused on developing techniques to advance the practice of risk management for software development projects.

Before joining the SEI, Alberts was a scientist at Carnegie Mellon Research Institute, where he developed mobile robots for hazardous environments. He also worked at AT&T Bell Laboratories, where he designed information systems to support AT&T's advanced manufacturing processes. He has B.S. and M.E. degrees in engineering from Carnegie Mellon University.

Alberts's publications have focused on information security, risk management, and robotic and automated system development. He is a coauthor of the *OCTAVE Method Implementation Guide* and the *Continuous Risk Management Guidebook*. Among other publications he has coauthored are Alberts, Christopher J.; Behrens, Sandra G.; Pethia, Richard D.; and Wilson, William R. *Operationally Critical Threat, Asset, and Vulnerability Evaluation[SM] (OCTAVE[SM]) Framework, Version 1.0* (CMU/SEI-99-TR-017, 1999); Gallagher, B., Alberts, C., and Barbour, R. *Software Acquisition Risk Management KPA—A Guidebook.*

Pittsburgh, PA, Software Engineering Institute, Carnegie Mellon University, 1997; Siegel, M. W., W. M. Kaufman, and C. J. Alberts, "Mobile Robots for Difficult Measurements in Difficult Environments: Applications to Aging Aircraft," *Proceedings of the Pittsburgh Meeting,* C. Thorpe, ed., International Conference on Intelligent Autonomous Systems: IAS-3, Pittsburgh, PA, February 1993; Alberts, C. J., W. M. Kaufman, and M. W. Siegel, "Automated Inspection of Aircraft," *Proceedings of Aerospace '92: Maintaining and Supporting an Aircraft Fleet,* Society of Manufacturing Engineers, Dallas, TX, June 1992; and Kaufman, W. M., M. W. Siegel, and C. J. Alberts, "Robot for Automation of Aircraft Skin Inspection," *Proceedings of the International Workshop on Inspection and Evaluation of Aging Aircraft,* Behnam Bahr, ed., Federal Aviation Administration, Albuquerque, NM, May 1992.

Audrey J. Dorofee

Audrey Dorofee is a senior member of the technical staff in the Networked Systems Survivability Program at the Software Engineering Institute (SEI). She is responsible for developing, transitioning, and training security risk management methods, tools, and techniques. She is currently working on OCTAVE and other areas in the security domain. Prior to this work, Dorofee was developing and delivering software and systems development risk management practices and was project lead for risk management in the Risk Program at the SEI.

Prior to joining the SEI, Dorofee was a member of the technical staff with the MITRE Corporation in Houston, Texas, supporting various types of work for the National Aeronautics and Space Administration (NASA), including Space Station software environments, user interfaces, and expert systems. Before MITRE, she was a NASA electronics engineer at the Kennedy Space Center, working with the Space Shuttle Launch Processing System.

Dorofee's most recent publications have focused on risk management. She is coauthor of the *OCTAVE Method Implementation Guide* and the *Continuous Risk Management Guidebook.* Among her other publications are "Putting Risk Management into Practice," R. Williams, J. Walker, A. Dorofee. *IEEE Software,* May/June 1997, Piscataway, New Jersey; "Team Risk Management: A New Model for Customer-Supplier Relationships," R. Higuera et al. (CMU/SEI-94-SR-5). Pittsburgh, PA: Software Engineering Institute, Carnegie Mellon University,

1994; "Overview and Analysis of National Space Transportation System Fault Management," A. Dorofee. (MTR-92W00026). McLean, VA: The MITRE Corporation, 1992; "Space Station Freedom Advanced Automation: Evolution with Environments: A Plan for the Software Support Environment," A. Dorofee. (MTR-89W00271-03). McLean, VA: The MITRE Corporation, 1989; and "SUIM: An Alternative for Developing and Effecting User Interfaces," L. Ambrose et al. (MTR-90W00020). McLean, VA: The MITRE Corporation, 1989.

Index